Foreword

Mr Siim KALLAS

Vice-President of the European Commission
responsible for Administrative Affairs, Audit and Anti-Fraud

As Commissioner in charge of Administrative Affairs, Audit and Anti-Fraud, I am very pleased to see the great success of such initiatives as the OLAF Round Table on Anti-Fraud Communication (¹).

This project first came into being in October 2004 as a virtual round table within the OLAF website. It today provides a precious analysis forum on communication and information as a means of preventing fraud and corruption, and as such it constitutes an important element of the OLAF Anti-Fraud Communicators' Network (OAFCN).

This round table brought together and encouraged discussion between different experts on institutional communication such as anti-fraud investigators, police and other law enforcement agencies, academics from the fields of law, economics and the media, members of investigative and judicial services, officials from the European institutions, journalists and other individuals working in related fields.

I truly believe that communication can help deter and prevent fraud and irregularities by raising awareness and promoting public debate. Communication policy can help shape public opinion, and the key to success in the fight against corruption is changing public opinion, different in each of the Member States and candidate countries, to ensure that corruption is viewed critically by members of the public.

For this reason it is crucial for law and anti-corruption authorities from all over the EU to share their experiences in such forums, particularly as putting across a positive message about our work is not always easy. We need to constantly communicate that we strive to be professional, impartial and reliable in fighting fraud that harms all citizens.

Looking at the experiences and successes of investigative and law enforcement services from the Member States and candidate countries offers a valuable insight into the ways in which such agencies can adequately inform the public about their activities and, in doing so, actively involve them in the fight against fraud. It also gives an insight into the role that the media play as a vital platform for communication with the public about anti-fraud cases and as a vehicle that can be used to educate citizens about the risks that economic crime poses to them.

I would like to offer my heartfelt thanks to the OLAF Anti-Fraud Communicators' Network for providing us with this compilation. By highlighting the role of the public in the fight against fraud, this publication moves towards the goal stated by the Barroso Commis-

---

(¹) http://europa.eu.int/comm/anti_fraud/olaf-oafcn/rt/c/i_en.html

sion and most notably by my colleague Margot Wallström, Vice-President of the European Commission and Commissioner for Institutional Relations and Communication, of connecting with the European citizen and opening up dialogue and debate.

I encourage the continuation of such meaningful projects and extend my most sincere congratulations to OLAF for such worthwhile initiatives.

Foreword to the third edition

The year 2009 marks the 10th anniversary of the creation of OLAF. During the past decade a culture of accountability has developed further within the European institutions and other public administrations. Political leaders and officials are now very sensitive to the need of the public to be informed and assured that malfunctions and fraud are identified eliminated and appropriately punished. Projects like the Round Table on Anti-Fraud Communication foster this spirit and are, at the same time, instrumental in 'deterring fraud by informing the public'. Therefore I am particularly happy that this initiative has now culminated in the third edition of this volume.

Since the last edition, OLAF and its Anti-fraud Communicators' Network (OAFCN) have worked hard to get their message across. Their debates about transparency and media relations as a means of fighting fraud and corruption affecting EU financial interests have contributed to further closing the gap between anti-fraud communicators on one side and journalists on the other. The network's discussions about television drama as a means of fighting fraud and corruption affecting EU financial interests and a seminar on anti-fraud communication and Web 2.0 may well lead to new opportunities for reaching a broader audience directly.

I warmly welcome these activities that will surely help bringing Europe closer to the citizens and I encourage OLAF and its partners to continue their valuable work.

Siim KALLAS
Vice-President of the European Commission
responsible for Administrative Affairs, Audit and Anti-Fraud

European Anti-Fraud Office (OLAF)
In cooperation with the OAFCN (OLAF Anti-Fraud Communicators' Network)

Deterring fraud by informing the public

...TABLE

...RAUD

...ATION

...2007 and 2008

Third Edition

All t... ...can be found on
...seminars/en.html

4 Week Loan

This book is due for return on or before the last date shown
below

Further information on OLAF and the fight against fraud against the Commnity's financial interests can be found on OLAF's website at the following address: http://olaf.europa.eu

The contributions appear in alphabetical order of the name of the persons concerned.

Photo credits:

European Communities, 2006, 2008; European Parliament

Europe Direct is a service to help you find answers to your questions about the European Union

Freephone number (*):
00 800 6 7 8 9 10 11

(*) Certain mobile telephone operators do not allow access to 00 800 numbers or these calls may be billed.

More information on the European Union is available on the Internet (http://europa.eu).

Cataloguing data can be found at the end of this publication.

Luxembourg: Office for Official Publications of the European Communities, 2009

ISBN 978-92-79-06047-2

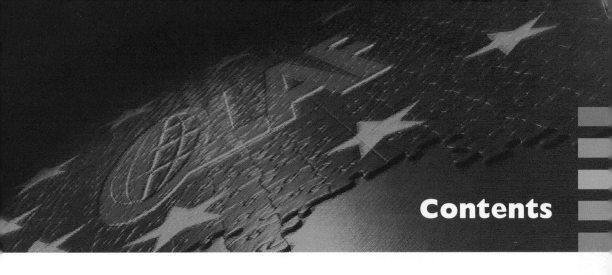

Contents

1. INFORMATION AND COMMUNICATION AS A MEANS OF EU FRAUD PREVENTION

2. FIGHT AGAINST FRAUD ON VISION:
Television drama as a means of fighting fraud and corruption affecting EU financial interests

3. ANTI-FRAUD COMMUNICATION AND WEB2.0: New technologies, new tools, new audiences

4. ANNEXES

1. INFORMATION AND COMMUNICATION AS A MEANS OF EU FRAUD PREVENTION*

* Based mainly on the contributions for the round table on anti-fraud communication during the fourth training seminar of the OLAF Anti-Fraud Communicators' Network (OAFCN), Brussels, 24 to 26 November 2004, concerning 'Deterring fraud by informing the public: How information and communication can be a means of EU fraud prevention and a true service for citizens in the respect of their rights'.

1.1 ACADEMICS

Iuliana BOTEZAN

PhD in Information Science, Professor
of the Universidad Complutense,
Faculty of Information Science, Madrid, Spain

**Iuliana
BOTEZAN**

PhD in Information
Science at the
Universidad
Complutense of
Madrid, MA in
Public Relations
(Advertising),
University of
Bucarest, 'International
cooperation to
the development',
Universidad
Complutense of
Madrid, and 'Conflict
analysis expert',
University San
Pablo-CEU, Madrid.
Assistant Professor
teaching information
policies and mass
media information
management at
the Universidad
Complutense of
Madrid, Faculty of
Information Sciences.

'Striking the right balance in disclosing information: a dream or reality?'

Much has been said or written to the effect that the 21st century will belong to all the world's inhabitants, that it will be the century of full, free and protected expression of human personality and of the potential of each citizen's intelligence and hard work. And as the 21st century began in the context of the information and knowledge society, it will also see information and knowledge playing a decisive role in the economic development of States and in the shaping and assertion of each individual's personality. The 21st century is the century of information's great challenges, the century where learning the alphabet goes hand in hand with computer skills, the century of adapting to the new demands of society.

As knowledge has always been at the heart of economic growth and the gradual improvement in social welfare, economists have come up with new concepts with thought-provoking names, such as 'knowledge society', 'knowledge-based economy' (²), and so on. This phenomenon appears to signal a discontinuity or break from previous times.

Society expresses the need for the world to be presented in a clear, orderly and coherent way, with everything making sense and obeying a specific hierarchy (upon which we can base the decisions we must take on professional or everyday issues). This is also the century where States and governments must ensure that citizens are well prepared and desire to live and develop in an information society. Some analysts believe that information society has already come to an end and that the next stage in human evolution is a knowledge-based society, in which specialised institutions will no longer be happy simply to provide information but will also 'plant' knowledge, through the direct involvement of information-science specialists (now known as 'knowledge workers') in the knowledge process.

Transparent communication does, however, entail certain risks. Strict information policies must be laid down in accordance with institutions' data-privacy policies, something which only the institutions themselves and their specialists can do, despite the opinions and 'advice' they may receive from outside, and good information policies can only function in tandem with effective international institutional cooperation programmes, through networks allowing data to be exchanged quickly and with the best results.

When security requirements are not met, we feel in a position of insecurity, that epistemological state whereby we do not believe (or know) something which is certain. It has to be said that insecurity is a subjective, not an objective, state ([3]).

Since the beginning of the 20th century we have seen a new characteristic of economic growth in the form of greater 'intangible' capital as compared with 'tangible' capital (as demonstrated by Abramovitz and David) ([4]). And in developed countries, the expression 'knowledge-based economy' has sprung up. The problem is that access to knowledge-based economies is still very restricted and there are big disparities between different countries and different social strata.

Paul David and Dominique Foray are of the opinion that knowledge economies come about when a group of people co-produce (i.e. produce and exchange) new knowledge on a mass scale using information and communication technologies ([5]). They analyse the start of the digital era as a revolution in knowledge instruments, and as being of great importance since it influences the technologies used to produce and distribute information and knowledge. Although these instruments allow us to access remotely both information and knowledge, they also have had terrible effects since they appeared in their first forms during the 1950s. They allow us to transmit written and digitalised messages or even to gain access to knowledge systems from afar — for example, distance learning (tele-education — the framework of a dynamic relationship between student and teacher) or distance experiments and full virtual access to databases.

Differences between information strategies arise due to the different technical, technological and economic starting conditions of each country as well as their human, economic and financial potential.

On 19 July 1994, the first European action plan for information society, 'Europe's way to the information society', took many European countries by surprise. Some had better communications infrastructures than others, some had more developed electronic-product industries while others had not even thought about this issue as they were too busy trying to find solutions to domestic economic and social problems, such as economic recession, rising unemployment and inflation, and so on. They realised very quickly that this new information and communications technology together with the EU's modern plans for building a global information society constituted a solution with much potential and which was able to deal with the problems they were facing, whether it be creating new jobs, improving public services at low cost, reducing pollution and traffic congestion in large cities and on motorways or improving educational standards and skills (particularly among young people) and sustained economic development in general. EU candidate countries are making a valuable effort to reach certain standards in global cooperation on information. For example, in 1996 Romania took its first steps in the fields of computerisation and creating a fundamentally information-based economy on a national scale based on the free exchange of information, the precondition for any genuine 'information-broker' activity.

The EU and EC have been and still are the logistical and administrative hub for a coherent European strategy and action plans for the information society. To solve the security problem which stems from full access to information, it is necessary to devise strategies for information processing and decision-making. The quantitative analysis of risk, the principle of precaution, reversible decisions, end-user involvement and participatory procedures are some of the approaches researchers and professionals have adopted to develop these strategies. In order to solve security problems and the risks involved with full access to information, it is doubtless necessary to gain a better understanding of the flow of information in modern societies and its social repercussions [6].

To this end, OLAF's decision to consult specialists in the field is a worthy one and should be imitated by other Community institutions as a guarantee of adaptation to the demands of the global information and human-rights society. Although external solutions may be found (such as 'filtered' transparency through interinstitutional networks), the decision to 'lift the veil' which, for security reasons, conceals information on their investigations, should ultimately be left to the sole discretion of the institutions concerned.

[2] David, Paul A. and Foray, Dominique, 'An introduction to the economy of the knowledge society', *International Social Science Journal*, March 2002, No 171, 'The knowledge society', p. 9. http://www.unesco.org/issj/rics171/fulltext171en.pdf (last consulted 13 July 2003).

[3] Ove Hansson, Sven, 'Uncertainties in the knowledge society', *International Social Science Journal*, March 2002, No 171, 'The knowledge society', p. 39. http://www.unesco.org/issj/rics171/fulltext171en.pdf (last consulted 13 July 2003).

[4] Abramovitz, M. and David, P. A., 'Technological change and the rise of intangible investments: the US economy's growth path in the 20th century'. In Foray, D. and Lundvall, B. A. (eds), *Employment and growth in the knowledge-based economy*. OECD, Paris, 1996.

[5] David, P. A. and Foray, D., Ibid, p. 15.

[6] Ove Hansson, Sven, Ibid, p. 48.

Academics

Gérard DUBOIS,

Professor of Public Health, Head of Public Health Department,
Faculty of Medicine, Amiens, France

Gérard DUBOIS

MD, MPH, is
Professor of Public
Health, Medical
School of Amiens.
He is Chairman of
the French Alliance
against Smoking,
a corresponding
member of the
National Medical
Academy and an
expert in the WHO
and in the EU.
He is also author of
'Le Rideau de Fumée'
(The Smoke Screen),
Le Seuil, 2003, and
of tobacco industry
documents.

'Communication, relationships with the media, tobacco industry and smuggling'

Public health is the discipline aimed at preventing diseases or their consequences in human populations. As a public health specialist, I have held several administrative positions (within the French National Health Insurance Fund for Employees between 1981 and 1990) in the fields of flu vaccination, neo- and ante-natal screening, cancer screening and the coordination of health testing centres. In a modern public health system, delivering these services requires a communication effort in order to ensure that the objectives are shared by policymakers, health professionals and the general public. This means that resources must be provided for training and communication. Establishing relationships of trust on a long-term basis calls for openness, accuracy and honesty, something which rules out any recourse to media 'stunts'.

I was one of the co-instigators (with Professor Claude Got) of the reintroduction of the ban on television advertising for alcoholic drinks (1987), the first public health initiative in the media sector which led to a legislative decision of the utmost importance. The aim of the ban was to limit the promotion of a product that was causing an epidemic of industrial rather than infectious origin.

This initiative was broadened to include tobacco and in 1991 led to the adoption of the Evin act, which covers both tobacco and alcohol. Here too, relations with the media and public support ensured that the French parliament remained immune to the all-pervasive pressure from industrial and advertising lobbies.

Chairmanship between 1993 and 2003 of the French National Anti-Smoking Committee (a non-profit-making association), which brought dozens of lawsuits against the tobacco industry, attracted intense media exposure. I have since 1995 frequently acted as an international expert on tobacco and alcohol issues for the WHO (in particular during preparation of the Framework Convention on Tobacco Control) and the European Commission. I have taken part in several seminars with journalists under the auspices of those international organisations and with the French Committee on Health Education (CFES). Since 2003, I have chaired the Anti-Tobacco Alliance, which groups together some 30 organisations.

The point of outlining these activities is to show how communication issues and relations with the media form part of the job of a public health professional, and I am therefore well aware of their importance.

Following the publication, ordered by the US courts, of the tobacco industry's internal documents, one of the topics to have come under special scrutiny has been the tobacco industry's involvement in the organisation of cigarette smuggling [7] [8]. Tobacco consumption is linked to its selling price: consumption falls by 4 % when the price rises by 10 % [9]. Raising taxes must therefore form part of any soundly based anti-smoking policy (WHO Framework Convention on Tobacco Control). It goes without saying that cigarette manufacturers are strongly opposed to such moves and are using all possible means, whether legal or illegal, to combat them. One of their responses with a view to holding on to their market at all costs is to organise cigarette smuggling, which accounted for 30 % of all cigarette exports worldwide in 2000. This means that close relations must exist between the tobacco firms and organised crime at international level, with technical and financial structures that are both powerful and sophisticated. Internal documents, convictions, confessions and many investigations all point in the same direction [10].

The European Anti-Fraud Office has played an internationally recognised and respected role in this area, and I will not dwell on this point. It is an example of how communication has been essential, both by OLAF itself but also with the support of the media, experts and associations, which spoke with one voice. The upshot has been that the European Commission brought a lawsuit, with the support of 10 Member States, that recently resulted in a transaction between the Commission and Philip Morris. This concerted action, coordinated with a large number of national authorities, could not have taken place without OLAF.

Since 2000, smuggling has been on the decline throughout the world. International experience confirms that giving in to the threat of smuggling by cutting prices revives consumption. On the contrary, the head-on attack on organised crime and smuggling pursued by the authorities in the United Kingdom and Canada has reduced both cigarette consumption and cigarette smuggling. Smuggling is not a passive reaction to tax and therefore price increases but well and truly a response encouraged by the tobacco industry in conjunction with organised crime in order to maximise its profits. The World Bank has shown that cigarette smuggling is linked more closely to the level of corruption in different countries than to the price differential. In fighting successfully the scourge of cigarette smuggling, OLAF has not only defended the EU's financial interests but has also made an effective contribution at international level to the effort to curb smoking [11], the largest avoidable cause of death in the world. One of the new aspects to emerge is therefore that efforts to promote public health are linked in this way to issues that may at first sight appear unconnected.

OLAF is entrusted with the key task of protecting the EU's financial interests and fighting fraud and corruption. To achieve these objectives, it has wide-ranging investigative powers, both internally, within the European institutions, and externally, in the Member States. Enjoying a large degree of functional independence, OLAF therefore operates as a financial police force whose investigations often have a criminal dimension and are ultimately passed on to the judicial authorities. In these circumstances, can OLAF communicate?

Professional secrecy and the secrecy of investigations militate in favour of silence. But such silence comes in for criticism when an investigation does not cause the funding of an activity to be immediately suspended! Silence exacerbates curiosity, sly inventiveness, inaccuracies and even lies, some of which are ostensibly intended to provoke reactions. Silence can even facilitate genuine or simulated leaks. Silence is interpreted as a lack of transparency, something that is today always treated with suspicion.

Communication, on the contrary, must have due regard for the needs of the investigation and the rights of suspects and witnesses. Its virtue is that it makes the public conscious of the dangers of fraud and legitimises action to combat it by de-trivialising fraud and combating fatalistic views of the 'what difference does it make?' type. It limits the impact of disinformation on individuals, groups and even industries by re-establishing the true facts of the case. It therefore helps to shift the attitude of the public in the right direction. The public (and the media) may occasionally be misled for a time but the truth will emerge in the long run. An institution cannot retain its credibility for long if it manipulates the facts. It is this self-limiting factor which should remove any fear of a body such as OLAF retaining the ability to communicate.

More generally, we cannot ignore the recent collapse of the EU's image in the Member States, due to citizens' inability to perceive directly the benefits they derive from the Union. The fight against corruption and fraud is by definition a combat for the defence of the European citizen. It should therefore be more widely publicised among all Europeans, in the interests of the institutions themselves and of their development, particularly in the context of adoption of the European Constitution.

Communicating, for an institution, therefore means demonstrating that it is independent, that it is active, that its action is effective and that it abides by the rules, but also involves revealing its uncertainties and its policy discussions. Communicating, for OLAF, means making European citizens aware of what is being done to protect their interests against fraud and corruption. Communicating is essential to its existence.

---

[7] Dubois, G. and Tramier, B., 'The responsibility of the tobacco industry for the tobacco pandemic', *Int J Tuberc Lung Dis*, 2001, 5: 304–306.

[8] Dubois, G., *Le rideau de fumée*, 2003, Le Seuil.

[9] World Bank, *Curbing the epidemic. Governments and the economics of tobacco control*, 1999.

[10] Favereau, E., 'Les cigarettiers sont des contrebandiers', *Libération*, 21 July 2000.

[11] Dubois, G., 'La nécessaire internationalisation de la lutte contre le tabagisme', *Bull Acad Natle Med*, 1998, 182: 939–953.

Florian NEUHANN,

Graduate from the Geschwister-Scholl-Institute for Political Science, University of Munich, and freelance journalist, Germany

Florian NEUHANN

was born in 1980, studied political science, communication science and European law at the Universities of Munich and Bologna. He wrote his thesis (diploma) on European fraud prevention and the work of OLAF. He is also a graduate of the German Journalism School (Deutsche Journalistenschule) in Munich. He has worked as an intern for several national and international media companies and, in summer 2004, at the European Anti-Fraud Office in Brussels. He currently works for the Berliner Zeitung in Berlin.

'OLAF and the public: Why the European Anti-Fraud Office should attach more importance to the active involvement of the public' ([12])

An institution set up specifically to combat corruption must measure its success in the light of two overriding questions: first, is it effectively combating corruption and fraud? And, second, is its work perceived as credible by the public and does its existence increase the credibility of the political system as a whole? Operational effectiveness and political credibility go hand in hand. For both criteria, one factor is key: the involvement of the public in the fight against corruption and fraud. If that fight is to be successful in the long term, an anti-corruption agency must win the community, other anti-corruption bodies and, most of all, the population over to its cause. It does this, for example, through public information campaigns, press work and active dialogue with the other bodies involved in combating and monitoring corruption — in short, through what Lala Camerer has described as 'public interaction':

'If little has been done to involve the community in the work of the agency, the inevitable result is that the public comes to distrust the agency and provides no information about what is going on. Without that information the agency's investigative powers are useless' ([13]).

This is especially true of an institution like OLAF, whose creation in 1999 was the focus of media attention and, together with the announcement by the newly appointed Commission President at the time, Romano Prodi, of a 'zero tolerance' policy towards fraud and corruption, led to high and sometimes unrealistic expectations of the office among the public.

Five years on, however, it is difficult to measure OLAF's success in involving the public in its work. Any assessment must also take account of the early stages when the office focused more on itself, establishing internal procedures and processing old cases left behind by its predecessor UCLAF than on proactive communication and public relations work with the outside.

On the one hand, the increase in information about possible fraud cases received by the office since its creation (1999–2000: 322 notifications; 2002–03: 585 notifications; 2003–04: 637 cases reported ([14])) clearly points to a boost in its profile and credibility compared with its predecessor UCLAF.

However, the office, still little known by the wider public, has so far tended to fall short in this aspect of its work. Since its creation, it has regularly been criticised for its setting of priorities and has clearly not yet been successful enough in giving a convincing account of its policies to an interested public and to Parliament and explaining its priorities.

While the setting up of the office was positively received by the public at the time, OLAF came in for some heavy criticism in 2004 in particular. A shift in public opinion came especially after the so-called Tillack affair, when information in the office's possession about the presumed bribery of a member of its staff by the *Stern* correspondent at the time, Hans-Martin Tillack, led in March 2004 to the latter's office and private residence being searched by the Belgian police ([15]); since then, some journalists most of all have taken a hostile view of the office ([16]). OLAF must do far more in this area if it is to reach the level of 'public interaction' which is vital to its success.

The opinion of OLAF's Supervisory Committee to the effect that the office's press policy is 'secondary' and should 'remain limited' in view of the risks it entails for the respect of fundamental rights and the reputation of the institutions ([17]) must be decisively refuted. Although there is undoubtedly a potential conflict between the goals of active press work and protecting the rights of the individuals involved, information about successful anti-fraud work makes a key contribution to boosting the office's deterrent effect and credibility. (Pro-)active press work is a tried-and-tested means of informing the population about the fight against fraud and winning their support for it. In view of the problem that has been identified with the legitimacy of European integration, including on account of perceived corruption, the office's information policy cannot be secondary.

To date, the office has taken a reactive and extremely guarded approach to its official press work ([18]) — doubtless on account of its specific legal situation: the successful completion of an OLAF investigation usually signals the start of criminal proceedings in a Member State; over-detailed information might endanger the success of the national criminal investigation. However, information about OLAF investigations has, on numerous occasions, reached the public — not through official channels, but through leaks from the office itself. Obviously, this deficit has to be put into perspective as it is symptomatic of the European Union as a whole ([19]); but, in precisely such a sensitive area as combating fraud, it undoubtedly does not serve to enhance OLAF's credibility. To counter this problem, the office should first take steps to increase staff identification with OLAF and reduce the likelihood of internal leaks (increase internal transparency and communication in order to boost motivation). Second, OLAF must alter its perception of the media: up to now, the latter have been regarded as more of an opponent than a potential partner in the fight against fraud. Both sides could benefit from a more open approach on the part of the office; and extending OLAF's official activities to include press and public relations work, without infringing the rights of individuals or data protection, makes perfect sense (more press briefings, greater transparency regarding the conduct of investigations, especially where they are closed without a result, more public conferences on the prospects for anti-fraud work, etc.).

The office's education and prevention work (which admittedly is not listed as one of its tasks in the underlying legislation) has also been neglected up to now. Day-to-day practice in the European Union's Member States shows that a change of thinking is needed here: the EU budget is rarely perceived by the public as being taxpayers' own money. Instead, it is frequently seen in terms of a 'self-service shop', not needing to be spent with particular care.

As a Commission department, OLAF should not be merely reactive, but in future should also take a more preventive approach to the fight against fraud. Successful anti-fraud work is built not only on detection and prosecution, but also on a third, equally important, pillar: that of prevention and education (^{20}). To date, both the European Union as a whole and OLAF itself have neglected this aspect of combating fraud. Five years after its establishment, it is now up to the office to make good this shortfall.

(^{12}) The following contribution is based on the author's recently completed book on fraud prevention in the European Union which will be published this year by NOMOS as part of the series 'Münchner Beiträge zur Europäischen Einigung'.

(^{13}) Camerer, Lala, 'Prerequisites for effective anti-corruption ombudsman's offices and anti-corruption agencies', 10th International Anti-Corruption Conference, Prague, workshop papers, 10/2001: http://www.10iacc.org/download/workshops/cs06.pdf (15.8.2004).

(^{14}) OLAF activity report for 1999–2000 and activity report for 2002–03. Figures for 2003–04: Office's own figures, not yet published.

(^{15}) See OLAF's account of the case at: http://europa.eu.int/comm/anti_fraud/press_room/pr/2004/14background_en.html (22.9.2004). Regarding the accusations by Stern's journalist, see Tillack, Hans Martin, Kontakt zu gut informierten Kreisen at: http://www.forum-online.lu/textarchiv/2004/237/hmtKontakt%2zu%20gut%20informierten%20Kreisen.html (1.9.2004) and Leyendecker, Hans, Abgrund an Amtsversagen in Süddeutsche Zeitung, 9.6.2004, p. 22. OLAF responded to these accusations: see its press release 'Clarification regarding OLAF internal investigation and Belgian judiciary investigation on a leak of confidential information', Brussels, 23.3.2004, at: http://europa.eu.int/comm/anti_fraud/press_room/pr/2004/07_en.html (1.8.2004) and the journalist's own account.

(^{16}) Interviews with German media correspondents in Brussels, 25.5.2004, 24.6.2004, 24.8.2004, 26.8.2004, 9.9.2004 and 29.9.2004.

(^{17}) OLAF Supervisory Committee, Opinion No 2/03 accompanying the Commission's report about the evaluation of the activities of the European Anti-Fraud Office, Luxembourg, 18.6.2003, see Chapter IV.3 (Communication), p. 21. Available online at: http://europa.eu.int/comm/anti_fraud/reports/sup_comm/2003/avis/en.pdf (1.9.2004).

(^{18}) From 2000 to the present (as at October 2004) the office has issued 82 press releases, that is, less than two per month on average. Of these press releases, less than half (38) related to specific OLAF investigations; most of them only contained OLAF's reaction to information which had already been published in the press. For the office's communication strategy, see OLAF's homepage: http://europa.eu.int/comm/anti_fraud/olaf-oafcn/rt/i_en.html#strat (15.9.2004) and the Round Table on Anti-fraud Communication set up by the office: http://europa.eu.int/comm/anti_fraud/olaf-oafcn/rt/i_en.html (15.9.2004).

(^{19}) See Wernicke, Christian, Der Beton lebt in Süddeutsche Zeitung, 9.10.2004, p. IV. The author writes of the Brussels eurocracy, 'Nothing stays secret, almost every document eventually — in the strictest confidence — becomes public. The visitor just has to know which document he is looking for.'

(^{20}) On the importance of involving 'civil society' in the fight against corruption and fraud, see the recently adopted UN Convention against Corruption, Art. 13: Participation of society. The text of the convention can be found on the website of the United Nations Office on Drugs and Crime (UNODC): http://www.unodc.org/unodc/en/crime_convention_corruption.html (18.8.2004).

1.2 EUROPEAN INSTITUTIONS

Franz-Hermann BRÜNER,

Director-General, OLAF, European Commission

Franz-Hermann BRÜNER

Since March 2000 Franz-Hermann Brüner has been the Director-General of the European Anti-Fraud Office (OLAF) of the European Commission. The Office has responsibility for conducting administrative anti-fraud investigations and has a special independent status within the Commission. Born on 14 September 1945 in Bad-Nauheim, Federal Republic of Germany, Mr Brüner is married with one daughter. He is a graduate in law, economics and political science of the University of Munich (1971–76). He then undertook judicial preparation practicum in the Ministry of Justice, in Bavaria (1976–79). From 1979 to 1998 he worked in a variety of judicial roles in the German justice system. From 1998 to his OLAF appointment in 2000 he was Head of the Anti-Fraud Unit of the Office of the High Representative of Bosnia and Herzegovina.

'Making sure that communication about fraud is not taboo promotes openness and this in turn will help prevent fraud occurring in the first place'

When considering the topic 'Deterring fraud by informing the public' one of the first things to come to mind is the importance of doing this, but also the difficulty that doing this poses.

Why is fraud such a difficult crime to talk about? And does this mean that it is all the more important to do just that, communicate about it?

Fraud is something of a taboo subject. It involves issues of individual ethics and competence. It can be very complex, a crime of a highly technical nature and as such can often be incomprehensible to those who are not experts in the field. Mist often shrouds cases of fraud. This is a problem that all those involved in the fight against crime face. The facts of the case are often not understood, and more importantly they are often misunderstood.

The technical nature of the crime does not interest the public, the human side of it does. Dishonesty, particularly when it occurs where one might not expect it, holds a fascination for many. Unsurprisingly the media have always paid a lot of attention to fraud. They are, however, not always interested in facts of fraud but rather in the story that can be made out of it.

It is precisely because of these difficulties that communication is of vital importance for anti-fraud bodies. But the tools of communication must be used wisely. The facts of anti-fraud activities must be made known without permitting opportunities for misinterpretation or manipulation. Ambiguity or confusion will be not go unnoticed by opportunistic media. Making sure that communication about fraud is not taboo promotes openness and this in turn will help prevent fraud occurring in the first place.

OLAF must communicate not only about what it does, but also about what it is. It is a young organisation, a respected law enforcement agency, but it must still forge its own path. If what it is, is unclear, then what it does will be less credible.

When communicating with citizens about anti-fraud activities one of the most important points that OLAF must stress, clearly and unambiguously, is the unique position it occupies amongst the European institutions in having investigative independence. Fraud and corruption within the institutions undermine people's confidence in the Union. This is an issue that has attracted considerable, and often negative, attention in the past.

One of the most important tools in OLAF's communication strategy is the OLAF Anti-Fraud Communicators' Network (OAFCN), which was set up in 2000. It forms part of the external independent communication strategy of OLAF. The OAFCN aims to prevent fraud through the free flow of information; create a permanent dialogue between OLAF's communication unit and its counterparts in national investigation services; inform the European citizen about what OLAF and Member States are doing jointly and individually to protect their financial interests; and lastly, provide information to the general public about the fight against fraud.

The OAFCN is very important for OLAF because, through its partners in the Member States, it provides a much more direct channel for information. For instance, in the candidate countries there is a real need to educate public opinion about what constitutes fraud. For OLAF it is much more effective to do this in conjunction with the OAFCN partners in the candidate countries.

OLAF is responsible for investigating fraud against the EU interests. Fraud against EU interests is fraud against money from the European taxpayer. So the work of OLAF in combating this is of great importance to all European citizens. If OLAF can put this point across successfully and inform the public about their work and the very real implications it has for them then this can help deter fraud in the long run. Initiatives such as the freephone number for each Member State will prove all the more fruitful if an informed public knows why the fight against fraud is important for them. The fact that the free number sometimes receives spurious phone calls goes to show that there is still much that can be done to communicate this.

As OLAF's work deals with protecting the financial interests of the Union this also provides it with an opportunity to make clear, in its investigations of irregularities, where EU funds are spent, and of course emphasise the fact that it is working to ensure that this is done properly. For instance over 80 % of EU expenditure is administered not by the EU institutions themselves but by national authorities. Most financial losses to the EU as a result of fraud occur away from Brussels. However, there is a common misconception that EU fraud occurs in Brussels. OLAF can debunk such misconceptions.

Again the care that must be taken to avoid providing information that is not totally clear can be highlighted here. If it is stressed that 80 % of EU expenditure is administered by national authorities, it must also be stressed that this in no way detracts from the importance of OLAF's investigative independence.

OLAF's investigative independence can mean that it can communicate with the media in a different way to other EU institutions. Journalists may perceive OLAF to be a more reliable source of information because of its investigative independence with regards to matters of fraud within the institutions.

For OLAF communicating to the media must not just be a matter of providing information. OLAF must also communicate with journalists to inform them about why it is important to provide accurate and unambiguous information about fraud cases. Due to the sensitive nature of fraud investigations it is also important that journalists should be informed about why it can be detrimental to the work of the Office to report, perhaps speculatively, on cases that are still under investigation.

'Speech delivered on 28 October 2005 in Brussels at a joint seminar of the International Federation of Journalists (IFJ) and the European Anti-Fraud Office (OLAF) for the OLAF Anti-Fraud Communicators' Network (OAFCN)'

Mr White,
Ladies and Gentlemen,
OAFCN members,

On behalf of OLAF I would like to give you a warm welcome. I am pleased that the communication network that has been built up here in the last few years is so successful. Your presence here today shows that you appreciate these meetings very much and that we are moving forward.

This is also borne out by the make-up of today's seminar, with direct participation by representatives of the press and journalists' federations, in particular Mr White. I see this as a real chance for dialogue and better understanding on both sides.

In this context I would like to take up in more detail the issues already raised by Mr Henrik Hololei, Head of the Cabinet of Vice-President Siim Kallas, concerning openness - or the lack of it - and the protection of investigations and the individual on the one hand and, on the other, the desire and need to describe in clear and transparent terms what an authority does.

The type of investigations conducted by OLAF and your own departments in the Member States, which are designed to protect institutions and must safeguard the rights of individuals, should not be seen primarily as a negative measure. On the contrary, the purpose is to root out the bad apples, so to speak, i.e. to identify those people who are abusing the systems in place.

This is the message we are trying to get across and we should therefore always be mindful of informing the public via the press. We would like to send out positive signals by using the results of our work to identify clearly the areas where there is scope for adjustment and improvement. We are certainly not in the business of cheap propaganda that seeks to call into question the workings of all institutions per se. As an illustrative example I would cite the Oil-for-Food programme introduced by the UN in New York. In that case there was a definite need to get to the bottom of the facts. I also agree with any member of the press who says that it is too late for that now. Much more should have been done beforehand.

That is of course correct. However, what has to be done now is to draw lessons from what happened and to clear up any injustices and infringements of the law. In that sense this clarification phase should also be seen in a positive light – even if it is a painful process for the United Nations. What we are striving for in our day-to-day work is to prevent abuses such as the Oil-for-Food programme from happening at all. We must be able to take preventive action.

It is important that we in the European institutions admit that we cannot be free of problems either. It is not enough just to recognise where the problems lie; we must also tackle them head on. Great progress has been made here. Anyone who has ever come into contact with the European budget and is familiar with the context knows where and how EU funds may be spent and that this is regulated by law.

I would like to stress here – also for the benefit of the representatives of the new Member States who are here with us today – that the big scandals many prophesied would accompany EU enlargement have yet to come to pass. Many people predicted that Europe would be overrun with corruption and that entire systems would collapse.

Two years after enlargement I am still waiting for these cataclysmic events to happen.

I believe that we have managed to prevent what the pessimists were predicting by sound preparation, continual cooperation in investigations, hard work and also a spirit of openness. There are good examples of cases where the national criminal prosecution authorities in the new Member States have uncovered irregularities involving EU funds entirely on their own, without any help or even pressure from Brussels.

I would also like to mention the next round of enlargement. We have with us today representatives from Romania. I shall never ever forget my first public appearances in Romania - the contacts with the press, who almost "ate me alive" at the mention of corruption. Anyone who tried to explain things rationally was denounced more or less immediately as an agent of the system. But, on the other hand, it also took a long time to clarify what corruption actually means. My last visit to Romania proved that things have evolved. The same issues I had raised before were now looked at in a different light. Talks with government authorities were more rational and less emotionally charged. If we can succeed in getting the press to take a similar view and

– I must express myself carefully here – not automatically to regard everyone as a serious criminal, then we will be on the right path there too. But all over Europe the biggest danger we always face is that our investigations may be misused for political purposes. We must therefore try to prevent such abuse through good communications.

On the question of public relations work and protection of the individual, I would like to stress that, in Maître Louis, we have someone among us at this seminar who comes to face-to-face with investigations because of his professional environment.

The same applies, from a different point of view, to the representatives here from journalists' federations, Aidan White for the IFJ and Michael Stabenow for the API. Both of them are very familiar with the tensions we experience and contribute through their daily work to better understanding.

I would therefore argue that we should carry on with this system of dialogue and joint meetings.

In particular I would like to stress – and I see this in the work of my press spokesman Alessandro Butticé, whom I really have to thank for the idea of regular meetings of the OAFCN network – how easy it is today to communicate with each other over and above Europe.

Ladies and Gentlemen, it is also thanks to you that we are able to exchange views and tackle together the many problems facing us. As I emphasised last year, you are not alone with your problems; these are problems which are global in scope.

With this thought in mind, let me wish you all a successful day.

European institutions

Alessandro BUTTICÉ,

Head of Unit, 'Communication, Public Relations, Spokesman' and Spokesman for the European Anti-Fraud Office (OLAF)

Alessandro BUTTICÉ

is Head of the Communication, Public Relations and Spokesman Unit within the European Anti-Fraud Office (OLAF) of the European Commission. He has created and coordinates the OLAF Anti-Fraud Communicators Network (OAFCN). Before joining the European Commission, Mr Butticé served as Colonel in the Italian Guardia di Finanza where he held several managerial positions, which included leading the operational unit of investigators into financial and economic crimes and drug cases, as Deputy Head of Communication and Spokesperson in the Guardia's Headquarters. He has also worked as a freelance journalist and a part-time professor at the University of Bari, in Italy.

'What anti-fraud information and communication policy for OLAF?'

The names of the seminars ([21]) as well as of the virtual public debate ([22]) on anti-fraud communication launched by the European Anti-Fraud Office (OLAF) within the framework of its anti-fraud communicators network (OAFCN) ([23]), are very useful in introducing the anti-fraud communication and information policy: 'The protection of European financial interests: information and communication as a means of fraud prevention'.

One specific term, perhaps, deserves to be considered for a moment, the word 'fraud'. One can define fraud as being an attack on the interests of all citizens. And, since fraud does not only harm a specific person or group of persons but society as a whole, it is generally perceived as a crime without victims.

Consequently, how can we make citizens aware of the danger of this type of fraud? How can we make it possible for communication and information, in other words, for a collective pedagogical action to become a major player in fraud prevention?

These are the main questions to which the public debates launched by OLAF wish to offer an answer to.

These initiatives' origins and *raison d'être* can be found in OLAF's communication and information strategy. This strategy was developed within 'the idea laboratory' that to some extent is the European Anti-Fraud Office (OLAF), taking into account its future projects, its immediate actions and its operational activities.

Therefore, it is a completely new policy that is based on two relatively simple concepts: information and communication not only as a service to the citizen but also as a fraud prevention tool. To achieve this goal, the communication strategy must be based, on the one hand, on the absolute respect for legality principles and, on the other hand, on the respect for individual rights, that is, to respect the presumption of innocence of those persons under investigation and to protect the confidentiality of investigations. This strategy must also consider another obligation we have — as all other public institutions — to inform the public on how public funds are being spent, including when they are assigned to investigative services, whether national or Communitarian.

OLAF's anti-fraud communication and information policy is based on concepts easy to define; but its application, in contrast, is not as easy. Indeed, its application requires pursuing and maintaining a balance — that sometimes may be very difficult to attain — between the requirements that I just mentioned which, in certain cases, can collide and oppose each other, making the implementation of this policy a very complex matter.

Executing this communication and information strategy, in particular by means of the press, is not always a simple affair for a national investigative service and that is all the more true for a young investigative service such as OLAF, instituted within a legal framework that is still relatively fragile and half way between administrative and legal. Contrary to national services, OLAF is not based on the experience and tradition of the majority of national administrative or criminal investigative services.

OLAF has the power to act within the European Union, which means within a territory where a global judicial space does not yet exist and where internal borders — that no longer exist for people, goods, or capital — do exist and are still clearly defined for investigators as well as for law enforcement and judicial authorities.

Information, as well as goods, persons and capital within the EU, no longer has borders and circulates faster and faster and through an ever growing number of channels. But achieving an information and communication policy based on respect for legality principles as a service to citizens does not mean that all information can be revealed: there are secret documents and confidential information that can damage the outcome of investigations and affect individual rights. The media, if not the only vehicle for this kind of information, are nonetheless the main source in charge of revealing facts that can sometimes damage investigations and persons.

Therefore, those of us who are responsible for communication departments in investigative services have the duty, on the one hand, to inform, and on the other, to protect certain information. As a result it is not always easy to reconcile the public's expectations and those of the media — that are always on the lookout for information — with protection of confidential information obtained during investigations.

But difficult does not mean impossible. The fact that the implementation of an anti-fraud communication and information policy is a difficult task does not mean that it is an impossible one. Our experience and the statements received from various sources prove it. Despite many difficulties, OLAF — in close collaboration with its Anti-Fraud Communicators Network — has created within the Member States and the candidate countries, even if modestly, something that constitutes undoubtedly a step further in the creation of a European platform of legality and justice, a platform also built on knowledge, information and to raise citizens' awareness towards issues that often affect them more than they imagined at first, and, once again, to inform citizens that protecting the Community's financial interests entails, above all, prevention, because prevention is better than the cure.

Among the directorates-general of the European Commission, the unit within OLAF that I have had the honour to coordinate since it was created is one of the smallest information, communication and public relations units. However, it is the only one to have included a spokesperson for the 'investigative' function of the office who is independent from the European Commission.

This independence must be, and is, practised within an absolute respect for legality principles and the defence of public interest. And the conscious effort to defend the independence of an office created to serve the interests of the European citizen has helped my collaborators and me to accomplish our daily responsibilities. These efforts have strengthened our resolve to react in the best possible way, in other words, firmly, when faced with situations that look to destabilise and that must be effectively handled by the services responsible for institutional communication. If not it will be necessary to consider looking for a different job.

But along what lines should this anti-fraud communication and information policy be based?

An anti-fraud communication policy: four cardinal points

As was the case for a ship's crew, which in times past embarked towards troubled waters and unknown destinations, OLAF's communication and information policy, created in 2000 — when my unit was created and the director-general entrusted me with its coordination — is based upon four aspects that are the cardinal points of our activities.

The four cardinal points are:

- absolute respect for legal provisions;

- EU communication and information guidelines;

- parameters given by the budgetary authority;

- indications contained in the reports and viewpoints given by OLAF's Supervisory Committee ([24]) pertaining to the office's investigative function.

1. Absolute respect for legal provisions

I do not consider it necessary to explain this aspect extensively because it is the pillar of every service with a mission to ensure the respect and protection of legal provisions. Thus it is unthinkable for any investigative service not to be based upon this central principle. The law must be respected always and at any cost. And respecting the law involves respecting the professional secret. Because if the possibility is open for a person who operates under the realm of professional secrecy to take a confidential document in order to transmit it to a third party, this makes it simply impossible for an institution to adequately perform ([25]). And when the institution is an investigative service, it makes it impossible to search and/or pursue the person suspected of having violated the law or other persons' rights.

2. EU communication and information guidelines

They are made available to us mainly through the Commission's communications pertaining to the 'Information and communication strategy for the European Union ([26])'.

As can be read in the most recent Commission communication, dated 2 July 2002, this strategy 'does not place on a lesser level the information and communication activities developed by the Commission's directorates-general in their particular sector-based competence domain. Developed as a complement to these activities, it aims, however, at contributing to a global dynamic for all the different sector-based information actions, so as to strengthen the Commission's coherence with regard to its information and communication actions'.

Although OLAF is independent in its investigative function, as a directorate-general of the Commission, it is impossible for the anti-fraud communication and information strategy developed by the office not to be inspired by this document. The strategy is being developed, maybe even more than in other EU areas of competence, in a progressive and empirical way.

But while contributing to create a public platform for European debate on the protection of Community financial interests, this policy also looks to contribute to reinforce the coherence of the Commission's actions relating to information and communication, as indicated in the communication text.

Indeed, at the time of the greatest enlargement of the Union, as well as of the approval of a European Union Constitution, and faced with incomprehension with regard to globalisation, the European project needs more and more direction and visibility. One of the conclusions reached by the Heads of State or Government during the Laeken declaration was that the European Union could not continue to make any considerable progress without the support and commitment of its citizens. Nevertheless, there are many citizens who are aware of the fact that they are ill-informed on 'European issues' and blame the media and the national authorities as well as the European institutions for the unclear vision they have of Europe.

For this reason, fighting ignorance and indifference today has become an essential need and duty of the European Union. It becomes an even more urgent obligation when criminal attacks on Community financial interests pose an important obstacle in the development of the European Union.

I am convinced that the lack of knowledge and disaffection that citizens feel towards the European Union, in particular with regard to the protection of financial interests, is not fatally irreversible. This situation is explained mainly by the complexity of the European financial procedures, but not only by this factor. Indeed, until now, the resources assigned for the development of an anti-fraud information and communication policy have been quite limited as far as European institutions and Member States are concerned.

This was even more evident after the results of the first Eurobarometer ([27]) survey on the attitudes concerning fraud detrimental to the EU and its budget, carried out at the request of OLAF and published in January 2004. The study showed that three out of four persons asked agree that the EU should give more information on anti-fraud campaigns and success stories, and that 56 % of EU citizens feel that the media does not inform them enough on the EU fight against this type of fraud.

In its White Paper on European governance, the Commission recognises that a real information and communication policy is the first strategic element necessary for better European governance. This standard should also be applied in the protection of Community financial interests. Thanks to targeted and precise facts given by the institutions, Euroscepticism borne from a sometimes imprecise mediatisation of certain budgetary irregularities should be by now certainly quite limited.

On the subject of citizens' awareness of European issues and specifically of the fight against fraud, Mr Siim Kallas, Vice-President of the European Commission on Administrative Affairs, Audit and Anti-Fraud, insists: 'Communication can help in deterrence. It is possible to prevent fraud by raising awareness of the severity of crimes related to EU funds, as well as by promoting a meaningful public debate on this issue. It can also be done by raising awareness of OLAF's and the local authorities' efforts to prevent and detect fraudulent acts committed against the taxpayer's money' ([28]).

He goes on to say, with a motivating message with regard to OLAF's communication policy, that changing the public's perception of the work performed by anti-fraud authorities and getting through a positive message is a difficult task. 'But this does not mean that it cannot be done. We need to communicate continuously that we strive to be professional, impartial and reliable in fighting fraud that harms all citizens, and that these institutions work well every day'.

He stresses that 'in the fight against corruption the key to success is a change in public opinion. Communication policy can help achieve that public opinion functions effectively as a means to deter fraud'.

Vice-President Kallas concludes by pointing out that even if he is a strong advocate for transparency, every investigative institution must take into account the respect for law and 'communicate and in practice confirm the message that information is given according to legal and professional principles'.

In the Member States and at European level, democracy depends on the citizens' capacity to take part in public debate. The institutions, with the support of the Member States, should contribute by assuming this challenge, which will have an even larger field of action with the enlargement.

3. Parameters given by the budgetary authority

The third cardinal point is occupied by the budgetary authority, and, specifically, by the Budgetary Control Committee (Cocobu) of the European Parliament. Cocobu has already honoured us by taking part in the seminar organised last year in Bucharest ([29]). On that occasion we counted on the gracious participation of its former President, Mrs Theato, who always liked to think of herself as OLAF's godmother.

Cocobu has indirectly participated in the creation of the communication strategy and has encouraged its application.

In an amendment to the 2003 budget draft, for example, Cocobu's Vice-President, Mr Bösch, encouraged OLAF to be more active with its communication strategy, particularly with regard to the quantity and quality of its press releases ([30]). OLAF, although it has very limited resources devoted to this area, received this suggestion very favourably to continue and increase the volume of its communication activities, by means of the media, within the boundaries, obviously, of the abovementioned constraints and other constraints which I will evoke in the following paragraphs.

However, during a public discussion with OLAF, on 7 April 2004, in connection with the investigation launched by the Belgian legal authorities concerning a German journalist working for *Stern*, Mr Bösch asked OLAF 'to end its foolish press policy'. According to Mr Bösch, the office had published way too many press releases and the investigators in Luxembourg had been surprised to read an OLAF press release concerning a file that had been sent to them. Mr Bösch concluded by stressing, 'There needed to be more investigators and fewer press officers'.

During the same public discussion, Mrs Stauner, European MP and Cocobu member during the fifth legislature (1999–2004), added, 'OLAF should be careful as to its declarations in press releases. It should not authorise its civil servants to address the press'.

Thereafter, members of the European Parliament of the current legislature (2004–09) have made more specific information available to us with concrete suggestions supporting the need for an anti-fraud communication policy.

Mr Szabolcs Fazakas, for example, newly elected Member of Parliament and Chairman of Cocobu, underlines that 'in the information society sharing information with the public is crucial' ([31]).

He details his point of view notably with regard to the relationship between investigative bodies and the media, which changed after reading the contributions sent to the OLAF Round Table on Anti-Fraud Communication ([32]). 'Initially, my idea was that fraud investigators should not appear in the press at all. Indeed, their work relies on confidentiality'. But he goes on to add, 'Then, having read through the contributions and expert opinions, I reconsidered my initial point of view. Indeed, in a world influenced by the mass media and by information available at random, it is increasingly important that organisations protecting our financial interests are present in the media and that the media portray a positive image of them'.

Mrs Silvana Koch-Mehrin commented on the need to intensify communication campaigns within the Member States ('the person who defrauds is a liar'), to reinforce the OLAF Anti-Fraud Communicators Network (OAFCN) and to create in all Member States a toll-free telephone number to report on cases related to fraud ([33]).

According to Mr Paulo Casaca, it goes without saying, on the one hand, that any law enforcement service requires a certain degree of discretion to properly operate and, on the other hand, that 'the public has the ultimate right to know about public wrongdoings, and everybody — innocent or culprit — has the right to be informed of what he is accused of before a trial, so that he can defend himself' ([34]).

On his part, Mr Lorenzo Cesa wanted to underline 'that thanks to the OLAF Anti-Fraud Communicators Network, we have an invaluable and essential instrument in the fulfilment of European citizens' information requirements: people want to be informed on the cooperation and success of investigative services from Member States, and don't want to be constantly harassed by those who tend to exploit scandals. Special attention must be paid to this because, as we know, the "all corrupted" or "all defrauders" are equivalent to "nobody is corrupted" and "nobody defrauds"' ([35]).

Mr Gianni Pittella finally considered that by 'drawing attention with targeted information sequences on specific kinds of offences, the media could provoke a strong public opinion reaction, which would in turn call for an institutional course of action in a considerable number of cases, taking the form of new and stricter prevention and punishment policies. This would bring about a sort of chain reaction between the world of communication, public opinion and institutions' ([36]).

Last but not least, Mr Terry Wynn's observations on his website are also very enlightening, in particular when he underlines the difference between the public's perception and the facts in the use of Community funds. In our opinion, when a difference exists between the public's perception of the facts and the actual facts communication is always required, and for a public organisation it becomes an obligation and a service to the citizens ([37]).

Finally, in reference to Mrs Theato's speech in Bucharest ([38]), I can only add that, on the one hand, the not too mediatised investigators are 'a sign of quality', but that, on the other hand, public opinion is informed and influenced by the press. Consequently, it is even more difficult to achieve a balance on this issue. However, it is always necessary to aim towards this balance.

4. Guidelines provided by OLAF's Supervisory Committee

The Supervisory Committee is in charge of guaranteeing OLAF's independence.

The committee, in its viewpoint No 2/03 accompanying the Commission's report on the 'Evaluation of the activities of the European Anti-Fraud Office', three years after OLAF's creation, highlighted that 'OLAF has set up its own autonomous public relations department and conducts an active policy of communication with the public and the media. However, the Committee feels that, while communication is important, it is none the less secondary and should remain limited in view of the risks it entails for the respect of fundamental rights and the reputation of the institutions and their members, officials, and staff' ([39]).

To my knowledge, the only other observation made by OLAF's Supervisory Committee with regard to our communication policy prior to the anti-fraud communication round table, was one made by the Committee's President, Mr Raymond Kendall, during the hearing before the UK House of Lords. During this hearing, published in an ad hoc report on OLAF by the House of Lords ([40]), Mr Kendall strongly criticised certain video images produced by the office with its partners from the national customs services within the framework of the OLAF Anti-Fraud Communicators Network. They are the same images that according to the European MP Lorenzo Cesa, had, on the contrary, the merit of having 'drawn the attention of the world's public opinion on cigarette smuggling and contributed to an international and media mobilisation. Without this we would have never started an effective fight that has given us results during these last years that at first were completely unexpected ([41])'.

According to Mr Kendall, the European Parliament's objective, following the resignation of the Santer Commission, was to support internal investigations in European institutions and so attention should be focused solely on these investigations.

Mr Kendall has recently commented on OLAF's communication policy, this time from a new, positive and very encouraging point of view. 'We are dealing with an area such as this which deals with ethics, with morals, also with issues of incompetence, and all these things make the work of OLAF extremely difficult. Therefore, there is this necessity of explaining the positive aspects of what they do, and there are very, very many ([42])'.

He goes on to say that he can confirm, on the part of the Supervisory Committee, that things are moving on very quickly towards the establishment of what is becoming every day a more efficient Anti-Fraud Office.

European Institutions

With regard to the relationship between investigative services and the press, Mr Kendall considers it better to give as much information to the media as possible, obviously excluding material prejudicial to the investigation. He justifies this by explaining that 'there is perhaps — and particularly in the context of the European institutions — a tendency to overemphasise confidentiality. It seems to me, and my experience has been over the last four years here in Brussels, that it is extremely difficult to keep anything secret in the institutions. Somewhere along the line, information gets out, even suspicions which may not even be confirmed as suspicions become the subject of rumour and so on, so in that situation, it's probably better to give as much information as you can, with due respect for confidentiality'.

It is quite obvious that to find and maintain a balance between all the interests, rights and duties and between all these different points of view — which, put together, appear sometimes contradictory — constitutes the greatest challenge we must face.

OLAF AND THE MEDIA

Even though contact with the media only represents one aspect of the anti-fraud communication and information strategy, it is nevertheless a determining factor in any type of communication. What if OLAF could not communicate with the media (even if it has operational independence) if only to prevent or clear up misunderstandings? Who should or could do it in its place?

Without the right to speak publicly, circumscribed within the boundaries of legal provisions, OLAF's independence in its investigative function — which constitutes its *raison d'être* — would be severely compromised. And often nothing is more harmful than silence in a relationship with the media.

It is precisely because of its operational independence that OLAF is the only service in the European Commission to have a spokesman function which is independent of the Directorate-General for Press and Communication. The relations of the office with the media are handled on a centralised basis, in order to:

- provide the media with a single version of each material in a format that is constantly accessible, in order to prevent misunderstandings which could emerge if the information were provided by several people;

- protect the investigators and other personnel from direct media contact pertaining to sensitive areas of their work;

- ensure that the office, rather than the individual investigators, is identified as being in charge of each investigation, to protect each civil servant's identity and avoid personalisation ([43]);

- control as much as possible the risk of violation of investigation secrets and individual rights.

As some recent events have demonstrated (such as leaks of confidential documents ([44])), even in a service such as OLAF, which is staffed by experienced investigators who are well aware of their professional duties, a determined journalist can always find a disloyal person that for different reasons, objectives or interests is willing to leak information (or even worse, confidential documents) that could damage the outcome of investigations, individual rights and the credibility of the investigative service.

The office has adopted a very strict code of conduct. For ongoing investigations it usually gives out very little or no information, taking into account the restrictions described in Communitarian and national laws, as to protect the investigations' outcomes and the fundamental rights of all persons involved.

However, OLAF makes use of all available elements to ease the media's work, in the public's interest, but taking care not to violate the legality principles on which all investigative activities should be based in a democratic system.

The most important mechanism that OLAF has established to satisfy this specific demand has been without doubt the OLAF Anti-Fraud Communicators' Network (OAFCN).

THE OLAF ANTI-FRAUD COMMUNICATORS' NETWORK

I wish to welcome the colleagues that have joined the network in the last year. I would like to remind you that the OLAF Anti-Fraud Communicators' Network (OAFCN) ([45]) is one of the key elements in the anti-fraud communication strategy. We have just covered the four key elements that guide us in the application of this strategy, as the four points once guided ships through troubled waters. Let us talk now about the 'crew', those who, hand in hand with OLAF, successfully guide anti-fraud communication, and share their knowledge and experience for mutual benefit, in an effort to avoid mistakes.

The idea to create the network came up in 2001. The OAFCN owes its success to the professionalism and enthusiasm of its members. The network's goal is to give added value to the work of national investigative services, as well as to showcase the work of the different Member States and the global Community dimension of the fight against fraud. OAFCN members constantly exchange information on a legal and operational level on questions pertaining to information procedures of mutual interest. Likewise, they help journalists to evaluate, understand and document information transmitted to them by other OAFCN members, regardless of their nationality. Usually, national law enforcement services are more effective and feel more at ease with national than with foreign media. In collaboration with OLAF and other national investigative services ([46]), OAFCN members provide common media coverage (videos, photos and press releases) to illustrate their operational activities.

One of OAFCN's priorities for 2003–05 is to inform the candidate countries' citizens on the various criminal activities that we are trying to fight and the risks that they represent for taxpayers. The network's last meetings have included for the first time the 10 new EU Member States, as well as Bulgaria and Romania. Our seminars and the virtual round table have also been conceived in accordance with this objective.

For the public and the media to be aware of the importance of protecting the Community's financial interests in the candidate countries, it is necessary to assure taxpayers that their money is being spent in the best possible way. This also means explaining how and why any type of fraud against the Community's financial interests, from diversion of taxes and rights that make up the European budget to the abuse of Community financial assistance, involves a real and important loss that directly affects each European taxpayer. The OAFCN members carry out common media actions to illustrate how the Member States' national investigative services collaborate with OLAF. The goal is to show the success of administrative cooperation within an operational framework.

ISSUES TO REFLECT ON ADDRESSED TO THE MEDIA

To my friends the journalists, with all the respect that I have for them as a citizen, for the essential role they play in a democratic system, including the one of democracy's watchdog, I would like to send out a message, or rather, to discuss some matters to reflect on.

First of all, I insist on the fact that OLAF was created as a service for European citizens to defend the inalienable values that are at the core of the European Union: legality, rule of law and respect for democratic values. Therefore, all of OLAF's activities are deeply related to these values. This is valid even if OLAF's operational legal framework, created in an emergency situation by the Community Legislator in 1999, at the time of the Santer Commission's fall, cannot always fulfil the expectations of all parties involved — and this becomes especially complicated when faced with opposing expectations, as we discussed previously.

Obviously, journalists want to obtain as much information as possible on a specific subject. But the office's obligation is to protect fundamental rights, legal standards and the integrity and effectiveness of its investigations.

I also want to stress that OLAF is, and remains, a small service. The office has a team of about 350 employees, from the director-general, to the investigators, to the ushers. This is a small group of people in comparison with national investigative services, which have thousands of agents. But, even as a small service, OLAF handles investigations which are usually very delicate, complex, transnational, and which involve very large amounts of money. These investigations take place both inside and outside Community institutions and European Union territory. The fact that every Member State has its own legal framework and that the Communitarian one must also be considered adds to the complexity of the office's work. To that we must add, last but not least, the language barriers...

I will now point out some of the problems and issues that are well understood by law enforcement specialists, but may not be so by the outside world. Some of our interlocutors do not necessarily understand what it means to carry out an investigation and are sometimes unable to grasp the complexities involved in our work.

On this same note, it is quite clear that OLAF does not have a policy of 'journalistic scoops'. OLAF has no wish to conduct a communication policy marked by 'sensationalism'. OLAF's objective, above all, is to achieve concrete results in its investigations. This means that we aim to achieve results that cannot be measured by the number of positive press articles, but rather by the number of guilty verdicts, recovery measures and administrative or disciplinary procedures. This means as well, as the experts on this subject know, that these results cannot be expected immediately after an OLAF investigation has ended. Indeed, the legal, administrative and disciplinary procedures that can arise from an OLAF investigation are long and subject to complex procedures.

Information several years after the end of an OLAF investigation: Why?

Why does so much time elapse between an OLAF investigation and the disclosure of the information relating to it? There are many reasons. An OLAF investigation, as any complex financial and transnational investigation, can take months and even years to complete.

Secondly, in order to confront any attacks against the office's conclusions by the accused parties (who are very often represented by very experienced and well-prepared lawyers, considering the amounts of money involved), investigators need adequate time to prepare their files.

Thirdly, the end of an OLAF investigation often marks, as already mentioned, the beginning of another investigation (police, legal and/or administrative) in one or more States (in the EU or a third country).

And finally, due to the fact that operational results of investigations pertaining to financial and economic issues (such as guilty verdicts, recoveries, etc.) often arrive, as in every country, only after several years. In fact, in addition to the complexity of financial and transnational investigations, the majority of countries in the world, as well as all the Member States, have two if not three levels of judicial recourse.

In most cases, the involved parties may consider it beneficial (and will not hesitate) to use all the grounds for appeal at their disposal.

Excessive speculation or criticism of OLAF's operational activities (which began practically on the day after its creation and which the office has had to face and answer to one way or the other) can considerably slow down its operational activities. This only benefits the criminal organisations that the office has the responsibility to fight.

So please pay attention, dear journalists. Even a small investigative service can be weakened, even paralysed, by scandals or repetitive media attacks, and in such cases this only works against public interest. Prudence is therefore essential. If an investigator is at risk of being misled or manipulated, then so is a journalist. Like an investigator, a journalist's duty is to be attentive. In Brussels — the largest press room in the world, where press releases in several languages are constantly exchanged — attentiveness can become prudence by verifying information instead of simply translating it. This lack of prudence can lead to the circulation of false ideas and erroneous information. It is always prudent to ask who stands to gain from the circulation of inaccurate information. One should always ask: 'Who does it benefit?' Economic or political lobbyists? Someone's personal ambitions? 'Who does it benefit?' is the question that everyone within the European Parliament, other institutions and even in the Brussels press room is starting to ask. And that only makes us feel confident, first and foremost, as citizens.

Is a relationship based on trust possible between OLAF and the press?

According to a Belgian high-ranking magistrate, Christian Panier ([47]), 'the relationship between the justice system and the media has never been harmonious. It will never be a good relationship because both professions are, if not contradictory, very different. For the media, the keyword is "quickly", whereas for justice and for investigative services the keywords are "not too quickly", because if one moves too quickly, one makes mistakes'.

The experienced German investigative journalist, Mr Johannes Von Dohnanyi explained, 'investigative journalists and investigators from institutions behave like cats and dogs. Information exchange between European investigative journalists and investigators is often so difficult — on both sides — due mainly to distrust ([48])'.

In order for this relationship to become more harmonious, it is first necessary to try to create a relationship based on trust between journalists and those in charge of communication in investigative services, a personal and trusting rapport that can only be built individually and by taking everyday life experiences into consideration. But when I say a relationship based on trust, by this I do not mean based on complicity. A relationship based on trust means respect for one another's work, legal obligations and professional ethics.

Unfortunately, this relationship can sometimes be broken. Indeed, as said by Von Dohnanyi, 'journalists go with their research to European institutions and find themselves very often being blocked in their work by these institutions and maybe even sometimes being put on the suspect list. There are also journalists who cause massacres with information given to them in absolute trust by making it public without considering the possible consequences, just to get a scoop. As always in life we need to choose carefully who we can trust', concluded Von Dohnanyi.

In other words, in order to be effective while respecting the duties that have been assigned to him as a public servant, the OLAF spokesman must not necessarily have the same relationship with all journalists. Mutual trust must be earned by all parties involved.

As the Romanian television reporter Cristian Unteanu ([49]) said, to be efficient, a spokesperson does not need to give journalists all the elements of the investigation, hand them entire files, nor introduce them to sources. Experience has shown that investigative reporters find it helpful when spokespeople provide them with key elements to understanding an issue, or facilitate their contact with investigative and judicial personnel around the world, who can give them information that the spokesperson him/herself often cannot provide. The spokesperson can also help the reporter with documentation — for example, television and magazines need images and OLAF has done a great deal to provide memorable images, such as those that illustrated cigarette smuggling for viewers and readers around the world.

The spokesperson's talent is key, as indicated by Unteanu, as is the respect given to the investigation's priorities. But I think it is important to emphasise at this point that the reporter's intelligence, ability and professionalism — as my contact with eminent reporters has shown me — will carry him or her the rest of the way.

In short, my journalist friends, a relationship of mutual trust and respect between you and the communications department of any investigative agency is essential. You should seek it out and cultivate it. But this relationship requires the respect of the law and of your professional duties.

To respect the law, according to Christian Panier, means to never do less than is required and to never do wrong. To respect professional duties means to always do more and always strive to do it better. Let us try to always respect our professional duties with the greatest intellectual honesty, because behind every investigation there lies real men and women and real lives.

OLAF's independence

OLAF was created to fight fraud committed against the Community's financial interests and corruption within European institutions. As such, it was created as a completely independent investigative institution. This independence entails, obviously, an absolute respect for the law under every circumstance, as well as independence from everything and everybody — from any personal ambition and from any desire for notoriety.

It is to be expected that the work of a completely independent office will not make everybody happy. When a reporter or someone very influential is unhappy, it is to be expected that they will attack the investigators' work. To think otherwise would be naïve.

Thankfully, most of OLAF's personnel have been trained to confront this type of situation. They have been trained to remain independent in the face of external pressure, including the media's.

WHY DOES OLAF SOMETIMES HAVE TO TAKE A PUBLIC STAND?

OLAF does not measure its results according to the amount of positive press that it receives. This being the case, why is it necessary for OLAF to sometimes take a stand concerning the attacks carried out against it through the media? The answer is simple and based on concrete facts.

As I explained, due to objective reasons that elude OLAF's will and capabilities, the results of its investigations — the judicial, administrative and disciplinary measures — often take months or even years to be put forward.

As European MP Lorenzo Cesa has stated in a very direct way, sometimes 'the publication of an investigation's results by the media before the court has taken action can transform these results not only into instruments of political squabbling, but worse, into instruments utilised by criminal organisations [50].' These public processes in the media, this publication of the results of an OLAF investigation therefore often need to be publicly denied or rectified by the investigative service that has been unjustly challenged, even before legal measures are taken in the case.

If an investigative body such as OLAF, as many would like it to, refrained from exercising its right to rectify or clarify the allegations and speculation that have often threatened to compromise it, this would damage not only its aesthetic image, but its credibility. And let us not forget that the office's cooperation with its partners worldwide depends on the credibility and the professionalism of its investigators, the majority of whom were recruited from among the ranks of highly experienced judges, police officers, customs officials and European investigators.

Over the years, OLAF has become an essential instrument of international cooperation, very much appreciated by its partners at national level with whom it has built close ties that are strengthened regularly [51]. If the office lacked the right and the technical resources to defend itself publicly with weapons similar to those with which it is unfairly attacked (for example, statements to the press), it would come to an end. This would end the hope of creating a true legal system that looks out for the interests of all of Europe's citizens.

This is why, with the prudence that is required, we believe that this office has the duty — not only the right — to publicly respond to public accusations, as well as set in motion any necessary processes at the indicated institutions to protect its institutional credibility.

CONCLUSIONS

Despite the numerous and rigorous rules that regulate the information and communications policies at an investigative service such as OLAF — which apply not only to media relations, but also to general information, publications, videos, Internet, public relations and others — we will always be confronted by different points of view, which can be explained by the diversity of approaches and perspectives linked to national cultures, as well as different professional environments and even personal interests.

The two most extreme points of view come from two different schools of thought. On the one hand, there are those who would like everything to be made public, from the moment the investigation begins, and on the other hand, there are those who would prefer it if the investigative bodies remained permanently silent and devoid of any and all communication instruments.

The anti-fraud communication and information policy put forth by OLAF — a service that the legislative designed to be independent — is located somewhere between these two extremes, aiming for a balance that is not always easy to achieve. Independence, in a rule-of-law system, implies the absolute respect for the law under every circumstance, especially in the face of personal ambition and the desire for notoriety.

Luckily, the majority of OLAF's personnel were trained and are prepared to confront this type of situation. They are trained to be independent from every form of pressure, internal and external to the European institutions, even the pressures of the media.

'Transparency, service to the citizen and prevention' are the keywords of the OLAF's information and communication policy, but always within the strictest respect for the law.

The implementation of this policy requires not only ideas, but also moral rectitude and professionalism. It also requires human and financial means. It requires above all the political support of the European Parliament and the European Commission.

And it also depends upon the understanding and the support of the professional associations of journalists, as we build a relationship based on trust and a mutual respect for our legal and professional obligations.

The seminars and the forum initiated by OLAF to discuss the topic of communication as an instrument to prevent fraud also intend to provide the opportunity for a detailed study of the specificities of communication and information in the area of fraud prevention and to examine the ways in which they should be carried out. Here are some questions that we should reflect on.

- Once we accept that all anti-fraud bodies (police, customs, financial services, control and administrative services, etc.) must carry out information and communication activities, how should these actions help in the prevention of fraud, inform citizens about how their money is being spent and reduce the distance that separates them from Europe without degenerating in propaganda?

- What is the difference between information, communication and propaganda and what are the boundaries that separate them?

- Given the fact that the media are among the main information and communication instruments of any public institution, at national or Community level, what rules should govern the relationship between an investigative body and the press? And which press are we talking about, at European level and in the new countries? Can we rightfully refer to a 'European press', or are we referring to a diverse group of national, regional and local media outlets?

- Press relations are important. But information and communication actions are not limited to relations with journalists. There are other instruments that we must know and use appropriately, and even perhaps differently from country to country, in order to bring our institutions closer to the citizens. What are these instruments?

If, during the reflections that are to follow, we are able to come up with some clear and concrete answers to these questions, I think that we will have achieved the main goals of our event. If each of us leaves here with some new ideas, some clear ideas, about how to improve our respective institution's work in the area of fraud prevention, we could, I believe, all be satisfied with our work.

---

(21) 'First training seminar of the OLAF Anti-Fraud Communicators Network', Helsinki-Stockholm, 16 to 18 September 2002: http://europa.eu.int/comm/anti_fraud/olaf-oafcn/documents/seminar1_ en.pdf. 'The role of communication in fraud prevention', Salamanca, 21 to 23 November 2002. OAFCN seminar for journalists. http://europa.eu.int/comm/anti_fraud/olaf-oafcn/seminars/sal_ en.html. 'Protecting the Communities financial interests: information and communication as a means of fraud prevention in the context of EU enlargement', Bucharest, 20 to 22 October 2003. http://europa.eu.int/comm/anti_fraud/olaf-oafcn/seminars/bu_en.html

(22) Round Table on Anti-Fraud Communication: how information and communication can be a means of EU fraud prevention and a true service to the citizens in the respect of their rights: http://europa. eu.int/comm/anti_fraud/olaf-oafcn/rt/i_fr.html

(23) OLAF Anti-Fraud Communicators Network (OAFCN): http://europa.eu.int/comm/anti_fraud/olaf-oafcn/fr.html

(24) Article 11 of Regulation (EC) No 1073/99 of the European Parliament and the European Council, dated 25 May 1999, relating to investigations carried out by the European Anti-Fraud Office (OLAF) (OJ L 136, 31.5. 1999).

(25) Christian Panier, 'Justice, media, power: an infernal triangle'; Labour Editions, Brussels, 2004, p. 135.

(26) Communication from the Commission to the Council, the European Parliament, the European Economic and Social Committee and the Committee of the Regions, 'Information and communication strategy for the European Union', from 7.2.2002, COM(2002) 350 final.

(27) Eurobarometer opinion poll, 'Attitudes concerning fraud detrimental to the European Union and its budget', carried out at the request of the OLAF unit 'Communication, Public Relations, Spokesman', by the Directorate-General for Press and Communication ('Analysis of public opinion' sector) in 2003: http://europa.eu.int/comm/anti_fraud/press_room/eurobar/en.html

(28) Siim Kallas, Vice-President of the European Commission for Administrative Affairs, Audit and Anti-Fraud. Opening address at the OLAF seminar, 'Deterring fraud by informing the public', 24 to 26 November 2004, Brussels.

(29) OAFCN training seminar for anti-fraud communicators in candidate countries, Bucharest, 19 to 22 October 2003: http://europa.eu.int/comm/anti_fraud/olaf-oafcn/seminars/bu_en.html

(30) Budget 2003, Amendment proposal 5201, made by MPE Herbert Bösch concerning budgetary guideline COM-A-III 3 0 3: 'As proposed, the doubling of information and communication financial resources in comparison to 2002 [EUR 200 000] is not justified. The financial aid that for now is stocked in the reserve will be unblocked once the office has explained to the budgetary authority its information and communication strategy and, in particular, has exposed the means of diffusing more and better press releases (for 2000 and 2001, less than 12 press releases were counted per annum)'.

(31) Szabolcs Fazakas, Member of Parliament and Chairman of the Committee on Budgetary Control in the European Parliament. Opening address at the OLAF seminar, 'Deterring fraud by informing the public', 24 to 26 November 2004, Brussels.

(32) http://europa.eu.int/comm/anti_fraud/olaf-oafcn/rt/i_en.html

(33) Silvana Koch-Mehrin, Vice-President of the Democrat and Liberal Alliance Group for Europe, temporary member of the Committee on Budgetary Control, 'Perspectives for OLAF': http://europa.eu.int/comm/anti_fraud/olaf-oafcn/rt/c/koch_fr.pdf

(34) Paulo Casaca, Member of the European Parliament, Coordinator of the PSE Group in Cocobu, 'Secrecy and information, a right balance to be found': http://europa.eu.int/comm/anti_fraud/olaf-oafcn/rt/c/casaca_fr.pdf

(35) Lorenzo Cesa, Member of the European Parliament, Vice-President of the PPE (DC) and DE Groups, member of the Committee on Budgetary Control, *Cui Prodest* 'OLAF without communication?': http://europa.eu.int/comm/anti_fraud/olaf-oafcn/rt/c/cesa_fr.pdf

(36) Gianni Pitella, Member of the European Parliament, (PSE Group), former President of Cocobu, 'The media therefore have a role to play, if not in terms of prevention, at least in encouraging the dissemination of a culture of respect for the law by highlighting the damage which fraudulent activities cause to citizens': http://europa.eu.int/comm/anti_fraud/olaf-oafcn/rt/c/pitella_fr.pdf

(37) Terry Wynn, Member of the European Parliament (Group PES), 'The EU budget — Public perception and fact', 'Contrary to public opinion, Brussels is not the European centre of fraud and waste. The funds that — according to regular media reports — allegedly "disappear through fraud and waste" do not "disappear" in the corridors of the European Commission. EU money is almost exclusively spent in and by the Member States. This is where most irregularities occur. Admittedly, the European Commission might be blamed for not having adhered to some administrative financial rules to the last letter, but the European Parliament's and the Court of Auditors' criticism have led to a profound reform process within the Commission, creating clearer responsibilities, systems that are more transparent and more efficient control procedures': http://www.terrywynn.com/home.html

(38) http://europa.eu.int/comm/anti_fraud/olaf-oafcn/seminars/documents/theato_fr.pdf

(39) http://europa.eu.int/comm/anti_fraud/reports/sup_comm/2003/avis/fr.pdf

(40) Mr Raymond Kendall, Chairman of the OLAF Supervisory Committee, before the Select Committee on the European Union (Sub-Committee E) of the UK House of Lords 'Strengthening OLAF: Inquiry into the European Anti-Fraud Office', Wednesday 19 May 2004 '...The difficulty comes back again to the way you approach the media communication issue. You will see that in its own publicity film, OLAF says "This is what we do", and you will see in the film pictures of people running around at a border point or something like that with a jacket with "OLAF" on the back, like "FBI" or something like this, as if they wished to present themselves as some kind of truly operational outfit, which they are not, in the sense of the way our customs service is or anything else, and they make a big thing, for example, about trafficking in cigarettes, notably in the Mediterranean. To me, it is very clear that the best people to deal with that are the customs people. So you should be very interested in what the customs people tell you about that, but there is no reason why you should necessarily want to get involved when you could be doing better things. After all, as a result of the Santer Commission, the objective of the Parliament was to get hold of the internal investigation business. So there should be a clear emphasis on internal investigations and making sure that the external investigations are done by the Member States who are in the best position to do them'.

(41) Lorenzo Cesa, Member of the European Parliament, Vice-President of the PPE (DC) and DE Groups, member of the Committee on Budgetary Control, *Cui Prodest*, 'OLAF without communication?'

(42) Raymond Kendall, President of OLAF's Supervisory Committee, opening address at the OLAF seminar, 'Deterring fraud by informing the public', 24 to 26 November 2004, Brussels.

(43) According to Christian Panier, in 'Justice, media, power: an infernal triangle', 'We can sometimes ask ourselves where certain public prosecutors or substitutes find the time to look at their files when we realise the amount of hours they spend talking to the press or explaining themselves to the media'.

(44) OLAF press release numbers 17/2004, 14/2004, 7/2004, 21/2003 and 3/2002 in the web page: http://europa.eu.int/comm/anti_fraud/press_room/pr/index_en.html. Number 83/2004 from the Court of Justice.

(45) http://europa.eu.int/comm/anti_fraud/olaf-oafcn/fr.html

(⁴⁶) Some 56 % of European citizens declare that the media give relatively little information on the fight against fraud detrimental to the EU in their country. Among them, 58 % consider themselves ill-informed of this issue in the other Member States, while 57 % are badly informed on the EU fight against this type of fraud. Three out of four people think that the EU must distribute more information on the anti-fraud campaigns and successes obtained in this area: http://europa.eu.int/comm/anti_fraud/press_room/eurobar/en.html

(⁴⁷) Christian Panier, author of 'Justice, media, power: an infernal triangle'.

(⁴⁸) Johannes von Dohnanyi, Sonntags Blick, Ringier AG, Zürich, 'Investigative journalists and the protection of sources': http://europa.eu.int/comm/anti_fraud/olaf-oafcn/rt/c/jvd_fr.pdf

(⁴⁹) Cristian Unteanu, European correspondent, Prima TV Romania, 'Communication towards citizens: a democratic principle of the institutions' work': http://europa.eu.int/comm/anti_fraud/olaf-oafcn/rt/c/unteanu_fr.pdf

(⁵⁰) Lorenzo CESA, Member of the European Parliament, Vice-President of the PPE Group (DC) and of the DE, member of the Budgetary Control Commission, Cui prodest 'OLAF without communication?': http://europa.eu.int/comm/anti_fraud/olaf-oafcn/rt/c/cesa_fr.pdf

(⁵¹) To wit, the very positive statements made by the heads and the general directors of the main national police, customs and judicial institutions who are partners of OLAF on the ground. These statements can be read on OLAF's website: http://europa.eu.int/comm/anti_fraud/partners/tribune/index_en.html

'Speech - Joint seminar of the International Federation of Journalists (IFJ) and the European Anti-Fraud Office (OLAF) for the OLAF Anti-Fraud Communicators' Network (OAFCN) – Brussels - 28 October 2005'

Some of the greatest friendships of my professional life have been made on the battle-field, if you will allow the expression. This battlefield is of course a metaphorical one, and I remind those not present, who might be tempted to talk ironically of a 'warrior' spokesman even though I became a journalist before ever becoming an Official of a police organisation, that I first discovered that excellent text book *The Art of War* by the great Sun Tzu at journalism school rather than at the *Guardia della Finanza* Academy.

When, borrowing from Sun Tzu, I talk of friendships on the battlefield, that doesn't mean having friends from the opposing side. Having nearly always worked in the fight against crime in general, and in particular the fight against fraud, I have always done all I could not to have friends from the other side of the picket-fence. What I'm talking about instead is being able to express opposing ideas and to defend varying points of view, with colleagues of a style of management unlike my own, for example, or with those of differing investigative cultures and national backgrounds. Or, again, with magistrates whose ideas and investigative techniques have in the past differed from our own.

After a first and occasionally stormy encounter with such colleagues, time and contact have often led me to value the good faith of many of them, to help both parties better understand the other's point of view and to overcome any initial misunderstandings. The close collaboration that has come from this is based on a mutual trust. This trust, because it has been built on the job, is true and solid and cannot be separated from the mutual respect of both parties' duties and obligations. Frequently it has even become, over time, a true and personal friendship.

I do not know if a friendship like this will develop one day with Aidan White, General Secretary of the IFJ ([52]), whom we have the pleasure of having with us today as co-organiser of this seminar. I do feel, however, that all requirements are in place that will allow there to be at the very least a close and I hope mutual trust and respect between us one day in the not-too-distant future.

I say this not only because Aidan has already won my esteem by the tenacity, courage and professionalism he has shown in his not easy and important role as Secretary General of the IFJ. I say it also because the first contact we – or our respective organisations – had with each other – was not the easiest ever. Indeed, it was long-distance contact, never face-to-face, between sides incorrectly described as opposing by a disinformation we hope to begin fighting with this seminar.

On the one side, we were told, were the defenders of the freedom of the press, the watch-dogs keeping an eye out for the evildoings of the EU and non-EU institutions. On the other was OLAF and its accomplices, the investigative and judicial services its accomplices, defending 'despotic' or 'police states', 'evil ogres' that, working together, had had a journalist be according to some, searched, according to others, 'arrested', according to still others, perhaps even 'tortured'.

Long-distance contacts, I was saying, because I only had the pleasure of meeting Aidan White personally a short time ago, and of recognising in him a responsible, courageous interlocutor. Aidan White always acts in good faith even when we have a difference of position in a case against OLAF and the Commission at the Court of Justice of the European Communities ([53]), or when he asks OLAF for things that OLAF has no legal means of providing. Aidan carries out his job with passion and dignity just as each of us tries to do in his own small way. His task is to represent over 500,000 journalists, 250,000 of whom are in Europe, in a world that needs the freedom of the press. In a world which needs to protect the freedom of information, one of the most important signs of democracy.

This contact between us has lead to the organisation here in Brussels today of this joint seminar of OLAF and IFJ.

It is a seminar which, as the title says, aims to be a further opportunity to construct that mutual trust upon which contact between journalists and investigative and anti-fraud services should be based in the context of the European Union. A context in which the freedom of the press and of information follow naturally on from the democratic and legal values on which this European Union was founded.

I said it was, and this I emphasise, a further opportunity; because this process of construction of a relationship of mutual trust is not new, even though I hope that this seminar can be an important step forward for it. This process is not new, because every OAFCN member began to construct or consolidate the relationship with journalists on a national level a long time ago. This just as I myself began doing, with a certain satisfaction, over twenty years ago, contributing to the creation of a new and modern information and communication policy for the Italian Guardia di Finanza. The memory of that experience is summarised in a booklet, now a little old, but available for all those able to follow the language of Dante Alighieri ([54]).

This process is not a new one, however, whether on a European level or on that of OLAF, because our network has been active now for five years, even though it seems some people don't like to be reminded of this. So for five years, that is to say from the creation of OLAF through our dialogue, through our common actions – which have represented one of the greatest professional satisfactions I have experienced at OLAF - we have been carrying forward, with few resources but with great enthusiasm, the project of an information and communication anti-fraud strategy as a service for European citizens. I must stress, though, that this strategy is not only a service but also an instrument of *fraud prevention*.

The majority of our joint endeavours are discussed in the publication *Deterring fraud by informing the public* ([55]), on which both the IFJ and IPA collaborated through the participation of Cristian Unteanu and Enrico Brivio ([56]). These endeavours are also to be seen in the different seminars organised for the network members and for the journalists, whose main objective is that of organising a better service to our journalist friends. And through these journalists, a better service to all European citizens.

The Anti-Fraud Communicators' Network, dear Aidan, which I have the pleasure of introducing to you today, was created above all for you, the journalists.

It is well-known in fact that national investigative services are more efficient, more at ease and more willing to collaborate with national media than foreign media. One of our goals, therefore, has always been that of ensuring that each of the national investigative services that OLAF works with has the opportunity, as far as possible, to come into contact with international media and not only those of its own country.

Alerting citizens and the media to the issues surrounding the protection of the European Community's financial interests means involving them in our efforts to guarantee to the taxpayers that their money is used in the best possible way. It also involves explaining to them how and why any form of fraud perpetrated against the financial interests of the Community, from fiscal evasion of the European budget to abuse of fiscal aid provided by the Community, involves real and dramatic loss that affects all European taxpayers. OAFCN members thus use the media to inform the public and to illustrate the existing collaboration between investigative services in the Member States and OLAF, thus showing the successes and not merely the limits of this co-operation.

The OAFCN is an instrument that all of us here, Aidan, place at the disposal of the IFJ and, for the international Brussels press, of the IPA. This is the first and most definitive step towards the consolidation of that mutual trust which should be at the base of every kind of constructive relationship. We are sure that the IFJ will be capable of making the best possible use of this network.

This OAFCN network, I want to emphasise, is not the result of any legal requirement. None of the colleagues here with us today has come due to a Community requirement which obliges his organisation to take part. The network has been working for five years, and it continues to survive because it has shown that it works. What is more, it works and aims to work especially to help the people represented by the IFJ, to help those thousands of your colleagues who have already benefited from its existence and who thank us on a daily basis. This thanks is given to us in a much quieter although no less heartfelt way than the noisier, although largely Brussels-based, defamatory campaigns that just a few of your colleagues – vocal and well-organised nonetheless – have aimed at us: campaigns that are sometimes unfair although not necessarily intimidating.

Excuse me if I say this again, but this network is also working for the IFJ as far as the sector you represent works towards upholding the law and the democracy in which we all believe. That is to say, towards information that is as transparent, as objective as possible, that is not used for political battles, not used for disinformation or fraud. All of us here, citizens first and foremost, consider this as highly important and expect your federation to oversee it.

Therefore, in order for it to continue to exist, the network needs the collaboration and the support of the IFJ.

I am perfectly aware that in this world nothing is perfect and that everything can therefore be made perfect. But all of us believe and hope in a press that is becoming more independent, free and objective, just like we believe in a legal and justice system which should also be, as far as humanly possible, independent and, naturally, objective.

I do not want to repeat what both I and other far more authoritative speakers have said and written several times last year, during the round table on anti-fraud communication. I do want however to remind you that independence, whether that of an investigative service or that of a journalist, is not an abstract concept. It is, above all, a question of respecting rules and norms that are firstly legal, but also deontological.

I believe that such rules as these already exist on a European level. If we consider that they can be improved, we will work together in order to improve them, but we will do this using the methods provided by the differing judicial systems on Institutional and national level, improving the rules with already existing normative tools. And while we wait for them to be changed, let us all strive to respect them and to make sure those with whom we work do likewise.

No-one can better be the teachers and guardian of journalists' ethics than their own associations.

Personally I am proud of having contributed in these five last years, together with our colleagues here today, to building a policy of information as a means of fraud prevention. An information policy which has also been a defence of OLAF's investigative independence, an independence which, as some people have shown, everyone claims sometimes to want, but which in practice some (and not only within the European Institutions) have at times tried to limit.

We have known many pressures of all kinds and there have even been some instances of intimidation directly at me personally. Despite these I as OLAF spokesman, together with my colleagues in my small unit, have defended the right and the duty of an independent investigative service to have a "*mouthpiece*" independent of any other structure outside OLAF.

OLAF must have this *mouthpiece*. A *mouthpiece* that some have criticised, contested, sabotaged perhaps because, as some people have suggested, there are those who would like to speak, or to carry on speaking, about OLAF's investigations in OLAF's place.

With the help of the network, and of my few but excellent colleagues, we have defended this right, this absolute necessity, to the maximum. I have also defended, however, the fact that this *mouthpiece*, like all mouthpieces should be, is dependent upon the *head* of its *body*, a *head* that in the OLAF *body* is the person who is legally responsible for OLAF's own investigative function and who, according the current law, is OLAF Director General. And this, of course, only as long as the *head*, if you will allow me the euphemism, stays *healthy*. The only means I know of determining the *health* of the instructions given by the brain to the *mouthpiece* is that of respecting the law and legality. Any other way would be illegal.

Unless proven otherwise, every time OLAF's *mouthpiece* has opened or closed it has been with the strictest respect for the law. Proof of the opposite, for an investigative service, does not come from the word going around, whether noisy or not, nor from a press campaign, whether positive or not. There is only one method of judging this: the decisions of the courts, because let us not forget that we live in a Europe, luckily, that, although far from perfect, remains - even within the possible limits of the European Union – a world-wide beacon of justice, of legality, of liberty and of the respect for human rights. This is the Europe in which I personally believe, but I am sure everyone here feels the same way. It is for this Europe that my colleagues and I work and, if necessary, fight.

However, independence also means resisting many things, and not only corruption. And resisting corruption not only means resisting when offered money. Independence also means not being part of the desire for consensus at any price, which means it is logical that those who work in a truly independent investigative body know that they will never make everyone happy, even when working on relations with the press or when signing press releases on behalf of the Office. When very influential people are not happy, for example, it would be naïve not to expect the work of the investigators to come under fire.

When a journalist is the unhappy one, it would be just as naïve not to expect the investigation to come under attack with the means used by journalists, whether these means is more or less correct according to the law or to the code of ethics.

Luckily the majority of OLAF's staff, including those who work in information and communication, have also been trained and prepared to face this type of situation and to be as independent as possible of external pressures such as those of the media.

Resisting media pressure does not of course mean ignoring well-founded criticism, which helps us to improve our structure and fix our mistakes. But OLAF, like every serious investigative service, must aim, in the interests of the citizens, for its results to be assessed according to their significance and not on how many positive articles have been published in the press.

In certain cases, however, it is OLAF 's duty to take a public position in relation to certain journalistic attacks. The reason for this is simple, and based on concrete facts. If an investigative service such as OLAF did not have the right to public speech, if only in order to rectify or clarify certain claims or speculations that, at times, have risked to damage it seriously, it is not its *aesthetic image* as an investigative service, not important for the public, that would suffer, but OLAF's own *credibility*. Let us not forget that the world-wide collaboration between the Office and its various operational partners is especially based on the *credibility* and professionalism of OLAF.

Such claims or speculations can be serious, especially when they happen far prior to the judicial or administrative decisions which will establish, if necessary, the real nature of the facts and the real responsibilities, but which will often take place many years later. During this time, the Office's credibility is slowly being undermined. And if this happens at a time when the Office is busy carrying out investigations that attract the attention of the institutions and of public opinion on a European or world-wide level, we can easily imagine what the consequents could be for public interest.

In March 2002 for example, there was one whole month in which a series of extracts of a confidential OLAF document was published by various different press bodies, weeks of public accusations and discredit, which were sending the credibility of the young Institutional investigative service into freefall. OLAF, which was being described as untrustworthy, as a sieve of confidential documents that, according to some, could even be bought, issued a press release (signed by myself, of course), outlining the problem and the measures that had been taken ([57]).

It was the public denunciation by the then President of the EP Committee for Budgetary Control of the fact that the members of the press had an important document that the Parliament had not heard about and its request that OLAF transmit this document to it, that meant that the decision to publish this press release could not be put off any longer ([58]).

I do not think that many other press releases have provoked that much attention, speculation and untruths, whether on the part of the media or not.

Indeed, although that particular press release has been called a textbook example of excellent *crise communication*; although it has not been the object of any censure on the part of any of the various National and European judicial Authorities interested by this leak of information; although I am convinced that, by signing and releasing this press release I fulfilled my duties as Official and as OLAF spokesman, contributing to the defence of independence and to the recovery of OLAF's operational credibility; although I am certain that OLAF fulfilled its obligation to declare in public with all transparency, *"we have a problem, we are not hiding it and we are telling you about what we are doing to solve it and to try and prevent the same thing happening again"*, out of respect for legal principals and for safeguarding the rights of all concerned parties; although, finally, this same European Ombudsman, the only body to have criticised OLAF's actions, formally stated, after a few polemical media moments, that it *"had no reason to doubt that – the man speaking to you now – has not carried out his professional duties in an irreproachable manner"*; despite everything that I have just listed…, I sincerely believe that few spokespersons have never been attacked, even on a personal level, for having signed a press release of this kind.

But, as I said before, being independent also means being able to withstand every kind of pressure, even if those experienced, believe me, have not been small. However, withstanding pressure without giving in, is part of the game and part of our work, that is of course until it goes as far as to require the intervention of the courts so that one can defend one's own interests. But if this pressure, this intimidation, must never make us stop carrying out our work to the maximum, we must nevertheless admit that they can make us waste enormous amounts of time. This time comes out of the time that, at least for my small Unit, we would have wanted to dedicate to helping more the hundreds of journalists who ask for our help every year.

I don't consider it the moment to go into greater details of this serious case of leak of confidential documents and suspected corruption that, over and beyond what was reported in our press releases and in the judicial decisions taken then by European and National Judiciaries, is still the ongoing subject of national judicial investigations. This is because I consider it right to respect the secret nature of the investigations being carried out according to times and ways of doing that I do not have any right to discuss.

I do however hope that this *incident* is now behind us. I also hope that we can draw lessons from what we have gone through in order to prevent, in everyone's interest, incomprehension that, in the end, becomes a danger for the citizens, for investigative services but also for those same journalists and for this relationship of mutual trust that we would like to strengthen.

Thinking about the future, about Aidan White and the IFJ, with all the respect that, as a citizen, I harbour for the essential role journalists play in a democratic system, including that of the watchdog of democracy, I would like to remind you of some of the thoughts that I had directed to the attention of the media last year, during our round table.

Excessive speculation about, or criticism of, OLAF's operational activities (which began almost the day after OLAF was created), which does not take into account the legal, institutional and complex multinational framework in which OLAF operates (speculation and criticism which the Office has had to face and respond to in one way or another) can bring about a slowing-down of OLAF's operational activity, which gives an advantage to the criminal organisations that the Office has the task of fighting.

So then, my friends from the IFJ, we must be careful. Even a small investigative service can be weakened, if not paralysed, by repeated attacks and scandals by the media and it is the public good which suffers as a result. We must therefore be prudent, because if an investigator runs the risk of going in the wrong direction or of being manipulated, this is also true for a journalist. Just like the investigator, the journalist must therefore be careful. In Brussels, one of the biggest press rooms in the world, where news and information is exchanged in many languages, this kind of vigilance could become a basic habit, that of not limiting oneself to *translating* an article without checking at least some of its contents. Although it is easier not to bother, this is a bad habit that often leads to incorrect ideas and information being spread. The first step should always be to ask oneself who could profit by the rapid spreading of this inexact information. We must always ask: *"who stands to gain from this?"* Is it economic or political lobby groups, personal agendas, or someone or something else? *Who stands to gain from this?* It seems that everyone, within the European Parliament, the other Institutions and even the Brussels press room, is now beginning to ask this question. And this in turn encourages the growth of our trust, first and foremost our trust as citizens.

In conclusion I would like to answer the question at the heart of this seminar: is it possible to build a relationship of mutual trust between investigative services and the press?

My answer is yes, but with certain conditions because, as always in life, it is important to choose with care the people in whom to place our trust. In other words, in order to be effective in our own duties as civil servants and journalists, we certainly cannot have the same relationship of trust with all investigative journalists or spokespersons.

Trust, precisely because it is mutual, must always be deserved and earned by both parties, by respecting some basic, clear and unbreakable rules.

Personally I do not know whether Aidan White and I will one day have a personal friendship – even if I hope we will - even though we might each totally respect the other's functions.

But I, still personally speaking, already feel I can trust Aidan White and the IFJ. This trust is 80% based on what I know, 20% a bet I am taking. But when I place a bet, I do not like to lose.

It is for this reason that I feel it is right to invite all my OAFCN colleagues to place this same trust in Aidan and in the contribution that IFJ can and wants to give to the building of this relationship of mutual trust between investigative bodies and journalists.

This is why I invite you, during the frank discussions that will take place during this seminar, and in the days to come, to take this bet with me.

A bet that is helpful for our work.

A bet that is helpful, above all, for the European citizens.

(52) *International Federation of Journalists*, http://www.ifj.org/

(53) Causa C-521/04 P(R). http://europa.eu.int/comm/anti_fraud/press_room/pr/2005/07_en.html

(54) A. BUTTICÉ, *Forze dell'ordine e comunicazione. Polizia di Stato, Carabinieri, Guardia di Finanza, Opinione Pubblica e Mass-Media*, Bariletti Editori, Roma, 1990.

(55) http://europa.eu.int/comm/anti_fraud/publications/brochure/index_fr.html

(56) http://europa.eu.int/comm/anti_fraud/olaf-oafcn/rt/c/brivio_it.pdf

(57) Press Release OLAF/03/2002, 27 March 2002 – http://europa.eu.int/comm/anti_fraud/press_room/pr/2002/2002_03_en.html

(58) Sintesi cronologica di questo caso alla pagina: http://europa.eu.int/comm/anti_fraud/press_room/pr/2005/7-background.doc

Paulo CASACA,

Member of the European Parliament,
Coordinator of the Party of European Socialists (PSE)
Group in the Budgetary Control Committee (Cocobu)

Paulo CASACA

has been Member
of the European
Parliament since
1999, is Socialist
Coordinator in
the Committee on
Budgetary Control,
Member of the
Committee on
Fisheries, Member of
the Committee on
Budgets, President of
the Delegation for
Relations with the
NATO Parliamentary
Assembly, Member
of the Delegation for
Relations with Iran,
Substitute Member
of the Delegation
for Relations with
Australia and New
Zealand, President
of the Intergroup
on the Welfare and
Conservation of
Animals, Co-Chair of
the Friends of a Free
Iran Group. He is a
graduate in economics
(1980) with a master's
degree in economics
(1987).

'Secrecy and information: the need to find the right balance'

The rule of law and individual rights are inextricable parts of our democratic system, the maturity of which can be measured, to a large extent, by its capability to serve both aims. It goes without saying that any anti-criminal State force needs a certain level of discretion to operate: finding out if a wrongdoing is happening obviously means that the suspected wrongdoer should not be warned in advance when and how the investigation is going to take place.

Conversely, the public has the ultimate right to know about public wrongdoings, and everybody — innocent or culprit — has the right to be informed of what he is accused of before a trial, so that he can defend himself.

In reality, things are not always that simple. Just to quote one of the most obvious examples, the police authority often warns of the location and the timing of speed limit controls, since it is often more interested in preventing speeding than in punishing speedy drivers.

Otherwise, there are cases where it is quite clear that the ultimate aim of the secrecy imposed on information possessed by the authorities is not to defend the ongoing investigation but rather to use this investigation as a tool to publicly attack somebody.

The recent scandal unveiled during the current summer in Portugal concerning tape recordings of conversations between a journalist and several police officers — including the national director of the Portuguese Judiciary Police — as well as the press officer of the Portuguese public prosecutor's office is very telling.

The public revelation of these tape recordings showed that State authorities abused the privilege of secrecy stamped on the information they handled. The problem here is that the very strict rule of information secrecy existing in Portugal was shown to be misused: instead of preventing any investigation to be torpedoed, it allowed the manipulation of information and the trial by public opinion of a public personality without possible defence.

The accusations were shown to be without credibility, and the prosecutor's office decided to drop them, but, of course, the public damage caused by this action was already done.

In the context of the European institutions, the recent raid on a journalist's premises raises important questions regarding the balance to be established between the freedom of information and the confidentiality of investigations.

Although the most questionable facts regarding the assault on the journalist's premises have to do with Belgian legal procedures rather than with European ones (according to the press, the famous Miranda procedure was not followed and the journalist was interrogated for 10 hours without a lawyer's assistance), there are important questions related to European institutions that cannot be forgotten.

If a journalist obtains classified information, the publication of which could damage an ongoing investigation, the first logical step should be to try to prevent the damage, and this should be possible either by mutual agreement or through the judicial system.

Regarding a possible unlawful action of the journalist, by which he would have had access to the classified information through the corruption of any officials, this should naturally be persecuted.

However, it would be most unfortunate if, just to confirm such a suspicion, irreversible damage were caused to the work of a journalist and therefore to the democratic right of citizens to be informed of what is going on with public affairs, even before the suspicion is confirmed in judicial instances.

In any circumstance, an objective balance has to be established between the several goals. It seems to be clearly disproportionate to seal all the work material of a journalist for an undetermined period of time just because of such an investigation.

This particular incident comes after the so-called 'Eurostat affair'. As I did point out on several occasions, the crucial aspect of this scandal was that the secrecy of procedures — established on the basis of the suspicion of criminal activity and in order to protect the public interest — was actually used as a means to leave situations untouched where obvious administrative wrongdoings were taking place and needed immediate correction.

The question that all these examples raise is that in each situation, when it is necessary to establish what has to be considered secret, reserved information or publicly available information, it is necessary to carefully establish the balance between different public interests.

The number one rule on this issue is that every actor in the process (officials, politicians, journalists) fully understands his own role and responsibilities and obeys basic ethical principles.

The number two rule is that it is necessary to have a common and understandable set of information procedures regarding every actor in the process.

In any circumstance, I do believe that in numerous occasions to decide what should get in the public domain, and what should not, will not be simple, and we will need a sort of information ombudsman that can decide on what information should be delivered or should be kept secret.

Presently, I think that this could be a task performed by a body like the OLAF Supervisory Committee.

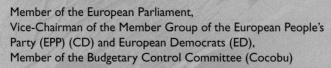

European institutions

Lorenzo CESA,

Member of the European Parliament,
Vice-Chairman of the Member Group of the European People's
Party (EPP) (CD) and European Democrats (ED),
Member of the Budgetary Control Committee (Cocobu)

Lorenzo CESA

(MEP) is Vice-
President of the EPP–
ED Group, Member
of the Budget Control
Committee in the
European Parliament.
He has been Director
of External Relations
and board member
of several Italian
companies and has
had many political
assignments such as
Municipal Adviser
of the city of Rome
and President of the
Advisory Committee
on Personnel from
1989 to 1993, Acting
Head of the Political
Secretariat of the
UDC Party and
Coordinator of the
2005 Regional Part-
Election Campaign of
the UDC Party. He
has also been one of
the founding fathers
of the UDC party
after the collapse
of the Democrazia
Cristiana.

'Cui prodest: OLAF without voice?'

Following my election to the European Parliament and arrival in Brussels, I was appointed as a member of the Committee on Budgetary Control. I soon became curious and intrigued by the debate on the role of the Community's investigative body, OLAF, a debate that, to put it mildly, does not enjoy a high profile in Italy.

With my experience of Italy it did not take me long to realise that OLAF was and still is in danger of being used in political power struggles and battles, although to say political is to insult the nobler calling that I personally have always considered the true nature of politics.

This experience has marked an important and not entirely painless period in Italy's history and has taught me that the loss of independence is the beginning of the end for any investigative body (judicial, administrative, or administrative and quasi-judicial, as is OLAF). Independence is not an abstract, philosophical concept; it is a core principle that must underlie any important institutional activity. Independence means independence from everyone. Or, to put it another way, independence entails total respect for such sacrosanct principles as legality and the rule of law and for the rights and democratic values on which the European Union is based. In other words, when we abandon our cherished principle of justice — and justice has nothing to do with investigations' media circuses, or with trials by kangaroo court or by newspaper before cases are properly tried in courts of justice — investigations can become merely pawns in political power games; and they can also be used by criminal gangs.

This was the first and in some ways disconcerting impression I had when I arrived in Brussels and, I confess, listened to some debates and discussions in the corridors of Parliament.

I tried to find out more. I gathered evidence. And it did not take me long to notice that many people were demanding that OLAF be independent, and had been for some time. But I have the impression that some of those voices crying out have not always wanted or really wanted the Community's investigation service to be truly independent or to act solely in the service of the supreme and unchallengeable values of justice (administrative, civil or criminal) and the rule of law. In fact, I have had the impression that some people want OLAF to be independent simply 'of the others,' and these others are basically their opponents, be they political or institutional, be they obstacles to their careers or anything that could harm their image. It was also my first impression — and I say this with the modesty befitting a new member who found himself taking on important institutional duties within the Parliament — that some people (perhaps more at a personal than a political level, and for a variety of reasons) seemed to want OLAF to be under their control. I am very suspicious of anyone — politicians, other people involved in politics, careerists or strivers for personal prestige — who seem more interested in how OLAF's investigations, news of OLAF's investigations, or perhaps even speculation about future OLAF investigations can be used for their own ends, perhaps through the not terribly original system of leaks. I will keep a lookout for such people throughout my term of office.

I want to stop here and turn to the subject of this round table, which fits in nicely with the impressions of a newly elected Member of Parliament.

Communication as a tool for fraud prevention — communication and prevention are two interesting concepts that inform the principles of modern enforcement. We must communicate because the institutions have the right and, above all, the duty to explain themselves to their citizens and let them know what they are doing, why they are doing it and how they are doing it. This means not only why they are acting in the citizens' interests (let's hope this is always the case) but also (and we know this is true) why they are doing it with the taxpayers' money. The Community institutions really do need to communicate, most probably more than national institutions. They need to be even closer to the people. It is not by chance that the Barroso Commission has created the position of Vice-President with the specific function of dealing with communication.

Prevention. I like this word. Because in a democratic system based on the principles of freedom and the rule of law, before we enforce we must try to prevent.

I understand, for example, that when the police are conducting investigations they must work in secrecy, if they are to safeguard the values of the rule of law and security of our democratic systems. As a private individual, I also like to see uniformed police officers on the beat. It gives me a sense of security and — I hope — it makes any potential criminal feel less secure. I also like the idea that traffic controls should be announced and publicised in advance. After all, the main objective is not to increase the number of offences; it is to reduce the number of accidents and loss of human life. The uniform and the announcements, to mention two examples, are preventive measures. This prevention results from two types of communication: the sight of the uniform and the announcement in the media that the checks will be conducted.

But is it possible to explain the activities of a young Community investigative body like OLAF to the general public in a way people can understand and, by so doing, prevent crime from being committed? Is it possible to explain to people that, in the final analysis, the real victims of apparently 'victimless crimes' such as fraud at the expense of the Community budget are the people themselves? Before sending in this contribution, rather than just listening to the raised voices in Parliament's debating chamber, reading the demands in certain newspapers or listening to rumours in corridors, I did what I always do and set about finding out for myself.

I visited the website and, after scrolling through the publications and audiovisual tools developed by OLAF's Communications Unit, I came to the conclusion that it is possible. Let me give you an example: the development of the OLAF Anti-Fraud Communicators Network is, I believe, extremely valuable ([59]). It is essential if we are to set about satisfying the demands of the people of Europe, who recent surveys have shown want information about ongoing collaboration and successful investigations conducted by the investigative services in the Member States; they do not want simply to be bombarded by continual, almost routine scandal-mongering ([60]). This is an important point because we all know that statements like 'they're all corrupt' or 'they're all fraudsters' are quickly interpreted as meaning 'no one is corrupt' and 'there's no such thing as fraud'. Giving the idea that defrauding is easier than it actually is (where there is also the risk of being caught up in the web of international collaboration OLAF is developing) may encourage other potential fraudsters. This warning goes out to everyone, including my colleagues in Parliament.

I then looked through OLAF's publications for the general public, economic operators and its operational partners ([61]). I found them to be highly professional, providing clear explanations of questions, organisations, structures and procedures that are often hard to understand, even for those working in the field.

I also discovered that a wealth of audiovisual material has been produced ([62]). Some is available to the press on image banks, while other material is available to the general public or can be used for teaching. I discovered that some photos of the fight against cigarette smuggling that have been circulated all over the world actually came from OLAF's image banks. They have helped to draw public attention to one of the most dangerous areas of criminal activity, activity that in Italy has cost the lives of several people. Without this international mobilisation, and without the involvement of the media, it would never have been possible to set about combating this form of crime and the results once thought unattainable would not have been achieved in the last few years. OLAF has played a key role in this area. I don't wish to dwell on this subject any longer, as respected journalists taking part in this round table discussion have already done so.

I found OLAF's website clear. It contains an abundance of information and is multilingual, as are the publications and the videos. I also found out about the information-training visits to OLAF ([63]) and many other initiatives to inform the people of Europe and its own partners more effectively about what OLAF does and how it adds value to international collaboration.

Glancing through all this material I had the impression that while there were other possibilities, much had already been done. I wondered how many people were working in this field. Examining the material, comparing it with material issued by a normal press office representing a typical institution or company, and bearing in mind the unavoidable language problems, I concluded there would need to be a whole host of institutional communications specialists. This idea was only reinforced when I read Opinion No 2/03 that accompanied the Commission report entitled 'Evaluation of the activities of the European Anti-Fraud Office (OLAF)' drawn up by the OLAF Supervisory Committee ([64]). Section IV.3 of the opinion (communication) states that 'OLAF has set up its own autonomous public relations department and conducts an active policy of communication with the public and the media. However, the Committee feels that, while communication is important, it is none the less secondary and should remain limited in view of the risks it entails for the respect of fundamental rights and the reputation of the institutions and their members, officials, and staff'.

I have also heard that some colleagues from the old Budgetary Control Committee have suggested publicly that OLAF should 'put a stop to its ridiculous press policy. The office has issued too many press releases … There should be more investigators and fewer press officers'.

Understandably surprised, and slightly alarmed, I continued my research, this time on the staffing levels in its 'autonomous public relations department' and on the number and content of OLAF press releases.

I was no less surprised when I discovered that OLAF's Communication, Public Relations and Spokesman Unit is one of the smallest, if not the smallest communications and information units in any of the European Commission's directorates-general. Because OLAF's investigative function must remain independent, it is also the only unit that has to deal with its own relations with the media, while other directorates-general can use staff from the pool of spokespersons in the Directorate-General for Press and Communication. Although a large amount of the material is multilingual, a large number of visits and conferences are organised and hundreds of contacts are maintained with the world's press, the unit consists of just two Grade A officials, two B Grade officials, an auxiliary, a national expert on secondment and a secretary.

I looked through the press releases published by OLAF on its own site (in at least three languages) ([65]) and, quite honestly, I fail to see which of these communications my colleague from the Committee on Budgetary Control was referring to when he said that too many press releases were published.

So I asked myself who stands to gain from such heated criticism. I also asked myself whether behind the much-trumpeted appeals for rights to be safeguarded, for greater independence for OLAF and the need for OLAF to spend less time speaking or even to keep silent, there was not a desire to enable others to speak. And this is how I found out, from a press release published in total transparency in 2002, that OLAF had started investigating itself, launching an enquiry into the leaking of confidential information and possible corruption of a Community official. I was surprised to learn that some people have been commenting publicly on current investigations that are still confidential when there is a sacrosanct duty to protect those presumed innocent (until a court finds otherwise) and safeguard the effectiveness of the investigations. While I applaud the dignified silence maintained by OLAF, I again find myself asking the question 'who stands to gain?'

I still do not know. But I will do everything in my power as a Member of the European Parliament to ensure that OLAF is an effective tool of the rule of law because it is the first to respect rights and the rule of law, and I will be merciless in bringing to light any deviations from this course. I will also do everything I can to prevent OLAF from becoming a dangerous toy in the hands of those who want to play games for their own benefit and against the interests of the rule of law and the rights of us all.

Communication as a means of prevention. An excellent idea! My compliments to OLAF for this initiative. I would like to join my fellow MEPs from all parts of the political spectrum in welcoming this round table as well.

For any investigative body communication also means prevention. But communication does not mean just talking to the media, and it definitely does not mean leaking information. Communicating in the name of the rule of law means acting as transparently as possible in accordance with the values of law and democracy that provide the foundations on which Europe is based and that Parliament safeguards and will increasingly have to protect.

The anti-fraud communication policy pursued by OLAF together with its operational partners deserves encouragement and support. I will therefore do my utmost to ensure that OLAF's right to use modern means of communication to get its message across is never undermined under any pretext.

---

(59) http://europa.eu.int/comm/anti_fraud/olaf-oafcn/en.html

(60) See 'Special reports on attitudes related to defrauding the European Union and its budget': http://europa.eu.int/comm/anti_fraud/press_room/eurobar/en.html

(61) http://europa.eu.int/comm/anti_fraud/publications/brochure/index_en.html

(62) http://europa.eu.int/comm/anti_fraud/publications/a-v/index_en.html

(63) http://europa.eu.int/comm/anti_fraud/rp/visit/en.html

(64) http://europa.eu.int/comm/anti_fraud/reports/sup_comm/2003/avis/en.pdf

(65) http://europa.eu.int/comm/anti_fraud/press_room/pr/index_en.html

European institutions

Thierry CRETIN,

Head of Unit, Investigations and Operations Directorate,
OLAF, European Commission

'The art lies in the doing'

**Thierry
CRETIN**

has a judicial
background as a
public prosecutor. He
started his career in
the French judiciary
as an investigating
judge in 1980. From
1997 to 2000, he
was a national expert
seconded to the
General Secretariat
of the Council of the
European Union for
the implementation of
the action plan against
organised crime (he
wrote two books on
the matter). He joined
OLAF in May 2001,
first as a member of
the Magistrate Unit
and later became
Head of the Custom
Unit. He is currently
Head of Unit for
Direct Expenditures
and External Aids
(Phare and Tacis
programmes).

Communication: the art lies in the doing. The word 'art' calls for an explanation. It should be understood not as referring to the rather vague activity of the artist but in its other sense of skill, of know-how.

The resources available to an anti-fraud department, whose main mission is to undertake investigations, include communication. This is not just a statement of principle; it is in the logical sequence of things.

There is a simple reason for this: investigations consist of detecting the mechanisms by which defrauders unduly appropriate public funds that are supposed to be used to improve the living conditions of the general public. So to investigate is to discover. Communication is the logical consequence of discovery, since communicating means disseminating knowledge of what has been discovered. If the successes and failures of investigations were simply stored out of sight in a filing cabinet, the public would be deprived of information to which they were entitled.

There is therefore no fundamental discrepancy between investigative activity and communication; both partake of the same spirit, the same logic.

But that is not the only reason: Article I-46(3) (principle of representative democracy) of the European Constitution, which has admittedly not yet been ratified, states that 'decisions shall be taken as openly and as closely as possible to the citizen'. In relation to the work of investigative bodies, there is no proximity to the citizen if information is not supplied on the way decisions are taken, the content of investigations and their findings.

This may seem simple and really quite obvious, but the picture becomes complicated as we go into the subject in greater depth. The values we all share are values inherent in the rule of law. Article I-2 of the Constitution provides that 'the Union is founded on the values of … the rule of law', one of these being 'respect for human rights'.

The rule of law means that we are under an obligation to abide by principles expressed in primary legislation and instruments adopted under it. I should like to begin by reviewing these constraints under which we operate and then go on to consider how they can be reflected in our communication activities.

Incompatible principles?

In a State governed by the rule of law, public freedoms are the ultimate guiding principle, along with legal rules imposing limitations on them. We can never overemphasise the point that the law sets the limits on the area of freedom; it does not impose compulsory forms of conduct; it merely sets the limits that cannot be overstepped. And overstepping them is a crime.

What are the limits that those in charge of communication may not overstep?

All investigation services are required to enforce the law; that is what they are there for. If they break the law, their very image is at stake as their function is to enforce the law and violating it automatically discredits whatever action they take subsequently. Being at pains to respect fundamental human rights and freedoms, investigation services can therefore neither say nor do anything that is in conflict with these elementary rights. The first of these prohibitions flows from the confidentiality of investigations, which serves both to protect the person likely to be found guilty of wrongdoing (but enjoying the presumption of innocence) and to ensure that investigations proceed properly without risks from inappropriate interference and intervention (protection of evidence and sources, since investigation services also have sources). In the absolute, for considerations both of evidence and of public freedom, none of the information gathered in an ongoing case can be revealed. But it must be borne in mind that the prohibition is not absolute; it covers the facts of the case and the individuals and bodies under investigation. There is no reason why a service should not state that an investigation is in motion, provided that it does not say who is involved.

Apart from this, there is the principle of the freedom of the press, a public freedom which must be seen as a clear sign of democracy. It does not exist in dictatorships and authoritarian systems. The function of the press is to inform the public, and the investigation services also wish to inform the public of their anti-fraud activities. Two needs dovetail, and in an ideal world it could almost be concluded that life is easy. But this overlooks the fact that what our journalist friends want does not correspond to what we can give them. They want personal data; we cannot accede to that. They want the details of the case; we cannot provide them. The divorce starts here.

The diagnosis is as tough as it is simple: the principles to which we refer are paradoxical. You will observe that I did not say incompatible but simply paradoxical.

The initial reaction might be to go for a strategic withdrawal, on the ground that any form of communication raises the risk that we might violate the rules we have mentioned. This is the temptation of isolationism, but it provides only apparent protection since it has two major defects.

- We cannot generate any kind of awareness of our investigation work and there is thus a contradiction with what I said by way of introduction regarding the value of communication as a means of preventing fraud.

- What is more, isolation weakens the investigation service since we would be deluding ourselves if we believed that it offered any form of protection. Not pursuing a policy of

European Institutions

openness towards the general public leaves the field open to one's detractors, who will be all the bolder since they will never be contradicted. This really must be borne in mind as in this day and age the investigation services are more exposed than they used to be; they handle issues which have become a matter of public concern and a political issue.

After careful thought, and this is why I did not say incompatible, the question is not whether we must communicate but how we must communicate in order for these paradoxical principles to coexist. And this encapsulates the point that communication is an art that lies in the doing — and in doing the task well.

An art that lies in the doing

It really is true to say that what counts is the doing; opposing forces have to be reconciled, and the way forward is narrow and hazardous and has to be reinvented every day. There are times when it seems more like a tightrope than even a mountain track.

In short, the job is not an easy one, and I would like to share with you a few ideas on how to answer the following questions.

What should we communicate, on what subjects?

This answer should not be the longest one because we already know it: we can communicate whatever is not prohibited by the law. It is intangible and irremediable. I cannot concur with what Oscar Bartoli told us the day before yesterday — that we must say everything, say it quickly and tell the truth. I will come back to this question of the truth, but one thing is clear: the communicator cannot say everything, for he would be creating major problems for himself. No investigation service can name either individuals or firms without violating the presumption of innocence. What would one say of an investigation service which said everything and said it quickly? It would be rightly accused of violating the law and fundamental principles. The very purpose of its work would be undermined and would be doomed to failure.

You are already starting to think that I am closing the hatches like a submarine ready to dive. Nothing could be further from the truth. For on Wednesday I heard both Daniela Filipescu and Johannes Von Dohnanyi say that what a journalist needs is often not the detail of the case (he already has it) but confirmation. The case (Puwak) mentioned by Daniela was exemplary. She needed confirmation. She obtained it from OLAF without OLAF breaking any law. Since I speak about art that lies in the doing, here is a first component that falls fully within the spokesman's art of communication: stick to what is not prohibited. And there is real room for manoeuvre here.

At this point, I would like to quote an African proverb: 'You hear the sound of the tree that you fell; not the sound of the forest growing.'

The art of the communicator is to take every opportunity to convey the sound of something other than the crashing of the felled tree, in this case the sound of the forest growing. Alessandro Butticé said on Wednesday that we have to explain a lot of things to journalists, and ultimately to the public at large, because all but a few of them are generalists rather than lawyers or specialists in investigations. He clarified this by reference to the limitation period for public prosecutions, a sophisticated legal concept that can produce absurd results if it is not used carefully. By the same token, a case can always provide a communicator with an opportunity to help his contacts, especially when they first 'meet', to understand the background to investigative activity, the way the service operates and so on. He can make the discreet sound of the growing forest audible.

Lastly, before moving on from this first point concerning the content of communication, it is important to remember that, in circumstances that the communicator must analyse, it is still possible to say nothing and apply a 'no comment' policy, at least temporarily. Here again, the art is in the doing, since the option must be exercised rarely and cautiously. I share the view of Raymond Kendall, Chairman of the Supervisory Committee, who told us on Wednesday morning that, given how difficult it is to maintain secrecy, in particular in the European institutions, we must say at least something. And Johannes Von Dohnanyi echoed this when he reminded us that there will always be somebody somewhere who wants to talk. Total silence must be the exception, justified in specific circumstances only.

When should we communicate?

The question could also be put in a quite different way: when should we start communicating? The answer will depend very much on the circumstances of the case and the objective being pursued.

If we spontaneously set about telling the public about the 'forest that grows in silence', which for present purposes means telling them about how the European Anti-Fraud Office actually goes about investigating cases and what results it achieves, our communication must be at regular intervals and must always be inspired by the objective of generating the widest and fullest awareness of the efforts made and the difficulties encountered. The preventive effect of communication depends on this. The communicator is then no longer responding to pressure but taking a proactive, dare I say didactic, approach. He conveys a message; he provides information that will help the general public and the professionals to comprehend the successes and failures of a particular course of action when the time comes.

In other circumstances, the spokesman will not have taken the initiative. His communication will be in response to a request and it is clear that the way he responds will depend on the type of request. A specific request relating to a specific case will obviously receive a different response from a more general request for better information about a service. I am tempted to say that the art of communicating consists partly in making it possible to hear the forest growing as well as the tree falling.

Lastly, there are situations where the communicator is not primarily responding to a request for information but putting up a defence against an attack. This is not a common situation but it does arise, as we know from experience. The communicator will no longer be able to convey the sound of the growing forest as all ears will be focused on the crashing tree.

When communication is not spontaneous, the communicator will always be meeting an urgent need under the barrage of questions and calls for explanations. And that is when he most needs to preserve his sangfroid, because as Edgar Morin said, 'When we respond to short-term pressures, we lose the capacity to think'. And if there is one area where we dare not lose our capacity to think, even just once, this is it, for otherwise communication will be over. And for a long time to come.

Where the service comes under attack, before we decide how to respond we must first decide whether we actually need to answer. Is it really necessary? The risk is that we will feed the vicious circle of polemics. Communicators must be cold-blooded animals, and it may be preferable to say nothing, in particular when the remarks made are exaggerated, because we have known since the time of Talleyrand that 'Anything exaggerated is not worth taking seriously'.

As these three situations show, the art of the spokesman and the communicator really does lie in the doing. He must both draw attention to what really matters and avoid being constrained by the need to react to events.

How should we communicate?

The first rule is to communicate without embarking on debates that lead nowhere, without drawing battle-lines, but always taking a neutral tone; taking care in particular to avoid polemics, obviously, but above all avoiding any hint of a value judgement. As the French composer Hector Berlioz put it: 'We need to take a cold look at the burning questions'. So let us follow the cold advice of deleting all adjectives and adverbs and presenting the bald facts. And let us follow the advice of our Commissioner, Siim Kallas, who recommended us to be 'professional, impartial and neutral'. These are golden rules which have proved their worth. But there are more.

After a genius from the musical world, allow me to quote a writer, Albert Camus, who stated: 'Every ambiguity, every misunderstanding can be fatal; only clear and simple language can save us from this death'. Actually death is far from my mind, but Camus was right in that ambiguity kills lucid and serene thinking because it opens the door to manipulation and evasion. It follows that precision is the *sine qua non* for quality communication. Approximation is out of place and must be rejected.

But communication must not only be precise, it must be simple. Otherwise, we will not be understood by the general public or by the professionals that it is our job to inform and to reassure as to the real impact of the work done by the investigation services. Again, the art lies in the doing, since we must take up the dual challenge of being simple with the risk of being inaccurate and of being precise with the risk of being complicated, bearing in mind that the rules governing the fight against fraud and financial crime are not generally regarded as being easy to understand.

What we can say here is that, within the limits of what the law allows, communication must be based on the facts, which, as Julia Bokeva said, 'have always been the greatest challenge because they create an obligation to think'. And not just to comment, may I add. The communicator, in addition to his talent, must have confidence in the facts which in themselves are a raw material that is rather difficult to manipulate. The facts are obstinate, and reality, as one philosopher said, is irremediable.

With whom should we communicate?

The name of this seminar implies that we are to communicate with the public. But the concept of the public is rather a broad one. That means, of course, that there is no scope for exclusivity in a communication policy: everyone is concerned. To tell the truth, I would rather refer to the citizen, because fraud is combated on his behalf and for his benefit. Moreover, as Head of Unit, I am not dissatisfied if a well-run communication policy informs potential fraudsters of the risks they run, secretly hoping that they might be deterred from their criminal ways.

The art of the communicator is precisely to open his communication policy to everybody while adapting his message to the target audience. One does not address the same message to professionals, to politicians and to the general public, who may not be so familiar with the fight against fraud, but what my own experience has taught me is that the need for communication is essential if the effectiveness of the investigation function is to be enhanced. From time to time, I return to France to address groups of fellow members of the active judiciary. Technical communication about our work and the possibilities of collaboration always generates enthusiasm and improves understanding of the synergies that we can put into effect. But sometimes I also make presentations to groups who ask me to do so, such as associations or think tanks, and every time I see that people are relieved to discover that there is a body in Brussels which detects frauds, brings fraudulent techniques to light and recovers as much money as it can. They are just as satisfied to learn that there are relay arrangements in place in all the Member States that continue and back up our efforts.

Lastly, my personal conviction is that any communication policy must also be addressed to the political authorities. There are two main reasons for this.

- They have legitimate institutional authority over us and we are answerable to them.

- Since they are not professionals, they need to be informed, if only so that they can exercise their decision-making function.

The art of the communicator is also to fulfil this mission in all its diversity but in all its wealth.

But that said, there remains the question of the media, because communication policies tend to depend on them. So asking with whom are we to communicate entails the question through whom we are to communicate.

This brings us to a key point of the problem where we all realise we are on less solid ground. Strong words were said both during our debates on the first day and at our second workshop on the partnership between investigation services and the media.

The press is free in a democracy and, consequently, it can deal with the data it receives as it sees fit. Freedom can go as far as challenging the work of the institutions and even of the investigation services. In his relations with the media, the spokesman will be constantly mindful of the Chinese proverb which reminds us that 'you are the master of what you say but what you have said is your master'. If you do not want your words to come back and haunt you, it is essential to establish a partnership with the press. I remember that Alessandro Butticé spoke of trust right at the beginning of this seminar. Trust shared with the majority, though not necessarily with all. As if echoing him, Johannes Von Dohnanyi answered: test us, test our cooperation and see whether it works. But he also said that one had to test without manipulating. I agree, and I would like to repeat what Alessandro said when he called for a relationship without lies and without manipulation. I will take the liberty of making my contribution to the debate by proposing that communicators should be prohibited from practising seduction. We have nothing to sell. Lies, manipulation and seduction are the very opposite of what Oscar Bartoli recommended: tell the truth. You cannot say everything, but whatever you say must be true. That is the price to be paid for the trust of the media and of the public. In addition, it is what the network must offer you: contact points which you trust because you know the people in it.

To conclude on this sensitive question, I should like to remind communicators of a very specific aspect of their mission that, in my opinion, further illustrates my point that the art lies in the doing and that they must acquire and develop this ability. The press often know far more than we think, but sometimes they need confirmation or orientation. Let the communicator say whatever he can say without breaking the law, in the context of his partnership with those he feels he can trust, and let the journalist do the rest; for we should not forget that the journalist is also a professional (or should be, at any rate).

Actually, I have not told you anything new. My objectives were of a different order.

- First, to show that information is a core concern for fraud investigation services. Pardon my metaphor, but what can you know about a perfume if you have never opened the bottle? Nothing! Not the slightest hint of its fragrance! Some things are simply not possible in today's world.

- Then, to stress that the communicator's art is a difficult art which, once the path to be followed has been signposted by the rule of law and public fundamental freedoms, resides in the ability to act with every form of subtlety in every situation. This is why the art truly lies in the doing. As the philosopher Merleau Ponty said, 'A philosopher is a person who has inseparably a taste for the obvious and a sense of ambiguity'; we could paraphrase him by saying that a communicator is a person who has inseparably a taste for making his investigation service well known and a sense for the limits set by the rule of law.

- Nobody will dispute that this is a difficult art, but I suggest that this is what actually makes it so interesting. And in any event it is the way to be followed. And to really drive the point home, let me quote three people, two of whom have already gone down in history:

  - Seneca, whose advice to communicators dates from two thousand or so years ago: 'it is not because it is difficult that we do not dare to do it; it is because we do not dare to do it that it is difficult.'

  - Leonardo da Vinci, who argued five hundred years ago that: 'thinking is easy, acting is difficult, but acting in accordance with one's thoughts is the most difficult thing in the world.'

  - Siim Kallas, the European Commissioner, who introduced our work with the words: 'the task is difficult but possible.'

Alain DUMORT,

Acting Director,
Directorate-General for Press and Communication,
European Commission

Alain DUMORT

is currently Acting Director at the Directorate-General for Press and Communication of the European Commission and has been Head of the Audiovisual Service since April 2004. He has previously been Head of the Communication Unit at the Education and Culture DG, and responsible for the eLearning sector. He joined the European Commission in October 1990 as Chief Economist in the DG in charge of Telecommunications and Information Society. Alain Dumort is visiting professor in economics and political science at the University of Grenoble and has been associate professor on the economics of new media at the School of International Relations, University of Southern California, Los Angeles.

'Putting Europe in the picture: the audiovisual communication of the European Commission'

The effects of European policies in daily life are concrete and visible: one currency for the majority of the Europeans, a 'common market' where goods and services are traded, a largely free-border area for travellers, diplomas which are increasingly recognised internationally, and real job opportunities in countries other than one's own... And yet, European construction is not a popular topic. It is facing public indifference or scepticism. Benefits of belonging to the EU are not fully perceived by its citizen ([66]).

Results coming out from the Community budget have to be better publicised, in terms of both effectiveness and efficiency of actions. Fighting 'euro-apathy' in the current critical political agenda and increasing confidence in EU institutions call for a change in the communication process. From that perspective, only television and radio can reach large audiences. On average, each European watches television for 200 minutes each day. Indeed, these media are the main, and sometimes the only, access to information for most Europeans. They are unequalled for their ability to connect the EU with its people when messages and storyboards are properly designed.

The main mission of the Press and Communication DG of the European Commission is to help media professionals to treat European subjects in all areas of information. Its Audiovisual Service provides television and radio journalists and editors with genuine news coverage of the activities carried out by the EU institutions, direct access to unique audiovisual archives and technical assistance to stations wishing to produce programmes on the EU.

A broad range of products and services are offered free of charge and rights.

- **News**: key EU events are available via Europe by Satellite (EbS) which is used by over 600 television stations around Europe. Press conferences and briefings, debates in the Parliament, open Council sessions, European Councils, and so on, are available live and/or recorded on EbS in all available languages.

All EbS programmes are also available worldwide on the EbS website (253 000 visitors during the first quarter 2004).

- **Background material**: video dossiers on key topics. Related to anti-fraud communication, a stock shot has been realised on the fight against cigarette contraband. The pictures timely broadcasted have been widely used by television.

- **Archives**: video, photo and audio library: 26 839 photos, 2 526 audio documents and 33 566 videos since 1951, open to all journalists (online overview on the web).

- **Technical assistance**: the Commission's fully-equipped radio and television studios and editing suites available on request to journalists. These facilities are fully used every day by a wide range of radio and television stations (during around 3 600 hours per year). Deutsche Welle, Radio France, France 2 and 3, RTBF, TVE, ARD, South Eastern TV are some of the regular users.

- **Working with national, regional and local radio and television stations**: the Commission's representations in the Member States give priority to working with national and regional programme-makers and journalists. The press officers are, in several representations, supported by specially recruited audiovisual correspondents for this purpose.

- **Visits to Brussels by radio and television journalists**: organised on a group or individual basis, in close cooperation with the representations, the visits are crucial to providing journalists with premium information on the achievements and transparency of the financing.

However, EU topics are often complex or sometimes too technical to make immediate attractive visuals. A revisited media strategy is required with the main objective of raising overall European awareness. The challenge is to make EU activities more attractive to television viewers, directly relevant to people's daily life, more transparent on how tax money is spent. Putting Europe in the picture through a new audiovisual strategy should therefore be the priority for the Commission communication policy.

This strategy relies on the seven following points.

- Ensure that communication via television and radio is fully integrated in all communication activity from the Commission through a global and coherent strategy. Give priority to television and radio when giving interviews, statements and participating in discussions.

- Make a clear selection of messages and targets through a critical mass of actions.

- Ensure a sound balance between the effectiveness (results and impact), the efficiency (cost-efficient indicators) and the transparency of the actions.

- Give priority to news programmes, debates and short key programmes for understanding the co-financing policy through the call for proposals.

- Introduce systematically the human dimension and stories in the information policy to render the European Union institutions, its people and achievements nearer to the citizen.

European Institutions

■ Find ways for an efficient dialogue with the key players in the European television market.

■ Last but not least, develop the analysis and evaluation tools necessary to elaborate professional and efficient media strategies that can be submitted with clear indicators of performance for political decision-making.

---

[66] According to Eurobarometer, December 2004, the public opinion monitor in the EU, 53 % of the Europeans interviewed consider that, on balance, their country has benefited from belonging to the EU, compared with 34 % who are of the opposite view (12 % without opinion).

European institutions

Szabolcs FAZAKAS,

Member of the European Parliament,
Chairman of the Budgetary Control Committee (Cocobu)

Szabolcs FAZAKAS

was born in Budapest in 1947. He studied economics at degree level and holds a PhD. He started his career as a lecturer at the Budapest University of Economic Sciences before going on to work for the Ministry of Foreign Trade from 1973 til 1989. Since then he has held a range of posts including Ambassador to Germany, Minister for Industry, Trade and Tourism and Head of DaimlerChrysler Corporate Representative Office. He has been a Member of the European Parliament, Chairman of the Committee on Budgetary Control and of the Committee on Budgets since 2004.

Opening address at the OLAF seminar: 'Deterring fraud by informing the public'

Wednesday, 24 November 2004, at 9.30 a.m.

I am delighted to address the OLAF Anti-Fraud Communicators Network for the first time in my capacity as Chairman of the Committee on Budgetary Control of the European Parliament. The subject you have chosen, 'Deterring fraud by informing the public', is topical and of extreme importance. I would like to congratulate you on your choice! In the information society, sharing information with the public is crucial.

Recently, public attention was drawn to the European Parliament, when the vote on the incoming European Commission had to be postponed. I think the event has sent out three important messages to the European citizen: that the European Parliament has gained in stature, that the Commission has gained more independence from Member States, and that the whole procedure was a victory for European democracy.

I am a newly elected Member of Parliament from Hungary and I am honoured to follow in the footsteps of Diemut Theato, who chaired this committee for 10 years. She always took great pride in attending OLAF seminars and discussing with you the issues which are at the very core of OLAF's daily work. You, the representatives of the communicators network, are a cornerstone of OLAF's work: fighting and facilitating the fight for the protection of the Communities' financial interests.

The new Member States look with great interest at the European Union: They want to embrace best practice, they want to meet the high European standards, they want to spend the European taxpayers' money scrupulously, and they want and will be the first to fight fraud. We have no right to disappoint them. This seminar is an important contribution to building our common Europe.

The role of the European Parliament

Before entering into the seminar's subject, let me begin with a brief outline of the European Parliament's role in the protection of the Communities' financial interests.

The European Parliament is part of the budget authority establishing and controlling the EU's annual budget, worth approximately EUR 100 billion. In addition, it is the prime task of the committee to control how the Commission executes this budget and to recommend discharge if we think it has executed its task in an appropriate manner. It is worth noting that approximately 80 % of the above amount is actually administered by and in the Member States.

In this context, the Court of Auditors' annual report (which was submitted to this committee last week in Strasbourg) is an important reference document.

Unfortunately, there is sufficient evidence that Member States often have a rather light-hearted attitude towards 'European' money, although it is collected from the same taxpayers' pockets as national budgets.

Parliament also receives the Commission's annual report on the protection of the Communities' financial interests and OLAF's annual report (upcoming Friday), which are usually commented on in a single parliamentary report.

The role of the media

I think it is fair to say that, when looking at national investigation bodies and prosecutors' offices, the first idea that sprang to my mind was that fraud investigators should not be in the press at all. Indeed, their work relies on confidentiality. Thus, not making headlines is a sign of quality.

However, I have to admit this may be just an instinctive reaction, fuelled on the one hand by the European Parliament's experience with press leaks and sound-bite journalism and on the other hand by the European Parliament's own doubts about how to handle confidential information. Incidentally, the latter is an issue which is currently under discussion between OLAF and the Committee on Budgetary Control.

It is with this mindset that I have read some of the approximately 30 written contributions for this seminar, many of which have impressed me and have made me reconsider my initial point of view.

Indeed, in a world influenced by the mass media and by information available at random, it is increasingly important that bodies protecting our financial interests are present in the media and that the media portrays a positive image of them.

How can this be achieved? The following proposals, which stem from written contributions, strike me as valid.

- Make information accessible to the public, unless access has been limited by law, contractual agreement or secrecy legislation (Swedish example).

- Establish media hot-lines, which allow the media to verify information with the authorities concerned at any moment.

- Give journalists the possibility of covering investigations ('embedded journalism') (example from RAI).

- Give the bodies concerned the possibility of publishing articles, information campaigns or advertisements (example given by General Italo Pappa from the Guardia di Finanza).

More examples could be quoted from the contributions. But I cannot and will not attempt to replace your workshops.

In a nutshell: you will find me on the side of transparency on the basis of the rule of law. The public must learn not only about the villains putting the rule of law at risk, but also about those who protect them.

Information and communication among crime fighters

Let me now turn to the aspect of information and communication from a more inward-looking perspective: in a world in which international crime is growing — and again the written contributions cite, sadly, compelling examples, such as cigarette smuggling — it is also of increasing significance that crime-fighters communicate and share information amongst themselves.

In this context, OLAF is a great facilitator, a service platform. The greatest success stories of international cooperation and crime-fighting are usually found in black boxes in the OLAF annual reports.

Let me just highlight one aspect from a parliamentary view: the rule of law and the protection of citizens' rights. Indeed, transborder crime-fighting forces face different national legal systems, which are not only a challenge for the services you represent, but also a challenge to the rule of law.

To a certain extent this problem is highlighted by the existence of the Magistrates' Unit within OLAF.

This is why the European Parliament and the Commission are striving to establish the European Prosecutor's Office, which could regroup the different existing bodies. But this issue is a comprehensive one and it will have to be addressed on a different occasion.

Future development

In concluding, let me just point to a few legislative texts currently in front of the Committee on Budgetary Control, which are the results of OLAF's efforts to improve the protection of European financial interests:

- the agreement between the European Community and its Member States on the one hand and the Swiss Confederation on the other to counter fraud and all other illegal activities affecting their financial interests;

- the anti-contraband and anti-counterfeit agreement and release between Philip Morris International, the European Commission and Member States;

- the proposal for a regulation on mutual administrative assistance for the protection of the financial interests of the Community against fraud and any other illegal activities.

My committee has only just started to look at these documents. However, already at this stage, I would like to congratulate OLAF on its preparatory work.

Finally, the committee will have to address the revision of the OLAF regulation in 2005. In its discussions with the Council and the Commission, the committee will be guided, to my mind, by the idea of strengthening OLAF's operational capacities. The OLAF Anti-Fraud Communicators Network is an important element of these capacities, with the help of which OLAF can strengthen its competence as a service platform.

I wish you every success with your seminar and look forward to receiving your report, which will undoubtedly help us in our parliamentary task.

Henrik HOLOLEI,

Head of Cabinet, Vice-president M. Siim KALLAS, Commissioner in charge of Administrative affairs, Audit and Anti-Fraud, European Commission.

"Speech - Joint seminar of the International Federation of Journalists (IFJ) and the European Anti-Fraud Office (OLAF) for the OLAF Anti-Fraud Communicators' Network (OAFCN) Brussels - 28 October 2005"

Henrik HOLOLEI

is Head of Cabinet for Mr. Siim Kallas, Vice-President of the European Commission, responsible for Administration, Audit and Anti-Fraud. Before joining the European Commission in May 2004, for 9 years he was the Principal Adviser to the Prime Ministers of Estonia on EU matters and responsible for the internal co-ordination of EU affairs in Estonia as Head of the Office of European Integration of the State Chancellery. In 2001 and 2002 he also served as Minister of Economy of Estonia. He represented the Estonian Government in the Convention for the Future of Europe in 2002 and 2003.

Ladies and gentlemen, dear OLAF anti-fraud communicators, welcome to today's seminar. The main topic of the seminar is how to ensure a good working relationship between antifraud services and journalists. Looking at it in a superficial way, it would seem that this title is a contradiction. On the one side the Law enforcement agencies are investigating cases of fraud, corruption and other illegal activity damaging the financial interests of the EU. Their case work should take place mostly outside the public attention. On the other side we have the media, looking critically for failures of the public administration, and wanting to report on scandals. But I don't think that there is a contradiction, on the contrary I am convinced of the importance of the good cooperation between media and anti-fraud services.

1. Why is this communication with the public so important to us?

Because journalists have a central role in communicating to the public about OLAF's work:

- They are the public watchdog;
- They are strong force to ensure accountability of public institutions; and
- They are an important multiplier of the messages we want to communicate to citizens.

You all know the importance Commission, especially its Vice President, Mrs Wallström, attaches to communication and reconnecting the EU with the citizens. Communication as well as transparency is high on the agenda as witnessed by the recent Plan D and up-coming launch of the **Transparency initiative**.

To restore confidence in the European Union we should not look for complicated formulas but rather simple solutions: let's start by increasing the level of transparency.

People have a right to know what Europe is doing and therefore, they must have more access to information on how and why decisions are taken as well as who is benefiting from that.

Viewed from the Kallas portfolio of audit, budgetary discharge and anti-fraud; the European institutions must be more accountable, about the way they spends money, but also about how they react to wrongdoings.

As far as the transparency initiative is concerned, let me quote from a speech by Commissioner Siim Kallas at the Centre of European Policy Studies in Brussels on October 20 2005, who stressed the following:

"The second pillar is the fight against fraud by raising awareness. On the one hand, we have to give objective information, not minimising or sweeping under the carpet, but allowing the public itself to conclude that size of fraud is not alarming. This shall convey the message that we are in control and shall have the additional benefit of deterring any perpetrators by demonstrating effective action. Nothing is worse for public confidence in European institutions than scandals. They may come out of the blue and destroy our efforts to strengthen accountability for years. ..... Provision of information and a high level of awareness are needed to prevent fraud Fighting fraud is a two-way street. Citizens have to inform Olaf of possible cases of fraud but Olaf has to inform the public on the state of affairs.

New options in this field are limited but whatever scope for improvement available must be used because the fight against fraud is one of our main tasks. Therefore, we want to **explore possibilities for Olaf to give information on fraud cases, following the conclusion of investigations while fully respecting the presumption of innocence and other fundamental rights of individuals concerned, and the confidentiality of the investigation.**" This is what Commissioner Kallas said on his speech.

Here we see the synergies with communication. Communication is the active side to transparency, and transparency is fundamental to the fight against fraud and corruption and in their prevention. Also Communication can help in **deterrence** by making people aware of the role of OLAF, and the severity of the crimes it tackles, and raising **public debate** on the subject.

It is of course in the interest of the institutions to be seen as being in control of a fraud case, being pro-active and taking immediate and strict measures. We also wish to give a clear message that defrauding EU funds does not go unnoticed and will be followed by an effective sanction.

Our starting point is thus clearly that we need to communicate. Let me thus come to the second question: **But with every specific case, the big questions to be addressed are when? and how much can be said?**

2. Why is mutual trust between anti-fraud services and journalists so important?

Communication between investigators and journalists is particularly sensitive. While the

former will want to say nothing, the latter will want to know everything. Investigators and Law enforcement agencies are under an obligation to cooperate with the media. As always, they have to find a balance, and they have to agree where this balance should be. For this, it is important that both parties understand the framework within which the other works and accept its limits. Only in these conditions can a fruitful cooperation be established, based on mutual trust and understanding.

I hope this seminar can contribute to clarify when and how such limitations must be applied and how the framework can respected.

I see three conditions for good cooperation:

1/ **legal limits relating to the protection of individual rights** must be unconditionally respected. Any communication has to always occur in accordance with the law and with absolute respect for individual rights. People are innocent until proven guilty, they have a right to be heard, names and business secrets must be protected under data protection obligations, and there is also the freedom of press and the opinion, to name but a few examples. These are the legal limits and they are undisputed, at least in theory.

2/ secondly, trust and a good relationship are important to reach mutual understanding of the limits of communication and transparency, **for the sake of the investigation work itself**:

- *First:* undue or premature media coverage, or leaks to the Press, can smear the name of the accused, and damage the democratic principal of 'innocent until proven guilty'. Any infringement of this kind will render the procedure invalid.

- *Second:* leaks during an early stage of an investigation may seriously hamper the effectiveness, lead to destruction of evidence and drying up of information.

- *Third:* Dealing with scandals deviates resources from dealing with the underlying matter. Often the best results are achieved when an investigation body is left to work in peace and quiet. This is the case for OLAF customs and smuggling operations in cooperation with Member States, as opposed to high profile cases concerning misbehaviour within the Commission for instance.

- *Fourth:* often scandals in the press will lead to defensive reaction from the suspects and concerned institutions alike, making any progress more difficult.

- *Finally* besides the interest of the individual and the investigation we have to consider the **interest of the institution**. Every institution needs to preserve some internal space and time for thinking and policy making. When dealing with irregularities, the institution has to be able to present very quickly its reaction to it. It is not enough to uncover fraud, we have to establish facts and we have to take measures. This is the reason why an immediate reaction is not always possible. The way and tone fraud cases are reported, and the objective and trustful relationship between investigation bodies and journalists is important for the image of the institutions. Frequently EU institutions are seen as slow, bureaucratic, and corrupt themselves, so that communication about OLAF's successful cases can have a negative effect, as the public sees the occurrence of such crimes as proof of the institutions' corruptness.

- National anti-fraud bodies and OLAF needs to be trusted entirely by the citizens, to be accepted as professional, reliable and impartial so they can go about their work without the negative repercussions of undue media coverage. In dealing with such a sensitive subject, communication can be an important key to the fight against fraud or, when misused, potentially damaging. OLAF and journalists must be able to work together and trust each other in order to convince the public that **the existence of National anti-fraud bodies and OLAF is a serious guarantee against mishandling and fraud in the EU**. Therefore, while I fu ly understand why reports on alleged scandals have to be written in a certain style, I would ask you to always keep the bigger picture in mind. Let me now conclude. Every profession has its interests. In this room today we have experts on communication, journalists and representatives of investigations and law enforcement bodies. The members of the OAFCN network combine in a unique way the experience of working for law enforcement and having to communicate about fraud, corruption and wrongdoings everywhere in Europe. I can see no better forum to address the issue of building trust between anti-fraud services and journalists. This trust is necessary for an optimal cooperation and will be for the mutual benefit of both sides. For a good cooperation, journalists and the administration or the anti-fraud investigators have to work together, and not against each other.

I thank you for being here today and wish you, on behalf of myself and the Commission Vice-President Mr Kallas, a very successful seminar.

Siim KALLAS,

Vice President for the European Commission on Administrative Affairs, Audit and Anti-Fraud, European Commission

Siim KALLAS

is Vice President of the European Commission, Commissioner in charge of Administrative Affairs, Audit and Anti-fraud. Before joining the European Commission in November 2004, he served in Estonia as Prime Minister, Minister for Foreign Affairs and Minister for Finance where he was closely involved in the EU accession negotiations of his country. Mr Kallas has also been President of the Estonian Central Bank and has been elected three times to the Estonian Parliament.

Opening address at the OLAF seminar: 'Deterring fraud by informing the public'

24 to 26 November 2004

The OLAF communication unit some time ago launched a virtual round table to discuss the issue of whether information and communication can help fight and prevent EU fraud and corruption. This battle presents a crucial and significant task lying undoubtedly in the focus of public attention.

OLAF is a new institution, created only in 1999, and as such it needs time to build its traditions and experience, but also communication to build up knowledge of its existence. Public institutions have a duty to explain to the citizens what they are doing, and how and why they are doing it. Communication and establishing a more direct contact with the citizens is fundamental for the Community institutions — it is not by chance that the Barroso Commission has created the position of Vice-President with specific responsibility regarding communication and information.

Communication is the active side of transparency. Transparency is one of the cornerstones of the fight against, as well as the prevention of, corruption and fiscal mismanagement. It is in itself often enough to prevent fraud, proving effective for instance in such a sensitive area as procurement.

Indeed, several European countries provide a number of examples on how transparency can be used to prevent fraud, for example by publishing the beneficiaries of Community agricultural support. In Denmark, these lists are available to the public on the web page of an independent NGO, while in Estonia they have been published by the agency responsible for the management and allocation of support. Increasing transparency through the public availability of this information helps to prevent fraud in an area subject to a high incidence of errors. The same holds true for procurement.

Furthermore, communication can help in deterrence. It is possible to prevent fraud by raising awareness of the severity of crimes related to EU funds, as well as by promoting a meaningful public debate on this issue. It can also be done by raising awareness of OLAF's and the local authorities' efforts to prevent and detect fraudulent acts committed against the taxpayers' money. In the fight against corruption, the key to success is a change in public opinion. Communication policy can help achieve that public opinion functions effectively as a means to deter fraud.

OLAF has sometimes received more than its fair share of public attention. Its image and work have been questioned on several occasions, the most recent being a lawsuit presented to the European Court of First Instance over a press release issued by OLAF.

National public authorities and the EU institutions even more so are, in the public perception, often seen as bureaucratic, inefficient and very probably corrupt. Independent of the actual reality, this perception provides a background which influences the reception and interpretation of every new bit of information about their actions — including their anti-fraud activities. Against that background, news about a successfully tackled case sometimes confirms the institutions' image of corruptness, rather than points to their effectiveness in fighting it.

Therefore, the anti-fraud authorities face a difficult task in getting through a positive message about their work, as changing a broad and partly emotions-based perception cannot be done in a short period of time and by delivering a little good news. But this does not mean that it cannot be done. We need to communicate continuously that we strive to be professional, impartial and reliable in fighting fraud that harms all citizens, and that these institutions work well every day.

The worst that can happen to an investigating service is becoming politicised and subject to excessive attention in the media and politics. This threatens to distract the agency from its core work and make its findings subject to controversies. An institution like OLAF needs to be trusted and its work has to be accepted in order to build public trust in the public administration.

I am a strong advocate of maximum transparency. But every institution also has to control the information it gives in view of the need to fulfil its tasks. In specific cases there can be valid reasons for withholding information. But this has to be judged on a case-by-case basis and needs specific justification, based on achieving the organisation's objectives of protecting an investigation. Decisions on the dissemination of information should not be motivated by political reasons, interinstitutional struggle or organisational inertia. We need to communicate and, in practice, confirm the message that information is given according to legal and professional principles.

Transparency must always take into account the respect for law (respect for each person's rights, that is, the presumption of innocence of those being investigated and the duty to protect the investigations' confidentiality) in addition to the complete recognition of the principles of democracy upheld by the EU and its Member States. It must respect the rights of the individual not to hurt the persons involved. Being too lavish on information given can seriously hurt those concerned. I was surprised to learn that some people have been commenting publicly on current investigations that are still confidential when there is a duty to protect those presumed innocent (until a court finds otherwise) and safeguard the effectiveness of the investigations. I find myself asking the question 'who stands to gain?' Clearly, the one who loses is the one under investigation, because his name has been tarnished right away.

Too much transparency and too much public attention can be dangerous to a service dealing with investigations, which have to remain discreet to bear fruit and protect rights of individuals and presumption of innocence.

Success lies in the ability to build an image of the institutions as a functioning and integrated entity, a whole. There has to be a public conviction that the existence of OLAF is a serious guarantee against mishandling and fraud in the EU.

Today's seminar is aimed at promoting a better public understanding of the work of anti-fraud organisations and, through that, at building a public opinion that would act as a deterrent to fraud. This round table has promoted the development of a number of good ideas in this field and I believe that, as such, it is highly useful.

I thank you all for being here today and wish you a very interesting time.

Thank you for your attention.

Raymond Edward KENDALL,

Former Chairman of the OLAF Supervisory Committee,
Honorary Secretary-General of Interpol, Lyon, France

Edward KENDALL

has been member
of the OLAF
Supervisory
Committee since
July 1999 and was
President between
October 2001 and
February 2005.
He was elected
Secretary General of
the ICPO-Interpol
for the first time in
October 1985 and
retired in November
2000. Before,
he served in the
Metropolitan Police,
New Scotland Yard,
London with the rank
of Deputy Assistant
Commissioner.
He then served in
the ICPO-Interpol
Headquarters, Saint
Cloud, France, as
Assistant Director and
then as a Director
(Criminal Intelligence).
In July 2000, he was
appointed Founding
Member of the
International Chamber
of Commerce's
Cybercrime Strategy
Group.

Opening address: 'Deterring fraud by informing the public'

24 to 26 November 2004

I can speak as someone who has followed OLAF since it was born, and who has accompanied its growth over a period of four and a half to five years. So I know how important it is, and have the experience of seeing how important it is that, where possible, the best kind of communication of information and relations with the media exists. Now that is easy to say, but when one knows someone, who, as I say, has been closely associated with this development, the complications that there have been, not only in the creation of OLAF, but in the process of building it up into what it is today, are such that it is almost impossible to communicate in a simplistic way, which is often necessary for good communication.

I think, and I have to be fair in saying this, that OLAF has tried and continues to try, successfully in certain areas, less so in others, but that is a fact of experience.

The media and relations with the media are not what they used to be. When I was a young detective in Scotland Yard, and we used to travel out of London for serious investigations, there was a group of reporters and media people who were known and specialised in the work of crime reporting. And these specialists would accompany us, they would stay in the same hotel, each evening we would drink the same beer together and we would discuss what happened during the day, and we were able to say to these professional crime reporters, 'Well, here is the full story, but you can only publish this, not the rest.' And the relationship between the investigators and the crime reporters was such that, if one of those crime reporters published something which we had said he should not publish, he would be excluded from any communication in the future. Now that was a nice, easy, simple arrangement, and it almost worked on a family basis.

That is no longer possible. It is no longer possible because media communications are different, and furthermore the public perception is different, and you are now in the business of communicating information.

Strangely enough, the public is not interested in honesty. People are much more interested in dishonesty, and when you have an office dealing with subjects like dishonesty and corruption, it is normal, indeed expected, that they will be the subject of a great deal of interest.

So OLAF has always been an easy target, and especially when a new organisation, which has been founded and is developing itself and building up its own structure and system, is an easy target for the people looking for the kind of sensational information that is available.

And therefore for you, trying to find the balance between how you give something which can be of interest as opposed to giving information that in the end should not be communicated, or which it is not in anybody's interest to communicate, becomes a very difficult game.

Another part of it is that we all know that different journalists, different media representatives, are all in competition with each other — who can get the best story? They will resort to all kinds of means to obtain the information they want.

We know — and OLAF has been to a degree a victim of this — that there are people willing to give information, for all sorts of reasons: they may be personal, they could be financial. That is something against which it is difficult to take preventive action as well, and so seminars of this kind are absolutely essential if one wants to communicate to the public the kind of information you think they should have.

One of the things I have always been convinced of is that if you can explain to the public what you want to do and what you are trying to do, and that what you are doing is in their interest, then, generally speaking, the response will be positive. But that does not mean that, at the very slightest indication of something which can be criticised, they will not jump in and take notice of that.

I agree certainly with some of the recommendations that Mr Fazakas just made; this relationship between investigators, journalists and so on is something which has to be addressed, and it is true also that in relation to transparency, it is better to give as much as you can, obviously without prejudice to an investigation. There is perhaps — and particularly in the context of the European institutions — a tendency to overemphasise confidentiality. It seems to me, and my experience has been over the last four years here in Brussels, that it is extremely difficult to keep anything secret in the institutions. Somewhere along the line, information gets out, even suspicions which may not even be confirmed as suspicions become the subject of rumour and so on, so in that situation, it is probably better to give as much information as you can, with due respect for confidentiality and so on. So, I regard this kind of seminar as particularly important, and I know that Mr Butticé and his colleagues have done their best to make it interesting.

I said earlier on, and I'll conclude with this, that basically people are not much interested in honesty. There was a very good television programme the other evening about the career of a German banker, who was asked on one issue whether he had collaborated with other members of the banking community, who could have been interested in a certain project. And he said, 'I have to tell you that I have a certain difficulty in finding the right kind of people, who have notions of honesty the same as mine.' He also said it is probably because honesty cannot be calculated in money terms, and if it cannot be calculated in money terms, then it is of no interest.

So we are dealing with an area such as this which deals with ethics, with morals, also with issues of incompetence, and all these things make the work of OLAF extremely difficult. Therefore there is this necessity of explaining the positive aspects of what they do, and there are very, very many. We in our committee see that we have struggled with them to make sure that things are put in place, work and so on, and finally, after many delays at the beginning, because it was difficult — even the appointment of Mr Brüner as Director took some considerable time, and his directors and so on — but now I can confirm, on the part of my Committee, that things are certainly now moving very, very quickly towards the establishment of what is becoming every day more and more efficient in terms of an anti-fraud office.

I wish you well in your work and have no doubt at all that the product of these seminars — and this is the fourth one — will be that finally we shall begin to see the good elements of what is happening.

Thank you very much.

European institutions

Silvana KOCH-MEHRIN,

Vice-Chairwoman, Group of the Alliance of Liberals and Democrats for Europe, Substitute, Budgetary Control Committee (Cocobu)

'Perspectives for OLAF'

Silvana
KOCH-
MEHRIN

in 1995, received an
MA in economics and
history, in Heidelberg;
and in 1998, a PhD in
historical monetary
unions, in Heidelberg
and Paris. In 1999,
she was President of
the Auslandsgruppe
Europa (FDP) and
Co-Founder and
Managing Director
of a public affairs
consultancy. In 2000,
she was member
of the board of the
FDP; member of the
party council, ELDR;
in 2000–04 she
was lecturer, United
Business Institutes,
Brussels; in 2004,
Head of German FDP
list for elections to the
European Parliament,
and Leader of the
German Delegation
and Vice-President
of the ALDE Group
in the European
Parliament. She is
Ambassador for the
Initiative Neue Soziale
Marktwirtschaft
and recipient of the
following awards:
Woman of the
Year, German
Magazine (2000);
Young Politician of the
Year, Germany (2005).

Who or what is OLAF? The name probably makes most people think of a range of Swedish furniture. Or a new acquaintance from northern Europe. That is disappointing for the staff of OLAF (which stands for office européen de lutte anti-fraude). Every citizen of the European Union should be aware of what the European Anti-Fraud Office does. This is because the financial interests of the European Community are closely linked to those of the Member States, and therefore of European taxpayers, who finance the EU budget. And it is OLAF's job to protect the financial interests of the European Union from fraud, corruption and other irregularities.

OLAF has a heavy responsibility; its aim is to ensure a high degree of transparency and maximum cost-effectiveness for EU funds.

Independently of its operational tasks, OLAF conducts internal and external investigations. It cooperates with the Member States to combat fraud by providing them with support and passing on its expertise.

OLAF can initiate investigations in the Member States and, at their request, carry out on-the-spot checks on business premises. With an EU budget of over EUR 100 billion, there are strong incentives to commit fraud, especially where direct EU expenditure, structural expenditure, customs, taxes, external agricultural trade and trade in cigarettes are concerned.

Cases of fraud against the Community's financial interests are regularly detected in these areas. Such fraud takes a variety of forms, ranging from smuggling or falsifying customs declarations to presenting false documents in order to obtain import or export advantages, agricultural subsidies or structural aid.

In order to gain as complete an overview as possible of fraud cases, the European Union has set up a database to store all useful information.

There was a case in Kosovo that showed how important OLAF's work can be. OLAF launched an investigation into the embezzlement of funds in the energy sector. Following its enquiries and in cooperation with German, US, Serbian and Spanish authorities, a UN staff member was convicted of embezzlement. At OLAF's instigation, EUR 2.7 million were recovered.

Despite all the safeguards, major scandals like the Eurostat case unfortunately continue to occur.

Efforts to combat fraud must take account of organised international structures. Organised criminals also take advantage of the market freedoms, as in the case of transnational VAT fraud. That is why it is important to support the proposal for a European Parliament and Council regulation on mutual administrative assistance for the protection of the financial interests of the Community against fraud and any other illegal activities (COM/2004/509).

The proposed regulation also highlights the need for OLAF as an EU-wide anti-fraud office.

In May 1999 (with Regulations (EC) Nos 1073/99 and 1074/99), the European Commission's powers to conduct anti-fraud investigations were transferred to OLAF. In 2005 these 'basic regulations' will be up for review. Recommendations to improve OLAF's work should include the following points:

- organising an information campaign in the EU Member States: 'Fraud is theft';
- making OLAF's recommendations binding on national authorities following investigations;
- setting up a single, Europe-wide fraud hotline;
- reinforcing the OLAF Anti-Fraud Communicators Network (OAFCN);
- giving OLAF administrative independence from the European Commission;
- extending OLAF's powers to cases of VAT fraud;
- giving OLAF's work a higher profile on the European Union's policy agenda;
- having OLAF's Director appointed by the European Parliament.

The proposals to introduce a system of incentives to combat fraud based on the US model are also important. In the USA the anti-fraud provisions of the 'civil false claims act' impose heavy penalties for financial fraud, while informers who reveal such fraud receive a share of the recovered sums.

OLAF also needs more staff. If there is no prospect of increasing its staff, then thought should be given to restricting its tasks to conducting internal investigations within the EU institutions.

Lastly, all EU citizens should be informed that their financial interests are protected by OLAF. The public's confidence in the European Union must be reinforced, not undermined. We therefore need to combat fraud transparently and effectively at all levels of the European Union, while also protecting the rights of suspects. Extensive efforts are required to prevent fraudulent activities.

European institutions

Giovanni PITTELLA,

Member of the European Parliament (Group DS/PES)

Giovanni PITTELLA

was born on 19 November 1958 in Lauria (PZ). He graduated in medicine and surgery, specialised in medicine for legal and insurance purposes. He has been municipal councillor, member of Regional Council and member of the Regional Executive with responsibility for training, culture and productive activities. He has been Member of the Italian Parliament and Member of the European Parliament since 1999. He has been standing rapporteur for the Structural Funds, member of the Socialist Group in the European Parliament, and is now member of the Committee on Budgets and substitute to the Committee on Economic and Monetary Affairs, general rapporteur for the 2006 EU budget, member of the temporary committee on policy challenges and budgetary means of the enlarged Union 2007–13, and member of the Delegation to the EU–Romania Joint Parliamentary Committee and to the EU–Moldova Parliamentary Cooperation Committee.

He is the author of, inter alia, 'Eurodiario' (1999–2000), 'Il Triangolo della ricchezza' (2003), 'Europa' (2004), 'Partiti europei e Gruppi politici nel nuovo Europarlamento dell'Unione a 25' (2005).

'The media have a role to play, if not in terms of prevention, at least in encouraging the dissemination of a culture of respect for the law by highlighting the damage which fraudulent activities cause to citizens'

First of all I would like to express my deeply felt appreciation to OLAF for organising this round table focusing on the role of communication as a tool for fraud prevention.

OLAF's work makes a key contribution to the task of ensuring that the Community budget is transparent and secure, protecting the EU's financial interests and combating fraud, corruption and all other types of illegal activity.

As an MEP and a Member of the EP's Committee on Budgets, I am convinced that fighting fraud against the Community budget is one of the foremost political concerns both of the European Commission and of the European Parliament.

The perpetrators of fraud against the EU's financial interests must be prosecuted jointly and effectively by all the EU Member States. This is the task of the European institutions and it is also what people expect from Europe. And it is important to make people aware of what is being done, at European level, to uphold the law.

Organised crime, which according to police intelligence is the main force behind large-scale fraud, is constantly on the look-out for ways of escaping detection. OLAF must therefore be given all the necessary resources so that it can wage this difficult battle with the right weapons. Within the Committee on Budgetary Control, the European Socialists Group has pressed for more appropriate measures in the struggle for law enforcement, calling for harmonisation of individual Member States' administrative practices, highlighting the fact that only a small proportion of the targets of the national investigation and inspection departments are geared to the fight against fraud and urging Member States to review their priorities in this area.

In 1999, the European Commission announced a zero tolerance policy with regard to fraud and corruption, but in the field of the fight against irregularities rules and regulations have been adopted that are often contradictory, giving rise in my view to conflicts of jurisdiction.

But the fight against fraud must surely be pursued on other fronts, not just by conducting investigations. What is needed is for society in general to be made aware of the damage done by fraud and the danger it represents, and this is a task for the media.

The alarm sounded by the media through a series of news reports on specific types of offence can trigger a strong reaction in public opinion, which is often followed by an institutional response in the form of new prevention policies or new and stricter penalties. A kind of chain reaction can take place, linking together the media, public opinion and the institutional sector.

The type of offence we are dealing with here, namely fraud, is clearly an issue of concern to society as a whole and a threat both to our own national budgets and to the Community budget. The media therefore have a role to play, if not in terms of prevention, at least in encouraging the dissemination of a culture of respect for the law by highlighting the damage which fraudulent activities cause to citizens.

Michaele SCHREYER,

Member of the European Commission responsible for the Budget and the Fight against Fraud, 1999–2004 — Speech — Anti-Fraud Communicators' Network (OAFCN), Training seminar of OLAF — Bucharest, 20 October 2003

Michaele SCHREYER

Member of the European Commission 1999–2004 (Prodi Commission), responsible for the EU budget and anti-fraud policy. Before joining the Commission, Mrs Schreyer was Member of the Regional Parliament of Berlin, Germany, working in the Public Finance Committee, in different parliamentary enquiry committees and chairing the Green group in parliament for two years. 1989–90 she was Minister for Urban Planning and Environmental Protection in the regional government of Berlin (Senat). Mrs Schreyer has an academic career as economist, giving lectures at the Free University of Berlin and publishing on issues of public finance.

'To learn to share information which we communicate to the public to let them know what fraud is, how dangerous fraud can be and what we are doing together to tackle the problem'

Your Excellency, Mr President, Mrs Theato, Mr Ponta, Mr Butticé, Members of the OLAF Anti-Fraud Communicators' Network, Ladies and gentlemen, As Member of the European Commission responsible for the Budget, I would firstly like to thank the Romanian authorities for hosting this seminar.

Secondly, I would like to stress how important it is that such a seminar is taking place in a candidate country to the EU. This sign cannot be overestimated.

It is a sign of the host country how seriously it takes fraud problems and the fight against fraud.

It is a sign that problems of fraud with public money are not hidden whether the fraudsters are private persons or officials but that we fight against them and make it public when fraud has been discovered.

We are on the eve of the first wave of accession to the EU of countries from middle and eastern Europe. For Romania we will increase our support — including the EU's financial support — for achieving the aim that the country joins the Union in 2007. For the years 2004–06, support of around EUR 3 billion for the three years can be committed.

For the time after 2006, the European Commission is working on the preparation for the next financial planning period. In my calculations as Budget Commissioner, from 2007 onwards I am dealing with an EU of 27 Member States, that means including Romania. This is of course not to be seen as a guarantee for the country but as a strong encouragement.

Fraud is an international problem and a growing problem; we shouldn't be blind to this fact. All should be aware about how dangerous fraud is — both in terms of money lost and in terms of damage to the credibility of public authorities.

This seminar is in order to learn how we can share information which we communicate to the public to let them know what fraud is, how dangerous fraud can be and what we are doing together to tackle the problem.

At EU level the Union has OLAF as a strong instrument to fight against fraud. Although established inside the Commission, OLAF has full independence in its investigations including the independence to decide when and if it brings a case to the national judicial authorities. There should be no and there is no political influence by the Commission in the investigations, including the internal investigations against officials.

As it is in the Member States, the European Commission has found that the detection of irregularities is not taken by the press and public to be evidence of operating controls but rather as evidence of the existence of fraud. More specifically, a public authority whether at EU level or in a Member State or candidate country whose effective controls show up irregularities is seen as riddled with fraud while in the others who do not publish irregularities nobody speaks about them. That is hardly an incentive to be frank in communication.

It is as in ancient times, that the bearer of bad news is often punished. This is in particular heavy to bear for a government or public authority if — as it was in the Eurostat case — the wrongdoing took place in the past, before the current Commission came into office.

Also for a candidate country, the challenge and the risk is high to communicate in public on fraud, in particular when EU funds are involved. It may serve widespread prejudices. But it is a matter of fact that the risk is higher if fraud issues are not tackled as they are a risk not only to reputation but to democracy. It is also from this angle that I want to thank you, Mr President, for inaugurating this seminar.

Hiding or a minimalist approach in reporting irregularities and fraud is not the answer. We cannot and should not avoid reporting irregularities. A proactive strategy calls for disclosure of detected irregularities and engaging in public debate on how to counter fraud.

In tackling fraud we share information at the operational level to investigate crime and tackle criminality. We should also be able to share information which we communicate to the public to increase the impact of what we do and to create permanent professional and personal links between our services. This is why the OLAF Anti-Fraud Communicators Network is important. As the borders across Europe come down it will only be through a coordinated European-wide approach that we can successfully fight fraud. This is necessary for the cooperation of administrations and for judicial authorities and for those responsible for communication.

Communicating effectively to the public is not easy as fraud and economic crime are often complex and difficult to explain to the general public. Also for this reason, we must continue to work together to raise public awareness of these issues.

One step we have taken is to examine public awareness of fraud issues at the European level and accordingly the Commission has for the first time undertaken an opinion poll in both the Member States and the candidate countries to see what the public perception is of these issues.

It is important that we all understand the various aspects of this message: fraud is a crime, a serious crime — but it can be fought. We can and will fight it on a number of levels, by working together on prevention, by investigating and prosecuting fraudsters; we must continue to work together to raise administration and public awareness of these issues.

In this sense I would like to wish you all the very best for the seminar over the coming days.

Diemut THEATO,

Member of the European Parliament, Chairwoman
of the Budgetary Control Committee (Cocobu),
fifth term: 1999–2004
Speech — Training seminar of OLAF — Bucharest, 20 October 2003

**Diemut
THEATO**

Studied translating
(English and Portu-
guese) at the University
of Heidelberg (1956–
60). Interpreter and
translator (1960–87).
Freelance translator and
conference organiser
(since 1961). Vice-chair-
man of Rhein-Neckar
CDU (since 1981).
Land vice-chairman
of Baden-Würt-
temberg CDU (since
1991). Chairman of
Rhein-Neckar district
CDU Women's As-
sociation (since 1977).
Member of the area
executive of the North
Baden women's as-
sociation. Member of
the Land executive of
Baden-Württemberg
Women's Asso-
ciation. Chairman of
the Europa-Union,
Rhein-Neckar district
(1981–89).
Member of ward coun-
cil (1975–87). Chairman
of local council (since
1980).
Chairman of
Neckargemünd-Wal-
dhilsbach branch of
the DRK (Red Cross)
(since 1980). Chairman
of Heidelberg/Rhein-
Neckar district DRK
(since 1991). Freedom
of the city of Timisoara
(since 1995). Honorary
doctorate of the Uni-
versity of Urbino (Italy)
(1995). Order of merit
of the Federal Republic
of Germany (1995).
Honorary doctorate of
the Western University
of Timisoara (1998).

'An international information network is absolutely necessary and indispensible'

Your Excellency Mr President Iliescu, Mrs Commissioner Schreyer, Mr Butticé, Mr Ponta, Ladies and gentlemen, It is with great pleasure that I have accepted the invitation to be with you here in Bucharest, a city which I have visited on several occasions and that thrills me each time I am here. And so does your beautiful country.

I see the progress taking place for better living conditions for your citizens and promising developments towards the accession of this country to the European Union, foreseen for 2007.

But I recognise that much has still to be done to reach this goal. So hopefully yesterday's referendum — although with a low participation — may pave the way for further adapting the Romanian legislation to the *acquis communautaire*.

In this context I feel very honoured to participate in your high-rank training seminar, organised by OLAF in cooperation with the Prime Minister's Control Department of Romania.

Within the large and important issue of the 'Protection of the Union's financial interests' you have chosen the crucial aspect of communication, information and addressing of the media.

I assure you that in my capacity as long-standing chairperson of the Committee on Budgetary Control of the European Parliament and 'rapporteur' on the protection of the financial interests of the European Union, I am confronted daily with these topics. Therefore, I congratulate you for organising this three-day seminar.

But let me first explain in a few words the role of the European Parliament and in particular that of the Budgetary Control Committee in this state of play.

The European Parliament is part of the budget authority: the annual budget of the EU amounts to about EUR 100 billion, more than 80 % of it being executed by the Member States.

This is not 'European' money, but the money of the European taxpayer, who we — being directly elected — represent in the EP.

The larger the Union has become, the more the tasks and the budget have increased and thus the amount of money that has disappeared — be it by irregularities, waste or fraud.

Therefore, the Commission, the European Court of Auditors and especially the European Parliament via its Cocobu (French abbreviation for our Committee on Budgetary Control) have intensified their attention to the PIF (French abbreviation for protection of financial interests).

The legal provisions for this obligation are laid down in the Treaty in Articles 276 and 280.

The principal tasks to be fulfilled and reports to be prepared by Cocobu for the Parliament's plenary are:

■ holding the Commission into account in the annual discharge report on the basis of the European Court of Auditors' reports. Our reports are not appraisals but they rather hint distinctly on the shortcomings which have to be remedied by the Commission, such as the:

  ✓ unreliable accounting system
  ✓ necessity to modernise the payment system
  ✓ questions on externalisation of tasks
  ✓ under-implementation of the budget.

Further reports are drawn up by our Committee on:

■ the protection of the Communities' financial interests

■ the regrouping of the Commission's annual report and OLAF's activity report, where we criticise, that is to say, unsatisfactory recovery of undue payments, the number of not yet closed cases, the delay in spending pre-accession aid.

Two or three times a year we carry out so-called fact-finding missions to various countries, i.e. Member States and accession countries. Thus we have found that Romania has a good record and great readiness for cooperation. We also gathered knowledge in Slovakia, Poland and Bulgaria.

■ What we strive for is EU legislation to be simplified, procedures to be more transparent and controls more effective.

■ Reliable databases and archives have to be set up for better knowledge of contractors and subcontractors.

■ In the candidate countries we see the challenge in further building an efficient administration and an independent judicial system.

European Institutions

- We appreciate swift reaction from the national authorities in case of suspected fraud and full cooperation with the European Commission and OLAF. Therefore, we favour an independent horizontal structure as well as OLAF antennas in the candidate countries.

- Last but not least, we firmly support the creation of a criminal law framework at the European level beginning with a European public prosecutor for the protection of the Union's financial interests and a shelter for the individual rights of possible wrong-doers.

This well-founded issue, profoundly elaborated by the European Parliament and the Commission has found its way into the convention. Commonly the Commissioner — Mrs Schreyer — and the European Parliament — with me as 'rapporteur' — try to persuade the IGC to adopt it with some necessary improvements.

Now let me outline some thoughts on the topic which you are going to tackle during the coming hours and days.

Unfortunately, irregularities, fraud and corruption must be considered as part of normal life, especially in the field of public money; to assume otherwise means closing our eyes to reality. Since we cannot avoid them, it is of chief importance that the public has confidence in that we are shedding light o i them instead of covering them up, in that fraud-preventing measures are being undertaken and efficient structures are being developed to combat these phenomena.

Now, as to the press and the media as a whole, we all know that cooperation with the media can be of great importance, for it is through the media that we can reach a wider public. However, I am convinced that it is not the task of fraud investigators to be in the press at all. Quite the contrary: their work relies on secrecy and confidentiality. Staying out of the media is a sign of quality. The press mostly is interested in sound-bites. Therefore, one has to be careful and precise when having to deal with journalists. There is a role for investigative journalism, a trap into which one should not fall.

On the other hand, functioning internal information and communication channels are crucial: they are the precondition for both — the management and the political level — to assume their particular responsibilities. Both are held accountable by the public that is mostly informed and influenced by the press. A balanced judgment is therefore very difficult to be achieved.

One example in recent times is the still ongoing so-called 'Eurostat affair'. As far as I can see at present, it is not a case of embezzlement and/or personal enrichment, but a case of disrespect of budgetary rules and an internal communication break-down.

The lessons to be learnt thereof are, in my opinion:

- rules have to be clear and known to people;

- the specific management level must dispose of information which enables them to make responsible decisions;

- the politically responsible level must receive (or also seek) the information to be able to be held accountable and shoulder this responsibility;

- informants (whistle-blowers) must be listened to and must be protected.

An international information network is absolutely necessary and indispensable: OLAF, European and national courts of auditors, Europol, Interpol, police, customs and so on, and you, the participants of this seminar as partner services of OLAF.

In the best sense of subsidiarity: the work has to be done at the level where you are most effective and share your information.

As to OLAF, we in Parliament would like to lay more stress on internal investigation. It shows often that it is difficult to judge what is an internal and what an external case is. They may be linked and it often shows that the starting point lies in an internal wrongdoing and/or wrongdoers.

Therefore, investigations should always be pursued in a way as if the file will go to court.

And in the end the aim is not only to fight irregularities, misuse of money and fraud, but also to channel information back to the legislator in view of creating fraud-preventing and fraud-proof laws.

I wish you three days of fruitful information and discussion.

Thank you.

1.3 MEDIA

Media

Oscar BARTOLI,

Journalist and distinguished lecturer on public relations
and mass media, Washington DC, USA

'The different perspective of a European living in the US'

**Oscar
BARTOLI**

has an accreditation
for Barrister from the
University of Bari. He
also has a law degree
from the University of
Florence and is Presi-
dent of the International
Liaison Group, Inc. in
Washington DC. He
has been Director
of the Istituto per la
Ricostruzione Industriale
(IRI) in Washington, DC
representing the compa-
nies of the group at the
multilateral financial institutions. Director of the
communication projects
for the privatisation of
the Credito Italiano
and Banca Commer-
ciale Italiana, as well as
Senior Vice-President
and Director of the
Press Office of the IRI
Group appointed by
CEO Professor Romano
Prodi, the former Prime
Minister of Italy and the
former President of the
European Union.
As a journalist he has
done freelance work
for some of the most
important newspapers
in Italy and broadcasts
for Radio RAITV. He
is also the Director
of the Società Metal-
lurgica Italiana (SMI)
headquarters in Rome.
In this position he has
provided contacts with
the various Ministries in
Rome, political parties,
and Confindustria (the
Italian entrepreneur
union). He is also the
Director of the Società
Metallurgica Italiana
press and publicity office
in Florence, which is the
most important Euro-
pean private company
for manufacturing semi-
finished copper, nickel
and alloy products.

While I wish to support the favourable comments for this undertaking by OLAF, I would also like to say that my brief contribution, to many, might appear to be in the vein of a 'different perspective'.

Before arriving in Washington DC, I had many years of professional experience in the communications field in Italy.

I've now been in America for 10 years and I must confess that I have witnessed a culture clash in the area of communications between the US and Europe.

Fraud

The very last thing I wish to be is pedantic. But please allow me a moment to define the matter in question, beginning with the current definition of the word 'fraud.'

It derives from the Latin *fraus-fraudis*. According to the Italian Zingarelli dictionary, it means 'astute deceit intended to deceive — grievance, crime against good faith — extortion'.

According to the Webster dictionary, 'fraud is an instance or act of trickery or deceit, when involving misrepresentation: an act of deluding'.

Short cut — cheating — fraud

I will now put on my hat of an Italian emigrant, eternally enamoured of his native country, and admit that Italians are known for always seeking short cuts. It is our response to having to live in survival mode and battle against the abuse inflicted upon us by higher-ups. It has become part of our DNA. It could be seen as a nice characteristic of our way of living, despite some counter-indications.

Because from short cuts one inevitably moves on to cheating and that leads to fraud.

Without unduly generalising, what follows are a few personally witnessed examples of short cuts and cheating.

Moscow, 1970s, Kremlin Museum. Inside the cloakroom, where you are supposed to put on flannel slippers so your shoes won't leave skids on the flooring, there were signs saying, 'No Smoking'. But they weren't in Russian. No! They were written in Italian!

State comprehensive exams in one of the most famous parochial schools in Rome. During the Greek exam the supervisor went to make photocopies of the best student's paper and handed it out to the less prepared ones. He was obviously motivated by a great humanitarian spirit and the desire that the school should have good results to avoid a decrease in enrolment.

Georgetown University, Washington, DC. Posted in the classrooms in the Business Administration Department are signs that warn that anyone caught cheating will be expelled from the school. The signs were put up after a student was caught copying from notes he had brought from home. The student was an Italian — we don't know if he attended the aforementioned high school.

He's a crook... but

Obviously other countries are not populated only by pure souls.

In our collective imagination, in every part of the world, anyone who 'cons' others enjoys great esteem because he or she is viewed as 'shrewd and intelligent'.

In the US, big time bank robbers, con men, swindlers, and Mafiosi have always been admired by the public thanks to Hollywood movies and television series based on their exploits.

(A few years ago after the first episode of 'The Sopranos' was broadcast, I was addressed as 'Bartoli Soprano' on several occasions. And it was said quite jovially. There was great surprise when I answered with a few choice words.)

It could be seen as a parody of the always popular legend of Robin Hood, who stole from the rich and gave to the poor.

The movie 'Catch Me If You Can' was a box office hit. The movie celebrates the true story of Frank Abagnale, a very successful swindler with great acting abilities. After a tumultuous career, his prison sentence was reduced thanks to the intervention of the FBI because they wanted to use his talents as a cheque forger. Today Mr Abagnale is a multimillionaire and very highly paid consultant who helps important financial institutions detect forgeries.

(Frank Abagnale, Jr (Leonardo Di Caprio) worked as a doctor, a lawyer and as a co-pilot for a major airline — all before his 18th birthday. A master of deception, he was also a brilliant forger, whose skill gave him his first real claim to fame. At the age of 17, Frank Abagnale, Jr became the most successful bank robber in the history of the United States. FBI Agent Carl Hanratty (Tom Hanks) had made it his prime mission to capture Frank and bring him to justice, but Frank is always one step ahead of him, baiting him to continue the chase.)

Communication in the US

Let's go to communications and, in particular, to the state of things in the country where I claim citizenship: the US.

Political communication

Here in the US, the President is elected thanks to hundreds of millions of dollars invested in commercials. Over the past few years these 30-second adverts, which have either been directly approved by the two candidates or put forth by groups of their supporters, have assumed an increasingly negative, dare I say aggressive, tone comparable to the worst type of advertising.

According to the latest estimates, both parties and their supporters broadcast 630 000 adverts during the 2 November presidential elections. Each advert was repeated several times a day, with the greatest frequency during prime time.

Consensus, therefore, is obtained via the classical *gutta cavat lapidem* that subliminally penetrates the brain and, in doing so, inhibits any form of reasoning or verification through a democratic exchange of opinion.

The polarisation in the USA today is the result of the domination of commercial television, the print media's inability to shape opinion, and the absence of widespread familiarity with the concept of dialogue. We are left with what some term 'John Wayne culture' in which 'either you're with me, or you're against me'. On top of all this one must add the generally low level of sophistication of US public opinion.

The three televised presidential debates, by definition, cannot influence millions of votes. What counts on television are not ideas and proposed solutions to problems, but body language. Plus, to win on television you have to have the right kind of face. A face with downward lines just will not do. John Kerry didn't win.

The US consists of 289 million individuals, most of whom live in small, isolated towns.

You cannot think of the US and only think of New York (which even Americans consider a crazy social anomaly), or Washington DC, San Francisco or Chicago.

Political marketing sells candidates using the same techniques it would use for burgers and fries.

But political communication consultants also rely on other things. The following is a summary of the four elements on which the success of Karl Rove, whom the President calls 'the Architect', is based.

First: keep very close ties with your constituency (the religious and political right).

Second: try to win over as many as possible of your rival's constituents.

Third: destroy your opponent's image by using dirty tricks. And do it without getting your hands dirty.

Fourth: Once you have won, make the reasons for your victory permanent. This means: use your power to reduce your potential Democratic rivals' constituency base. (These points come from an article by Massimo Cavallini, published on 2Americhe.com.)

All of which confirms that anyone thinking of coming out on top in this television commercial context by relying on noble arguments is fighting a lost battle.

The world of information in the USA lives by the motto 'What's your story?'. If the story you want to tell is easy to grasp, chances are that it will be taken up by the media.

Otherwise, it is better to put your message forth in some other way. One way is to establish Internet sites as was done by supporters of the Democratic Party (MoveOn.org is the most well known). These sites can function as bottom-up democratic engines by soliciting contributions, arranging community meetings and registration drives.

There is no point in thinking you can count on a network of 'friendly' journalists. It is not the case that US journalists are any more ethical than their European counterparts.

It is just that the journalists in the USA are strictly controlled, not only by the brass, but also by their colleagues who live in a constant state of high alert due to the high level of internal competitiveness.

After all, everyone remembers last year's scandal at *The New York Times* with Jayson Blair (who filed invented interviews from home), followed by the one at *USA Today* and other papers with consequent severe loss of prestige.

But there are also colleagues who die while on the job in combat zones so we can have objective reporting on what is actually happening in those countries.

How to communicate

'Fraud'… Communication

As for fiscal fraud, in recent months the US media have devoted a lot of space to Enron and Halliburton and all the other big corporations caught with their hand in the cookie jar. What follows is a list, compiled by Forbes, of the scandals involving US corporations from 2000 to 2002. Parmalat and Cirio should be added to the list.

Accounting

The corporate scandal sheet
Penelope Patsuris, *Forbes Magazine*

With the avalanche of corporate accounting scandals that have rocked the markets recently, it is getting hard to keep track of them all — but our corporate scandal sheet does the job. Here we will follow accounting imbroglios only — avoiding insider-trading allegations like those plaguing ImClone, since chronicling every corporate transgression would be impractical — and our timeline starts with the Enron debacle.

Company	When scandal went public	Allegations	Investigating agencies	Latest developments	Company comment
Adelphia Communications (otc: ADELA — news people)	April 2002	Founding Rigas family collected USD 3.1 billion in off-balance-sheet loans backed by Adelphia; overstated results by inflating capital expenses and hiding debt.	SEC; Pennsylvania and New York federal grand juries	Three Rigas family members and two other ex-executives have been arrested for fraud. The company is suing the entire Rigas family for USD 1 billion for breach of fiduciary duties, among other things.	Did not return repeated calls for comment.
AOL Time Warner (nyse: AOL — news — people)	July 2002	As the advert market faltered and AOL's purchase of Time Warner loomed, AOL inflated sales by booking barter deals and adverts it sold on behalf of others as revenue to keep its growth rate up and seal the deal. AOL also boosted sales via 'round-trip' deals with advertisers and suppliers.	SEC; DOJ	Fears about the enquiry intensified when the DOJ ordered the company to preserve its documents. AOL said it may have overstated revenue by USD 49 million. New concerns are afoot that the company may take another goodwill writedown, after it took a USD 54 billion charge in April.	No comment.
Arthur Andersen	November 2001	Shredding documents related to audit client Enron after the SEC launched an enquiry into Enron.	SEC; DOJ	Andersen was convicted of obstruction of justice in June and will cease auditing public firms by 31 August. Andersen lost hundreds of clients and has seen massive employee defections.	Did not return repeated calls for comment.
Bristol-Myers Squibb (nyse: BMY — news — people)	July 2002	Inflated its 2001 revenue by USD 1.5 billion by 'channel stuffing', or forcing wholesalers to accept more inventory than they can sell to get it off the manufacturer's books.	SEC	Efforts to get inventory back to acceptable size will reduce earnings by 61 cents per share through 2003.	Bristol will continue to cooperate fully with the SEC. We believe that the accounting treatment of the domestic wholesaler inventory build-up has been completely appropriate.
CMS Energy (nyse: CMS — news — people)	May 2002	Executing 'round-trip' trades to artificially boost energy trading volume.	SEC; CFTC; Houston US Attorney's Office; US Attorney's Office for the Southern District of New York	Appointed Thomas J. Webb, a former Kellogg's CFO, as its new chief financial officer, effective in August.	No comment.

Company	When scandal went public	Allegations	Investigating agencies	Latest developments	Company comment
Duke Energy (nyse: DUK — news — people)	July 2002	Engaged in 23 'round-trip' trades to boost trading volumes and revenue.	SEC; CFTC; Houston US Attorney's Office; Federal Energy Regulatory Commission	The company says an internal investigation concluded that its round-trip trades had 'no material impact on current or prior' financial periods.	Although the effect [of these trades] on the company's financial statements was immaterial, we consider improper trades in conflict with the company's policies. To address this we have made changes to our organisation, personnel and procedures.
Dynegy (nyse: DYN — news — people)	May 2002	Executing 'round-trip' trades to artificially boost energy trading volume and cash flow.	SEC; CFTC; Houston US Attorney's Office	Currently conducting a re-audit. Standard & Poor's cut its credit rating to 'junk', and the company said it expects to fall as much as USD 400 million short of the USD 1 billion in cash flow it originally projected for 2002.	Dynegy believes that it has not executed any simultaneous buy-and-sell trades for the purpose of artificially increasing its trading volume or revenue.
El Paso (nyse: EP — news — people)	May 2002	Executing 'round-trip' trades to artificially boost energy trading volume.	SEC; Houston US Attorney's Office	Oscar Wyatt, a major shareholder and renowned wildcatter, may be engineering a management shake-up.	There have been no allegations or accusations, only requests for information. The company has confirmed in multiple affidavits that it did not engage in 'round-trip' trades to artificially inflate volume or revenue.
Enron (otc: EN-RNQ — news — people)	October 2001	Boosted profits and hid debts totalling over USD 1 billion by improperly using off-the-books partnerships; manipulated the Texas power market; bribed foreign governments to win contracts abroad; manipulated California energy market.	DOJ; SEC; FERC; various congressional committees; Public Utility Commission of Texas	Ex-Enron executive Michael Kopper pleaded guilty to two felony charges; acting CEO Stephen Cooper said Enron may face USD 100 billion in claims and liabilities; company filed Chapter 11; its auditor Andersen was convicted of obstruction of justice for destroying Enron documents.	No comment.

Company	When scandal went public	Allegations	Investigating agencies	Latest developments	Company comment
Global Crossing (otc: GBLXQ — news — people)	February 2002	Engaged in network capacity 'swaps' with other carriers to inflate revenue; shredded documents related to accounting practices.	DOJ; SEC; various congressional committees	Company filed Chapter 11; Hutchison Telecommunications Limited and Singapore Technologies Telemedia will pay USD 250 million for a 61.5 % majority interest in the firm when it emerges from bankruptcy; Congress is examining the role that company's accounting firms played in its bankruptcy.	No comment.
Halliburton (nyse: HAL — news — people)	May 2002	Improperly booked USD 100 million in annual construction cost overruns before customers agreed to pay for them.	SEC	Legal watchdog group Judicial Watch filed an accounting fraud lawsuit against Halliburton and its former CEO, Vice-President Dick Cheney, among others.	Halliburton follows the guidelines set by experts, including GAAP (generally accepted accounting principles).
Homestore.com (Nasdaq: HOMS — news — people)	January 2002	Inflating sales by booking barter transactions as revenue.	SEC	The California State Teachers' Retirement pension fund, which lost USD 9 million on a Homestore investment, has filed suit against the company.	No comment.
Kmart (nyse: KM — news — people)	January 2002	Anonymous letters from people claiming to be Kmart employees allege that the company's accounting practices intended to mislead investors about its financial health.	SEC; House Energy and Commerce Committee; US Attorney for the Eastern District of Michigan	The company, which is in bankruptcy, said the 'stewardship review' it promised to complete by Labor Day will not be done until the end of the year.	Did not return repeated calls for comment.
Merck (nyse: MRK — news — people)	July 2002	Recorded USD 12.4 billion in consumer-to-pharmacy co-payments that Merck never collected.	None	The SEC approved Medco's IPO registration, including its sales accounting. The company has since withdrawn the registration for the IPO, which was expected to raise USD 1 billion.	Our accounting practices accurately reflect the results of Medco's business and are in accordance with GAAP. Recognising retail co-payments has no impact on Merck's net income or earnings per share.
Mirant (nyse: MIR — news — people)	July 2002	The company said it may have overstated various assets and liabilities.	SEC	An internal review revealed errors that may have inflated revenue by USD 1.1 billion.	This is an informal enquiry, and we will cooperate fully with this request for information.

Company	When scandal went public	Allegations	Investigating agencies	Latest developments	Company comment
Nicor Energy, LLC, a joint venture between Nicor (nyse: GAS — news — people) and Dynegy (nyse: DYN — news — people)	July 2002	Independent audit uncovered accounting problems that boosted revenue and underestimated expenses.	None	Nicor restated results to reflect proper accounting in the first half of this year.	Our focus now is to stabilise this venture and put some certainty to its financial results. The company is evaluating its continued involvement in this venture.
Peregrine Systems (Nasdaq: PRGNE — news — people)	May 2002	Overstated USD 100 million in sales by improperly recognising revenue from third-party resellers.	SEC; various congressional committees	Said it will restate results dating back to 2000; slashed nearly 50 % of its workforce to cut costs; is on its third auditor in three months and has yet to file its 2001 10-K and so, consequently, is in danger of being delisted from the Nasdaq.	We have been and will continue to cooperate with the SEC and the congressional committee.
Qwest Communications International (nyse: Q — news — people)	February 2002	Inflated revenue using network capacity 'swaps' and improper accounting for long-term deals.	DOJ; SEC; FBI; Denver US Attorney's Office	Qwest admitted that an internal review found that it incorrectly accounted for USD 1.16 billion in sales. It will restate results for 2000, 2001 and 2002. To raise funds, Qwest says it is selling its phone-directory unit for USD 7.05 billion.	We are continuing to cooperate fully with the investigations.
Reliant Energy (nyse: REI — news — people)	May 2002	Engaging in 'round-trip' trades to boost trading volumes and revenue.	SEC; CFTC	Recently replaced Chief Financial Officer Steve Naeve with Mark M. Jacobs, a managing director of Goldman Sachs and a Reliant adviser.	We are cooperating with the investigations.
Tyco (nyse: TYC — news — people)	May 2002	Ex-CEO L. Dennis Kozlowski indicted for tax evasion. SEC investigating whether the company was aware of his actions, possible improper use of company funds and related-party transactions, as well as improper merger accounting practices.	Manhattan district attorney; SEC	Said it will not certify its financial results until after an internal investigation is completed. The Bermuda-based company is not required to meet the SEC's 14 August deadline. Investors looking to unseat all board members who served under Kozlowski may launch a proxy fight to do so.	The company is conducting an internal investigation and we cannot comment on its specifics, but we will file an 8-K on the initial results around 15 September.

Company	When scandal went public	Allegations	Investigating agencies	Latest developments	Company comment
WorldCom (Nasdaq: WCOEQ — news — people)	March 2002	Overstated cash flow by booking USD 3.8 billion in operating expenses as capital expenses; gave founder Bernard Ebbers USD 400 million in off-the-books loans.	DOJ; SEC; US Attorney's Office for the Southern District of New York; various congressional committees	The company stunned the Street when it found another USD 3.3 billion in improperly booked funds, which will bring its total restatement up to USD 7.2 billion, and that it may have to take a goodwill charge of USD 50 billion. Former CFO Scott Sullivan and ex-controller David Myers have been arrested and criminally charged, while rumours of Bernie Ebbers' impending indictment persist.	WorldCom is continuing to cooperate with all ongoing investigations.
Xerox (nyse: XRX — news — people)	June 2000	Falsifying financial results for five years, boosting income by USD 1.5 billion.	SEC	Xerox agreed to pay USD 10 million and to restate its financials dating back to 1997.	We chose to settle with the SEC in April so we can put the matter behind us. We have restated our financials and certified our financials for the new SEC requirements.

Employee pension funds have been depleted. Tens of thousands of families have been left without any health insurance. You can bet that the injured parties do not feel much admiration for the people who landed them in this mess.

Famous accounting firms that, instead of defending the interests of small investors, plotted with their clients to set up a perverse tangle of corruption.

High-level executives, the so-called 'untouchables' because they were friends of leading politicians, have been sent to jail or are on their way there. Now these are stories.

One cannot help asking: before these scandals exploded, almost by self-combustion, where were the electronic and print journalists specialising in finance and economics? How can it be that none of them realised, in time, that all was not well in the world whose production and management wonders they so highly praised? These are useless and naïve questions.

Anti-fraud communication

In the USA, talking about the war on drugs is a déjà vu that falls flat. The USA has been fighting a civil war for years against drug abuse. It is a country where the every day stress to survive, the big city ghettos, the gangs, the loneliness felt while being in a crowd, and the absence of real families leads from French fries to obesity, from stimulants to heavy drugs, from alcohol to heroin or crack.

Police departments, to combat their bad image fuelled by incidents of reprehensible behaviour, attacks on innocent civilians and corruption, in recent years have teamed up with Hollywood to make movies and television series and reality cable shows.

Despite the fact that spectators may pull for the thief, the drunk driver or the desperate junkie, these shows serve a law enforcement purpose.

The visualisation of the risks and personal problems that can befall the citizen who does not respect the law is a positive antidote against those who might be tempted otherwise.

Should we conclude that we are dealing with a 'Mission Impossible'?

There is no single answer and it depends on the communication environment one is dealing with.

In the USA it takes a lot of money to buy time on commercial television; public stations do not have a large audience.

In Europe, things can be handled differently given, above all, the presence of important public networks where political campaigns can be waged at a relatively low cost.

You must allow me to praise, in all honesty, what OLAF, despite limited resources, has miraculously achieved by focusing its every day and highly professional efforts on behalf of all European citizens.

The motto of all public relations is, 'Do it and do it well'. I would like to add, 'And let it be known' as I wrote in my corporate PR manual *You don't know who I am!*, which was published with an introduction by Professor Romano Prodi. It quickly sold out.

We must always remember that when you do well and word gets around, the number of people who attack you will increase. This is not only due to jealously, but rather because you have reduced their sphere of personal influence.

In any event, it is important to stress the results achieved in the war against contraband and fraud, but also it might be more effective to make people understand that buying bootleg cigarettes, fake Prada purses, avoiding taxes with phoney invoices, or selling drugs all leads to immediate civil and penal consequences.

Let us not forget that when a series of articles in Italy came out lamenting the fate of the young man who was caught exiting a café without the required proof of purchase, everyone's behaviour underwent an abrupt change. The result: people started demanding receipts. Law enforcement means what it says.

Crisis communication

I wish to conclude my presentation with a few comments on the subject of 'crisis communication', [which in] the US has become the mainstay of corporate communication, due to the frequent scandals, that, as previously mentioned, involve famous and powerful corporations and their highly overpaid administrators.

Among the many publications on the topic I would like to mention Sandra K. Clawson Freeo's because I feel it is noteworthy in its direct focus on market exigencies.

Media

The author writes, 'A crisis is any situation that threatens the integrity or reputation of your company, usually brought on by adverse or negative media attention. These situations can be any kind of legal dispute, theft, accident, fire, flood or man-made disaster that could be attributed to your company. It can also be a situation where in the eyes of the media or general public your company did not react to one of the above situations in the appropriate manner.'

And she adds, 'If handled correctly the damage can be minimised. One thing to remember that is crucial in a crisis is tell it all, tell it fast and tell the truth. If you do this you have done all you can to minimise the situation'.

The most basic technique in 'crisis communication' is simulating responses to possible negative events. This enables you to prepare for ad hoc communication and tests the professional skills and effectiveness of the intervention being organised.

I had the opportunity to observe how OLAF reacted in dealing with the well-known incident when a journalist from *Stern* magazine started publishing a confidential internal document.

The decisions made by those in charge at OLAF by means of their press releases and their willingness to be available to the media were, in my opinion, a textbook example of how to manage a crisis situation. It was even more noteworthy because we are talking about an organisation with a multinational cultural history of decades of 'I'll say it here, and here I'll deny it' and of reluctance to deal with the press. OLAF and its management should be commended for their preparation and the immediacy of their decisions in what was, by all accounts, a difficult situation.

Media

Dragan BISENIC,

Journalist of *Danas Daily*,
Chief Editor of the Serbian magazine *CorD*, Serbia

**Dragan
BISENIC**

is a journalist from
Belgrade, Foreign
Editor of the Daily
Nasa Borba and
Editor in Chief of
the monthly CorD,
which specialises in
European issues. He
teaches in the Centre
for USA Studies at
the Faculty of Political
Sciences in Belgrade.
He was also fellow at
the Free University
in Berlin and at the
Institute for Human
Sciences in Vienna. He
is an expert on the
Council of Europe
focused on media
training and local
authorities. He is also
the author of several
books and publishes
articles in international
media.

'Three unsolved cases in Serbia'

U ntil after 2000, no one in Serbia knew of the existence of OLAF, the European Anti-Fraud Office, or what the organisation could do and in what ways it could affect the lives of people not even living in the European Union. After the regime changed, the process of integration into the EU began. As will be seen, several practices inherited from the period of sanctions and isolation of Serbia continued without interruption, which directly hurt the Union's budget. Since then, and until recently, awareness of OLAF's activities has grown, and there have been several cases where OLAF has opened investigations and undertaken actions affecting Serbia, but, unfortunately, none of this has significantly improved the general public's knowledge of what the organisation's aims are, or what OLAF's findings were in all instances where the subject was a non-EU country.

According to information known to Serbia's public, OLAF has undertaken four investigations relating to Serbia and Montenegro, or Yugoslavia, the country's former name. The first mention of OLAF in Serbia occurred when the issue of cigarette smuggling into the EU was raised; top officials of both member republics, Serbia and Montenegro, were implicated in the affair. OLAF had already been investigating another case of infringement or misinterpretation of EU regulations on the import of sugar into the Union from the Balkans, especially from Croatia and Serbia and Montenegro.

OLAF was twice mentioned in connection with investigations into the misuse of European Union funds. Both cases were similar: the first related to corruption in the reconstruction of Kosovo power plants. The second, more recent one, involved corruption in the reconstruction of the Nikola Tesla power plant in the Serbian city of Obrenovac, where, according to media reports, the German firm Siemens bribed officials from the European Agency for Reconstruction and Development to get the contract.

The first two cases grew into substantial scandals, and were thoroughly covered in the Serbian media. Both affairs, at least as far as the general public is concerned, ended with the media failing to go beyond speculations and guesswork, and using only their own sources and personal connections. It is standard practice for OLAF to leave the reporting of results of its enquiries to legislative authorities of the countries in question. However, such procedures are rather less well-defined in cases where countries under investigation are not EU members and are still involved in the accession process. Not a single Serbian institution mentioned in the investigations or authorised to inform the public of the results has ever made it possible for the public to inspect even the smallest part of any OLAF report. Conversely, both institutions and individuals named in the investigations have publicly denied any connection with the actions, without opening reports compiled by OLAF investigators to public scrutiny. The most perseverance and thoroughness was shown by journalists of daily newspapers, who constantly applied pressure on the government to allow public access to OLAF materials, yet the government did not lift a finger to resolve matters in any of the instances. The government's stance could be understandable when one remembers that scandals involving sugar exports and disregard for the spirit of agreements on sugar exports into the EU disgraced and eventually brought down the previous government. The politicians who followed that government into office, and who built their position on criticising it on the basis of results of OLAF enquiries, continued the trend of keeping mum when the public asked for those results to be presented. The man cited most often as the main culprit in the 'sugar affair', the scandal that caused great damage to Serbia's economy (as the EU first suspended sugar imports from Serbia for six months, and then prolonged the suspension several times), was temporarily arrested and held in custody, but was released after charges were brought against him. He kept insisting that he had only been following instructions given by senior officials of the previous government — who then went on to keep their positions in the new administration. Virtually nobody, apart from the general public, had any interest in discovering the whole truth. On the other hand, because of its built-in limitations, OLAF's information service was unable to present any details on the results of its enquiries. As Serbia still lacks legislation on free access to information — which would make it compulsory for public institutions to allow free access to data and information of public interest — the media's persistent requests for vital facts went unheeded. Instead, the journalists were sent on wild goose chases from one institution to another, from the Ministry of the Interior to the Customs Office, from the Customs Office to the Chamber of Commerce, and so on. Instead of a credible story, rumours started circulating, further complicating and obscuring an already unclear case. The incident was all but forgotten, and was never solved, as Serbian bodies had no interest in making public the whole truth of the background of the deeper rift in relations with the EU, which could have had more lasting consequences.

The OLAF 'network of communicators' showed its true value during the operation aimed at stopping the smuggling of cigarettes between Italy and Montenegro. Thanks to the existing network of customs, judicial and police bodies, it was possible to get all data about this important issue from the Italian side. Media investigation received concrete backing, so almost all information relevant for solving the complex relations between criminal groups and customs and police bodies was published, as were data on the web of corruption which harmed the budgets of both the European Union and Serbia and Montenegro.

If one looks at the results of this public campaign to expose the 'grey market' in cigarettes from a distance of two years, one can easily see that cigarette smuggling has all but vanished, that the government brings in income from excise duties, and that organisers of criminal activities have been brought before justice.

Serbia was, in all fairness, the only Balkan country to undertake a serious campaign against organised crime before and after the assassination of Prime Minister Zoran Djindjic. After the Prime Minister's assassination, on 12 March 2003, a state of emergency was instituted, lasting three months, and resulting in the suspension of certain civic rights. During the state of emergency, some 12 000 people were brought in and detained. Debate is still raging on how justified the measures were, but it is beyond dispute that the core of organised crime was broken in the operation. Numerous criminal groups were dispersed, while the trial continues for the murder of Prime Minister Djindjic, as well as for a number of other cases from the jurisdiction of the special prosecutor and other institutions created to fight organised crime.

The last case testifying to the great usefulness of OLAF's 'network of communicators' is that involving corruption during the refit of the Nikola Tesla power plant in Obrenovac. Serbian authorities failed to react to media reports on how assets from the European Agency for Reconstruction and Development ended up in the pockets of corrupt officials, and how companies were ready to use bribery to further their aims. Apart from European officials implicated in the case, Serbian media were unable to discover a single Serbian official involved in the scandal. While German media described the role of the German parties and Siemens, and the European press debunked the behaviour of the European officials, what were the Serbian media doing? The role of not even a single person from the Serbian side was revealed; yet, obviously, they were instrumental in the case.

It is only with the help of OLAF's network that some knowledge was gained. The information, however, is limited, as it is not easy for people as far apart as, say, a journalist from Belgrade and a prosecutor from Wuppertal, to communicate with clarity and precision.

The role of the 'network of communicators' in countries outside the EU which, like Serbia and Montenegro, do not have close institutional ties with the Union, is much more important than in the case of Member States. These are bound by numerous legal standards concerning openness of work and transparency, unlike countries which are still not even candidates for membership. Those who have authority in these countries often make use of OLAF's imperfect public relations system. Since OLAF is not allowed to make its findings public, it is obvious that local elites do not find it necessary to help the media. The 'network of communicators' is the only instrument, albeit not the only one necessary, helping investigative reporting in countries still outside the European Union.

Media

Enrico BRIVIO,

Journalist, Associated Press Association, Correspondent,
Il Sole 24 Ore, Italy

Enrico BRIVIO

*has been
correspondent in
Brussels for the Italian
financial daily,* Il Sole
24 Ore, *since 1996,
covering European
affairs. He was also
chairman of the
International Press
Association (IPA),
the association of
Brussels-based foreign
correspondents, from
2000 to October
2004. He has been a
professional journalist
for* Il Sole 24 Ore
*also in Milan and New
York since 1986. He
is author of the book*
Come comunica la
Casa Bianca *(How
the White House
communicates), Bridge
editore, Milan, 1992.*

'An EU press room perspective in anti-fraud communication strategy'

am a correspondent for *Il Sole 24 Ore*, which is a financial newspaper in Italy and I also represent here the International Press Association (IPA), which probably is the biggest press room in the world even if they may not think so in Washington. But it is, practically, because we have almost 1 000 accredited journalists and the majority are members of our organisation. So, just to explain what is, in a few words, the International Press Association: it was established in 1975 and was the first organisation to bring together foreign journalists of all categories and specialisations based in Belgium and from all the different organs — television, radio, press agencies or newspapers. It is not a journalist trade union in the classical sense, it is an association which has as its aim the assistance of its members in the exercise of their profession. We also represent correspondents, in the relations with the institutions for all the problems concerning communication, the organisation of press conferences and other issues.

So, why am I here? I am not what you may call an investigative journalist — some of whom you probably had the pleasure to hear in the previous days, and which is a category of journalists for which I have a great respect and admiration. But I think even here, in Brussels, correspondents have a stimulating job that allows us to come in contact with ministers, members of the European Commission, MPs, officials, and with the way of thinking of 25 and, even more, different countries, if you consider that there are also members of third countries.

The risk, maybe, as a correspondent, is living and writing within what I call a Communitarian bubble. So — a bubble where you have to deal with directives, comitology, qualified majority, block minorities and all things that seem very remote from everyday life and problems that may sometimes seem a little far from the problems of the world; real stories like some cases of frauds and misdemeanours that some professional investigative professionals in the audience here are used to coming into contact with.

Still, I think it is very important for you to understand my world and for me to understand yours. Why? Because if you want to have a complete picture of the world of media and information, no matter what country you live in, you will have to come to terms with the flow of information in Brussels, which is often channelled through almost 1 000 correspondents, actually more than 1 000, and also because it is also useful for me to understand better, when I write about Community frauds or OLAF investigations in Brussels, some of your experiences on the ground in different countries. That will allow me to give a real perspective to the stories from Brussels, and help me to understand exactly what happens outside this Communitarian bubble.

There are a few aspects I would like to touch on in the relationship between journalists and operators in the field of investigation. I would briefly touch on different subjects: the structure of the current information society, the time factor, the different national sensitivities and the converging and sometimes conflicting roles of journalists and investigators, that maybe is the point that interests you most.

As far as the structure on news is concerned, I would say that the world of news has dramatically changed in the last few years. Now, as we all know, we are totally overwhelmed with such a flow of information. Every day I receive hundreds of e-mails, like you do, probably. In this respect, I think we have to be realistic and acknowledge that the fierce competition between media and the large flow of information lead a large part of the media to be more sensational. To catch the attention of the reader or the television viewer you have to strike, nowadays, a higher chord. And even newspapers with the solid reputation in the business community, like the *Financial Times* or *The Wall Street Journal* or we can mention, if I may, *Il Sole 24 Ore*, are forced nowadays to carry more sensational titles, to gain the attention of the reader, which they would not have done 10 years ago.

And so I know that if I asked everybody here in this room if they would prefer a long, in-depth, accurate story, everybody would say 'yes', but we have to face reality. Even many newspapers or news media that carry serious articles now have to strike the attention of the reader if they want to survive in a very competitive market.

So lesson number one is, I think, and we cannot escape it: if you have a message, I think you have to make it sexy.

Unusual stories, broad conspiracies in many countries, frauds involving large amounts of euro unfortunately will have greater possibilities to pass through the media and reach a large number of citizens than very detailed essays and reports. So if you want to reach a large number of citizens with your message and make it known all over Europe, I am afraid you will have to play according to the rules of the game and grab the interest of journalists with those elements that can feed their appetite: so, as I said, unusual stories, broad investigations, large confiscations of illegal goods or drugs. And we also know other rules, like sometimes leaking a document in an exclusive way to one media can bring that media to give much more emphasis to the fact than if that piece of news had been released to every other media. It may be a cheap rule but sometimes it works, so if you want to be effective I think you have to consider also the fierce competition that exists between different media and use it for your own purpose.

Another point I wanted to touch on is the time factor. Being forced to cover the events for a daily newspaper day by day, I probably have the privilege to have a little bit more time than my colleagues who work for a news agency or television, because news agencies and television have to give the news in real time. But still, I have a time constriction much tighter than some other journalists that, as I said, I respect and admire: those journalists who may work for days and days on an investigative story for a magazine. No matter what, I have to file my story at the end of the day. So for this, I think availability and prompt response by the press official of an institution is extremely important. I think that most of the correspondents in Brussels are very serious professionals; most of them are, I know them very well. And they like to check with two or three different sources the information they get, sometimes using also a network of their colleagues in their own country or in other countries, and exchange information with other correspondents in more provincial and local situations where some stories may have happened or where some events may have taken place. But in these cases, it is extremely important to have the possibility to have access to a spokesman or to an official source, to have a confirmation or to correct wrong information. But this has to be made almost in real time in many cases. In my case, I have a few hours' time. The article must be written by 9 or 10 o'clock at night, at the latest, and be published the day after. So, I understand that some of you may have legal constrictions and you may have to ask permission to release the information, and the permission could be hard to get. But in some cases, to give an answer tomorrow will be too late, because a story may already be too old and readers will not need a following article on the same story the day after. So my suggestion is, if you trust a journalist or if he comes from a reputable media, it is better, I think, to give an off-the-record comment or an unofficial confirmation in the background than nothing. At least, your point of view will be registered and have an impact on tomorrow's stories, otherwise it may be absolutely lost in the sea of news produced every day.

As regards different national sensitivities, I think that the Brussels press room is a privileged point of view to understand different ways of thinking. When I arrived here eight years ago, I had been used to hearing in Italy, about bribes of millions of euro during the Tangentopoli affairs and scandals and I could not understand why German and Nordic journalists were so excited about some Communitarian frauds involving a few thousand euro. But then, living here, you understand why there are different conceptions and ideas about public office. For the Scandinavian mentality, transparency, for instance, is the main character that every institution should display in a very open way. In contrast, a Spanish or Italian journalist would be a little sceptical towards an institution that claims to be very transparent, suspecting that giving out a lot of information is the best way to hide secrets. Germans are very careful about numbers and details. The UK press is constantly concerned with every little expense that may involve a waste of taxpayers' money, whereas other journalists of southern countries think that they should concentrate their attention on big scandals. I think that to know and respect each mentality is one of the beautiful things about being here in Europe and I think that for you to try to get in tune with each one of these different mentalities should be an important feature for any institutional communicator.

And then, if I can go to the question of roles of journalists and investigators, I think, as Alessandro Butticé pointed out in his speech, the ultimate interest of the good investigator or communicator for a public institution and that of the good journalist should be the same: to disclose some frauds in the interest of the citizen and as a tool of prevention. But of course, the investigator looks for evidence to be shown to the judge and the journalist to make it available to his reader. So the timing and structures of their two roles are inevitably different and sometimes, even if they have a common ultimate goal, they may run into a collision. And so I am perfectly aware that the release of some information by the media may have the effect of obstructing the development of an investigation, creating problems. And I think that even in those crucial moments when there could be a collision, we do not have to lose the respect of the reciprocal roles, which are essential for our democracy.

I personally think that there is not good democracy if crimes are not investigated, regardless of who committed them, but there is also not good democracy if there is not freedom of the media to report about crimes, regardless of who committed them. So, I consider as a good suggestion that made by Alessandro Butticé in his speech to have a more structured dialogue — now I'm using an expression that may come from the Communitarian bubble of Brussels — to have some form of constant dialogue between OLAF and the press corps in Brussels. I do not know if this constant dialogue should take also the form of a code of conduct because I am a little sceptical about a code with no sanctions that help to enforce it. And, also, the International Press Organisation is not an organisation that deals with ethical sanctions. But I think it is very important to maintain a constant, open channel of communication, have a sort of mutual trust between the operators of the media and the representatives of the institutions, respecting, obviously, the two different roles. And I think we have already shown in critical moments that this mutual respect already exists. There was one case of a journalist belonging to the Brussels-based press corps being searched by Belgian police. We had always kept, even in that situation, an open and constructive dialogue. In those days, one of the OLAF magistrates, Mr Perduca, came into the press room, and was given the opportunity to explain the situation: what were the powers that OLAF had, its responsibilities, and those of Belgian police. That was very helpful for many people who did not have a clear picture of the situation. The IPA, a priori, refrained from expressing a judgment on the matter of the case because we felt that was not our business, and we have to respect the role of OLAF and people investigating, as well as the right of the journalist. The point that concerned us the most was the strange and disturbing situation of being a European correspondent in a country, Belgium, that at that time did not have a law that recognised the right of journalists to protect sources. Then, after a few months, the Belgian parliament started discussing the law for the protection of sources by journalists; a law that from our point of view may improve the situation. But it is very important that at the root there is a mutual trust and a sincere relationship. I do not think, for instance, that a public officer should ever resort to lies, although you know that Winston Churchill used to say this: 'In wartime, truth is too important and should be protected by some bodyguards: lies.' But I do not think that even if you are at war with crime you should follow this Winston Churchill idea and you should resort to 'no comment' or to silence, without having to come to the point of saying lies.

In general terms and without references to any specific case, I think that if a journalist gets a confidential document which could be of some interest and thinks that it is not a fake document, he should publish it. If he is a journalist, he will do it and has the right to do it. Most European laws give this right and it is also the right that was recognised in the United States by the first amendment of the Constitution. The first — not the second, not the third — to show how important that right is. And I think also that journalists should have, like priests in a confession, the right not to disclose their sources and not be forced to disclose who gave them a document. Of course, searching operations of investigators can be legitimate if there is serious doubt of a crime. We have to be realistic, that can happen. But, from the point of view of journalists, it is not acceptable, the so-called 'fishing operation': let's go and search in a journalist's office just to check if we can find anything interesting; as any attempt to intimidate a journalist would not be acceptable. And I hope that in our democracies this will never happen. In the same way, honest fact-based reporting should always be accepted, whereas trashy, not accurate reporting needs to be criticised, even by the same journalists. I think that even us journalists have to criticise sometimes those colleagues who do not do an adequate job because they do, after all, a bad service to the community and give a bad image also to our profession.

Of course, we have accepted fast times and, as I said before, the constrictions of modern media, so we have to understand that if I do not get a quote by the evening, and the story would come out in any case, maybe it will not be so accurate. But the important thing is that this has to be done in good faith and with an honest professional attitude by the journalist. On the contrary, bad, trashy journalists, as I said, should not be excused and we do not have to be too complacent with bad journalism.

Justice, media and power may be a hellish triangle like someone has claimed. But this can also be a triangle that, with its checks and balances, helps our democracy to be a better democracy. For this reason, I think that a dialogue between journalists and investigators should be kept always open in the mutual respect and deep understanding of the different roles. And for this reason, I was very happy to be here with you today.

Media

Media

Paolo DI GIANNANTONIO,

Journalist, RAI 1 news service

Paolo DI GIANNAN-TONIO

49, was born in Rome and has been a journalist since 1978. Since 1982 he has worked for Tg1. As a special and war correspondent he followed crises in the Middle East, Afghanistan, Somalia, Croatia, Bosnia and Kosovo and in Saudi Arabia and Kuwait during the First Gulf War. He is a specialist on the Arab and Muslim world. He is currently the anchorman for the 1.30 p.m. edition of Tg1 News and specials about breaking events such as the death of Pope John Paul II and the Tsunami tragedy. In Italy he has reported on organised crime in Sicily, Naples and Puglia, dealing in particular with smuggling issues.

'Why informing and communicating also means fighting and preventing fraud: a personal experience'

I would like to share with you a personal experience that is — I feel sure — highly relevant to this discussion. It concerns my investigations into smuggling, a problem that had reached alarming proportions in Italy in the 1990s but was generally underestimated by the general public, the media, political circles and the State.

The first indications emerged in articles published in regional newspapers reporting that Apulian smugglers were using four-by-fours with homemade but effective armour in real battles against the Guardia di Finanza vehicles attempting to prevent cigarettes being landed on Italian shores. The first example of collaboration occurred when I asked the Guardia di Finanza press office for permission to be present at the 'on-the-ground' investigations and enforcement operations. I was somewhat sceptical because, like the armed forces engaged in operations abroad, Italian police forces rarely allow the press to be present when operations are being conducted. The usual reasons given are safety and caution, but there is another reason. The journalist in me will not allow me to mince my words here and so I must say that there is a broadly held conviction that it is better to avoid problems with journalists, who are generally viewed as 'interfering and troublesome'.

However, I found the officers to be open and courageous. It was decided to open up all possible information channels, accepting the risks involved. I was given the green light to go to Apulia to cover the investigations, the ambushes and the chases overland and at sea (as were others). On several occasions, we accompanied officers in the provinces of Bari and Brindisi and managed to take truly unique photos, not only of arrests but also of cars being overtaken and rammed. In other words, alongside the Guardia di Finanza's officers we tasted the risks of fieldwork. A couple of times, it is true to say that we were lucky to get out in one piece.

What were the results? Firstly, we obtained top-quality photographs that not only made it possible to illustrate smuggling operations in the newspapers but also provided a source for a series of special in-depth operations. Then, we had direct contact with an activity that had, until that point, seemed less of a series of serious, organised crimes and conspiracies and more a romantic attempt by picturesque characters taken from some or other history of Naples to make ends meet. Those days and nights taught us that we were not dealing with Sophia Loren-style smuggling; we were locking horns with the mercenaries of the Sacra Corona Unita and the Camorra.

There were 'normal' people, and lots of them. But the embrace of criminal organisations threatened to become suffocating. It covered all aspects of the investigations. I met smugglers and, with the Guardia di Finanza, I pursued them overland and at sea. I discovered how many people were involved in the fast, synchronised operations to unload the speedboats. Some evenings a hundred and more people went off to earn between EUR 50 and 100 in just a few minutes. These were normal people, not criminals. They were students, unemployed persons or pensioners, all of whom finished up being sucked into a criminal economy that was having a highly alarming social impact. Ultimately, these smuggling operations further highlighted the poverty and backwardness of the area, effectively offering itself as a possible solution.

We knew that behind the whole problem was corruption at all levels, connivance on the part of other countries, a lack of scruples on the part of broad swathes of the business and financial community, as well as ambiguity and shortcomings on the part of the major tobacco multinationals. And this was the point: I realised that those nights spent in Apulia with the Guardia di Finanza were only the start of an investigation that would reach out well beyond Italy's borders. Clearly, in addition to the willingness and cooperation of the Guardia di Finanza we needed other, more broadly based cooperation. And so our second step was to contact the judiciary, the anti-Mafia section of the Public Prosecution Service, which was able to second some top-grade 'brains', and OLAF, which gave us a European perspective and a general overview.

Thanks to contacts with judges in Bari and Naples and with Brussels officials, we succeeded in finding out the extent of the involvement in smuggling of the highest echelons of the governments of Yugoslavia at first and Montenegro subsequently. It had even become one of the key components of the budget in certain countries that were struggling to survive the turbulence of the war-torn Balkans. The second stage took us to Montenegro, where blood had been spilled at the hands of leading members of the Sacra Corona Unita.

We met the Minister of the Interior. It was a tough meeting but finally we obtained permission to film the quays at the port of Bar. It was unbelievable. We arrived to meet with an atmosphere of the greatest tension and found dozens of smugglers' speedboats filled to the gunnels with cases of cigarettes ready to set off for Apulia. The crews were hiding in some sheds. At that very moment, I received a call on my portable phone from Bari. It was a highly agitated smuggler friend in Bari phoning from the Italian shoreline. 'How long do you plan to stay there in Bar?' he asked me, 'because we're going to lose all today's load and that means billions of lire …'.

Montenegro was not the only Balkan State involved in the smuggling. The others included Macedonia, Kosovo, Albania and Serbia. It seemed that the whole of eastern Europe had become a haven for traffickers of all kinds. And it was possible to shed light on the situation only by working closely together with other journalists, public prosecution services and police forces, some from the Balkan States in question.

I became convinced, and I would like to stress this point, that it would never have been possible for a television company or newspaper, however important it might be, to conduct such an extensive investigation. The operations were transnational. They were 'global' and this is why they were so successful: they could extend their tentacles beyond their own borders. We journalists had to get used to this.

This is what we did, working together with Montenegrin, Croatian, Serbian, English, German, Swiss and French colleagues. It was a complicated puzzle to put together but, once the initial difficulties had been overcome, the network began working well for all concerned. We could tell the story of the unloading and shipment of the cigarettes; we had the low-down on the criminal organisations in Italy. Our colleagues from the Balkans had the task of establishing the details of their governments' involvement. Our Swiss counterparts were indispensable when it came to arriving at the 'third level': the financial transactions.

Switzerland was the third stop on my smuggling tour. This was where the 'brains' of the organisations met the financiers and cigarette suppliers. This is where contracts were concluded, payments made, banking operations transacted and money exchanged. I do not think it any exaggeration to say that there was a time when the smugglers effectively enjoyed full rights of citizenship in Switzerland, simply because the offence was not recognised as such there. It was just one of many lawful operations.

This fundamental question proved to be an economic, political and legal battlefield. And this is where OLAF and Brussels played a key role, explaining, demonstrating and encouraging. We were able to show how the contraband was at the centre of large financial flows and how the people behind it, who were wanted in EU countries, enjoyed privileges and facilitations of all kinds. We learned how the business transactions could be concluded without any problems. I will not mention any names but the roles of extremely well-known moneychangers, banks and companies became clear. Light was shed on that twilight zone where the world of crime intersects with the world of business.

But this was not enough. There was a fourth stage, the most difficult one. It involved the relationship between the smugglers and the tobacco multinationals. This relationship is anything but transparent, and much still needs to be done and said on the subject. It is fraught with risks because the economic and legal power of the companies, whose turnovers are greater than the GDP of certain third-world countries, can be intimidating.

In general, we can say that it has been established that the giant multinationals are able to control both the lawful and illegal markets as a type of continuum, and even the most important players in the press have experienced real difficulties in their attempts to shed light on the situation.

There has been a sea change, however, thanks to measures taken by the EU, which has gone as far as to take the case to the Manhattan court. We have identified a number of major players in the network, some of whom are Italian businessmen who used to work for the multinationals and were entrusted with dealing with the 'grey-zone traders'. They enjoyed and still enjoy support in the highest places, including at federal level. But we had arrived at a far more rarefied atmosphere and were working in terrain where it was far more difficult to conduct investigations. It is one thing to see smugglers in armoured vehicles but quite another to detect the near invisible threads of financial and banking transactions.

Media

This is the point the press has reached in its dealings with the smuggling operations: the world of finance and the tobacco multinationals. Without the network consisting of journalists, investigators, courts and international bodies (most notably OLAF) I have sketched out, the extent of the operations would not have emerged and its ramifications would have remained hidden. As we know, large-scale crime is increasingly white-collar crime, where the colours have become shady. It worms its way into niches in business and civil society, benefiting from the neutrality of paper and documents.

To combat it we have, first and foremost, to bring it to light, drawing it to the attention of the public and raising awareness of its impact. We have to make it clear to everyone that — in the case of cigarettes — buying a packet on a street corner means helping a complex criminal operation that has tentacles at all levels, that the money is used to finance other criminal activities, and so on.

This is why we cannot go back. This is why, in fact, we need to step up cooperation between the press and the international bodies involved in the fight against fraud. OLAF has always been an attentive and willing partner, and we are all aware of our respective roles.

What is happening with regard to cigarette trafficking and other fraud operations can serve as an example and a model for everyone in Europe.

I would just like to say a very sincere thank you.

Media

Media

Daniela FILIPESCU,

European correspondent,
Prima TV Romania

Daniela FILIPESCU

European correspondent for Prima TV Romania. Before joining Prima TV, Ms Filipescu was a consultant in charge of relations between the Romanian Chamber of Deputies, the European Parliament and the European Commission within the Committee for European Integration and the Department for International Relations. She obtained a Robert Schumann scholarship for paid traineeship in the DG for Information and Public Relations, European Parliament, Brussels, a certificate in negotiation techniques in the diplomatic academy within the Ministry of Foreign Affairs in Romania and in the United Kingdom Foreign Office, a DEA in Political Sciences, a certificat d'études specialisées (a certificate of specialised studies) in business law and international cooperation and a BA in Business Administration.

'Communication towards citizens: a democratic principle in the work of institutions'

The democratic principle discussed here is, basically, a common one, either when referring to what we journalists want, or to the wishes of various institutions' representatives — national, European or international.

It is about our obligation to inform public opinion accurately, to satisfy to the best of our abilities the citizens' fundamental right to know what is happening in the world around them and how public expenditure is structured, through political and administrative institutions that operate on a fair and sound basis. But the problems that arise are different and sometimes extremely complicated, as they affect sectors and flow from causes that differ fundamentally from one part of Europe to another.

Even if distances on the map are no greater than a few hundred kilometres, the huge gaps created by our recent past are not so easy to cross — even now. They have so often created different mentalities and patterns of behaviour which affect the fair operation of institutions and, even more, the way the democratic principle mentioned above can be truly complied with.

I wish to speak about Romania in particular, but I believe it is relatively easy to generalise from my country to the entire former communist structure because, with a few minor national exceptions, the system had the same characteristics and much the same effects.

The first characteristic of this system was that it was built from the outside on a system that eliminated all genuine public communication. Because the system was assumed to be perfect and it belonged, as we used to say, 'to all the people', it was presumed there was no need for it to explain itself — or its actions — to anyone, at any time and under any circumstances. For example, the institution of the 'spokesperson' or of the 'Public Relations Department' emerged only after the fall of the communist regime, and it has imposed itself as a must in order for the democratic system to function properly.

But for the Romanian citizen during the communist period, the institutions represented the supreme formula of bureaucracy, raised to the level of instrument of repression and absolute bureaucracy. Nothing was more atrocious than an absolute dependency on the institutions of the communist State, the ones your life depended on, without you having even the least power of control over them because, from the outset, they purely and simply refused to accept any other form of control than the one set by the superior party structures. Actually, for this control to be as wide as possible, the public administration required every local or central administrative authority to be managed by the leader of the party organisation at that particular level. The party thus became the manager of public life and it was exclusively represented, at all levels of decision-making, by party members, from which, obviously, the ordinary citizen was completely excluded.

This is the cause of the complete lack of confidence in the messages transmitted by those institutions, rightfully considered as an endless propaganda activity. Not a single piece of information transmitted to the citizen could escape from the gigantic and suffocating system of party propaganda, and appropriately enough it was treated as such. That is to say, it was rejected and regarded as not trustworthy or, in most cases, with hostility.

This situation was prolonged in communist Romania for almost two generations, long enough to allow a distinct group attitude to emerge that extended to the whole of society — refusal to trust official messages, no matter what their source was.

This is the real situation faced by the institutions which started to function after the revolution; this is the specific climate in which the public relations and communication departments started their activities. Cristian Unteanu, my colleague at Prima TV, who is also the head of our press bureau in Brussels, was asked, in the first few days after the December 1989 revolution, to become the first spokesman of the Government of Romania in the post-communist period. He has regularly asserted that the biggest problem they had to face in those days was the absence of specific public communication structures. But, at the same time, freedom to pass on information was still something asked for only by public opinion and was not something understood and accepted by the new State institutions. Inertia in this area was enormous, partly because people in all sectors of the system were obsessed with avoiding mistakes, not knowing in the new context what was confidential information and what was, or could have become, public information. To give an eloquent example, for years after 1989, the personnel of many of Romania's public institutions made no distinction between the 'Public Relations Department' and the 'Public Information Department', given the lack of qualification (and a real desire for transparency) of the officials and leaders of those institutions.

This is the context in which the first investigative journalists started to be trained and to work. Inevitably, their activity was strongly influenced by the social context and residual aspects of the mentality that I have just considered. Consequently, their attitude was, from the very beginning, influenced by a deep lack of trust in the information passed on by State institutions, or what little there was of it, regarding it with distrust or hostility, almost even as a premeditated attempt of manipulation. On the other hand, the State institutions — those that were not hostile in the beginning — started taking a hostile attitude and their spokespersons started to deliberately avoid contact with representatives of the mass media. This is how the investigative journalist reached the conclusion that it was best — or wiser — for his or her entire activity to completely disregard official information sources, and even ridicule and discredit them.

This relationship has sometimes been handled in inappropriate ways and, unfortunately, sometimes still is, and this should be offset not in the abstract but on the basis of a system of rules and principles accepted by both parties. This brings me to the core of our dialogue: who provides information, how and under what system of regulation?

Naturally, to answer this question, I have turned, both attentively and hopefully, to you — to the European institutions and their departments specialised in public communication. Investigative journalists were even more interested to see how the system works, especially how it sets its limits. At what point does the system become opaque and do spokespersons use the formula 'no comment' or simply refer you to their press releases? What does the term 'sensitive information' mean in your value system, and from what moment on can it legally be withheld from a journalist?

These are more than purely hypothetical questions, at least in our perspective. I would like to share with you a practical example to highlight the importance of the answers you can give us and the consequences they can have for the real compliance with the democratic principle of the right to information. In 2002, the editorial staff of the newspaper *Curierul National*, which my colleague worked for at that time asked my colleague Cristian Unteanu to start an investigation into the possibility that OLAF may have started an investigation on a possible embezzlement of European funds; embezzlement in which Mrs Hildegard Puwak, then Minister for European Integration, may have been involved in. The subject was extremely sensitive, because a government member was involved and even more, one who supervised the correct execution of the entire package of pre-accession funds allocated to Romania.

There were two possible approaches. The first was the classic method of using direct or possibly collateral sources, either from OLAF, from the Commission or from the Parliament. The second involved using unconfirmed sources for background comment, tagged 'sources from…', because the deadline was very short, only a few hours, and using, if possible, an official source from OLAF to confirm the news. It was very difficult to imagine such a confirmation would come, especially because of the obvious implications for the Romanian political stage. This, however, was not the case, because the phone conversations with Alessandro Butticé, at that time on holiday away from Brussels, allowed us to have official confirmation of an investigation procedure opened in this case. Mr Butticé's statement just mentioned that an investigation procedure had been launched to seek information in the case, but this was strongly denied by the officials of the Public Communication Department of the European Integration Ministry where Mrs Puwak was minister at that time. This statement was sufficient, because we had corroborated it with all the other elements already in our possession. And the effect on Romania's mass media was strong and immediate, the entire press starting to broadly deal with this story, developing and enriching it. It would have been most presumptuous to imagine that we could do anything beyond provoking public debate, but the impressive thing is that, on the first day of the OLAF seminar held in Bucharest in October 2003, it was announced that three ministers, including Mrs Puwak, had resigned, all of them being involved one way or another in issues concerning mismanagement of Community funds.

However, this story is interesting from another point of view as well. The day after the publication of the first article from Brussels, Minister Puwak addressed an open letter to the newspaper where my colleague was working at that time, accusing him of misinforming public opinion and, worse still, of endangering Romania's process of integration into the European Union. This reaction could be explained as a prolongation of a certain mentality that had been common in the communist totalitarian structures of the past, whereby it was not possible to present 'negative aspects' of an official's activity without automatically damaging national prestige. Of course, the entire Romanian press did not pay attention to that press release, published only by the newspaper Mr Unteanu was working for as a Brussels correspondent, but that does not diminish the gravity of that type of reaction which was, unfortunately, not an isolated one at that time.

From then on, our colleagues in Romania found it increasingly difficult to obtain the most accurate data possible from the Ministry of Integration, as all its Public Communication Department would release was only outraged denials but no figures, files or statistics. This was the first politically significant case which allowed Romanian public opinion to receive accurate information on the true powers of OLAF, the role of national authorities and the Romanian judicial authorities, which are responsible for bringing the case to completion.

Let us now expand on the discussion regarding the status of Romania's investigative journalist specialising in the analysis of cases of embezzlement of European funds. A status which is fundamentally no different from that of our colleagues anywhere in the world. The first rule is always to work under pressure and to have the competition breathing down your neck. The story must be finished, usually 'yesterday' because the obsession of every editor in chief is that 'our story' must be the first to come out and we should not have to face the unfortunate situation of being second best or, even worse, to gather our information from the competition, without us even knowing it existed. The case of the international press correspondent is somehow even more difficult, because, at the national level, the television he or she works for has an entire network of correspondents and official or unofficial information sources, whereas he or she is, in most cases, working alone or with a very small team.

Consequently, the attention paid to forming his or her own personal information network will be greater, and will even be a priority when his or her remit extends beyond 'Brussels' to the whole range of topics relating to NATO and the EU. Logically, the information sources the correspondent seeks will depend on the nature of the institutional response.

The first evaluation therefore concerns the question whether communication departments in the institutions believed to have a high interest for journalists, such as OLAF or the institutions represented at national level by the persons in this room, have the capacity and the real desire for transparency. The evaluation refers to your capacity for producing information in good time, your desire to get involved, your possibility for maintaining close contact with the real decision-making levels in the institution you represent, the freedom of movement and trust given to you when dealing with journalists, the possibility or impossibility for you of communicating directly with the head of the unit when crisis situations occur. All these are the elements which lead us fairly quickly to an evaluation, most certainly a subjective one, of the possibility of using you as a credible source during our investigations. Our subjective evaluation refers to the quality and the utility to us of the press releases, statements or analysis you make or have made in a crisis situation, this proving how open you can be in such moments, compared to the type of information other sources can provide on the same story.

Media

One thing is absolutely certain: the more you are tempted to restrict information, the more the value of alternative sources will increase. This in itself will be a serious problem only when the gap becomes too wide with the direct result of a loss of credibility of the official source or even of actually discrediting it. It must not be forgotten that any investigative journalist can access and will definitely have his or her own sources of information inside any structure, even those that are theoretically the best protected. What you call 'accidental leaks of information' are and will be means used by persons inside those institutions to solve their own personal or institutional problems or, in many cases, to protest against the institution's general policies, concerning one topic or another. It is not fair to extend this statement to all the officials working in an institution, but it remains true for some cases, 'Deep Throat' being a classic example in this respect.

Of course, there are cases in which information will not come for free, but this is not the sources' first motive. This, from our point of view, can make them credible when, along with documents, they offer their own comments or analysis, many times much more complex and enlightening than the data contained in the actual documents. What do you have to offer?

The answer may be interesting to us, or we may ignore it or mention it only in passing as a minor factor, which, as you know, is what often happens. It all depends on the nature and timing of the answer, because the first reaction will always be to consult the institution's spokesperson. If the answer received is vague or unconvincing, then the journalist's investigation will rely more and more on other sources. Logic and pressure of time make this process an almost mechanical one.

Why don't you want to speak out? This is an almost rhetorical question, when, in OLAF's case for example, leads do exist, such as the one coming from the Supervisory Committee, which states there must be much less communication with the press. The true problem is that, in this case, bridges with the communication department are burnt and that all unofficial sources inside OLAF automatically become credible, the ones that will gladly agree to provide documents or analysis 'on a deep background basis', to use the classic terminology. Is this the right solution?

Not at all, we dare say, because we would then miss out on an essential link in the journalistic approach, concerning the possibility, however limited or theoretical, of verifying our conclusions by relating them to the official version. At least for the satisfaction of proving ourselves right or of demonstrating that our sources are more trustworthy and complete than what you want to disclose to the public.

We know very well that your dilemma is connected to specific institutional constraints, especially to the principle of not disclosing information that will damage the development of an investigation. The problem is that, most of the time, this information reaches us through other sources, sometimes in good time, regardless of the number of barriers you wish to install.

From our point of view, the solution is not to raise more information barriers and definitely not to adopt legislation — even only internal regulations — which restrain information-sharing with the press. It has been seen in many cases that these measures are far from having the desired effect of discouraging the investigative journalists, rather the contrary, and we all know the consequences of that.

Is this dilemma impossible to resolve? We believe not, and our experience with OLAF has proved to us that establishing a relationship based on trust and on mutual respect of professional requirements has led — however long it has taken — to the establishment of a privileged channel of communication, through which real information rapidly reaches its real addressee, the public, without in any way affecting the interests of the investigators or of the institution itself. What is more, a very interesting phenomenon has occurred, which we regard as demonstrating the expansion of the social value of our specific contribution to changes in mentality and to the evolution of a society that is still undergoing a transition process. First of all, our approach, strictly related to the investigation itself in order to be correctly understood, had to incorporate an information component referring to European procedures in this area, explaining to everyone what OLAF means and what it can accomplish, how far its powers extend, compared to those of national institutions, demanding that their public communication departments adapt to fit the European institutional set-up. We have talked about your communicators network and we have requested our law enforcement agencies, the courts and the National Anti-Corruption Prosecutors' Office to change their communication behaviour and open real communication channels with our colleagues from Romania.

The results have been spectacular and most welcome at a time when dialogue between institutions and the press usually consisted of no more than a barren press release or a spokesperson forced to recite his homework.

For example, the National Anti-Corruption Prosecutors' Office has established a personalised dialogue with every representative institution of the Romanian press at the level of the General Prosecutors' Office — the highest national authority — and asked each of them to accredit a journalist specialising in anti-corruption affairs. We have also observed a substantial increase in the frequency of public statements of views by representatives of the National Anti-Corruption Prosecutors' Office and General Prosecutors Office, and some prosecutors have been appointed as spokespersons, leading to an improvement in the quality of their press releases and public statements.

It is very important for national anti-corruption authorities, not only in Romania but also in the Member States, for OLAF to have the right communication policy and to avoid changing it in the sense suggested by some Members of Parliament in Opinion No 2/03 of the OLAF Supervisory Committee of 18 June 2003 by saying 'communication … should remain limited in view of the risks it entails for the respect of fundamental rights and the reputation of the institutions and their members, officials and staff'. Most likely what would happen is that the national anti-corruption authorities would look to OLAF and copy any new model it adopts. This would be indeed a very negative change, not to mention that the previously explained Puwak case would never happen again, and this would act against the public's interest.

What Mr Herbert Bösch, MEP, said about there needing to be 'more investigators and fewer press officers' is also against the public's interest, because OLAF press officers are responsible for providing information about the use made of the European taxpayers' money. But it seems strange how Mr Bösch fails to notice that fewer press officers would ultimately destroy OLAF's positive image. Around the world, investigators need answers as well as the cooperation of the general public. A negative image of anti-fraud authorities would make citizens lose trust in these institutions and in the motivation to fight fraud and would certainly not dissuade them from giving bribes. In the end it would run counter to the very efforts of OLAF and of national authorities involved in the fight against corruption.

Media

Another MEP, Mr Szabolcs Fazakas, Chairman of the Committee on Budgetary Control of the European Parliament, declared that 'the first idea that sprang to my mind was that the fraud investigators should not be in the press at all' and concluded that 'not making headlines is a sign of quality'. Happily he changed his mind after reading other people's opinions on the role of communication and information in deterring fraud. And I used the word 'happily' not only referring to public opinion's interests but also to the very interests of the Members of European Parliament. Because now, after the recent EP elections, it seems that they have forgotten that other elections will follow. And choosing to reduce the number of press officers and promoting a 'limited' communication policy on the European taxpayers' money, will just further reduce the European citizens' dwindling interest in the EP elections and will increase the serious problem of the so-called European democratic deficit.

Coming back to the Romanian context, I would stress that, by developing a real public communication department, we were able to expand the discussion by involving the top members of the political class. The time I previously mentioned, when the only official answer was a press release containing threats and nervous justifications, is long behind us. This is because we sought — apparently successfully — to send a message that the opening of an investigation regarding the use of Community funds in Romania does not mean a direct attack on the country's prestige or a threat to its integration process, but is a basic process in a democratic context. An essential change of mentality which proves a journalist's work is not reduced to no more than presenting a series of facts. If we can participate by launching a journalistic investigation in the implementation of fraud-preventing systems — and this was our goal — this means the moral result of our approach has been even more worthwhile.

Furthermore, since I have been addressing the issue of mentality changes, I cannot imagine how, several years ago, a report such as OLAF's, which showed that in my country there is the largest number of investigation cases, would have been received in Romania. Maybe there would have been violent political protests; maybe a public debate would have started between the parties in power and those in opposition, each side claiming that the other was the most corrupt, and so on. Instead, we have organised a debate on the report, starting from an analysis made here in Brussels, with Mr Alessandro Butticé as our guest. The analysis showed the existence of a large number of cases that pointed towards two elements: fraud cases and an appropriate reaction on the part of the national authorities. What could have turned into a political scandal had transformed itself into a serious analysis that was agreed on by the Romanian political parties.

One may reply by saying that the investigative journalist is not compelled to trigger a social reflection process. That is true, but from the very beginning I have stated that the target of our specific approach is Romania's information market, which obviously includes its political stage. Consequently, it is only natural to wish our approach to be even more open to supporting fraud-prevention activities because, in the last few years, we have realised that only 'the story on fraud' is not enough.

There were far too many, and ending each story with the statement that 'in Romania there is fraud in relation to Community funds' could trivialise not only the conclusion, but also the entire issue, because too many news articles and investigations on this topic not followed by the engaging of a broader phenomenon could produce apathy and disinterest from the audience. We believed it was important to involve the State authorities in the analysis of the core of this phenomenon as much as possible, beginning, of course, from real cases and correctly handled investigations, but what was essential was observing a re-

Media

action, an answer at a national institutional level. The audience was tempted to simply watch, just as they would watch a play at the theatre, not being emotionally involved at all, because they still had something of a lack of trust in institutions and in their transparency capacity. The investigation itself was important, but our approach would be truly successful only when we could prove that what we call 'the voice of society' does matter, and when the authorities open their gates and are compelled to respect democratic principles. Going even further with this reasoning, we prove that the rule of law means that every one of those who are watching, whenever a problem occurs, will have free access to this circuit based on what we call the free movement of information and strict compliance with citizens' rights.

I am convinced that, for most of you, these things may be part of those 'general truths', but please believe me that, for other generations of journalists from your countries, they were at one time as important as they are now for us, the truths that prepare us — and public opinion in our countries — for accession to the EU respecting this system's quality standards.

Thank you very much.

Media

Michael STABENOW,

President of the International Press Association (API-IPA), Brussels

Michael STABENOW

has been working as a journalist in Brussels since 1981. Since 1990 he is correspondent for the German daily newspaper Frankfurter Allgemeine Zeitung, currently covering EU affairs and the Benelux countries. His main area of professional interest lies in the creation and completion of a functioning internal market and on the European constitutional process. Mr Stabenow has been a representative for the German press in the International Press Association (API-IPA) and currently its chairman.

'Speech - Joint seminar of the International Federation of Journalists (IFJ) and the European Anti-Fraud Office (OLAF) for the OLAF Anti-Fraud Communicators' Network (OAFCN) Brussels - 28 October 2005'

I am grateful to OLAF for having organised the meeting. Recently we have heard of the Commission's recent Plan D on communicating Europe, dialogue, democracy and debate being the key words. Although as journalists we don't get involved in any of the political aims, as far as the content goes, the future of the Constitution, we all have our views. For us what is paramount is that information can flow freely. To achieve that we also need this dialogue between you, the ones trying to provide the information, and us, those who wish to pass this information on to the public.

So it's a question that has been very much at the heart of discussions here, because people feel there is a big gap between what is happening on a European level and the perception of Europe in the Member States and beyond. Our organisation is here to represent Brussels-based correspondents, so we're much smaller than the IFJ, but of course it's an advantage for us to have the IFJ because it allows us to keep up with developments and we're lucky to have these close contacts with Aidan White and the people he's representing.

Brussels is one of the most important places as far as journalists are concerned, we have about 1200 accredited journalists with the European Institutions. This t makes us probably the most important place in terms of numbers and figures beside Washington. It has also contributed in the last couple of years to make life on one hand more exciting but on the other also quite difficult because spokespeople are very important, but if they are flooded with telephone calls they cannot always be available.

This explains the dilemma that we are facing here in Brussels, which is increasingly competitive. This is also because the media landscape has changed quite a bit, certainly as far as the written press is concerned. In many European countries and be-yond there has been a crisis of the sector. We don't know whether newspapers will be able to continue to exist in the current form. This has added to the pressure and the competition. Sometimes journalists do try to give that extra appeal to a story which might encourage people to buy the paper. This is the general context we work in.

We are also facing considerable problems with regard to the main actor here in Brussels, the European Commission. There is a new Commission that came into office a year ago, new commissioners of new member states. But there is also a sense that, against a background of political crisis in Europe, people don't know exactly how to handle the press and, when we talk about access information and transparency there clearly are different views on how to obtain this result.

Aidan White talked a little bit about one of the elements that make you and us talking a bit more spicy. When police in Belgium raided the office of our colleague Hans Martin Tillack of Stern our organisation was among the first ones, with the IFJ, to condemn this and to seek clarification. I recognise and welcome that at the time OLAF very swiftly agreed to be present in the press room and to explain its role in the whole process. Now finally we have achieved progress as far the as the legal protection of journalists in Belgium is concerned. This was a very slow process and should provide some safeguards against this happening again. I won't go any further into the Tillack case, and I think there will be other opportunities to discuss it.

A lot has been said about the way that Brussels journalists work, and it has been implied that there might be a difference between investigative journalism and journalism tout court. I think it's not right to make that difference because as journalists we have to cover the whole range. We cannot just concentrate on copying press releases or writing up interviews with people. Journalists have to work according to the challenges posed.

As far as the relationship between Brussels press and OLAF is concerned, yes there have been problems. But this has certainly nothing to do with individuals, it is a question of structures. We find this difficult to deal with because, as you know yourself, OLAF is an institution that is independent but still closely linked to the Commission in terms of organisation.

On the other hand, the information that you are dealing with is very important to try and discover to what extent European money has been used or misused. And we totally agree that confidentiality is a major challenge for much of this information. A similar approach applies to European competition policy, a classic example where we have to accept that certain information must be kept confidential as long as possible. The same applies to the European Court of Justice; you have to be very careful not to interfere with the actual process.

So, we're perfectly aware of these challenges, On the other hand what we miss is a more proactive, open way of dealing with the issues. We would very much like OLAF to come up with more basic briefings on the main tasks like VAT and customs. It would be very helpful if we had the opportunity to discuss this on a regular basis. This also allows continuous dialogue between you and the journalistic community.

I don't know how many people are regular clients of OLAF, but in our newspaper's office here we have five or six people and there is one colleague who concentrates very much on the OLAF issues. This also makes it more difficult for you to know how to treat us as journalists because we don't specialise in reporting on fraud. Of course, if a case comes up we do report on it, for example the information on cigarette smuggling, which OLAF dealt with very well. So these are some of the things I would like to see explored on a much wider scale.

There is another thing, I wouldn't call it whistle-blowing, but a more general aspect that applies to Brussels journalists and possibly to others. We need our sources, and have to be careful, but we cannot be put in a straitjacket on how we use these sources. If information is deemed to be important and we feel we must pass it on then we will, and it's up to us to justify it when it might appear to be in breach of certain rules.

I'll give you an example from another European Institution, the European Parliament. We have been as far as API is concerned in close contact with our friends from the IFJ, agreed on a code of conduct as far the audiovisual press goes in the Parliament- One of the points is that filming with a hidden camera should be forbidden. Of course we think that this is a good principle that should be adhered to. Butt if there are certain elements which we feel can only be brought to light by using these means there are certain cases where this must be done. But it's up to the journalist to do that, and it's up to the ones that have been attacked to criticise it on the grounds of what happened, and then the discussion will happen at a later stage.

Coming back now to what this means as far as relations between OLAF and the press are concerned, we really appeal to both groups to try to be as open as possible. We are trying to apply our own standards and I think I can say, from a Brussels perspective, that those who don't stick to the rules only punish themselves. Someone who is misusing information will not get full access to sources and I think quite rightly so. But this means that it is helpful to be as cooperative and open as possible. And you should always bear in mind that not only spokespersons are talking to journalists, but other people within the services, who should also know what their duties and responsibilities are.

To give an example, I've been following recent debates on information that has possibly been leaked by people in the Supervisory Committee of OLAF. The question is where has it come from, where might it lead to? Like very often there must be underlying interests to this. By looking into such questions journalists are trying helps to find out about and to explain problem. If there is an impression that one is trying to hide things, then people will only get more suspicious.

We are also curious to see the outcome of the procedure brought up at the ombudsman by our colleague Tillack and the report that has been drafted in the European Parliament. We are very interested to see what the assessment – both at OLAF's and the political level – is concerned. As journalists we don't have any problems discussing with you. Unless we talk together we cannot identify problems. This way we know what your job is and you know what ours is and this can be only beneficial for both sides.

I would like to touch upon another aspect of interest to Brussels based cor-respondents: We are a bit wary when we have to put everything into black and white. As far as access to documents is concerned: of course this sounds great, it's a contribution to transparency and is in the Amsterdam Treaty in the famous Article 255. But what does it mean as far as journalists are concerned? We depend a lot on documents, but a document must be de-fined. The Commission has tried to define any sheet of paper as a document so creating new problems for new information being handed out and making it more difficult for officials, even for spokesmen, to communicate.

So what we prefer is once again to get the principles right. But let's not be too meticulous about going into too much detail as it might make life too difficult for us. This goes back to 1999-2000 when we were afraid that we would get less access to information. In the meantime I think people have understood that it is in their own interest to be flexible and as you can read in the newspapers there are still plenty of documents and information being leaked. Thank you.

Media

Cristian UNTEANU,

European correspondent,
Prima TV Romania

Cristian UNTEANU

was born on 14 July
1950, in Bucharest.
In 1973 he started
working as a reporter
for Romanian radio
and television,
specialising in
international relations
and defence and
security issues. Since
1996 he has worked
as a journalist in
Brussels for PRIMA
TV.

'Communication towards citizens: a democratic principle in the work of institutions'

Opinion No 2/03, adopted by the OLAF Supervisory Committee on 18 June 2003, accompanying the Commission's report, *Evaluation of the activities of the European Anti-Fraud Office (OLAF)*, Chapter IV.3, Communication: 'OLAF has set up its own autonomous public relations department and conducts an active policy of communication with the public and the media. However, the Committee feels that, while communication is important, it is none the less secondary and should remain limited in view of the risks it entails for the respect of fundamental rights and the reputation of the institutions and their members, officials, and staff'.

It is not easy to find other public statements revealing what is, sadly, the desire of some politicians to keep hushed up the findings of certain investigations that could prove awkward or embarrassing. The communication policy of a public institution — and all the more so a Community institution such as OLAF which is supposed to be the guarantor of the proper safeguarding and protection of the financial interests of European taxpayers — cannot be 'secondary' and 'limited' precisely because citizens must be informed correctly and at the appropriate time. The provision of such information is not only their right but also confirms the democratic principles on which the institutions operate, by giving citizens the facts on which to base their judgment and, why not, their vote in national and European elections.

A communication policy can be harmful or entail risks for 'the respect of fundamental rights and the reputation of the institutions and their members, officials, and staff' only if it is poorly framed or implemented. In that case, the individuals involved in conducting such activities must of course be called to account for their incompetence and where necessary replaced or disciplined. But to assert that, among all the activities of an institution, communication policy must remain of secondary importance poses a very serious problem that could, if such a call were to be taken seriously, have extremely grave and fairly unexpected consequences.

The first one would be greater public mistrust of the European institutions, because any reader of the quotation I have used as the headline for this article will gather, without needing any journalistic comment, that this was in fact a fairly clumsy attempt to gag the source of public information within OLAF, while reserving for others the right to make comments and feed news to the press.

Second consequence, if such a directive could be applied: journalists would quite simply 'forget' the OLAF spokesman and his department and, in carrying out their own research on a story, would attempt to gain access to no matter what source of information within the institution. And, as the history of journalism has shown, such attempts will always be successful precisely because our professional ethics require us to fiercely protect our confidential sources. That is perfectly normal. But what would not be normal at all would be if, in our concern to present a story objectively, we were not given the possibility at all times of also presenting the viewpoint of the institution concerned, if only to provide a counterweight to our own demonstration.

Third consequence: if the communication department is deliberately weakened, if from the outset it is given a secondary and limited role, then its credibility in times of crisis will be considerably reduced. As everyone knows, journalists will not be interested in bland official pronouncements at such times, when they know that 'something is going on'. The institution would have a timid spokesman who could do nothing more than read out a press release, without making any comment, without any scope for 'personalising' what is happening, while being well aware that the journalists themselves are in possession of much more complex data and confidential information that could confirm or contradict what he is saying. But, because of his weak starting position, he would not be able to emerge from his institutional 'shell'. All this would be to the detriment of his reputation as a spokesman, the credibility of the institution and the interests of taxpayers.

But let us now leave theory behind and briefly consider a specific case. In 2002, I was working for a Romanian daily, *Curierul National*. One day, I was asked by my chief editor to check with OLAF a story that had appeared in a regional newspaper reporting the spokesman of the European Commission's Delegation in Bucharest as having said that OLAF had files on possible cases of fraud involving Community funds allocated to Romania under the pre-accession programmes. OLAF's spokesman was on holiday; his department asked me to wait for an hour and, at the promised time, put me through to the person I was seeking and enabled me to carry out an interview by telephone. I obtained confirmation that information existed on possible cases of financial fraud and that one or more investigations might be opened on the basis of that information.

That was all, but it was the only thing we needed in order to begin publishing our own findings, calling on Romanian officials to comment and urging them to react swiftly. The first response from political circles took the form of an open letter which the then Minister for European Integration sent to my newspaper (and which we carried on our front page) in which she dismissed outright all the information I had passed on from Brussels and formally accused me of undermining my country's efforts to join the EU. In this she was supported by the Commission's Delegation in Bucharest, which first tried to retract its initial statements. My newspaper reacted strongly and openly continued its investigations into the conduct of certain Phare programmes, for example. At the same time, the whole Romanian press launched a massive campaign on this issue, which became increasingly hard-hitting and well argued, since it now had, for the first time, a line of communication permanently open with OLAF's spokesman.

Media

This spokesman had not only established his credibility in relations with the Brussels correspondent of a Romanian newspaper but, because of his initial action, had suddenly become — for all my Romanian colleagues dealing with the issue — a necessary and competent interlocutor. We did not ask him for the results of investigations, since that was a question to be put to the Romanian authorities; we asked him to validate a single type of information: whether or not, on such and such an issue or such and such an individual, information existed that could provide the basis for an investigation; or whether or not the Romanian authorities had received files from OLAF on those issues or individuals.

This shows that in an investigative body, the spokesman, if he is to be effective, does not necessarily have to feed journalists with the facts of a case, pass on documents or identify the investigators. It is enough for him to carefully choose the moment for laying his cards on the table, for lighting the fuse. That choice reflects the spokesman's talent and, at the same time, the need to respect the priorities of the investigation. Journalists will do the rest, if they have not already done so and are precisely awaiting such confirmation in order to validate weeks, months or even years of personal research.

What we really need to see is a relationship of mutual trust developing between, on the one hand, a communication department staffed, not by timid administrative officials anxious only to defend their privileges, but, as I believe is the case at OLAF, by decent professionals who know their job and, on the other hand, journalists who have to discharge as effectively and as quickly as they can their foremost duty, which is to inform the public. Such a relationship of trust is unique and invaluable precisely because, behind the information gathered in investigations, there are individuals, lives and reputations to be protected. On this specific point, the opinion of the Supervisory Committee is not wrong. Such protection can be afforded, however, not by restricting access to information but by ensuring that information circulates normally, in a democratic system, for the good of everyone.

Media

Johannes VON DOHNANYI,

Journalist, *Sonntags Blick*,
Ringier AG, Zurich, Switzerland

'Investigative journalists and the protection of sources'

Johannes von DOHNANYI

was, born on 10 February 1952 in New Haven, the USA. Raised in the USA and the Federal Republic of Germany, he obtained a university degree in economics. From 1979 to 2003 he was foreign correspondent for various prestigious German and Swiss newspapers, magazines, radio and television stations, among them Stern magazine, Die Weltwoche, Spiegel-TV, based over the years in Italy, Singapore, Thailand and the Balkans. Since 2004 he has been foreign editor, Sonntags Blick, Zürich, specialised in organised crime and international terrorism. He is the author of several books on the economic development in South-East Asia, Islamic terrorism and weapons of mass destruction, infiltration of Islamic fundamentalists in European societies.

Europeans really do have every reason to be satisfied. For the first time in their history they have experienced more than half a century of uninterrupted peace — with the exception of the Balkan conflict. The old dream of a politically united continent has drawn rapidly closer since the signing of the Rome Treaties. Twenty-five nations have come together in the European Union. More people than in the USA live in this Europe. The combined economic power of the 25 bears comparison with that of the United States. Never before have so many people in Europe known such political freedoms and such affluence.

And yet many Europeans are unsatisfied with this Europe. It has never been brought close to them, explained to them. There is a myth that Europe is a Moloch, gradually devouring people's national identity. An administrative monster, which is blindly tying up the continent with red tape with the aid of a non-elected bureaucracy. And of course a gigantic machine, which not only swallows up taxpayers' money but is reproached first and foremost not for efficiency but endemic corruption.

It makes no difference that most of these prejudices, like all prejudices, are based on false premises. And it makes no difference that it is less the Commission and its apparatus in Brussels which are installing the existing machinery in Brussels than the national governments who are resisting the liberalisation demanded by Brussels. The fact remains that Europeans' confidence in their Europe is often alarmingly low.

This state of affairs can be changed only by a massive, targeted enlightening of the public about what is actually going on, and equally about mistakes and omissions and the attempts to correct them.

Political as well as factual enlightenment must be the starting point. And to do this, the European institutions need the help of the media. The latter's task is not only, as is often maintained, to check on the institutions and their representatives. Newspapers, radio and television stations also provide the institutions and their representatives with a platform for presenting and generally debating ideas and objectives. And this is how at the same time the press fulfils what is probably its most important function — the social and political cohesion of national and European society.

This function of the media must not be lost sight of in what follows. The cohesion function is probably the most important reason why there must be better cooperation with the EU in general and in this case with OLAF in particular. Only when the public realises that corruption and inefficiency in the EU administration are being combated on a permanent basis from the inside, will it in future be able to identify more easily with 'Brussels', which has rather negative connotations generally today.

OLAF and relations with the press, therefore. Or, as we have seen in recent months, the representatives of the press and their relations with OLAF. Without disparaging my colleagues at all, I am not going to speak about those who talk and write about OLAF like any other European institution. We are concerned here with those journalists who in addition to descriptive work conduct investigations themselves. The representatives of investigative journalism.

I don't want to overrate my fellow professionals of course. But, ladies and gentlemen, as investigators — what would you do without us investigative journalists? People talk to us voluntarily about things which they would never open up to you about without compulsion. And then we write up that which to the best of our knowledge and with a clean conscience we have verified — so that you get to read it. This first point of contact between investigators and journalists can be the start of a wonderful friendship. In one way or another, you, the investigators, can build on the basis of our work. Sometimes our work will lead to legal proceedings and ultimately to court decisions on the criminal relevance of the results of your, and our, work.

Even though there are of course exceptions, such an ideal situation seldom occurs in practice. As a rule, investigative journalists and institutional investigators react to each other like cats and dogs. One of the main reasons why the exchange of information between investigative journalists and institutional investigators is so often difficult is mistrust — aroused, mark you, on both sides. The opposite of mistrust is trust. Unfortunately, this is broken all too frequently. Journalists turn with the results of their research to the institutions — only to be prevented in their researches by those same institutions, or even suddenly to appear on the list of suspects. On the other hand, and this should not be concealed, there are journalists who misuse information given in confidence and publish it immediately without regard to the consequences in order to guarantee a scoop.

As always in life, one must choose very carefully the people one confides in.

There is also a third, most dubious variant: a total misunderstanding of one's own role. For some time the number of national and international institutions which feel the professional inquisitiveness of the investigative journalist to be a presumption, sometimes even a violation of the journalist's job, has been increasing. It is as if these institutions and their representatives were exempt from scrutiny by a democratically legitimised press. Symptomatic of this, a few years ago, was the angry reproach of an Italian minister during an interview: 'Who gives you permission,' he asked, 'to devote your attention to me and the performance of my duties?'

On the other hand, there is also a considerable misunderstanding among individual journalists. They are convinced they have a special role in the parallelogram of democratic

Media

forces, the role of the untouchable. Not only do they believe — which is their right — that they should practise their profession unhindered, they are firmly convinced they operate outside the reach of the organs of State and the investigative authorities.

Whoever thinks and acts like this is not only outside democratic society, he has also not understood the basic rules of investigative journalism. Ultimately, he is denying the fact that nobody, not even the investigative journalist, is above the law.

Such a misunderstanding of the freedom of the press also covers the journalist's assumption that he is basically entitled to information from all quarters.

It is the duty of every institution to protect its internal matters and the data it administers from unauthorised access by outsiders. In every authority there are areas which should not be available for general information. On the other hand, all authorities should be self-critical: if institutions try to evade reporting by a democratic press, and if they do this by using the police and the law against the press, this is much more serious than a few journalists tripping up over their own arrogance. The representatives of such institutions, whether elected or appointed, do not work for themselves and their office. They carry out their duties for and on behalf of the State and are therefore accountable to society.

It is precisely at this interface between the duty to provide information and the refusal of information the investigative journalist operates. Because he has no institutional access to the information he seeks, he depends on informers from inside the institutions. They may contact him voluntarily in order to reveal abuses. They may also act from personal motives. The journalist should not bother about this, as long as he verifies the substance of the information and at the end of his research gives everybody involved the chance to express their opinion. It is also quite legitimate to actively seek informants. This does not offend against the principles of professional ethics.

Assuming of course that the journalist does not first get the informant to divulge internal matters with the promise of financial gain. That, in a word, is corruption. And corruption, both for the briber and the bribed, is a criminal offence. This is one of those areas which, even for journalists, are taboo. If the journalist decides, for whatever reason, to cross this boundary, he cannot then rely on his journalistic right to obtain and disseminate information freely. He must bear the consequences which the suspicion of corruption entails.

What are those consequences? They range from the questioning of the journalist as a witness to a 'visit' from the investigating authorities, say the search of his home and his office. An arbitrary interference? An attack on press freedom? Not at all — provided that their use against the journalist has been blessed by a judge's order. Irrespective of the journalist's beliefs, it is the investigating authorities' job to fight corruption.

An EU authority reads in the press about a hitherto unpublished investigation. The authority has to investigate internally but has no legal basis for taking external action itself. To do this it needs the help of the executive of a Member State. The latter now examines the results presented to it, recognises the suspected infringement of legal rules and takes action. House searches are carried out. Material is seized. Corruption proceedings are initiated.

Without going into details, such a case has caused a lot of commotion in recent months. Who was entitled to do what when — that and other questions will be clarified by the courts. If national or European institutions have exceeded their powers, if they have vio-

Media

lated the journalist's right to collect and disseminate information, they must be brought to account.

Irrespective of the legal assessment of the case, there is another, no less delicate question: what do we journalists, who are so quick to criticise others, think of it, in the light of the principles of our own professional ethics?

There can be no investigative journalism without informants. One thing is clear, whatever their motives, informants have a right to be protected. In other words, when he gets involved in the 'story' of his informant, the investigative journalist is duty-bound to protect the latter's right to privacy as long as that person requires.

This means that the journalist accepts responsibility for protecting the source of his information, even when this is to his own disadvantage. In our part of the world this is not demanding too much of the individual. In the European Union no one is tortured by the State into giving up his secrets. The most that can happen to him is to be detained in a cell on the order of a judge. Which, to analyse it with the necessary professional coolness, would be a new 'story' in itself. Anybody who is not prepared to take this risk, who does not entertain the possibility that he may be hauled before the beak by the 'victims' of his revelations, anybody in short who can't stand the heat in the kitchen, should not opt for investigative journalism.

Investigative journalism automatically leads into 'Indian country', into 'enemy territory'. The other side, be it institutions or individuals, will do everything to hinder the journalist in his research, or even stop him. Anybody who is unaware of this from the outset will be unpleasantly surprised. Just as the investigative journalist will use the legal means at his disposal to track down the truth, so will the other side use its means to prevent this from happening. These, let me repeat, include house searches, provided the judge can be persuaded there is enough suspicion of a criminal offence.

A journalist who enables the other side to discover by legal means the names of his informants and so on is breaking the most elementary rules of his profession. Above all he is breaking his obligation to protect his informants and what they have told him. Any subsequent protest is hypocritical.

Clearly, such incidents create mistrust on both sides. In future, therefore, not only must investigative journalists practise their profession in accordance with its well-tried rules, but a fundamental consensus — in this case between my fellow professionals and OLAF — must be established on a basis of mutual trust.

OLAF and, through the Brussels institutions, national investigators too should build up a regular exchange of information. It must be possible, in such a restrictive circle, to exchange information not only about completed investigations but current ones as well. It could also be to OLAF's advantage, despite recognising the protection of sources or even because of it, to benefit from the investigative journalist's network of informants.

Media

Media

Aidan WHITE,

General Secretary,
International Federation of Journalists (IFJ)

**Aidan
WHITE**

is the General
Secretary of the
International
Federation of
Journalists. He was
born in Ireland and
educated in the
United Kingdom
where he learned his
trade as a journalist.
He joined the IFJ
from *The Guardian* in
1987. He has written
extensively on the
social and professional
conditions of
journalism. The
IFJ is the largest
organisation of
journalists in the
world with a range of
projects and solidarity
programmes that
cover the globe.

'Speech - Joint seminar of the International Federation of Journalists (IFJ) and the European Anti-Fraud Office (OLAF) for the OLAF Anti-Fraud Communicators' Network (OAFCN) Brussels - 28 October 2005'

First of all, thank you for the invitation and the initiative in organising this meeting. I want to take this opportunity to reflect on some of the problems facing journalists today and on the need for increased dialogue between anti-fraud investigators and journalists' groups in the member states of the European Union.

Having said this, I should tell you that this meeting is not without controversy among some journalists who have expressed surprise that the IFJ, through the European Federation of Journalists, is associated with the organisation of this meeting. How can you talk to these people, one journalist has asked me, when you are taking them to court?

My answer is simple. As an organisation that lobbies and campaigns in favour of journalists' rights, and that calls for public authorities to be open and accountable, we have a responsibility to meet and to discuss concerns of media, to promote respect for journalists' rights and to create mutual understanding about our different roles and responsibilities.

I think that the lack of constructive dialogue and structures for problem-solving between us has been exposed by the recent breakdown in confidence between some sections of journalism and OLAF.

There is bewilderment among many journalists over the case of German journalist Hans Martin Tillack, which has even led the IFJ, for the first time in my 18 years in Brussels, to launch a legal action against the Commission and OLAF in defence of journalistic freedoms.

It is 20 months since this journalist was raided by Belgian police. His home and office were turned over, his files sifted, his confidential documents detailing contacts and sources taken away. Yet, to this day, there has been no formal charge laid against him.

There is still no police report on the case.

Extraordinarily – and such was the state of Belgian law at the time, although I'm told this is now changed – the complainants in this case, that is OLAF and the Commission, have the right of access to the seized documents. They can fish through his files to find out who he has been talking to – a gross violation of his right to protect his sources of information. It appears they have this right even while all allegations against him remain unproven and untested.

We have written to the Commission and to the Belgian Police asking for this matter to be finally settled – for the complaints to be withdrawn, for the investigation to be ended, and for the immediate return of documents. We are seeking confirmation that the Commission has not exercised the right to examine Mr Tillack's files.

It is time to move on, to put this issue aside and to rebuild relations. But we still need answers to the questions we have put. But it would be remiss of me not to speak plainly – there is little hope of building a successful and productive dialogue with journalists in Brussels unless the air is cleared and unless we resolve to do everything we can to make sure such a case never arises in future.

We have to learn from bad experiences, and to move towards building trust through a fresh start in our relations and not just here in Brussels – but right across the EU.

And we do so at a difficult time. We are living in a period of great uncertainty. There is a decline in tolerance in society and a fall in public confidence that democratic institutions can properly defend their interests.

Today the unsettled nature of European society is seeing the emergence of a new intolerance. In some countries, a dangerous cocktail of unscrupulous politics, public uncertainty and incidents of religious extremism have seen previously tolerant societies transformed into communities where discrimination has become routine.

Also in journalism we are witnessing an alarming tendency among policymakers to try to restrain the work of media. We have counted no less than three separate references in different policy documents currently being dealt with by the European Union which talk ominously about "codes of conduct" for media.

Last week, the European Federation of Journalists warned that proposals from the European Commission to recruit journalists into its anti-terrorism strategies are reinforcing concerns of news people that politicians want to manipulate media content.

Some of you may have sympathy with the perceived need to regulate journalism. You may think that intrusive and investigative journalists who speak to people who are breaking the rules of confidentiality in their employment are also a problem. We don't accept that.

As part of their professional work, journalists need access to a wide range of relevant sources. Often they find themselves in contact with people connected to fringe organisations with political objectives, or with organisations that have links to criminal groups or even terrorism.

We also deal with people working inside public authorities who, for different reasons, feel the need to speak out. They are important contacts for us as they are for investigators.

Whistle-blowing is and always will be an integral part of exposing wrong-doing in society. People who tell the truth that others would prefer to be suppressed serve the cause of public investigators and journalists alike. They deserve better protection.

Equally, free reporting is an essential part of the architecture of investigative and professional journalism. As an Irish journalist, for instance, I know how valuable the journalism of tolerance can be. It kept lines of communication open between different extremists groups in Northern Ireland, some of them unambiguously terrorist, and was a factor in creating public confidence around recent moves towards peace and reconciliation after 30 years of violence.

I know, too, that nosy, intrusive, rule-breaking journalists have over the years done much work that has been vital to the fight against corruption. They have often irritated and angered politicians and sometimes they have paid for it with their lives.

These are the good soldiers of the press. There are many others who are seduced by the easy pickings available in a spoon-fed world of journalism driven by corporate public relations and spin-centred politics. Too often journalists today suffer from passivity and low-morale in an industry that, consumed by the imperatives of commercial advantage and political influence, sometimes appears to have lost its way.

Even people in public relations are getting fed up with offering cash bribes and other inducements for media coverage as well as the incompetence which leads over-worked and financially-strapped newsrooms to publish press releases and public relations briefings without questioning any of the facts and opinions contain.

In the last year or so, the crisis of falling standards in media has led the IFJ to join with a number of other organisations – including the International Public Relations Association – to issue a joint statement of principles calling for higher standards [67].

And in Brussels we have issued a media code of practice for journalists in association with the International Press Association, the Belgian Journalists' Union, the European Journalism Centre and the International Press Centre [68].

Media

None of us here are naïve about the world in which we live, but that is no excuse for cynicism. All of us have a responsibility to move beyond a sullen acceptance of how things are. We should aspire to better ways of doing things.

Not so long ago corruption in business, like paying bribes for foreign contracts, was regarded as a necessary evil, but the ground-breaking work of groups like Transparency International, has begun to change all that.

Media today may be a rum mixture of excellence and third rate trivia, but we need to keep faith with journalism and encourage reporters to play an active role in raising awareness about the corrosive effect of fraud and corruption.

Some of you will recall the days when there were journalists dedicated to police work or crime reporting who formed part of a reliable media network. You could establish a working relationship, drink together after work and share information in a relaxed atmosphere making clear distinctions between what could be published and what was off the record.

Today most media don't have the money or inclination to invest in specialist crime journalism. Reporters are expected to be multi-skilled generalists, usually freelance, who move without skipping a beat from text to radio and from television to internet. This does not mean that we have lost good old-fashioned values and standards, but it does mean that reporters are under more pressure to deliver their stories faster than ever.

We need to better understand this new and difficult environment. We have to develop new structures for dialogue, perhaps more seminars like this, organised on a more systematic basis and not just here in Brussels, but in the member states.

One issue to consider is how the limited protections for journalists such as those that exist for safeguarding confidentiality of sources need to be strengthened. We have too many cases of prosecutors and police applying undue pressure, sometimes through the courts, to discover to whom journalists have been talking.

Inevitably, whenever this happens there is a danger that sources will dry up. And that is not just dangerous for journalists, it is also potentially damaging for the business of crime fighting.

It is only in recent years that this right has been strengthened under article 10 of the European Convention on Human Rights and, indeed, it is only a few months ago that it was recognised here, in Belgian legislation. A systematic debate and discussion about the importance of this right would do much to improve our relations.

The issues we are talking about here, whether standards in journalism or standards in public life, are fundamentally questions of morality and good conduct.

Sometimes journalists have to make choices that do not fit a model template of good behaviour. Sometimes, for instance, it is appropriate to pay for information (if the source is the victim of loss or suffers penalties as a result of giving information); occasionally it will be necessary to succumb to self-censorship and to suppress information (if it might cause panic, for instance, or if it might incite others to violence); and sometimes it is even justifiable to betray a source (as some of my colleagues did who were witness to human rights abuses in Bosnia, for instance).

But these are ethical dilemmas which only journalists themselves can resolve. Ethics are a matter for professionals alone and the same goes, I'm sure, for people who work in the area of policing. It is not appropriate for outsiders to try to make our judgements for us.

So let us, finally, look at some possible basic principles for future co-operation:

Firstly, we should meet more often. I would like to see, if possible, an annual meeting between communicators like yourselves and journalists in which we can review how we are working together. This may also give us an opportunity to identify problems, to anticipate new policies and developments and to exchange opinions.

Second, let us try to establish some sub-regional discussions, perhaps looking at difficulties and challenges arising within the new-member states and the countries in the process of joining the European Union and aimed at improving the flow of information to the public about the fight against corruption.

Third, we should identify some key issues that concern all of us. These could include :

- respect for professionalism and ethical standards

- protection for whistle blowers within the European Union institutions

- improving levels of transparency and the flow of information and

This dialogue must be about creating a trusting and enabling environment where honest journalism can thrive and where lines can be drawn that properly identify our different roles and responsibilities. In the fight against corruption we should recognise that antifraud authorities and journalists are on the same side. We work best when we can work together.

Thank you.

Brussels, October 28th 2005

Media

---

(67) See www.instituteforpr.com

(68) See Journalists@YourService web site www.brusselsreporter.org

I.4. NATIONAL INSTITUTIONS, INVESTIGATIVE AND JUDICIAL SERVICES

National institutions, investigative and judicial services

Anu ADRA,

Head of the Public
Relations Bureau,
Estonian Police
Board

Annika LOIGU,

Advisor — Public
Relations Depart-
ment, Ministry of
Finance/Anti-Fraud
Coordination
Service, Estonia

Marke TARMO,

Head of Public
Relations Depart-
ment, Estonian
Customs Board

'How information and communication can be a means of EU fraud prevention and a true service for the citizens in the respect of their rights'

I t is of paramount importance to all of us that the taxpayers money, originating from the EU budget funds, is being used only for the intended purposes and that nobody could misuse the resources of the common purse.

Communication is an essential tool in the fight against fraud. The building blocks of successful communication are reliable partners. Our partners are the Anti-Fraud Coordinating Service (AFCOS) together with its partners, the OLAF Anti-Fraud Communicators Network (OAFCN), as well as the media.

Two years ago the Ministry of Finance started acting as AFCOS and a year ago Estonia signed an agreement of mutual cooperation with the European Anti-Fraud Office. By this agreement the FCD became the body for ensuring the coordination of all legislative, administrative, and operational activities related to the protection of the national and the Communities' financial interests.

The objectives of AFCOS are very similar to those of OLAF — to protect the national and the Communities' financial interests. Misuse of the EU and national budgets can affect the successful implementation of the national development plan.

The creation of AFCOS has been one of the most important steps to ensure that the new Member States have proper and effective anti-fraud systems. Prevention is always better than treatment, and in this case also a lot cheaper. There are several areas where AFCOS and the national partners are going to focus on particular questions in order to further re-

Anu ADRA

is Head of the Public Relations Bureau of the Estonian Police Board, which develops the public relations strategy for the Estonian police and coordinates internal and external communication in the Estonian police. Before joining the Estonian Police Board, Ms Adra worked in the Estonian Ministry of Internal Affairs as a press officer. For two years she worked in a PR company, Hill&Knowlton Estonia. Directly after graduating from the university she worked for three years in the largest Estonian shoe company as Purchasing Manager. Anu Adra has a diploma in business administration from the Open University at the University of Tartu.

Annika LOIGU

worked for the Estonian Minister for Finance and was a member of the OLAF Anti-Fraud Communicators Network (OAFCN) until 2005. From 1994 she held a range of positions in the Ministry of Finance, including leading the PR Unit and Division. She has also been a member of the governmental communicators network and several workshops dealing with EU enlargement and euro communication.

Marke TARMO

is Head of the Public Relations Department in the Estonian Tax and Customs Board. Before the merger of the Tax and the Customs Boards she was Head of the PR Division in the Estonian Customs Board. Before joining customs, she worked in television, for a State television channel, ETV, as a journalist in news programmes, and for a private television station, Kanal2, as Head of Original Programming. She has a BA in cultural work (theatre directing) and has worked as an actress in theatre.

inforce the national system. Areas with a higher risk are, for example, eligibility rules, effective recovery, control of payment requests, procurement procedures, on-the-spot controls, and so on. AFCOS Estonia is working on these issues to further raise the professional level of relevant officials.

The first and most important task is to have all relevant parties work in the same direction. This can be achieved by setting common goals in an overall strategy. In cooperation with the national partners, AFCOS is currently developing a strategy for the reinforcement of the protection of the Communities' financial interest. The aim is to improve national systems in a profound way by analysing the weaknesses and implementing an action plan for bracing those areas with higher risk.

In cooperation with OLAF an extensive training programmes as well as seminars on irregularities, risk assessment, judicial cooperation, and various other topics have been organised for a large number of police and customs investigators from October 2003.

Strong emphasis has been put on awareness of the concept of irregularity and reporting obligations. AFCOS has issued a guideline for reporting irregularities explaining the EU requirements and national arrangements.

In order to ensure effective cooperation between AFCOS and law-enforcement agencies, the AFCOS Steering Committee was established including representatives from the Prosecutor's Office, Tax and Customs Board, Security Police Board, Central Criminal Police Department, and State Audit Office.

The responsibilities of the committee are to:

- ensure the information exchange and cooperation on the national level and with OLAF regarding the protection of the Communities' financial interests;

- analyse cases where EU financial interests are affected and decide on investigative measures;

- make specific proposals to the Ministry of Finance to strengthen the protection of the Communities' financial interests;

- AFCOS keeps investigative authorities informed on the latest developments originating from OLAF.

The committee has analysed several cases of suspected irregularities and the bodies represented in the committee have started investigations into these cases. The activities of AFCOS and its partners have played a significant role in timely reactions to cases of attempted irregularities and fraud, thus preventing financial damage.

In 2003 the government approved an anti-corruption strategy named 'Honest State'. The strategy sets an action plan for the fight against corruption from 2004 to 2007. The two primary branches of the plan are prevention and a more effective detection of crimes that have already been committed. In addition to the activities targeted at the officials, one needs to assimilate comprehension of the essence of corruption within society, in other words, explanations of the kind of behavior that is allowed or not allowed, and organisation of campaigns to increase awareness of the matter. A special hotline has been established in order to gain information for the detection of corruption cases.

The corruption tip phone that has been in operation since May 2004 helps with cooperation with the population, giving people a possibility to report on different corruption cases or their suspicions of a possible corruption case. The security police analyse every tip thoroughly and according to its competence tries a case by itself or forwards it to the police, where each case is further analysed and tried.

The security police as well as the National Police Board have actively notified the public of the existence of the tip phone and raised the topic in local media to induce people to report about all cases of alleged corruption.

Cooperation between Estonian customs officials and OLAF began at the time when Estonia regained independence and customs reorganised their operations. Mutual cooperation has been especially effective during the investigation of export fraud, specifically the export of butter and milk powder to EU Member States. Good results have also been achieved in the prevention of cigarette smuggling. For instance in the beginning of May 2003, with the help of the OLAF communication network, we managed to draw public attention to the importance of mutual cooperation between States in the detection of cigarette smuggling.

Media is our good partner in the shaping of public opinion. Electronic and print press gives us the chance to inform our target groups of depreciative actions, prevent violations of the law, and so on. In the long perspective we should gain public disapprobation of the misuse of our, the taxpayers, money. The reflection of the topic of violations is a challenge for communication specialists; one must find a balance between the journalists' interest for details and the protection of the investigation process. If too much information is published too early on in the process, it may damage the investigators' work. However, if there is too little information, the story does not reach the news threshold and relevant information does not get reflected in the media.

It is obvious that cooperation can be productive only when information exchange between partners works effectively and without a glitch. It is difficult to underestimate the importance of the OLAF Anti-Fraud Communicators Network. Through the network, communication specialists from different countries are able to meet to discuss various complicated topics in our common fight against fraud. By taking part in OAFCN work since 2003, initially as a EU candidate Member State, we have experienced an impressive synergy and seen the best practices, which cooperation between specialists of different countries can offer.

National institutions, investigative and judicial services

National institutions, investigative and judicial services

Ioan AMARIE,

General Prosecutor, National Anti-Corruption
Prosecution Office (NAPO)
Speech — OLAF seminar — 20–23 October 2003 — Bucharest

'The Romanian PNA's experience'

Good morning. The problem of corruption is of great importance not only in Romania but throughout the world. Not only is corruption a phenomenon in Romania but it is encountered virtually everywhere, but it is true that the phenomenon of corruption is more marked in a country moving towards a market economy. Unfortunately, Romania has been in this situation for close on 12 years and clearly needs to take steps to combat corruption, which is still found at all levels of society and the economy.

It should be stressed that in recent years Romania has created important instruments for combating corruption, adopting national strategies together with legislative measures which I do not intend to mention here because they are not the subject of this seminar. It is important that Romania has set in place legal machinery capable of combating corruption, a point mentioned on many occasions by the Prime Minister and by President Ion Iliescu. The National Anti-Corruption Prosecutor's Office (PDA), which was set up in September last year, must take the lead in cracking down on corruption. I believe that, as a result of everything we have done, the measures we have taken and the structural organisation set in place in this field by the Public Prosecutor's Office, the PNA is capable of fighting corruption. Admittedly, at the outset no one had any confidence in us because, for a number of years, the results of the fight against corruption were patchy. However, since September last year the number of individuals investigated and charged by the PNA has doubled. One important point should be stressed: the perpetrators have changed.

While, a few years ago, the individuals charged were not high-ranking officials, the situation is now different. The PNA has taken legal action against some 500 individuals roughly half of whom are high-ranking officials. It is capable of monitoring what is happening in various sectors of activity and we are able to act when we feel that something is not right.

Let me give you an example. We have been monitoring for a year now developments at the Defence Ministry, in various military units at the command level, where senior officers have committed serious offences linked to defence procurement. Since we had sufficient data, and with the monitoring operation coming to an end, we took action and a few days ago we ordered the arrest of four senior officers at the Defence Ministry. The investigation is under way and public opinion will be informed about what has happened. The public will see evidence of the measures taken by the PNA.

Another example concerns thefts of huge quantities of petrol, something which cannot be stopped. The PNA has monitored this phenomenon and, through specific investigative measures, we have discovered that those who must uphold the law have been helping those involved in the thefts. The PNA has ordered the arrest of some 40 police officers. The investigation has not yet been completed and at present 35 individuals have been charged.

Another field in which we are monitoring developments and taking action is the banking system. We have charged some 35 bank employees, civil servants, heads of ministries, magistrates and other categories of high-ranking individuals. Last week we also charged a local mayor with committing several acts of corruption described by the prosecutor in a case file almost 100 pages long. All this has been made public through various channels since, under Romanian legislation and in other countries' legislation, there is a fundamental principle of access to information of public interest. Romanian legislation is similar to European legislation and the laws and rules adopted govern such access.

I can now say that the relationship between the PBA and the public, through the intermediary of the mass media, is very good. Admittedly, we face many difficulties, we have been in existence for only one year and not everyone is allowed to work in this institution. For a prosecutor to join the PNA, he must have at least six years' practical experience. He must be a good analyst of social developments and must be specialised in combating corruption. At the same time, as regards the criminal investigation police, we now have 150 officers. Anyone wishing to be recruited must be a law graduate and specialist in various fields. Alongside ordinary corruption (e.g. offering and receiving of bribes), we have to deal with offences linked to corruption. These are offences involving organised crime. The PNA investigates money laundering, tax evasion, drug trafficking, trafficking in human beings, arms trafficking, and other offences. Generally speaking, all these offences involve corruption. For these aspects of our remit, we have set up activity-based units. At present, we are working with approximately 80 % of the staff we need. I reckon that in two to three weeks the PNA will be working at full capacity.

Where corruption is concerned, issues of definition pose major difficulties since the facts constituting corruption are not evident. They are not, for example, embezzlement, theft or homicide, where you have victims, can search premises and can discover what happened.

With corruption, the situation is different. Such offences are committed in secret. Those who receive and those who give bribes need to be kept under surveillance.

As regards legislation, our office cooperates with all the institutions of the State, which are required to provide us with all the information they possess on corruption-linked offences. As things stand, we have lots of information and will be taking action in many areas. We are going to shut down many criminal networks that operate at international level. We are cooperating with Interpol and, through a liaison office, we cooperate extremely efficiently with all similar institutions in other countries.

I would like to emphasise our excellent relationship with OLAF and I am not saying this simply because OLAF is the organiser of this seminar but because this is the truth. We are engaged in numerous measures and, if we do not speak to people about them, then clearly we will not have a good image. I have seen an opinion poll which puts Romania in a bad light in this respect. As a Romanian official who is well acquainted with this situation, I would like to say that things are quite different. Romania is now capable of fighting corruption, taking action and charging individuals, irrespective of their political affiliation and of their position within the State organisation. Any individual accused of committing an act of corruption in Romania will come before the courts and an investigation will take place if we have sufficient proof that the act took place. We are aware that the PNA is an institution that will not please everyone. We would like to become involved in many sectors where corruption is a problem. I believe that, in a short time, we will succeed in showing the world what is going on in this field. We will succeed in showing what we would like to do in future and in convincing everyone that we are very serious about what we do and that we are taking the lead in combating corruption. Alongside this, the legislative measures adopted, which are very important, will supplement this package of measures that Romania is taking to crack down on corruption.

We have endeavoured to do everything that is necessary in our communications with the mass media. Many of the things we have done are not in the public domain since both international legislation and Romanian legislation, beginning with the Romanian constitution, impose certain restrictions on communication. Such restrictions exist in most European countries. I would begin with questions concerning national security, the protection of young people, public information and other particulars relating to access to classified information. One recent example can be given: our institution was accused by an individual of not having provided him with the names of the people working in our institution. I do not know of what use this information was, but the law governing access to information stipulates that only the names of the institution's management are of public interest. Certainly, the law rejects such action on the ground that there is no legal basis for it. This was a signal for us that everyone must uphold the law and that there are restrictions which we have to accept.

The PNA has set up a press liaison office that provides the press each day with information on our work. But there is a fair amount of information that we cannot divulge, details of our strategy and investigations, and there are many things which Romanian legislation prohibits us from disclosing. I am certain that the negative perception of Romania that exists will change fundamentally since our institution is one of the most competent in the country when it comes to tackling corruption. And measures to combat corruption can be taken over a somewhat longer period now that we have begun tackling this problem.

We have convicted 160 people. Not one person charged by this office has been acquitted. Acquittals do not exist! Do excuse my lack of modesty but the PNA has an excellent record. The methods we are developing are means of investigation that allow us to obtain results without disclosing the fact. I would repeat that, if we make public what we are monitoring at the moment as well as the measures we would like to take, I am sure that many of those who compile statistics and place us somewhere between the 80th and the 100th position will change their opinion. Since we are speaking about communication, we have attempted, and I am attempting, to maintain contact with those individuals, with NGOs, with Transparency International and with others so as to convince them that we are a serious institution, that we have nothing to hide, that we are transparent and that we are and will be able to bring corruption in Romania under control.

I would repeat that there is a fear in Romanian society, a fear of the PNA, and offenders know that the PNA can be anywhere at any time. It is a known fact that anyone who offers money does so with some trepidation because the PNA may at any time be there monitoring the situation. We know what is happening in various areas and take action according to a given strategy. Similarly, a few days ago the Prime Minister, when speaking about corruption, spelt out the areas in which more action must be taken, and especially in the justice field.

We have taken measures and are currently engaged in a number of exercises while the Public Prosecutor's Office will be ordering procedural measures. Whenever we act, we inform the public of the important measures we have taken. We cannot inform them of investigative measures, secret data, State secrets or information which we are unable to place in the public domain, but important procedural measures can be communicated.

Through the press liaison office, we announce any important procedural measures such as preventive arrest. This is a measure that discourages would-be offenders.

It is made known to the public in a press release. At the same time, the public prosecutor and specialists give interviews on the radio and television.

Lars ANDRÉN,

Head of
Information,
Swedish customs

Eva-Lisa
LENNSTRAND,

Head of Information,
Economic Crimes
Bureau, Sweden

Lars ANDRÉN

Head of Communication,
Swedish customs.
Before joining Swedish
customs in 2002, Mr
Andrén worked as a PR
consultant specialising in
relations with the media.
Prior to that, he worked
for 12 years as a reporter
for radio, television
and newspapers. His
assignments included
editor and anchorman of
a daily Swedish business
programme on national
television. Mr Andrén has
a degree in journalism
from the Department
of Journalism, Media
and Communication at
Stockholm University.

**Eva-Lisa
LENNSTRAND**

Head of Communications
of the Swedish National
Economic Crimes Bureau
since June 2000. Before
joining the Economic
Crimes Bureau, Mrs
Lennstrand was the
Communications Officer
in SEB, one of the leading
banks in Sweden. Before
that she worked as a
Communications Officer
and Spokesman for
Trygg-Hansa Property
Insurance, one of
the major insurance
companies in Sweden.
Mrs Lennstrand has
a Bachelor of Arts in
Swedish and Social
Science.

'A strategy of communication adapted to the Swedish laws of transparency'

Stockholm, 1 November 2004

1. A brief summary of Swedish legislation on public access and secrecy and comments on the effects of the legislation on communication within a law-enforcement authority

Swedish legislation on public access and secrecy aroused great interest during the many and fruitful discussions held in recent years within the OLAF Anti-Fraud Communicators Network (OAFCN) on principles of communication and information to the press. The Swedish representatives within the network were questioned about the subject and the Chairman, Mr Alessandro Butticé, himself showed a personal commitment to it. This commitment included a suggestion from Mr Butticé that the Swedish contribution to the Round Table on Anti-Fraud Communication should include a description of the special requirements placed by this legislation on communication within a national law-enforcement authority.

As the information heads of the Economic Crimes Bureau and Swedish customs, we feel that the interest shown by OLAF in Swedish openness is a very positive thing. We have therefore opted to publish our two contributions together and to adopt Swedish legislation on public access and secrecy as our common theme.

The material we have put together consists of a brief description of the most important Swedish acts and the principles underlying this topic. This description has been compiled by the Swedish Economic Crimes Bureau and forms the introduction to our presentation. The Head of Information at Swedish customs has in the meantime added a number of observations and comments in relation to communications within Swedish customs specifically. We hope that this compilation will lead to greater understanding of Swedish legislation and the openness of Sweden's public service towards the media and the public.

2. Public access and secrecy: a comprehensive description by the Economic Crimes Bureau of some of the principal laws on openness

The principle of public access to official records and the constitution

The principle of public access — which is one of the cornerstones of the Swedish legal system — has a long tradition in the administration of justice and public administration in Sweden and means that the general public has a right to monitor the activities of the State and local authorities. This monitoring promotes the rule of law and efficiency within the administration. This freedom of expression and information which is guaranteed for every citizen is laid down in the Swedish constitution.

Freedom of the press act and the secrecy act

The freedom of the press act, which is one of Sweden's fundamental laws, establishes the right to have free access to official documents. Although this right is wide-ranging it is nevertheless subject to a great many restrictions since the completely free exchange of information can damage important interests. For this reason, the freedom of the press act includes a number of restrictions. The provisions which list the restrictions on the principle of public access in detail are to be found in the secrecy act. The secrecy act brings together provisions which protect certain sensitive types of information from public scrutiny and accordingly restricts the right established by the fundamental laws for everyone to have access to information held by various authorities. The restrictions placed on the principle of public access to official documents by the secrecy act are permitted under the Swedish fundamental laws. There follow a number of examples of interest to law-enforcement activities.

Secrecy and law-enforcement activities

The prevention of crime is so important that it justifies imposing a restriction on the principle of public access and hence also on freedom of expression and information. Another example, also of great significance to the fight against crime, is the protection of the personal or financial circumstances of private individuals. In practical terms this means, for example, that secrecy applies to investigations in accordance with the provisions on preliminary investigations in criminal cases.

On the other hand some decisions in connection with preliminary investigations in criminal cases are not subject to secrecy. Decisions to open legal proceedings, not to launch a preliminary investigation or to discontinue a preliminary investigation are not subject to secrecy.

In most cases judgments do not include any confidential elements. However, if a judgment includes information of a sensitive personal nature such information can be kept secret; for example, where a judgment is for sex crimes even parts of the prosecutor's application for a summons may be subject to secrecy.

Freedom of reporting

Something should be said here about freedom of reporting. Freedom of reporting is the right, as a general rule, to communicate freely information on any subject for publication in a medium protected by the constitution (e.g. press and broadcasting media). This does not imply a duty to provide information to the media but a right. There are a number of restrictions on the type of information which can be provided on the basis of freedom of reporting. For example, information about secret telephone tapping and certain types of security measures may not be disclosed.

Freedom of reporting is restricted by the fact that it can only be used by an individual and not by an authority. Information issued by an authority's information department, for example by a press officer, is not protected in this way.

Provided that they do not represent an authority, anyone who provides information to an authorised recipient with a view to having the information made public in a medium protected by the constitution is entitled to invoke freedom of reporting. This means that the person in question may be held accountable for the disclosure of the information only if it violates the rules on freedom of reporting.

As regards freedom of reporting and staff working in the judicial system, it is only to be expected that such people as a rule adopt a relatively strict approach to the mass media as regards individual cases. Above all, contact with the media must not be such that the impartiality of the prosecutor or the authorities can be called into question.

The Swedish Economic Crimes Bureau and Swedish customs would also refer to the English version of the Swedish government's website. Under the heading 'Ministry of Justice' is a PDF document which can be downloaded entitled 'Public access to information and secrecy with Swedish authorities'. This document provides a more detailed description of the broad information given above. The page can be found at: http://www.sweden.gov.se/sb/d/2768/a/16293

3. Limitations and possibilities: Swedish customs gives its views on information and communication policy in a very open society

In September 2003 Swedish customs drew up a new communication policy document. In it it states that openness is one of the fundamental principles of the authority's information, communication and public relations policy.

It states: 'Openness means that all information should be accessible with the exception of the limitations imposed by law, contractual agreement or secrecy legislation. We are happy to help everyone who asks for information about Swedish customs. We are honest and open in our personal communications. We share our knowledge and information with others and we listen to and talk to each other'.

This paper has its origin in the special laws governing public access and secrecy in Sweden, but it is also a product of the Swedish customs' internal culture. We believe that openness towards the world around us is one of our core values and a factor in the successful creation of a modern and efficient customs service.

Openness, a way to learn and make the service more effective

We are eager to open up to the outside world in order to draw inspiration and good practice from other authorities and from the companies to which our rules and regulations require us to provide services. Obviously, this kind of openness must be reciprocal. We not only want to learn from others, we would also like authorities, companies and the public to have an insight into our activities. In this way models and ideas may possibly give inspiration to others and at the same time provide us with important feedback in areas in which we can or should make improvements. In this context, Swedish customs regards both openness and constant improvement as core values of our organisation.

Swedish customs' customer ombudsman and our press hotline

In 2003 Swedish customs put into practice this policy of openness with the appointment of a special customer ombudsman to be accessible and to listen to people's views on Swedish customs and to help companies and individuals to exercise their rights. The customer ombudsman does not handle any complaints himself but makes sure that they are passed on to the body which will handle the question. In this way the customer ombudsman helps individuals to present their case in a proper fashion. The role of the ombudsman has a long tradition in Sweden. As long ago as 1809 the Swedish Parliament, and hence the Swedish people, got their first parliamentary ombudsman and since the 1950s the concept has also been taken over by other languages.

The customer ombudsman is easily accessible and answers questions by telephone or e-mail during generous opening hours. The same applies to the Swedish customs' press hotline which was introduced a year earlier when it was found that the media had difficulty in reaching heads of departments responsible or customs' spokesmen after 5 p.m. when the switchboard closed.

Swedish customs takes the view that setting up a press hotline creates a 'win-win situation' from which both the media and the authority can benefit. The media found it easier to obtain information from Swedish customs in the evening and at weekends and holidays, and at the same time the press hotline enabled the authorities to refer questions to the official customs' service spokesmen and women.

Being available to the media in the evenings or at weekends not only means that we can issue factual statements if we are criticised, but we can also make things easier for journalists in all those cases in which Swedish customs receive good publicity.

List of topics on the Internet

The description of the Swedish laws on public access and secrecy in the previous section makes it clear that the right of free access to official documents is a central principle of Swedish legal tradition. It also states clearly that not all documents or electronic texts are official or accessible. For example, the secrecy legislation allows access to be restricted in the case of criminal investigations or cases affecting an individual's financial or personal situation.

Final documents and letters received by and sent out by the authorities are recorded in Sweden on a special list, or register. This list can be consulted by both Swedish and foreign nationals, and the documents requested, provided that the secrecy act does not prevent disclosure.

Journalists used to visit national and local authorities at regular intervals to consult the register in search of news or to follow up a particular subject. Swedish customs has not only made a paper copy of this list available at head office, but it has also put it in electronic form on its website. This is another step by Swedish customs to follow the government guidelines on creating a '24 hour' administration via the Internet.

However, it is important to stress that the actual documents are not available via the Internet. Anyone who wants a document on a given subject must contact the authority which issued the document. The fact that the register outlining current topics is available on our website is in Swedish customs' view a major step forward and an important indication from the point of view of public access.

Freedom of reporting within a law-enforcement authority

Lastly, a few thoughts on freedom of reporting. This means that a civil servant is free to disclose information for publication in a medium protected by the constitution. In principle this means that he may not release a secret document but may on the other hand disclose secret information to the media. However, it is dangerous to talk in general terms, since there are also a number of exceptions to freedom of reporting in the case of information covered by the secrecy act, such as information relating to the security of the realm, for example.

It is also important to stress — and this is also clear from the Economic Crimes Bureau's report — that freedom of reporting implies that it is possible but not a duty to disclose oral information to the media. Civil servants are therefore not obliged to make use of their freedom of reporting.

Under the legislation, the authorities are not allowed to investigate people who disclose information either. A simple way of explaining the system might be to say that in Sweden the parliament has formalised the possibility for so-called 'whistleblowers' to inform the media when or if an abuse of power or corruption is taking place within an authority.

Of course, there is no guarantee that civil servants will only make use of this possibility in such cases and there can, of course, be a variety of reasons why the media might be given information by a particular individual. However, Swedish customs is firmly convinced that freedom of reporting does not create any major problems for its fight against crime. Within Swedish customs there is a clear culture whereby civil servants protect the effectiveness of criminal investigations, in particular from demands from the media for access to as much information as possible prior to a court hearing in a topical area of investigation.

National institutions, investigative and judicial services

Corinne CLEOSTRATE,

Head of the Information and Communication Office,
French Customs and Indirect Taxation Directorate-General

Corinne CLEOSTRATE

is Head of the information and communication for French customs and Indirect Taxation Directorate General. This department is responsible for all matters relating to communication: internal and external communication and information technology.

Her previous post was Head of Cabinet for the Director General, and prior to that she was Customs attaché at the French embassy in Rome and Head of a customs investigation service.

Corinne Cleostrate started her career in customs working at Roissy-Charles de Gaulle airport, before going on to hold a range of posts in HR management for French Customs and Indirect Taxation Directorate General.

'Why an investigation service should have both the possibility and the duty to engage in communication activities relating to its activity: the experience of French customs'

There are a number of reasons why the investigation services that undertake checks and inspections to identify fraud against the European Union's financial interests are entitled to engage in communication activities. Communication can help to make citizens of the Member States more aware of the risks from fraud for the Union budget to which they contribute. This in turn will help to lend legitimacy to the activities undertaken by the investigation services (and their operating costs).

Communication can therefore be handled either by the investigation services themselves or by a communication service operating in cooperation with the operational service that was behind the investigation.

There is no objective *a priori* reason why an investigation service should refrain from communication activities, especially where the operational service itself decides what kind of information can be made available to the general public. And if the investigation services have nothing to say for themselves, that in itself will arouse curiosity and adverse interpretations in the media that can be avoided by communication, however minimal.

But the constraints inherent in the confidentiality of judicial investigations, in the professional secrecy incumbent on French civil servants and in respect for the individual rights of investigators and suspects alike must be fully reflected in communication activity. It is sometimes necessary to postpone media comment on a case for the sake of its further development. Public information is necessary but it does not justify jeopardising the potential offered by an in-depth investigation or violating the judicial limits on communication.

In general terms, investigation or press services need to modulate their communication activities on the basis of the type of media addressed. An investigation involving a number of visually interesting aspects and relatively little in the way of explanation as to how the fraud operates is more suitable for television than for radio or the press.

Journalists working for the popular press are mainly interested in the sensational aspects of a case. They can be informed about the facts of the investigation (anecdotes about the things that fraudsters do and the clever ways they find to conceal their fraud), while scrupulously preserving individuals' anonymity as required by French law.

In addition, the general refusal to divulge any information to the press would be contrary to the equal treatment of the media that a public service must respect and would increase the risk of misinformation.

It must be stressed that communication on fraud cases can also have a preventive effect, as European taxpayers will be made aware of the consequences of fraud for the Union budget that directly concern them but that they do not always realise does.

Communication can, for instance, have a dissuasive effect on individuals who buy low-price goods that have often been smuggled, as they will now realise that in the long run the tax loss to the Union budget that their anti-social conduct partly causes will have to be made up from their other taxes.

Communication must also highlight the fact that fraud against the European Union budget generates ill-gotten gains that feed the underground economy. And apart from the financial impact, it can involve breaches of health regulations and thus be a health hazard for the consumer.

More generally, publicising cases concerning Community assistance wrongly received that has distorted competition to a greater or lesser extent, including competition on the domestic market, can help to improve compliance with the trade rules, in particular where the fines imposed on offenders can be revealed.

And the main difficulty in supplying the media with information, sometimes sensitive information, in their relations with public institutions lies in the risk that the information supplied will be distorted or that information not intended for the general public will be disseminated.

One way of reducing these risks is to work with a network of journalists with whom relationships of mutual respect have been built up. This has the dual advantage of communicating with journalists who have enough knowledge of the rules and regulations to appreciate the interest of a given subject (for instance, trade frauds require some knowledge of customs procedures) and who respect the need for discretion when the communication service asks them for it.

But this trust takes time to establish, and the investigation or communication service may have to share high-value information as a reward for the quality of the partnership relationship.

The existence of a network of anti-fraud communicators under OLAF's leadership provides undeniable support for communication on the different frauds against the European Union's financial interests. It makes it possible to harmonise practice and to share and thereby enrich the available information.

National institutions, investigative and judicial services

General B. Walter CRETELLA LOMBARDO,

General, Head of Unit II of the General Commando,
Guardia di Finanza, Italy

Brigadier-General
**Walter
CRETELLA
LOMBARDO**

is Head of the
Department for
Research and
International Relations
at the Headquarters
of the Guardia di
Finanza. General
Cretella Lombardo
has held important
leading roles in the
operational and
teaching fields of
the Italian Guardia
di Finanza, most
recently as the Head
of the NCO Officers
in L'Aquila. He has
also taught in many
important Italian
training institutes
such as Scuola di
Perfezionamento
Forze di Polizia;
Accademia della
Guardia di Finanza;
Scuola di Polizia
Tributaria.

'The Guardia di Finanza's anti-fraud communication policy'

There can be no doubt that OLAF's Anti-Fraud Communicators Network offers a great opportunity to weigh up and assess the next steps the European institutions and authorities involved in the fight against fraud will need to take if they are to tailor their actions more closely to the objectives they are pursuing and to make them even more effective.

The arrival of 10 new Member States in 2004 has increased the challenge, shifting Europe's focus more towards the east and the markets there.

The relationship between activity and communication is a key topic today. It is generally recognised that effective communication increases the effectiveness of the work done by any organisation involved in fighting fraud, raising its profile and increasing support. Basically, communication adds value to daily operations by bringing the public into contact with the organisation and sending out the message that it is working for everyone.

Clearly, we need a carefully devised media policy for publicising objectives, capitalising on achievements and projects, and informing the public in general if we are to gain the legitimising support of public opinion and business for the role officially assigned to us by current laws.

However, to avoid the pitfall of paying more attention to the tools and techniques of communication, that is, to the form, rather than to the content, which is the organisation's finished product, or its everyday usefulness, we need to have a clear understanding of the organisations' respective tasks and of developments in the world outside, availing ourselves of the benchmarks and changing scenarios for our operations.

The Guardia di Finanza sees this question as so important that, in March this year, it issued a special internal circular setting out our communication plan for 2004.

While its work is recognised and appreciated by the State and its institutions, when policing the worlds of business and finance, the Guardia di Finanza can, at times, unfairly acquire the image of the revenue officer with nothing to do but check tax documents or examine accounts. While such figures are irreproachable professionally speaking, they are far removed from the general public.

The problem is not therefore the lack of a media profile. It is, if anything, how to harness the individual channels of information (press releases, interviews and television reports) in such a way as to prevent excessive fragmentation from distorting the image, at the risk of placing too much emphasis on how the organisation would like to appear rather than on its awareness of what it actually is.

All police forces provide security, a value they traditionally promote by communicating at length and in detail on arrests, seizures and offences reported. The message is simple and hits home because everyone has suffered injustices and abuses of power.

The Guardia di Finanza's position is slightly more complex. In addition to personal freedom, freedom to settle, freedom to own property and freedom of expression, the Italian Constitution makes provision for economic freedom (freedom to conduct business, freedom to enter into contracts, the free market and savings).

Fraud endangers economic freedoms by unduly encouraging tax evasion and avoidance, unfair competition and organised crime. Without the minimum degree of economic security, trade declines and economic and financial insecurity lead inevitably to recession.

By policing the world of business and finance, the Guardia di Finanza plays a key role in the Italian system of controls set up to safeguard national and European financial interests.

Legislative Decree No 68 of 19 March 2001 requires the Guardia di Finanza to safeguard the budgets of the State, the regions, the local authorities and the European Union. It assigns to the Guardia di Finanza the specific tasks of prevention, investigation and prosecution of offences involving 'customs and border duties as well as the European Union's own resources and expenditure.'

In close cooperation with the authorities responsible for safeguarding economic freedoms, the Guardia di Finanza performs operations that help to create a secure framework for safeguarding commercial relations (tax audits and technical checks, air and naval patrols, police and other financial and assets-based investigations) and, of course, conducts prevention activities that cannot be measured and therefore objectively demonstrated.

In the final analysis, the Guardia di Finanza's daily operations make it the police force with most experience in safeguarding the economic and financial interests of the State and the European Union. This is the key message that the Guardia di Finanza has recently been trying to get across in preparation for one of the most important challenges that we will shortly have to meet.

I would like to thank OLAF for organising this important event, which I am sure will give rise to valuable suggestions and approaches, and for having given the Guardia di Finanza the opportunity to bring its ideas to the round table.

We are aware of the scale of the problem and know that we need a common communications strategy, which we can develop only — and in part thanks to this type of initiative — with the support of OLAF and the OLAF Anti-Fraud Communicators Network.

National institutions, investigative and judicial services

Arturo CUERVO,

Former Director of the Communication, Information and Social Relations Office, Guardia Civil, Spain

'Using communication in smuggling prevention'

Arturo CUERVO SÁNCHEZ

is currently Director of Empresa Municipal Promoción de Madrid, a Madrid City Council multimedia company that promotes Madrid internationally. Former Director of Communication in several Spanish public institutions including: Diputación Provincial de Valladolid (provincial government), Junta de Castilla y León (regional government) and the Directorate-General of the Guardia Civil, Mr Cuervo has also worked as an editor for the Spanish press agency EFE and held a management position in the communications consultancy Asesores 2000. Mr Cuervo holds a degree in information science from the University Complutense of Madrid and diplomas in defence studies from Ceseden (Spanish Ministry of Defense) and in senior management from the Enterprise Institute (Instituto de Empresa). He is a professor specialised in communication in public administration and lectures for different post-graduate programmes at the Universities of Madrid and Salamanca as well as at the CESMA Business School. He has contributed to many publications in the field of communication in public administration.

Please find below my thoughts on the questions to be discussed at the round table you have set up.

1. For — Information and communication: why should an investigative service have the powers and the duty to communicate on its work and what are its limits?

I believe that whatever information one holds back will be given out anyway by somebody else. It is always a good idea, as far as the law permits, to explain personally what your organisation is doing because otherwise somebody else will do it for you. It is mistaken to believe that an investigation will not become common knowledge — it always reaches somebody's ears eventually and will be passed on to the public, generally through the media. So why not get your version in first? Why wait for somebody else to reveal everything as and when they see fit? Why assume that it will never get out? The only limits are those laid down by the law.

2. Against — Information and communication: why should an investigative service always remain silent and never communicate on its work?

I can come up with no answers to this question. Such an attitude is for those narrow-minded individuals who refuse to face up to reality and have no knowledge of the world in which they live.

3. Rights/duties of information, rights/duties with regard to the secrecy of investigation: where is the proper equilibrium?

Legal and operational limits should be respected. The point is not to give out information for the sake of it, but to have well-prepared and exhaustive guidelines as to what should or should not be made public, and to give out information at the most appropriate moment.

4. Audiovisual information and communication of the investigative services: television, tabloids and financial enquiries.

Images are possibly the most important element in any newspaper article. Anything which is difficult to understand through explanation can be simplified by a good picture. I believe it is important for investigators to take on board this need for something visual and record as much of what they do as possible. Subsequently, and bearing in mind legal obligations and whether it is suitable to provide images, the decision will be taken on whether, how and when to provide them. Merely possessing the visual record will in any case always help the investigator and those in charge of public relations to give out information.

5. Why informing and communicating also means fighting and preventing fraud

Society needs to be aware of things in order to prevent them … and what better way to become aware of the problems caused by fraud than through the process of institutional communication, be it the media, public relations or countless other channels?

6. 'Information partnership'

A free media must question the performance of public institutions. This can build walls between journalists and institutional spokespersons. But is it possible, through the development of mutual trust and professional respect, to have a shared objective to tell a story fully and with frankness? What is the give and take in such a 'partnership'? What are the risks?

The media must become yet another channel of information about institutional activity. As an important tool in achieving this, however, they must be treated normally. There are many advantages and risks, but 'normality' might be the key word in such a relationship.

Ekaterina GENOVA,

Former Head of the Public Relations Department,
Bulgarian customs

'Bulgarian customs and the media'

Ekaterina GENOVA

was head of the PR department of the Bulgarian Customs Agency until January 2005. Before joining the customs administration, she was an author and the host of a weekly live talkshow on Channel 1, Bulgarian national television. Ekaterina Genova started her career working as a journalist for the culture section of the *Evening news* newspaper. Later she held the position of editor for the 'Science and education' section of the newspaper *Rabotnichesko delo* — Sofia. At the beginning of the 1990s she became a reporter for the central news edition of Bulgarian national television — Channel 1. As of February 2005, Ms Genova is back at Bulgarian national television working as head of the satellite channel, TV Bulgaria. Ms Genova studied journalism with the specialisation 'Press' at Sofia University. She writes interviews for the the Standart newspaper and has also written a book, dedicated to the 10th anniversary of the television talkshow, 'Trainer on-camera'.

A key priority in the Bulgarian government's programme is the integration of the country into the European Union. Regarding this, a communications strategy was developed. Its task is to bring the issue out into the public sphere and to give an opportunity to every part of society — institutions, groups and individuals — to become aware of the predominantly positive aspects of this process. The communication strategy is a dialogue with society and a way of guaranteeing its active participation.

The implementation of the communication strategy is aimed at bringing Bulgarian citizens closer to the everyday dimension of EU membership. The entire campaign is divided into two main aspects (depending on the goals and on the public to whom it is directed): the national plan, addressed inwards to Bulgarian society and aimed at explaining and bringing the citizens closer to the 'European idea' of Bulgaria, and the international plan, directed at the citizens of the EU Member States.

All Bulgarian institutions are taking part in this communications strategy as part of the national plan and are following common rules like transparency, honesty, flexibility and openness.

Those principles are also the most important ones for the Bulgarian customs agency. The idea of transparency led us to the creation of four documentaries that show the daily work of the ordinary customs officer. The everyday battle against customs offenders found its way into the film thanks to two very big cases of fraud and smuggling. After a few months of long investigation by the internal service, called the Inspectorate, 10 customs border officers were dismissed and charges against them were filed. They made serious procedure violations when they allowed goods to enter the country without proper control. It turned out that behind this criminal scheme was a notorious underground 'businessman'. In another case, customs officers found that a large amount of medicines worth more than EUR 23 million were missing from a warehouse under customs control. This means that the budget tax loss was of about EUR 4.5 million. When presenting these two cases we are not just informing society but also exercising a warning effect on any potential future offenders. Public opinion was on our side and it played a big part as well.

The main purpose of the PR department is to present a new image of the customs officer in a fair and open way. Every week we are trying as well to show the media interesting events that reveal different aspects of customs work, such as reports, interviews and publications. However, we must not restrict ourselves to the presentation of every single offence discovered by customs officers such as smuggling, fraud and so on. When presenting these cases we are searching for a comprehensible language. Even though the journalists are looking mainly for a sensationalist story, unfortunately we are restricted by Bulgarian law on the issue of supplying them with the complete information.

One of the best ways to strengthen the authority of an institution is honesty. When mistakes have been committed we must have the ability to be the first to admit and discuss them. The hiding or concealing of sensitive information leads only to speculation, and this is arguably the worst media reaction. A competent spokesman must confront every crisis situation.

The development of close contacts with journalists who follow customs work is an absolute must. We need to respect and help every reporter in every case. This means never denying a request for information and giving the needed data as soon as it is available. When it is possible, some information could be presented in advance or assistance lent to reporters when we cannot directly provide them with the information they request.

The information must go both ways: we not only give but also receive it. Any information from the investigative journalists about customs or a case where customs officials are involved will help us get a different perspective and understand a little bit better how society views the work of the agency.

The information policy of Bulgarian customs has another important dimension, as there is a big segment of people who are clients of the customs service and should be informed of every new detail in customs legislation or procedures. That is why information brochures were printed and distributed in every customs office. Our web page has also special sections for clients and people who travel abroad. If the information on the Internet is not enough there are also telephone numbers which could be used whenever necessary.

All of our activities are aimed at informing ordinary people and businesses as well as trying to create connections between the people and the institutions that in fact are working for them.

National institutions, investigative and judicial services

Adam HEMPEL,

PhD, Director of the Bureau for International Treasury Relations, Ministry of Finance, Poland

Adam HEMPEL,

PhD, has been Director of the Bureau for International Treasury Relations within the Polish Ministry of Finance, which is the Anti Fraud Coordination Service in Poland, since January 2004 (he was Deputy Director of the Bureau from January 2003). He is also Deputy Chairman of the Multidisciplinary Team for Combating Fraud against the Republic of Poland or European Union (GAFU) and coordinator of the Multidisciplinary Working Team's work concerning the fight against different kinds of irregularities. Mr Hempel possesses wide experience in the scope of combating economic crime and counselling in security (between 1999 and 2002 he was an investigation specialist for one of the Polish insurance companies). Between 1990 and 1993 he acted as a deputy for the capital commanding officer of the police in Warsaw and between 1995 and 1998 he worked in the General Customs Inspectorate in Warsaw.

'The scope and methods of cooperation with the mass media, institutions and concerned units involved in protecting public Community funds in Poland'

The Bureau for International Treasury Relations (ITR Bureau) is the Polish unit of the Anti-Fraud Coordination Service (AFCOS) responsible for coordination of anti-fraud activities. The office is the central contact point for European Commission services as well as for Member States' services responsible for issues associated with the protection of European Union financial interests. It is a partner of the European Anti-Fraud Office (OLAF) and is a participant in the system responsible for securing financial interests in Poland — to which also belong the Government Anti-Fraud Plenipotentiary responsible for fighting against financial fraud affecting the Republic of Poland and the European Union, as well as the Interministerial Anti-Fraud Unit (GAFU) responsible for the same tasks.

The main duties of the government plenipotentiary (these duties are currently being fulfilled by the General Inspector of Treasury Control, a Secretary of State in the Ministry of Finance) include initiation, coordination and execution of actions aimed at securing the financial interests of the Republic of Poland and the European Union. The government plenipotentiary is supported by the Interministerial GAFU group. The group consists of representatives of institutions and services responsible for securing the financial interests of the Republic of Poland and of the European Union. These are operational and investigative services and as such their activities are usually of a confidential nature directed towards combating crime and irregularities. GAFU group tasks include planning, coordination, monitoring and controlling activities undertaken by the appropriate government administration services, as well as preparation of proposals aimed at securing efficient information exchanges between these institutions. Employees of these services are required to keep confidential information obtained during the course of investigations due to non-disclosure clauses to which they are subject. They carry out operational activities and, as such, very often come into conflict with the need to communicate.

Institutional communication teams within the individual services are responsible for communicating with society. This obligation is carried out by means of proactive information policies. These teams cooperate with the mass media on the basis of provision contained in the press act as well as in the 'access to public information act'. They operate under extreme time pressure, especially in regard to making available information associated with actions currently being carried out by operational services. Journalists are interested in news — something that happened today and is of a sensationalist nature.

Proactive information policy means no more and no less than 'coming forward with information'. The media play a very important role in carrying out this active communication with society. They in essence constitute a part of public opinion and, above all, have a very large influence on how this opinion is formed. They have a high level of social trust (in particular news services) and, what is very important, are able to reach a wide range of recipients and as such play the role of an intermediary in contacts with society. If we want to reach the widest possible group of recipients, we use the media as an excellent communication channel.

In carrying out proactive information policies we must always know what we want to make available, how we want to achieve this and when is the best time to make such information available. The text of the information made available must also be very carefully prepared. Unconfirmed and false information cannot be made available under any circumstances. Our information must be interesting and contain a clear and truthful message.

By implementing such information policies, the organisation has the chance of being the first source of information, even if such information is not beneficial for it. This gives way to the unquestioned ability to offer an initial interpretation of the events, as well as to define the directions and means in which such information will be made available. It allows anyone to present his point of view. In addition, thanks to actively making information available, there exists the possibility of creating a climate of disregard for fraud and financial crimes against the Polish and EU budget among recipients. It also clearly shows to society that services that are looking after safe use of Community funds are working and that criminal activities will be discovered and punished.

Active communication with society also gives the opportunity for society to become better acquainted with the work of any given organisation. An example may be the documentary series entitled 'Granice' (Frontiers) currently being produced by TVN Television in cooperation with the Public Communications Office of the Ministry of Finance and the spokesmen of customs chambers. This programme explains to society the nature of the work done by the customs service and border guard, thus helping to increase the credibility and authority of these services. It constitutes a form of combating crime and fraud. The large number of people watching this television programme allows one to assume that social acceptance for the work of customs officers and social awareness of the role they play in securing the financial interests of Poland and the EU is increasing. A clear sign of this process is the fact that smuggling dropped significantly after the airing of the first edition of the series.

Of course, a conflict between the media seeking information and public services protecting finances against fraud cannot be avoided. An important issue is finding a middle-ground between reliable and exhaustive information regarding the operations of the aforementioned services and non-disclosure of facts which, if disclosed, could have a negative impact on the success of an investigation underway. One must remember that it is this information made available to the media, and thus to society, that influences how these services are seen in the eyes of the public.

The only efficient manner to make this type of information available is through the use of proactive information policies in conjunction with cooperation with the given services. The press teams, in executing these types of policies, must know what they want to make available, how they want to make information available and when will be the best time to undertake appropriate actions. The means of communicating with society must always be based on the context of the information being made available — it can be promotional information, cautionary information or preventative information.

One of the barriers involved in executing a proactive policy regarding information is associated with the non-disclosure of professional or treasury information of a confidential nature, therefore potentially limiting the flow of information between the individual services and the media.

A certain danger is also associated with potential 'rivalry' between organisations working together. Sometimes these services compete against each other in creating information available to the media regarding their achievements in the battle against crime. The services that are first in making information available are looked upon as the only (or most effective) ones involved in discovering the given crime.

Another barrier in active communication with society may be the limited and uninterested manner of making information available associated with activities being conducted.

Of significant importance too is that the services respond quickly and accordingly to information appearing in the media. A lack of reaction is seen badly by the public.

Due to the nature of the current situation in Poland arising from a growing crisis in public trust in the government, the media are oriented towards touching subjects of a negative nature, that are sensationalistic, thus putting press teams in a difficult situation.

Units involved in shaping information and communication with the media in all services are found responsible for financial irregularities.

Police: as part of its prevention and promotional activities, the police make available information regarding methods of preventing and combating crime, as well as information associated with new technical solutions and procurement of equipment. The police website is also a constant source of information regarding police activities. Various types of units are used by the police when handling media associated with a given event, for example, mobile information points (representatives of the press office at the scene of the event and giving information directly to journalists on site), crisis press services (experienced employees of the press relations department prepare press releases made available at the press centre) as well as the press centre (a centre in which police work achievements are presented).

Border guard: fulfils its assignments regarding communications with the media through the press centre of the border guard head office as well as spokesmen for the border guard regional offices. In addition, the media have constant access to statistical data containing information related to border guard activities. Such information is made available in the form of information materials, press conferences as well as answers to specific questions asked by media representatives. A constant form of communication is the border guard head office website as well as press bulletins sent to local media by press secretaries. The border guard service is also the initiator and organiser of excursions with groups of Polish and foreign journalists in order for them to become acquainted with given areas of the border and how these are defended by such excursions generating positive press publications of a European and international reach.

Customs service: cooperates with the media by placing information on its website regarding attempts at smuggling discovered by its officers, information regarding actions associated with fiscal crimes, fiscal misdemeanours as well as the scope of tax supervision. In addition, articles published in the *Wiadomości Celne* (Customs News) newspaper describe some of the most interesting smuggling attempts, customs and tax swindles, discovered by customs officers. The customs service also makes available to the media information related to discovered attempts, penalties which smugglers face, as well as information regarding trade of strategic commodities, such as weaponry. Additionally, the customs service conducts a number of precautionary activities such as organising exhibitions, press conferences related to a specific subject and the preparation of leaflets regarding, for example, changes in tax and customs laws.

The issues discussed previously clearly show the important role that communication between these services, the press and society plays. Without doubt, greater awareness among society, as well as the knowledge that a penalty for a given crime cannot be avoided, is partially the result of constant information regarding the success that organisations such as these achieve in their fight against crime. In order for communication with society to be successful, the individual services must always keep in mind the needs and reactions of society. If the media and these organisations lead proactive policies regarding information, this will undeniably help in combating irregularities and fraud. Information made available to society by these organisations will make society more aware of how these organisations work towards securing public safety and combating criminals.

(The text was prepared in cooperation with the Public Communication Office at the Ministry of Finance, the press services of the customs service, the general police headquarters and the border guard general headquarters.)

National institutions, investigative and judicial services

Ion ILIESCU,

President of Romania,
May 1990–November 1996 and December 2000–December 2004

Speech: Seminar for the Communicators of the European
Anti-Fraud Office — Bucharest, 20–23 October 2003

'Information and communication as a means of creating a public culture of honesty and transparency in the disbursement of public funds'

Ladies and gentlemen, The fact that this seminar is being held in Romania is attributable to the progress being made by the country in integrating into the structures of the European Union and to the need for the adoption of the Community *acquis* to go hand in hand with the introduction of EU procedures in numerous fields, ensuring in particular that European funds, which come from the public purse, are spent in a lawful and efficient manner.

Within the institutional framework of the European Union, OLAF — the European Anti-Fraud Office — plays an extremely important role because of the tasks assigned to it. Romania's cooperation with OLAF is in its infancy, and the fact that, thanks to the efforts of both parties, such an event as today's is taking place in Bucharest can be regarded as evidence of the country's resolute determination to combat all forms of fraud involving domestic and European public funds, acts of corruption, tax avoidance and, generally speaking, any violations of the law, regardless of the political or social position of the perpetrators.

Since those responsible in the European Union are aware of how important this campaign is, they are supporting Romania and the institutions of the Romanian State in our efforts to create an appropriate legislative structure, to prepare specialists for the fight against fraud, and to set up operational and credible control bodies.

A very wide variety of projects are being implemented with various partners, more often than not in different geographical areas and at quite different intervals. This complexity offers many opportunities for fraud. If we come to regard this essentially objective situation as our destiny, we will end up viewing fraud as an everyday occurrence. This would be the worst possible thing that could happen.

Fraud involving the public purse is all the more reprehensible, and must be severely punished, in that it cannot take place other than with the involvement of politicians and public officials, in other words, those who are entrusted essentially with defending and promoting the public interest. Their dishonesty undermines trust in the State, in the country's institutions and in democracy.

Whereas, from the point of view of the media, tackling corruption and fraud can, in general, be anonymous since more often than not it falls well short of being spectacular; in a world of media spectacle, acts of fraud are more spectacular and attract greater media exposure. This may give the false impression that the State and its institutions are powerless or, more seriously, may foster the idea that efforts to prevent fraud are pointless or impossible.

These realities have made it necessary to organise, within the framework of OLAF and similar agencies in the Member States and the candidate countries, a number of structures specialised in public communication and capable of interacting coherently and at all times with public opinion and with the media. An honest and professional relationship with the press becomes extremely important for the creation of a public culture of honesty and transparency in the disbursement of public money.

People must be aware of the danger posed by unlawful activities as well as by activities that result in the misappropriation and waste of taxpayers' money. Such fraud means greater poverty as well as fewer and lower quality public services and is harmful to the legitimate interests of society and its members.

It is our duty, the duty of all of us, to help the people understand that, alongside rights and freedoms, they have legal and constitutional obligations, that it is in their interests and in the interests of society that fraudulent acts should be severely punished, and that they should not become accomplices, including as a result of passivity or non-involvement, in such anti-social behaviour.

I welcome the fact that Romania has already set up a kind of public communications unit within the government's Control Department. It is important that, together with other specialists in the field, it devises and develops a number of information and awareness-raising campaigns concerning fraud involving Community funds and, in particular, that it gauges their public impact.

I would like to stress that, regardless of the obstacles we face, the institutions of the Romanian State and I personally are most concerned with ensuring respect for the laws and interests of our society as well as for European norms and with punishing those guilty of acts of corruption or fraud.

The Romanian authorities are absolutely determined to combat such kinds of fraud and, at the same time, to inform the European institutions and public opinion of the results obtained.

Transparency is nowadays an efficient weapon in stamping out corruption and fraud of any kind involving public funds. The existence of transparent procedures that are the same for everyone, the disappearance of those conditions that have paved the way for immunity and impunity in the case of many offenders, and the effective application of the principle whereby 'no one is ever above the law' are all arguments for continuing your activities within the control machinery, for supporting moves to give individuals responsibility and for creating a partnership between individuals and institutions, including the government's Control Department as well as active cooperation with Community institutions, including OLAF, with a view to clamping down tightly on all acts of fraud.

I wish you success in your work and can assure you that Romania will respect all the undertakings it has given to its European partners.

National institutions, investigative and judicial services

David JONES,

Head of Information,
Serious Fraud Office, United Kingdom

David JONES

is the Head of
Communication at the
Serious Fraud Office,
a United Kingdom
government body
for the investigation
and prosecution of
large and complex
cases of economic
crime. Previously
he held senior
communications
positions at the
Financial Services
Authority and also
with the London
Stock Exchange
in its regulation
and compliance
department. He has
worked at Henley,
the management
college on marketing
and financial services
training material.
His early career was
in the commercial
manufacturing sector
as a marketing and
public relations
specialist working in
foreign markets.

'Information partnership between the media and an investigative service'

This discussion paper addresses certain questions that arise out of the precept that a free media must question and, where appropriate, criticise the performance of public institutions. This quite proper function can build walls between anti-fraud agencies and journalists. But is it possible, through the development of mutual trust and professional respect and understanding to have a shared objective to tell a story fully and with frankness? What is the give-and-take in such an 'information partnership'? What are the risks?

Such questions must recognise that any collaboration brings certain dilemmas to both sides of the 'partnership' and, in order to explore the answers to these questions, I will first put each side of the 'information partnership' in perspective.

THE MEDIA

On one side of the relationship there are journalists who have a professional obligation to provide their readers/viewers with news or in-depth analysis that is accurate or an honest interpretation of the known facts. Whether those audiences are reached by television, radio, printed publications or electronic news services is not central to the principle although it can influence the nature of collaboration. The basic principles are that the media should be vigorous, objective and ethical in their approach to news and in the way they deal with newsmakers. Journalists do not make the news, they report it. They may be selective in what they report. They might ignore what some people may think is newsworthy and would wish to see reported. They might expose what some people would prefer not to be made public. These are key elements of free journalism. To place any controls or limitations or coercions on these elements would be tantamount to reducing journalism to State propaganda.

I said that journalism should be vigorous, objective and ethical. I shall explain.

Vigorous journalism

It can be argued that some examples of vigorous journalism equate to invasion into a human right of privacy. It can be argued that journalism is vigorous because they have the hunger of a mercenary paid by results to fill a column in a newspaper or serve the insatiable appetite of television news stations to constantly report breaking news. Vigorous journalism is not quite the same as aggressive journalism. Different cultures apply different styles. At an OLAF training seminar for spokesmen in 2002, two guest journalists, one from the United Kingdom and the other from France, were used to compare and contrast two styles. One was the assertive and direct, sometimes hostile, questioning often used by northern European media. The other was the more discursive style popular in southern Europe. These were explained to be loosely defined as the Anglo-Saxon style and the Latin style. From my personal experience, I accept this broad definition, but exactly which style is typical in the new EU members from central and eastern Europe, I am not qualified to say.

Objective journalism

As for objectivity, I bring to mind something about perception. Two people can look at the same thing but not see exactly the same. The example is a glass of wine. In the glass, the wine level is at half way. Does that mean it is half full? Or does it mean it is half empty? One is positive, the other is negative. Transfer this to the anti-fraud arena and we could see a press report about the failure of a State prosecutor to convict 50 % of defendants, meaning that a large number of suspected criminals are escaping justice. On the other hand, the State prosecutor might think that, because the other 50 % are convicted and jailed, society is protected from a large number of criminals. Who is right?

Ethics in journalism

Ethics in journalism are a minefield of debate. Honesty, dishonesty — what are these concepts? What is the calibration method and who is the judge? What might be considered ethical press behaviour in one country might not be regarded so favourably in another. What is ethical for one newspaper might not be a value fully shared by another, even both in the same country. This is a complex subject and deserves a more detailed examination than is possible in this discussion paper. But the experience I have with the media in the United Kingdom is that editors and journalists do behave in, what by my interpretation is, generally an ethical way. A good journalist would not knowingly report something he or she did not believe to be accurate on the available facts. To have to print a correction or an apology is not an experience journalists enjoy. They will try to avoid it and will often argue about the interpretation of a passage of text. There are laws of libel that act as a deterrent to prevent the media from making unjust reports about people. Newspapers can be taken to court by individuals or by companies and sued for damages. There can be orders issued by a criminal court to prevent reporting on particular legal proceedings so as to avoid a prejudiced judicial outcome. But generally, if there is no real defence, journalists will usually accept their error and print a correction. For most journalists, accuracy is driven by a strong sense of professional pride and reputation. But (in the United Kingdom) if there is an unresolved dispute with a newspaper, a complaint can be made to the Press Complaints Commission which will make a judgment where the newspaper might be instructed to publish a correction or apology.

It is because journalism should be, and in my experience is, vigorous, objective and ethical that the concept of an 'information partnership' can be developed. But what about the other side of the partnership — the institutional spokesman?

INSTITUTIONAL SPOKESMAN

Government institutions should communicate as openly as possible to ensure that the public has the opportunity to know what is being done in their name and to be able to make informed decisions about how they want their society to be governed and administered.

Institutional communicators should be accurate, knowledgeable, fair in their treatment of journalists and always available for comment — even if it is 'no comment'. Whenever I read a press report that says that 'a spokesman was unavailable for comment', it usually suggests to me that a spokesman has chosen not to be available perhaps because the questions are too tough to handle or that the organisation's capability to deal with the press on that occasion is not at its best. Either way it sends a negative message about the way the organisation feels at that moment and could be interpreted as having something to hide? A spokesman should never be stuck for something to say even if it is simply to explain the reasons why he is not able to comment on the circumstance at that moment. Journalists understand that there are occasions when a spokesman can legitimately decline to comment but to not be available at all is no way to build any kind of information partnership.

Because through the media is the most influential and effective opportunity of communicating to the public, the institutional spokesman should regard the media as an important ally in public education. In so many ways they share parallel objectives. That is, to inform and for that information to make a difference to people's lives. The concept of a just and fair society is a key motivation for both.

Need to protect confidential information

There is no dispute that the spokesman has a counterbalancing objective. That is a duty to protect confidentiality of the institution's work, such as investigations. And it is in this respect that the 'partnership' can come under severe strain. The natural hunger of a journalist to know more detail, to be able to share with his audience a fuller insight into the situation is a very strong impulse. Sometimes it takes great skill by the spokesman to retain professional respect with the journalist, whilst at the same time not disclose the information that might be asked for and which, if disclosed, could cause problems for the investigation or the court proceedings.

Balancing caution with trust

The spokesman can, if carelessly saying too much or not agreeing the rules of the discussion beforehand, wreck a case. It does require the establishment of a certain trust which is not an easy thing for a spokesman to feel comfortable about. The natural reaction for a spokesman is to say less rather than more and, though this is essentially a prudent and safe attitude, if it becomes an inflexible standard way of doing things, it can backfire. It is my experience that, though a general set of rules about how to deal with journalists can apply and a set of procedural action tick-boxes created and the basics of interview techniques taught, they do not guarantee a first-class spokesman. They are all necessary and helpful to achieve a level of competence, but good media relations is an art rather than a science. The best spokesmen are able to apply initiative in those difficult and fast-moving situations, and must be able to use judgment about what to reveal and importantly who to. It is vital that the development of trust is a two-way creation.

'PARTNERSHIP' IN PRACTICE

Some time ago, I had a meeting with a respected UK journalist who specialises in economic crime. He has been very interested in reporting major fraud cases over many years and routinely visits the USA and Europe to research stories. His style is to expose fraud and to bring public attention to the suspected dealings of businessmen who operate behind a mask of respectability or who carefully manipulate the rules to ensure it is very difficult for them to be successfully prosecuted. The quality of his reports and the insights he achieves is acknowledged and often envied by other journalists so I consider his opinions about media relations worth listening to. He said that the important thing to remember was that journalists and crime agencies are 'on the same side' and that spokesmen should trust them with more information at an earlier stage, so that when a situation happens, an investigation comes to nothing, a prosecution fails in the court, and an acquitted defendant briefs the press about his innocence and about the 'incompetence' of the prosecuting agency, the journalist would not have to rely entirely on the statements made by the former suspect. The anti-fraud agency must be as ready as the acquitted person to grab the attention of the media.

What do the investigators think?

A spokesman needs to develop trust in two directions. One is with journalists. It cannot be with every journalist because some may be infrequent contacts but there is usually a cadre of important journalists where contact is frequent and individual personalities are better understood. The second direction for trust is inward within the spokesman's organisation. Investigators and prosecutors must feel that they can confide confidential information to their spokesman in the knowledge that it will be carefully used or protected. This is also an important relationship for the investigator/lawyer to trust the spokesman's judgment about introductions to journalists and arranging special meetings for background briefings ahead of permitted publicity. The degree of contact that investigators or prosecutors have with the media will vary from agency to agency and from one country to another. Some will be experienced — others might fear themselves to be like innocents amongst a pack of devils. Therefore the comfort-zones can be elastic but, if the frequency of contact is minimal, it places greater responsibility on the spokesman to reassure his colleagues. Whatever the situation, the spokesman must accept responsibility for creating the right environment for 'information partnership' activities.

Partnership at the operational level

There are two general levels of partnership with the media. One is at the operational level where the focus is on a single case or type of fraud. The other is at the strategic level where the fraud agency itself, its *raison d'être* is the subject of examination.

The operational level brings certain sensitivities for investigators and for prosecutors. Investigations are naturally and properly secret affairs and investigators are understandably protective of their case. For them, the overriding goal is to collect sufficient evidence to bring charges which will stand scrutiny in court. Investigators have a natural nervousness that premature publicity will compromise the investigation, possibly alerting suspects to destroy any incriminating evidence. There is a current SFO case where the London office of a suspect was visited by investigators with a warrant from a court to search the office. Investigators entered the building and caught one suspect putting documents through a shredding machine. I cannot reveal here whether his action has made any difference to the overall investigation but it illustrates a real operational problem that investigators face and goes some way to explaining why it can be difficult for spokesmen to encourage their investigator colleagues to take journalists into their confidence. I do not advocate that the media should have been alerted to the raid in advance. They would have wanted their cameras there to record it but this can create its own unwanted 'circus'. However, details of a raid could be shared with the press at a future date, when the time is right for publicity.

Facts, facts and more facts are what make a good news report. An example of this is a case about a law firm in Cheltenham, England, which over a long period of time, made false claims on government funds for subsidies to provide legal advice and services to defendants in the courts in that part of the country. The fraud was estimated to amount to GBP 4 million (EUR 6 million) and, after a long investigation, 29 employees of the law firm were prosecuted. A number of trials took place and publicity was prohibited by the court until the end of the last trial. However, the story was so complex that the decision was made to cooperate fully with the media months before. Investigators gave detailed briefings to the media. Television cameras were allowed into evidence store rooms and there were pre-recorded interviews with officers. Statistics to illustrate the scale of the fraud — such as 38 properties searched on one day using 120 investigators, collection of 21 tonnes of documents including over 96 000 legal aid forms, nearly 15 000 of them forensically examined and over 3 000 witness statements taken. Working with the media in this way ensured a very positive message on national television and in the major newspapers.

A similar approach can help to blunt severe criticism in the media. Not all cases go well for an anti-fraud agency. Taking some journalists, or sometimes only one, into confidence by giving an advance briefing to help explain why the prosecuting lawyer made certain decisions, why the charges were selected the way they were, why a potential suspect instead of being prosecuted, was used as a witness for the prosecution. There are many twists and turns in a long and complex fraud investigation and its legal process through the courts. If a prosecution fails, and the case is one that has had high profile in the media, the acquitted defendant will often make a public statement to ensure that the business community and society in general is aware that the cloud of suspicion is lifted from him and that he is no longer tainted with the label 'possible fraudster'. In this process it is not unusual for him to criticise the investigating agency. It happens sometimes in the United Kingdom that an acquitted defendant will say that the anti-fraud agency made some bad decisions and has been irresponsible with public funds. In a recent SFO example, it was claimed by a defendant that the failed case cost the UK taxpayer GBP 10 million (EUR 15 million) in investigation costs and legal costs over a four-year period. The figure was not an objective calculation. It was simply a guess and though the Serious Fraud Office was able, through a quick reaction, to ensure that most news reports used a more modest and realistic figure, it does show the dangers of poor preparation by an anti-fraud agency for bad news when a case goes wrong.

It is with the failure of a high media profile case that anti-fraud agencies are at their most vulnerable. There is no secret that, some years ago, when the Serious Fraud Office was experiencing a number of prominent failed cases, it was given the name of 'Serious Farce Office' and though, as time passed, that tag has faded into the background, it remains ready in the journalists' repertoire, should another major failure occur. The way to minimise this happening is to be ready and able to share with the media as many positives about the case as possible and, when it is appropriate, to admit in retrospect that perhaps a certain decision was wrong or that a certain argument was not very strong. Journalists are prepared to listen to a well-thought-out argument and will allow some sympathy to modify a potentially scathing report.

In many situations, the spokesperson — if properly briefed by operational colleagues — can do much of the liaison and briefing, but journalists always prefer to talk with people who are actually investigating or prosecuting. So it is a positive policy, from time to time, to give some exposure by putting the investigator and the journalist together not just after the case is finished (which is valuable) but also during the progress of the investigation. The investigator must be made familiar with the rules of the meeting in terms of how the journalist can use, or not immediately use, the information. It is the responsibility of the spokesman to ensure that there is no confusion or misunderstanding about this.

'Partnership' at the strategic level

Anti-fraud agencies exist as a result of national laws or, in some cases, because of agreements between national governments that create a supranational body such as the EC or the UN. Anti-fraud agencies exist to protect society from financial crime and their existence represents a political will to stamp it out and to punish the transgressors. In practical terms, however, stamping out financial crime, though a noble political and social objective, is not completely realistic. The published objective of the Serious Fraud Office is to reduce fraud and its cost to the UK economy. Complete eradication can only be a dream. Objectives must be realistic.

How therefore to justify the existence of an expensive anti-fraud agency when financial crime still persists; when fraudsters find new ways of committing fraud and when the media is constantly filled with stories of fraud? It is impossible to quantify how much fraud is not being committed because of the existence of an anti-fraud agency. However, it is important to demonstrate, through the existence of an anti-fraud agency, that fraud is not tolerated in a developed society, that public and commercial concern must be manifested in the form of an anti-fraud agency. The threat of retribution in the name of the people, through the criminal justice system, is a tangible warning that fraudsters can be punished. This is the 'deterrence message' and for this to have any real 'bite', the successful actions of an anti-fraud agency must be made visible to the community. The most powerful information method to achieve this is through the media.

A sizeable majority of adults in the United Kingdom (population of nearly 60 million) read newspapers and/or listen to television and radio news broadcasts. By comparison, the number of persons throughout a year who read communications issued by the Serious Fraud Office such as annual reports or press notices, or who attend conferences where the Serious Fraud Office is speaking, or visit the SFO website is probably less than 20 000. Most of these will be professional people with an interest in fraud such as politicians, lawyers, accountants, police officers, some financial sector businessmen and of course journalists. They are a selective part of the community and do not represent the public at large nor do they represent everybody in their professional sectors. For this reason, it is also crucial at a strategic level to work with the media to help educate the public and the professional sectors to inform society of the governmental system that is in place to combat fraud in their name. In contrast, if all the major UK national newspapers report an SFO action, the news reaches an indirect audience of many millions instead of just the 20 000 or so reached through direct communication. The media is indeed a potent, if unpredictable, tool.

Fact or fiction?

One of the most effective ways to educate the mass population is to become famous on television or in film or in books. Some agencies have become famous in public awareness — in the United Kingdom at least — in this way. There is 'Scotland Yard' (a name which many will know better than its official title of London's Metropolitan Police), there is the FBI and there is Interpol as examples and I suspect that these and one or two others will be known throughout the world. The importation of television programmes from the USA has raised awareness about the NYPD and even the LAPD. But, invariably, the fame of these agencies revolves around other more dramatic forms of crime, such as murder. Anti-fraud agencies have a harder time of it. It is not often that economic crime meets the criteria for exciting mass population television and, in the United Kingdom, though the public are aware that the criminal justice system does tackle 'white-collar crime' (a generic media expression for fraud), they might only know of the Serious Fraud Office in the vaguest of terms. If anything, they might just as easily recall a famous high-profile case that failed, before they think of a success — such is the power of the media to shape public perception.

It therefore becomes all the more important for an anti-fraud agency to use what opportunities that might come along to turn their story into an entertaining television show. This might alarm some purists and understandably might cause some operational colleagues a sharp intake of breath in concern. However, I can cite a couple of examples where this has been applied to the Serious Fraud Office. One is a BBC television documentary series on the 10th anniversary, in 1998, of the creation of the SFO. It was called 'Fraud-busters'. It was a look at the legislation, the rationale, and the history of the organisation, examining some of its successful — and not so successful — cases. It also gave an insight on how the organisation works, how it makes its operational decisions and how it deals with some unexpected problems. It was important to show the human face of the organisation so a number of operational colleagues as well as the most senior executive featured in the documentary. This was more than an examination of one case where the measurement of organisational professionalism is based on one example. It was a full overview, made for a mass audience in a way that reduced the legal complexities to concepts that the general public would not only be able to understand but that the presentational style made it entertaining to watch episode after episode.

The above example included some editorial control by the Serious Fraud Office. It was pre-agreed with the BBC that nothing would be televised that might jeopardise an existing case but otherwise freedom was given the programme maker to include some of the possibly embarrassing moments in the life of the SFO. Throughout, it required frank discussions between the SFO and the programme maker and sometimes a compromise had to be reached about a particular item or scene, but the programme was based on reality and though there were some elements of re-enactment, it was the real SFO laid bare. In balance it proved to be a public relations success and even now, six years later, the programme remains remembered as a turning point in the SFO's presentation of itself to the public.

Another example is so recent that it is too early to judge as to its public awareness value. It is a drama programme to be broadcast on UK television later in 2004. It is a complete fiction on the scenario of terrorist activity in the Middle East playing havoc with trading on London's International Petroleum Exchange and the illegal actions of a market trader (with a character based on Nick Leeson of Barings Bank fame). Filming using professional actors was permitted inside the SFO building using rooms and facilities that could not be reproduced in the television studio, except at great cost. Some SFO staff featured as background 'extras'.

The drama is based on a fictional massive and complex fraud where the Serious Fraud Office has been called in to investigate. Because it is designed to be entertainment for a television public audience it is unlikely to reflect in absolute accuracy the style and pace of an SFO investigation but to use an English expression — 'that's show business'. If a few million viewers in the United Kingdom are reminded that an elite anti-fraud agency exists to help protect legitimate economic development and to track down those who commit fraud, then this example of information partnership will have been worthwhile.

Imagine a Hollywood movie starring Brad Pitt as an OLAF agent and Nicole Kidman as a beautiful Estonian government agent. They collaborate to uncover the smuggling of thousands of tonnes of potatoes into the EU from Belarus. Filming takes place in Brussels and in Tallinn with exciting chases in fast border-patrol helicopters or on horseback through the Baltic forests. And naturally the hero and the heroine form a romance. Just imagine the James Bond style. Though reality is not so exciting as such fiction, at one stroke, OLAF and the Estonian customs board would become as world famous as the '007' image.

CONCLUSION

Relationships with the media is as much about relationships with individual editors or journalists or programme makers as with the newspapers or with the broadcasters as corporate news service entities. Some news services will add their opinion to the facts in the form of editorial comment. They might have an editorial stance on certain issues. It might be because of the sector of the community they serve and might reflect the political preferences of their audience. But, in a free press society, the facts of a story are inescapable and an anti-fraud agency should find every possible way to use the media to tell its side of the story. Often this will mean using judgment, sharpened through the experience of building relationships with journalists, to lift the veil of secrecy on operational matters and to bring the press to understand more fully the difficulties and challenges faced by an anti-fraud agency. I repeat again what a noted UK journalist once said to me — 'We are on your side. Help us to understand the issue and we can tell a better story, more often in support of you than against you'.

It is true that there is the potential for the press to reveal a confidential matter that might jeopardise the investigation, and journalists of quality will accept that they all cannot be told everything all of the time. It is a give-and-take situation. Break a trust once and it usually becomes impossible to repair the relationship and journalists are in tune to that concept. It is my view that media relations is not an exact science, it is an imprecise art where the spokesman plays a pivotal role in helping to develop trust between his organisation and the press. The alternative is to risk a constant war of attrition which, in the long term, is no service to the public.

National institutions, investigative and judicial services

Anssi KARTILA,

Senior Investigation Officer,
National Board of Customs, Finland
Speech — OLAF training seminar, Finland, 2002

**Anssi
KARTILA,**

Senior Investigation
Officer, LLM, Section
Chief of Legal Affairs
and IPR Enforcement
in Enforcement
Department, National
Board of Customs
Finland. Before joining
the Finnish Customs
in 1997, Mr Kartila
worked as a judge at
the local town court
and for eight years in
the banking sector as
bank lawyer.

'Communication tools and international operations as a means of fraud prevention'

EU Member States' customs administrations have a central role in the fight against cross-border crime. For this reason, it is important to have all-round cooperation between the Member States and the Commission, as well as with third countries and the accession candidates in particular.

The EU Member States have agreed on a certain definition for joint customs operations: the term 'joint customs operation' stands for operational, targeted and fixed-term measures in order to stop sensitive and other goods from being smuggled. The operations may be full-scale, that is, carried out by at least five Member States; or limited, in which case the minimum number of participating countries would be three.

EU Member States' customs administrations have harmonised their activities and increased mutual collaboration in many ways. One significant area of customs cooperation is joint operational action for preventing fraud. It may be that, in the commotion of an operational action, not enough attention is given to informing the media. On the one hand, it is understandable, as crime prevention operations deal with a lot of confidential and sensitive information and documentation. In addition, there seem to be varying cultures of publishing information in different EU Member States. It has been striking, however, that the debriefing meetings after many of the operations have not given much attention to releasing the results for publication. And, on the other hand, it has not yet been discussed how and what aspects of the operation will be communicated to the Community and Member States. Yet, a significant function of these operations is to promote awareness on the customs authorities' preventive fight against crime.

The EU Member States' customs administrations arrange numerous crime prevention operations between two, three or more countries in various fields. For the most part, all EU Member States participate in joint enforcement operations. Preparations for the operational actions are naturally highly confidential as are the relevant documents. The operation targets are, by definition, of interest to decision-makers and to the general public, such as cigarette and alcohol smuggling, and trafficking in narcotics and weapons. The joint enforcement operations between the EU Member States' customs administrations are agreed upon in the EU Council Customs Cooperation Working Party (third pillar). Annually, there have been four or five such large-scale operations. Also, a similar Police Cooperation Working Group agrees on arranging certain joint operations each year, in which EU customs administrations participate within the limits of their powers. Furthermore, the Baltic area Member States have a cooperation working group operating against organised crime, which arranges numerous multilateral and multidisciplinary enforcement operations annually.

Although the primary goal in the EU fraud-prevention operations is to develop readiness to fight against fraud and organised crime, another aspect, nearly as important, is to see that information is shared in an appropriate manner. The operational action plans very often point towards actions that include the entire EU in an active fight against crime, and the aim is to prevent crime from happening.

Of course, the operations represent something in their own right and send in their essence a positive message about actively participating customs administrations.

Also, the results of the operations greatly influence communication, even if they often do not constitute the most significant part of a single operation. The public very often gets a very simplified black-and-white picture of the operations. Here perhaps communications experts could step in.

Who we inform of the enforcement operations:

- the general public
- operators of trade and traffic
- parliaments
- the media
- ministries and other national authorities
- EU working groups and authorities
- criminals.

Of course it must be stated that the confidential reports of the operations are better and better these days; clearer and analytical. This is definitely an important communication tool for catching the EU bodies' attention, especially at the OSA Council, on the work done. But it is hardly enough.

Practical situations are complex, however, as many things must be kept in mind when informing the media. Criminal investigations or other possible follow-up measures instigated as a result of the operations must not be jeopardised by going to the media too soon. In some Member States, the customs powers, as far as criminal investigations are concerned, are smaller, which may also affect the readiness to communicate information. National legislations and judicial practices determine when specific details on companies or persons involved in illegalities can be published. These operations hardly ever have any special common information policy. The EU Council Customs Cooperation Party has discussed how to inform the media but a clear coordination in this respect is still lacking. The Customs Cooperation Party has, on the one hand, underlined the successes of the operations and, on the other, brought to the forefront the risks of information leaks following a more open policy.

In actual fact, operational action can and should be reported on in a detailed and fresh manner. In real life, information on the criminal *modi operandi* spreads extremely fast, and operational action does not really produce the kind of tactical information which could not be published. In these cases, the viewpoints of the operational and communications staff and of the leadership may vary, but the aim should be at transparency. Retrospective communication of statistics is a different matter, as mere statistics rarely have the same news value as concrete events tightly set in time and place.

A concrete example

'Operation RAID' (co-financed by EU Falcone programme)

An operation targeted at combating organised crime involved in the trade and traffic between the EU and Russia. It was a question of double invoicing and organised economic crime. Nine EU Member States' customs, police and prosecution authorities, and representatives of ministries from several countries, as well as the authorities of the Russian Federation participated in the operation. It was arranged after the Finnish EU presidency, in accordance with the Tampere Summit resolutions, and Finland coordinated the operation.

There was an urgent demand for a concrete operation, as Russian authorities had recurrently paid attention to the matter, and demanded concrete measures from the EU. On the other hand, there had been a lot of discussion in the media and among the decision-makers in Finland about this issue. Then there was a political need both nationally and internationally to prevent concrete crime.

The goals of the operation according to the operation plan were:
- to prevent double-invoicing;
- to uncover the criminal organisations in the EU and Russia;
- to trace criminal proceeds;
- to stop and uncover money laundering and economic crime;
- to improve information exchange and to create smoothly operating communication between Russia and EU Member States.

Some of the goals were reached and some probably were not. The concrete results that could be measured in financial terms were substantial. The operation created a basis for future measures and showed that an associative system worked in fraud prevention. The operation may not have eliminated the problem, but it worked very well as a communication tool. Companies and persons involved in illegal activities as well as trade and traffic on broader terms received the message about sound practices and that authorities may intervene. The operation received positive publicity in the Finnish press. A press release was drawn up immediately after the debriefing meeting and the highest Finnish customs enforcement official gave out interviews. The operation gave a clear message and allowed the law enforcement authorities, customs and police to continue their work around the problem. The operation also created a credible project-based approach to this specific type of crime prevention. Nevertheless, even here we may have lost something, as there was not a single communication expert present during the different phases of the operation.

The Russian administration and communication culture presented certain problems, while imposing a lot of restraints. This is understandable, as for instance in connection with the operation RAID, where Russian authorities met us with a lot of pressure and surveillance. The safety of the participating officers must also be taken into account.

Recently, the police authorities have markedly become more media-active in many ways. The police emphasise in that way their contribution to an open society, and present themselves as an upright and transparent organisation in society. It can be said for police organisations that they have taken the media actively into their most significant operations to depict their action in an interesting and captivating way. Of course, part of the material will serve as excellent for training purposes, but in a special way they have also provided an extra value for breaking news and informing interest groups.

In certain fields of fraud prevention, the MOU partners provide an excellent channel for increasing publications. That way we are able to show other viewpoints and not just those of the authorities. With the contribution of our partners we point out the vital role of customs in securing legal traffic and trade. The emphasis on informing the media is among the tasks of the customs administration, such as collecting taxes and protecting society.

National institutions, investigative and judicial services

Antonio LAUDATI,

National Anti-Mafia Deputy Prosecutor,
National Anti-Mafia Bureau

Within the structure
of the National
Anti-Mafia Bureau,
Antonio Laudati
has been a member
of the Camorra
Department,
the Ndrangheta
Department, the
Apulian Mafias
Department, the
Study and Analysis
Unit, the New
Mafias Department,
the International
Cooperation
Service as well as
of the Suspicious
Transactions Service.
On behalf of
Prosecutor Vigna,
he has coordinated
investigations into the
smuggling of tobacco
processed abroad
run by organised
crime as well as
gold/silver smuggling
on a national and
international scale.

As representative of
his bureau, he has
been chairman of
the multi-disciplinary
group on organised
crime set up at
the Council of the
European Union in
Brussels.

'Using mass media to fight organised crime'

1. Introduction on media sociology

It is commonly said that we live in an information society. A society which is mainly based on services and where information of all kinds is the key to well-being and power.

Modern societies are increasingly dependent on complex communication systems, in which there is enormous interest and which play a considerable role in political, social and economic life.

It should also be said, however, that increasingly complex social structures, both at national and international level, have provided the media with new tasks and challenges. The decline of traditional social authorities (political parties, the Church, the family, the community, etc.) should increase the need for effective public institutions which can compensate for this loss. Moreover, public demand has expanded due to the trend towards globalisation, which affects all aspects of everyday life, while individualism, relativism and precariousness make most people more dependent and vulnerable and, therefore, increase their need for information.

Among the many changes in modern society, the mass media clearly have a pivotal role.

One important aspect of the problem is the role the media can play in the fight against crime and, in particular, organised crime. The issue has been widely studied and can be summarised in terms of three basic theoretical concepts.

- The first is Albert Bandura's theory of social learning, whereby individuals learn from the media what behaviour will be punished and what behaviour rewarded.

- The second is Berkowitz's priming effect, whereby people's observations of crime lead them to think along similar lines and make comparable judgments, which predisposes them to violence in interpersonal situations.

- Finally comes Huesman's script theory, according to which social behaviour is controlled by a script which indicates how one should behave in different circumstances according to a model provided by the media.

As well as such theories, there is also the widespread belief that being exposed to violent crime can lead one to become desensitised to and, therefore, more tolerant of violence.

It is, however, utterly true that the media can play a crucial role in the prevention and control of crime.

It may be perceived to be generally associated with the latest trends, but it has never been particularly open to radical change. People have been talking for years about the imminent death of the mass media. The new interactive media should have made it look outdated, but they have had almost no impact on the absolute supremacy of the traditional media.

It may be that several characteristics of the media are simply irreplaceable. Technology and form can change, but only mass communication can meet the demands of stable political, economic and social systems. National and international politics cannot, for the moment, do without effective communication methods and mass information.

Although these ideas are shared by many, the question still remains as to what type of State–media relationship might most effectively combat organised crime.

2. Characteristics of organised crime in the new millennium

It should also be emphasised that organised crime has altered considerably in modern society.

Things have changed in two main ways: criminal groups have become more international and, as they have gradually adopted a business-like approach, they are more likely to be copied.

In our global society, even crime has taken on transnational features, with cross-border crimes becoming increasingly frequent. First there was drug trafficking, then smuggling of foreign tobacco, prostitution, trafficking in persons, counterfeit industrial goods and so on, all requiring the transfer of goods, persons and capital from one part of the world to another. This led inevitably to a gradual grouping together of organised crime gangs controlling particular areas, the adoption of common modes of operation and the possibility of exploiting differing legislation and the varying levels of effectiveness of crime prevention in different countries. Things greatly improved for organised crime when Europe's eastern borders were opened up after the fall of the Berlin Wall and whole new territories and potential markets became available.

As a result, criminal organisations must nowadays carry out their illegal activities across a greater number of countries, targeting richer markets.

The second effect follows on directly from the first. If we look at cross-border crimes we see that they adhere to the principle of maximum profit for minimum legal risk which is characteristic of criminal businesses. They are also generally offences which completely overturn any traditional aggressor–victim relationship.

Cross-border crimes committed by organised criminals usually involve providing illegal goods or services to consenting persons. Drug trafficking, tobacco smuggling, prostitution and the trafficking in persons are all businesses run by criminal gangs who are willing and able to satisfy demand for illegal services in rich western markets with the flexibility associated with traditional business activity.

This makes things considerably difficult for national police forces who rarely receive testimonies or complaints and who, above all, no longer come across extreme displays of violence. Rather, they are faced with complex criminal systems operating in the impenetrable world of the underground economy. The way in which organised crime is fought clearly needs to change and focus on both prevention and control.

How can the fight against smuggling and prostitution be said to be effective while thousands of people are still buying smuggled cigarettes or obtaining the services of prostitutes?

Tens of thousands of people are arrested in Europe every year for crimes related to drug trafficking and many tonnes of illegal drugs are seized, yet the use of illegal drugs has not decreased; it has, on the contrary, become more widespread with currently unacceptable numbers of deaths from overdoses.

That is why any new crackdown on crime will not work without getting people actively involved and putting direct pressure on potential new clients. It is necessary to convince people that buying a packet of smuggled cigarettes is tantamount to financing a criminal gang, that prostitution is the last link in the unspeakable crimes of trafficking in human beings, that the use of drugs ruins one's health, and so on.

The role of the media in this issue is absolutely clear.

3. Using media to prevent and fight crime

In the modern information society, people should have as much information as possible on public institutions to ensure that democratic values are upheld.

In this connection, the provision of information on the activities of police forces and the public prosecutor in the fight against organised crime could be essential.

It is evident that the focus of criminal proceedings has changed in recent decades, from gathering, presenting and evaluating evidence for and against the defendant to becoming, through mass-media coverage and globalisation, more of a reflection of public opinion on important news items and issues of political and social interest (as, for example, in government corruption cases).

Criminal proceedings have thus become a means of influencing public opinion through the mass media, and they, in turn, can be influenced by media requirements and dominant political groups.

In our particular field, the effectiveness of criminal proceedings and control of the mass media can be excellent ways for us to gain people's trust in government institutions and even to prevent crime being committed.

The broadcasting of news items about the effectiveness of police forces or about the speed and timeliness of deterrent sentences certainly discourages potential offenders and may even force them to abandon crime altogether.

It is well known that one of the functions of sentencing is to serve as a deterrent to crime.

It is particularly important to gain people's trust in the fight against organised crime as this can help break the conspiracy of silence imposed by criminal gangs and encourage people to give evidence or make a complaint against a crime.

Positive examples publicised by the mass media can be particularly effective in geographical and social groups which have been forced into silence by criminal organisations.

The most decisive part, however, of the mass media's role in the fight against organised crime could and should be providing people with examples of social behaviour that are perhaps not collectively considered particularly alarming but which are big-business opportunities for organised crime.

Buying smuggled cigarettes or counterfeit clothes is not considered by most people as particularly serious anti-social behaviour; it is almost universally tolerated and there is even a certain satisfaction in paying less tax or less money for big, monopolistic brand names. However, if the mass media can make people all over the European Union conscious of the fact that buying smuggled cigarettes or counterfeit clothes will actually mean giving significant financial support to organised criminal gangs, helping them to commit violent crime, engage in large-scale drug trafficking and put many people's lives at risk, sales of such goods would probably fall.

Information on criminal investigations could also be extremely useful for people to help them avoid buying counterfeit products or becoming a victim of the large-scale fraud currently perpetrated by organised criminal gangs in the European Union.

We are therefore faced with the decisive challenge of guaranteeing freedom, security and justice in Europe, a challenge which, in the new millennium, will necessarily involve a much closer relationship between government and the mass media in the fight against organised crime.

It is worth recalling one of Pope Pius XII's teachings, expounded in his speech of 17 February 1950: 'It would not be an exaggeration to say that the future of modern society and its internal stability depend to a large extent on the balance between the strength of communications technology and the ability of individuals to react.'

National institutions, investigative and judicial services

Julio LESMES ANEL,

Deputy Director responsible for External Communication, Spanish Taxation Agency, Spain

Julio LESMES ANEL

is responsible for external communication at the Spanish Taxation Agency. Born in 1963 in Valencia, Spain, he has a law degree from the Universidad Complutense of Madrid and is a civil servant of the Cuerpo Superior de Investigación de Vigilancia Aduanera (the Investigation Body of Customs Vigilance).

He joined the Taxation Agency in 1991, the same year it was created, and has worked for customs in Vitoria and Madrid, and at the General Technical Secretariat of the Department of Economy and Revenue. Since 2001, he has worked at the Organisation Department of the Tax Agency, specifically, in the General Sub-bureau of External Communication, for which he has been responsible during the last year, and where the organisation's communication strategy is designed and carried out.

'An integrated strategy in the fight against fraud'

On the basis of our current experience in the Spanish Taxation Agency ([60]), I would like to present some ideas providing an overview of all aspects of our communication strategy.

Organisations like the Spanish Taxation Agency whose task it is to monitor taxation and customs so as to ensure the collection of public revenue, or whose remit includes such tasks, must project an image to society that reflects efficiency and openness in the performance of their duties, so as permanently to boost citizens' confidence in the tax authorities.

To achieve this aim, the organisation's communication strategy must be based on three fundamental principles:

- openness in its actions: the organisation must take responsibility vis-à-vis individual citizens and the general public for the results of its actions, even where these are negative;
- combating fraud: public organisations enhance their image by improving the results of the fight against fraud and the public's perception of these results;
- assistance and service to the general public: the services which the agency provides to the public must be maintained and their accessibility improved, particularly via Internet, to make it easier for citizens to meet their tax obligations.

This communication strategy must take the following two essential aspects into account.

- Staff are one of the organisation's main channels of communication. The organisation's public image is based to a large extent on the image projected by its members. This explains why many organisations, both public and private, have now dropped the conventional distinction between external and in-house communication, which used to be the responsibility of two separate departments — marketing and human resources.
- Communication between the organisation and the public must be two-way. The communication strategy must include mechanisms for gathering information on the public's views, their expectations and what they want the agency to do.

This is why the communication strategies of organisations like the Spanish Taxation Agency are designed as an integrated whole, including coordinated action involving both in-house and external communication tools.

1. In-house communication tools

As already stated, the image that professionals in the investigation and monitoring sector project to society is a key facet of the public image of the organisation they work for. The better the following aspects, the better that image will be:

- the motivation of the staff in the performance of their duties, their sense of belonging to the organisation and their identification with its goals;
- the extent to which investigators are properly trained to carry out their duties;
- the information that workers receive about the organisation as a whole and the service they provide or the task they perform in particular.

The communication strategy must therefore include mechanisms to facilitate staff participation and enable staff to communicate their ideas, needs, expectations and the level of satisfaction. To achieve these aims, the Spanish Taxation Agency uses the following in-house communication tools (the list is not exhaustive):

- a bi-monthly in-house magazine
- a suggestions box for the use of staff
- an intranet portal for staff use
- an intranet designed as an information management tool to facilitate staff training and information
- in-house surveys and opinion polls (such as the in-house survey on the atmosphere at work).

2. External communication tools

There are many channels of communication that organisations can use to convey to the public the image of an open, trustworthy organisation that is efficient in combating non-compliance — an organisation that reflects the society it serves.

The main external communication tools which the Spanish Taxation Agency bears in mind when designing its communication strategy are as follows:

- visual symbols of corporate identity;
- institutional publicity campaigns (press, radio and television);
- institutional publications (annual activity reports, leaflets, service charters or lists of services available to the public, etc.);
- information and help services (in offices and by telephone and Internet);
- studies and opinion polls;
- civic information about taxation in schools.

There are also a variety of channels for conveying the organisation's image to the general public:

- open offices that provide services to the general public;
- telephone;
- Internet;

- the media: press, radio and television;
- forums, conferences, exhibitions, seminars and other events in which the Taxation Agency can play a useful part.

In this context, relations with the press play a decisive role in developing the communication strategy. They involve anticipating the information required by the media, tailoring the message to the medium used to convey it, and ensuring the message is consistent with the rest of the communication strategy.

Every communication measure will use the most appropriate medium to convey the message aimed at the public or to gather relevant information from citizens.

An integrated communication strategy must combine the use of these tools in the best way to achieve the aim pursued — providing information, educating or providing services to the general public — bearing in mind that the ultimate goal is to convey the organisation's 'real image' to the public, and that this real image must closely resemble the 'desired image' that society wants to see: only then will the public develop a sound awareness of tax-related matters.

In conclusion, I believe the existence of a strategic communication document including an overview of all the objectives, principles, tools and channels of communication is a key factor in the success of organisations whose tasks include the investigation and monitoring of taxation and customs.

(60) Agencia Tributaria.

National institutions, investigative and judicial services

Richard LINNING,

FIPR Euprera Former President, European Confederation of Public Relations, IPRA Campaign for Media Transparency,

Expert on the Romanian Prime Minister's Department of Inspection and Monitoring of the Transparent Use of Community Funds

'Fighting and preventing fraud also means informing and communicating: a personal perspective'

Richard LINNING

is an experienced public relations practitioner who has successfully applied his craft in many cultures, countries and continents. Most recently he has been a counsellor in European public affairs, assisting governments, organisations and companies to reconcile business and public policy issues, particularly in EU member and candidate countries. His experience also encompasses the broad spectrum of public relations and broadcast media activity. He is a frequent speaker, writer and trainer in all aspects of communication.

Richard Linning is currently providing technical support in the field of media and public relations for the Romanian AFCOS. Members of the United Nations initiative, the Global Compact, have decided to fight corruption. The Compact's corporate and civil society organisation members — 1 200 in all — have agreed to add anti-corruption to their nine existing principles of good corporate citizenship in the areas of human rights, labour and the environment.

Why has it taken them until June 2004, adding corruption as it were an afterthought? To the outsider it is as if Moses clambered down from the top of Mt Sinai with an armful of tablets and realised he had left one of the Ten Commandments behind.

However tardy their action, in my opinion the Global Compact's decision will come in time to be seen as marking a seismic shift in the war against corruption — not because of any implied intention but because it marked the point at which the marketplace recognised the legitimacy — and commercial advantage — of embracing anti-corruption. Until now it has only been the big stick of the law or the carrot of future earthly or heavenly reward.

This reference to religion is deliberate and inevitable. All the world's religions are united in their promotion of ethical behaviour, of a set of principles which should guide every person in making choices. Their choice of words is strikingly similar: 'No one of you (truly) believes until he wishes for his brother what he wishes for himself' (Islam) [69]; 'A state which is not pleasant or enjoyable for me will also not be so for him; and how can I impose on another a state which is not pleasant or enjoyable for me' (Buddhism) [70]; or 'Do unto others as you would have them do unto you' (Christian) [71] [72]. Even Kant could be interpreted as providing a modernisation, rationalisation and secularisation of this golden rule. 'Act in such a way that the maxims of your will at any time can be taken at the same time as the principle of a universal legislation' [73].

Despite such exhortations no country or culture can claim to be entirely free of corruption. In some countries, corruption is so pervasive it undermines not only the fair and efficient functioning of the State, but even the very fabric of society. Without doubt as a consequence it also contributes to reducing economic growth, hindering international efforts for sustainable development, and, unchecked, can breed poverty. The Global Compact agreement is a result not only of fear of the consequences of corrupt activity but also in response to information about its impact and the wish of those who have put their names to it to communicate their concern.

That corruption in all its forms has to be opposed on principle and for practical reasons is manifestly obvious. But before going on to how information and communication can contribute to this, it is useful to dwell for a moment on that seminal observation for all ethical questions: the distinction between what is and what ought to be; on the fact that there is a vast abyss between the level of corruption today and the corruption-free world we aspire to.

The gap will not be reduced by investigations, pre-dawn raids, in courtrooms or by throwing people into jail. Fighting and preventing fraud also requires the use of information and communication, changing the public's attitude so that the criminal wolf is no longer able to hide beneath the sheep's clothing of being the perpetrator of a victimless crime.

As long ago as 1882, Sir Leslie Stephen, in arguing that 'conduct may be regarded as a function of character and circumstance...' ([74]), concluded that it is futile to forbid or require certain conduct. His conclusion is that moulding and guiding the character of people is at once effective, simple and exhaustive. Trying to control behaviour is to be always trying to adjust to novelty in violation, thus the rule/law grows ever more complex, and is always a compliance and enforcement problem; it always fails in what it was designed to achieve ([75]). The rising sophistication and level of crime — and the tools to fight it — since those words were written are witness to their enduring wisdom.

By 'moulding and guiding the character of people' the first step is taken in addressing that second ethical observation, that of the distinction between being and doing, namely that being is prior to doing. Zero tolerance is required before corruption can really be eliminated. As the Romans said in their time — *Actio sequitur esse* — action follows being. Changing public attitudes and securing the public's commitment to zero tolerance is the *sine qui non* of reducing if not actually eliminating corruption.

Societies and individuals alike learn either by shock or by anticipation. The costs of learning by shock would be much higher than those needed to nurture an anticipatory attitude ([76]).

The noted historian Arnold Toynbee ([77]) might have been referring to corruption rather than nuclear war when he wrote, 'When it has come to be a choice between our abolishing it or its abolishing us, we realise that we can no longer afford to take the line that it is incurable. We have to make attempts to cure it, without letting ourselves be paralysed by our previous conviction that a cure was impossible'.

How difficult will it be to administer the necessary medicine? Easier obviously if there is a proper informed debate in a receptive social context. An advisor to the UK Prime Minister, Anthony Giddens, has claimed 'that corruption is no more common in democratic countries than it used to be — rather, in an information society it is more visible than it used to be' ([78]). Giddens may be right, but unfortunately objective public discussion is nigh on impossible because the debate increasingly resembles what the author David Miller has described as 'the dystopian vision encapsulated in the film 'The Matrix'. Here the reality … is disguised by a sophisticated virtual reality — the matrix — from which it is difficult to break free' ([79]).

To illustrate his point, in Miller's 'matrix world Iraq had and may still have weapons of mass destruction. In the real world it did not. In matrix world there were links between Iraq and Al-Qaeda. In the real world there were not … In matrix world Katherine Gun (an intelligence analyst) and Clare Short (a government minister) are deeply irresponsible for breaching trust and revealing secret information. In the real world they blew the whistle on illegal and immoral official behaviour' ([80]). In Miller's matrix world any government is fair game and financial crimes involving public funds are 'victimless crimes'. Yet the truth is that everyone is a victim, directly or indirectly as a consequence.

Not so long ago the world business community regarded corruption as a necessary evil, with some top executives openly defending the practice of bribing foreign firms with a shrug of the shoulder and an offhand remark: 'I hate to do it … and I hate all the problems it will cause down the line … but I have to' ([81]).

On the other hand, the Anti-Corruption Assistance Centre of Transparency International, Romania, in the report of its first three-month counselling programme, concluded that few of those who came through its doors were able to correctly identify corruption. Only 10 % of the 428 cases presented clear cases of fraud and only seven were brought to the attention of the National Prosecutor's Office ([82]).

International efforts to unearth and eliminate corruption and encourage transparency and accountability are undoubtedly gaining momentum, thanks to an increased understanding of corruption's social and economic costs. The World Bank, for example, now estimates that 11 % of the income of a poor family is paid out in corruption-related costs. Wide-scale endorsement of the 2003 UN convention against corruption and the recent inclusion of anti-corruption in the principles of the United Nations Global Compact confirms that 'there was now a solid consensus behind the need to fight corruption' ([83]).

Clearly there is still a lot of moulding and guiding the character of people to bridge the abyss between what is — endorsement — and what ought to be — implementation.

Here I have to declare an interest as a public relations practitioner who knows something about communication (and a former civil engineer who knows something about building bridges).

In my opinion a wave of anti-corruption enthusiasm is about to break, and if we manage to catch the cresting wave then it will give popular momentum to the anti-corruption message.

Invisible beneath the waves licking the tip of the iceberg represented by the 2003 United Nations Convention Against Corruption, which celebrates its first anniversary in December 2004, and the marketing muscle of the signatories to the Global Compact, certain to promote their good governance practices, are alert entrepreneurs and marketers who will soon send a tidal wave of commercialised anti-corruption messages washing over popular culture.

The tsunami has already arrived in China where a media 'genre' on the specific theme of 'campaigns against corruption and mismanagement' has become the favourite of Chinese publishing houses and television stations. They all thrive on the fact that 'officials who accept kickbacks or bribes have become one of the most maligned groups of social pests in China' ([84]).

The 'genre' is not only emerging elsewhere. The global marketing power of the film industry will shortly be promoting 'Shattered Glass', the gripping and frightening story of (journalist) Stephen Glass' stories about computer hackers and drunken Young Republican orgies — all fabricated — which are as legendary as the fictional notes, phoney corporate websites and bogus business cards he created to cover his fraud ([85]).

Marketing power on this scale sets the media agenda. One just has to recall the public controversy, debate and airtime and column inches that anticipated and followed the film 'The Passion of Christ'. The democratic media do not dictate to people what they should think, but what they should think about.

One of the reasons the market sees a commercial opportunity in anti-corruption now is that people as a whole are fed up with living in an age of fakery, spin and PR manipulation. In Miller's matrix world.

Examples? In Johannesburg the third-world farmers demonstrating at the UN Summit on Sustainable Development in favour of GM foods were 'fake'. Bussed in, marshalled, press released and given T-shirts with English slogans, a language they didn't speak ([86]). In the USA, the Bush administration paid actors to produce fake news reports in favour of its policy on Medicare ([87]). In Turkey, BP's consultation on the Baku, Tiblisi Ceyhan pipeline included a telephone survey of a Turkish village of Hacibayram that 'had been deserted for many years, its houses having fallen into ruins. There were neither telephones nor anyone to answer them' ([88]) ([89]).

Even my fellow public relations practitioners — notorious for offering bribes in cash and kind for media coverage — are saying enough is enough. The Campaign for Media Transparency ([90]) launched by the International Public Relations Association aims to restore the credibility of the media which can only be based on its independent objectivity. Organisations ranging from the Global Alliance for Communication Management, International Press Institute to the International Federation of Journalists have already endorsed the campaign.

International good intentions are fine but what matters most is what happens on the ground. The European Union's agreements to protect Community funds implicitly accept that this will differ from country to country; they refer to effective and equivalent protection of the financial interests of the EU ([91]).

All public relations are local. But the same tactics for information dissemination will not get everyone in every country onto the communication escalator, moving from awareness through understanding to favourability, involvement and finally commitment or action. The principles, however, will be the same. Public relations messages unlike mass advertising are addressed to specific groups of people or special sections of the general public. Information flows through communication. The benefit of the cresting wave of market support for the anti-corruption message is that everyone is heading in the same direction. Each country, each culture will have to determine for itself how best to capitalise on that.

As a former engineer I know that no abyss is so wide or so deep that it cannot be bridged; as a public relations practitioner I know information and communication can bring what is and what ought to be closer together. As someone now engaged in the anti-corruption campaign I can see a rising tide of business and public support, and that catching the cresting wave is a once in a lifetime opportunity not to be missed.

(69) An-Nawawi, *Forty Hadith*, Ezzedin Ibrahim and Denys Johnson-Davies, Trs., (Beirut: Holy Quran Pub., 1991, No 13, p. 56) .

(70) *Samyutta Nikaya* V, 353.35-342.2.

(71) *The Holy Bible*, Luke 6:31 and Matthew 7:12.

(72) Other formulations are: Confucious, *The Analects*, D. C. Lau, tr., (New York: Dorset, 1979), 15.24, p. 135, 'Do not impose on others what you yourself do not desire'. Judaism, Rabbi Hillel, *Shabbat*, 31a, 'Whatever you want people to do to you, do also to them'. Hinduism, *Mahabharata*, XIII 114,8, 'One should not behave towards others in a way which is unpleasant for oneself: that is the essence of morality'. Jainism, *Sutrakritanga*, I, II, 33, 'Human beings should be indifferent to worldly things and treat all creatures in the world as they would want to be treated themselves', Hans Küng, *Global responsibility*, (New York, Crossroad, 1991), p. 59, *Towards a global ethic: an initial declaration* (Chicago, Council for a Parliament of the World's Religions, 1993).

(73) *Critique of practical reason*, A 54.

(74) *The science of ethics*, Sir Leslie Stephen, London, 1882, Books for Libraries Press, Freeport, NY, 1972 (reprint of the 1882 edition).

(75) John H. Bryant, 'A guided conversation on global ethics', International Institute for Public Ethics, *Ethics in the new millennium*, Ottawa, Canada, September 2000.

(76) Mircea Malitza, *The conflicts of the 21st century millennium III*, published by the Black Sea University Foundation, Bucharest, 2002.

(77) Quoted in Mircea Malitza, *The conflicts of the 21st century millennium III*, published by the Black Sea University Foundation, Bucharest, 2002.

(78) Anthony Giddens, 'The runaway world debate: democracy and third way politics': http://www.lse.ac.uk/Giddens/RWDdemocracyandthirdway.htm

(79) David Miller (eds), *Tell me lies: propaganda and media distortion in the attack on Iraq*, Pluto, 2004: http://staff.stir.ac.uk/david.miller/publications/Tellmelies.html

(80) David Miller, *Caught in the matrix*: www.eurozine.com/article/2004-05-03-miller2-en.html

(81) Peter Eigen, Chairman of Transparency International, New York, 24 June 2004.

(82) 'Simona Fodor TI releases anti-corruption guide', *Bucharest Business Review*, 24/30 May 2004.

(83) Peter Eigen, Chairman of Transparency International, New York, 24 June 2004.

(84) 'Campaigns against corruption and mismanagement', *China Daily*, 7 January 2004.

(85) Timothy W. Maier, 'The crumbling of the Fourth Estate': www.insightmag.com/news/2004/05/11/National/The-Crumbling.Of.The.Fourth.Estate-673861.shtml

(86) Jonathan Matthews, 'The fake parade', Freezerbox, 12.3.2002: http://www.freezerbox.com/archive/article.asp?id=254

(87) Robert Pear, 'US videos, for television news, come under scrutiny', *New York Times*, 15 March 2004: http://www.nytimes.com/2004/03/15/politics/15VIDE.html?th

(88) International Fact-Finding Mission, preliminary report, Azerbaijan, Georgia, Turkey pipeline project, Turkey section, Campagna per la Riforma della Banca Mondiale, Kurdish human rights project, The Corner House, Ilisu Dam Campaign, Platform, August 2002.

(89) Ibid, Miller.

(90) www.instituteforpr.com/international. phtml?article_id=bribery_index

(91) Para 3.b, Romanian Law 172 (XVI), No 266, 25 March 2004.

National institutions, investigative and judicial services

Jean-Noël LOUIS,

Member of the French-speaking Brussels Bar, mediator

Jean-Noël LOUIS

has been a member of the French-speaking Brussels Bar since 1973. He is also a mediator for the Brussels Business Mediation Center.

He has specialised in representing officials and other servants of the European Communities for over 25 years. He represents and assists them before Community courts, the European Court of Justice, the Court of First Instance and the European Union Civil Service Tribunal.

He also assists and represents them in the internal proceedings of the various Community institutions, particularly in investigation proceedings opened by the Investigation and Disciplinary Office of the Commission (IDOC) and the European Anti-Fraud Office. He takes part in negotiations at the highest level in the Community institutions and also acts as a consultant for a number of European Community regulatory bodies on matters concerning human resource management and implementation of the Staff Regulations.

'Speech – OLAF-IFJ joint seminar for the OLAF Anti-Fraud Communicators' Network (OAFCN) – 28 October 2005 – Anti-fraud communication and safeguarding the rights of persons under investigation'

A democratic state or community organised in accordance with the rule of law is governed by formal legal rules on life in society. These rules must be adopted by legally appointed public authorities which are also responsible for safeguarding the fundamental rights of every man, woman and child.

In the same way, it must be possible for every citizen to appeal against any decision taken by public or judicial authorities.

A rule-of-law State or Community therefore requires a system of justice that is administered by judges who are independent, impartial and competent, and who give their rulings within a reasonable timeframe.

Article F of the Treaty signed on 7 February 1992 in Maastricht requires the Union to respect the fundamental rights as guaranteed by the European Convention for the Protection of Human Rights and Fundamental Freedoms signed in Rome on 4 November 1950 and as they result from the constitutional traditions common to the Member states, as general principles of Community law.

The press and the judicial system are two fundamental pillars of any democracy.

The ineffectiveness and lack of transparency of the judicial system has repeatedly come under criticism.

At the same time, the role of the press has often been called into question because of the conduct of some journalists and the investigative methods they have not hesitated to employ in flagrant violation of the principles of the presumption of innocence, the confidentiality of investigations and even the independence of the judge.

The European Community is committed to encourage active participatory dialogue on such matters as governance in connection with the fight against corruption, access to justice and the reform of the judicial system. At national level, this commitment is particularly important in relation to the development cooperation programmes implemented by the Union.

OLAF's role in the fight against corruption is therefore a key element in the policy of Community development.

We therefore need to examine the approaches and limits to the information that OLAF can supply to the press to inform the citizens of the Union about the measures taken to combat the fraud that damages the Community's interests.

Under Article 10 of the Convention for the Protection of Human Rights and Fundamental Freedoms (ECHR), everyone has the right to freedom of expression, which includes freedom to hold opinions and to receive and impart information and ideas without interference by public authority.

However, these freedoms entail duties and responsibilities and may be subject to certain formalities, conditions, restrictions or penalties as are laid down by the law and are necessary in a democratic society in the interests of national security, territorial integrity or public safety, for the prevention of disorder or crime, for the protection of heath or morals, for the protection of the reputation or rights of others, for preventing the disclosure of information received in confidence or for maintaining the authority and impartiality of the judiciary.

Consequently, disclosure to the press of information concerning OLAF's activities, especially its investigations, is constrained not only by the need to safeguard the confidentiality of the investigation but also by the need to respect the principle of the presumption of innocence, as well as the right to a fair trial and respect for private life as required under Articles 6 and 8 of the ECHR respectively.

It should also not be forgotten that members of OLAF are subject to the rules and regulations applicable to officials and other servants of the European Communities.

Article 17 of the Staff Regulations prohibits the disclosure of any information brought to the attention of an official or other servant in the course of his or her duties that has not already been made public or is available to the public.

Failure to comply with this obligation is a breach of duty that may result in disciplinary proceedings and, in the most serious cases, in the dismissal of the official or other servant concerned.

It follows that OLAF must appoint from among its members spokespersons who will have the task of disclosing only authorised information concerning ongoing investigations.

It is also necessary to adopt a code of good conduct governing relations between OLAF's spokespersons and the press and clear and transparent rules on the disclosure of information regarding OLAF anti-fraud and anti-corruption investigations that take account of the rights of the defence and the rights enshrined in the ECHR.

National institutions, investigative and judicial services

Lieven MUYLAERT,

Head of the Communication
Department, Belgian Customs
and Excise Administration

Luc DE SOMERE,

Head of Investigation Service,
National Investigation
Department of Belgian
customs and excise

'How the diffusion of information can contribute to optimise the fight against fraud'

Lieven MUYLAERT

Director of the
Communication
Department of the
Belgian customs and
excise administration,
created this
department in August
1992. During the
years that followed
this service became
responsible for
press relations,
internal and external
communication
and public relations.
Before this period
he was involved in
the operational field
of the customs and
excise administration.

Luc DE SOMERE

started his career
with the Belgian
customs and excise
administration in 1971.
He had held several
managerial positions
before. In 1998, he
became Head of the
National Investigation
Directorate of the
Belgian administration
of customs and
excise. Before that, he
had been in charge
of the Prosecution
Unit of the regional
directorate and of the
Investigation Unit of
customs and excise of
the Brussels Region.

Before describing how a well-organised information policy can contribute to fraud prevention it is worth looking at the information policy of the Belgian customs and excise administration in the context of overall communication policy.

The communication policy of any organisation, and particularly that of the administration, is dictated by general policy. Because the customs and excise administration is a government body, its outlook is influenced by what goes on around it — at international, European and national level. In addition, Community law determines much of what European customs administrations do. The policy statement of the Belgian government outlines the themes for the coming term, and Belgian customs, as part of the Federal Public Finance Service (FOD), have to work within this framework.

In addition to the federal policy statement, which, in the area of communication, focuses primarily on implementing e-government, the policy missions of the Federal Public Finance Service and the customs and excise administration are largely responsible for shaping its communication policy.

I think it is therefore useful to reproduce both policy statements to give a clear picture of the parameters within which communication policy can operate.

1. General mission statement of the Federal Public Finance Service

The mission and vision set out as part of the management plan are presented below.

Running a modern State means satisfying collective needs. The main task of the Federal Public Finance Service is to collect and manage a large proportion of the financial resources needed to satisfy these needs.

The principle of parliamentary approval for taxation is one of the fundamental tenets of democracy. By accepting taxation, the citizens demonstrate their desire to live in a society that is mutually supportive. The Federal Public Finance Service strives to collect these taxes fairly and correctly, which means ensuring that every taxpayer pays the tax legally required of him. No more and no less.

The Federal Public Finance Service is also responsible, through the Treasury, for ensuring a balance between the revenue and expenditure of the Federal State. It does so by finding financial resources, through borrowing, to offset deficits, and/or by investing surpluses. As part of its mission it must also carefully and accurately execute payments under the heading of general expenditure, particularly the salaries of State employees and tax refunds.

The tasks of the Treasury also include extensive European and international responsibilities in the economic, financial and monetary field.

The Federal Public Finance Service also assumes other important tasks of public interest. It maintains the public property records (*Patrimoniumdocumentatie*), thus helping to ensure legal certainty, particularly in legal transactions involving goods. When checks are carried out on the flow of goods, the Federal Public Finance Service contributes to the protection of public health, the environment and the safety of people and goods, and particularly the fight against illegal trafficking and terrorism.

The Federal Public Finance Service's mission revolves around the delicate balance between the rights which the law extends to citizens and the obligations it imposes on them. This is at the heart of its mission. Seen in this light, the Federal Public Finance Service must rise to the challenges facing a modern administration that has to keep pace with changes in society, the economy and information and communication technologies.

In line with its continuing commitment to public service, the Federal Public Finance Service applies and guarantees rigour and professionalism in its core activities. It does so, on the one hand, by developing new working methods that are more efficient and more responsive to the needs of the public and, on the other, by fostering a new management culture that places more responsibility on its staff.

Whether or not it succeeds in its task will depend on the Federal Public Finance Service's ability to motivate its staff to pursue the quality and service objectives, particularly by constantly improving the standard of its employees in the most appropriate way.

By fulfilling the legitimate expectations of the public, the Federal Public Finance Service hopes to build a relationship of trust with the citizens to win their support for taxes and ensure that everyone fulfils their obligations by complying fully with the law.

2. General mission statement of the customs and excise administration

We intend to:

make a fundamental contribution to promoting the fiscal, economic and social interests of Belgium and the European Union as they relate to:

- the transport, manufacture, processing and possession of customs and excise goods;

- other regulations connected with this core business.

We shall do this by:

- correctly collecting the taxes for which we are responsible;
- participating in the implementation of measures to protect and stimulate the European market;
- participating in the implementation of measures to protect the public in the field of health, environment and safety;
- ensuring the correct application of the regulations and detecting and combating fraud;
- advising those with political, administrative and economic responsibilities;
- serving the public, with due regard for their legitimate interests.

We stand for:

- professionalism
- fairness
- respect

in our relations with the public, taxpayers and firms;

- a sense of common identity and group loyalty
- team spirit
- personal development

for our staff.

3. Mission statement of the Communication Directorate of the customs and excise administration

We intend to:

contribute to the provision of a general public service and to the personal and professional development of the staff by implementing a communication plan.

We will do this by means of an integrated approach to communications:

internally:

- by providing information and developing our own house style;

externally:

- by providing information to clients, partners, economic operators, the general public and the media;
- by encouraging compliance on the part of economic operators;

- by promoting a positive image to the outside world.

We shall do this:

internally:

- by, for example, publishing our own newsletter;

- by developing standard letters;

- by supporting initiatives to promote the esprit de corps.

externally:

- by producing an annual report for our clients and partners;

- by providing specific information to certain economic operators, in the form of leaflets;

- by providing general information to our non-professional customers;

- by responding to the information needs of the media;

- by encouraging cooperation through consultation;

- by supporting activities to improve the organisation's image.

We believe in:

- courtesy towards our internal customers in a climate of trust that allows everyone to develop their personal and professional potential;

- mutual cooperation with our clients and partners based on a proactive approach and targeted support in achieving social goals through collective action;

- providing a high-quality, efficient and effective service to all our users, within the limits of the law and what is economically and technologically feasible.

On the basis of the two policy statements we now need to work out what the priorities of the Belgian customs and excise administration's communication policy are to be. For the purpose of implementing this policy, two very important principles stand out, in my view. The first is the principle of subsidiarity. Corporate communication should be at the level of the entire organisation. Lower down in the organisation the principle of subsidiarity applies, and communication is best left to the level at which it is most effective. In the administration, which should be regarded as a business unit, people communicate best with specific messages tailored to the target groups.

The second principle is that all of an organisation's communication activities should be integrated. External communication has repercussions on the behaviour of the staff, and vice versa.

The fact that this policy is also service-oriented and customer-centred — meaning that compliance is encouraged — has the advantage that communication policy can derive its own mission statement from this.

A second important aspect of cooperation is promoting compliance. This has very significant implications for the provision of information about fraud prevention, because it is based on the one hand on the importance of prevention, so that essential resources are used for genuine fraud prevention, and, on the other hand, on repression as a means of deterring potential offenders.

One aspect of this information policy on fraud prevention involves presenting an account of activities (the annual report), but another even more important one is responding to the information requirements of the media.

Information is provided primarily after seizures are made. This also helps to enhance the organisation's image, not only for the officials involved in investigations, but also in the eyes of the general public.

We must try to strike a delicate balance here between the public's right to obtain information through the media and the confidentiality of the investigations, which is intended to protect the rights of those involved, and particularly the suspects' rights of defence. We must be very careful when weighing these principles against each other, and both the media and the authorities involved must show proper respect for each other's apparently conflicting objectives. Correct and effective information provision thus depends on a good understanding between the communication partners.

It is clear from the foregoing that information provision is not essential to better fraud prevention, but it is an important pre-condition for justifying and implementing such a policy. In view of the Community law that partly forms the basis of European fraud prevention, OLAF's initiative for this round table conference is to be welcomed.

I therefore wish it every success.

National institutions, investigative and judicial services

Francesco NAPOLETANO,

Director of the Communication and
External Relations Department,
Agenzia delle Dogane, Italy

**Francesco
NAPOLETANO**

is Head of
Communication and
Public Relations for the
Italian Customs Agency
and Director of the
review 'Oltre Frontiera'.
Before joining Italian
customs, he was Head
of Communication
and PR at T-Systems,
a company from the
Daimler-Chrysler and
Deutsche-Telekom
group. Until 2004 he was
Head of the Secretariat
for the Deputy Minister
for Economy and
Finance, Professor
Mario Baldassarri. Mr
Napoletano has also held
several managerial posts
including that of Assistant
Chairman of Iritecna, a
company belonging to
IRI (public institute for
industrial reconstruction).
From 1981 he has also
been the General Consul
of Swaziland in Italy.

'Information partnership'

'Information partnership': A free media must question the performance of public institutions. This can build walls between journalists and institutional spokespersons. But is it possible, through the development of mutual trust and professional respect, to have a shared objective to tell a story fully and with frankness? What is the give and take in such a 'partnership'?

This subject encompasses two ways of thinking that are very different in nature: communication with the public, which is a matter of general interest, and what has become known as media culture, which is increasingly pursuing the objective of tearing down the barriers between the public (and therefore the subject of information) and the private.

The multiplication of the number of information channels, of which there has been an explosion in the last few years, has turned the news into an industry at the expense of investigations and enquiries.

With regard to fraud prevention and the role played by the customs authorities, there is a pressing need to move beyond simply circulating information to creating situations and setting up workshops where representatives from the media, spokespersons from the institutions and companies can meet face to face.

The path to partnership will therefore involve overcoming the temptation for each sector to defend its own independence by opening up opportunities for dialogue and contact between the many seekers of information on fraud prevention activities and making clear the sensitive nature and importance of investigations and enforcement operations.

The seminar that took place on 30 June at the offices of the customs service under the title 'True or false? The customs service's new instruments in the fight against counterfeiting' is an example of how to give representatives from the public and private sectors the opportunity to analyse the socioeconomic impact of counterfeiting and develop new prevention strategies.

Communication was greatly enhanced because the seminar was attended by both the messenger and recipient of the message, which meant that both were able to take on board the feedback immediately and work together on joint communication strategies.

The broad exposure the press can offer should encourage similar initiatives, and we intend to adopt this course to further the development of an information partnership.

Clearly, the media will always determine whether operations conducted by organisations responsible for protecting the general public are viewed positively.

By increasing the number of occasions for coming together and explaining, we can work towards achieving this outcome.

National institutions, investigative and judicial services

Adrian NASTASE,

Prime Minister of Romanian Government,
December 2000–December 2004

Speech: Training seminar for OLAF communicators —
Bucharest, 22 October 2003

'The importance of the measures to combat fraud and to raise awareness of the general public and of journalists in particular'

Ladies and gentlemen, I would first like to welcome the initiative of the representatives of the OLAF communicators network in organising this seminar in Bucharest, the first of its kind to take place in a candidate country awaiting accession to the European Union.

The role of this network is crucial since its main objective is to promote measures to combat fraud and to raise the awareness on the part of the general public and of journalists in particular of the importance of such measures. It is essential that we find efficient means of combating fraud and, at the same time, enlist the support of the representatives of the mass media for this initiative.

The fact that this event is taking place for the first time in Romania is a clear indication of the importance we attach to this extremely complex matter of fraud involving European funds.

I also believe that this gathering provides the best possible proof that the government's desire to stamp out fraud involving European funds has struck a note at international level. The representatives of OLAF consider that our country, although still not part of the European Union, has the capacity and resources to take its place alongside Europe in combating this kind of unlawful conduct.

It is important that, as of now, we make all the necessary preparations for combating fraud, particularly where European funds are involved, starting from a very simple idea, namely that acts of corruption and illegal acts in the economic sphere will not be able to distinguish clearly or draw a line between European monies or funds and other funds, whether belonging to the State or to the private sector. For this reason, the fight against fraud involving

European funds must be very closely linked to the fight against corruption and fraud in general.

The Romanian government has recently taken several measures, some of a regulatory and legislative nature, that will lead to the adoption of a highly ambitious draft law incorporating anti-corruption measures and to the establishment of a number of special anti-corruption agencies — the National Anti-Corruption Office is one example — as well as practical measures at governmental level and, more broadly speaking, at administrative level that will remove some of the more deep-seated causes of corruption. Firstly, transparency of public procurement. Since the introduction of this system, over 190 000 electronic invitations to tender have been issued that have also had a beneficial effect from the budgetary viewpoint: some 30 % of the sums allocated were saved thanks to these procedures.

In addition, we have introduced what we call the 'one-stop-shop reform' consisting of a highly ambitious programme for performing electronically a number of administrative procedures — obtaining forms, completing them, sending them off. Over 165 forms can be obtained through a computerised system that is operational at all times. Similarly, we have also brought in a measure to streamline bureaucracy and have adopted legislation whereby, in so far as the authorities do not respond by the statutory deadline to a request for authorisation or approval, on expiry of the relevant period of 15 or 30 days such authorisation is deemed to have been granted. And so we have the principle of tacit approval when such authorisations are sought, and this clearly puts greater pressure on public officials to comply with the relevant legal provisions and to show greater discipline where relations with the public are concerned.

Following the adoption by referendum of the new Constitution at the end of last week, we have taken the step of partially reorganising three of the main portfolios within the government because we considered that such changes can enhance credibility and efficiency, over and above the personal problems which each of my colleagues concerned will resolve in one way or another, and we felt that such a measure was important, particularly at this very moment.

In addition, we are now going to press ahead with the administrative measures which we wish to take precisely with a view to dispelling various suspicions regarding the operation of a number of national procedures, some of which are very important. For example, road haulage licences have always given rise to some dissatisfaction and tension on account of the fact that demand is very high and supply very low. Since the number of licences is very small, there is pressure to reorganise the system. As of a few days ago, the granting of these licences has also been computerised and is transparent. This provided an opportunity to replace the person who was in charge until recently. This step was taken yesterday.

The Director-General of the national rail company (SNCF) as well as the Director-General of the national investment company have also been replaced in the interests of greater efficiency and of removing certain susceptibilities or sensibilities, both longstanding and more recent, linked to the management of these bodies, which involve, to a large extent, the management of public money and projects of public interest.

My view is that these measures must continue. It is not my or our desire that, with these measures, we should determine individual responsibilities; this is not a matter for the government.

Its problem is to ensure objectivity, credibility and efficiency in a categorical manner. For the rest, it goes without saying that if laws are infringed, these infringements must be closely scrutinised by the institutions of the State responsible for these problems. We had a very clear example of this recently in connection with the tenders for a project in the area of Bușteni concerning a ski slope. There are, of course, two different problems but, as regards use of the Phare funds, Mr Ponta, together with the government's Control Department, has examined, analysed and investigated the case and, from what I have heard, the results are now available and can be made public.

The fight against fraud clearly does not concern Romania alone; it is a problem with which the European Community as a whole is faced. This has been the reason behind our attempts in recent years to identify, in conjunction with representatives of OLAF, the main objectives and instruments for launching a coordinated strategy for preventing and combating such unlawful conduct.

I am pleased to say that we have succeeded in creating a coherent legislative and institutional framework for combating fraud involving Community funds. On the one hand, we need an appropriate panoply of instruments — laws, institutions and an efficient strategy — while, on the other, we are obliged to consolidate our relations with the specialised European agencies.

We have devised the necessary legislative framework and have created institutional machinery for taking comprehensive measures to control and combat fraud involving Community funds and national co-financing budgets. To this end, we have designated as the sole contact point for OLAF the Control Department, whose role is to coordinate the whole range of activities aimed at ensuring effective protection of the financial interests of Romania and the European Union.

In addition, we have adopted the 'Anti-fraud strategy for protecting the financial interests of the European Union in Romania', a document which sets up the institutional structure for tackling fraud. It envisages for the Control Department a structure with two distinct components. The first will have a monitoring function for analysing the way in which funds granted to Romania by the European Union are selected, negotiated and used. The second will have an investigative function for tracking down any cases of fraud in conjunction with our specialised institutions.

We attach special importance to the **aspect of fraud prevention**. To this end, our monitoring arrangements consist of a series of analyses for determining the areas that are predisposed to fraud and for creating an early-warning system. In addition, the objectives of investment projects (building sites, production lines, etc.) carried out with EU funds are vetted with a view to devising a programme of on-the-spot controls. Our specialists carry out certain comparative analyses for all of the consultancy or construction firms and suppliers of software or IT equipment that have been selected to tender for EU financing programmes. Our objective is to identify any links between these firms and individuals exercising public functions. There are, of course, still many aspects to be resolved. But, to my mind, what is important is the fact that we have managed to prepare the way for a well-coordinated strategy for combating fraud.

Ladies and gentlemen, It is very important that we have an appropriate institutional framework, and it matters a great deal that **we should take on board the experience of our European partners**. For Romania, stepping up the process of integration with the European

Union necessitates systematic preparation in all fields and a responsible approach to problems facing the European Community. For me, it is extremely important that we should be receptive and that we should coordinate our working methods and instruments with those of our European partners.

I would like to remind you that, in this connection, the Control Department has signed a cooperation agreement with OLAF for carrying out various preparatory programmes and modules regarding the main aspects of the protection of the financial interests of the European Community. Under this agreement, assistance and advisory services are made available to the other institutions and structures in Romania, in close consultation with OLAF. I am convinced that our specialists, who are involved in the common measures for combating fraud, have taken on board the experience necessary to rationalise relations with OLAF and to meet our common objectives.

To my mind, it is very important that we should hold such meetings and seminars. They allow us to develop our relations with OLAF and to place them on a systematic basis as well as to lay down general guidelines for cooperation in combating the fraudulent use of Community resources.

By way of conclusion, ladies and gentlemen, I would like to assure you of our full willingness to discuss matters and cooperate with the departments of OLAF with a view to preventing and combating the scourge of fraud. In particular, I would like to thank Mr Brüner, the Director-General, for the close interest he has shown in cooperating with our specialised agencies and with the Control Department and to assure him that we will endeavour to draw the necessary conclusions from the experience of other countries as well as from what has happened to date in Romania, so that we can safeguard our credibility in relations with our partners in the European Union, not only at a general political level but also at a much more practical level, namely the use of Community resources.

I wish you much success!

Italo PAPPA,

General, Guardia di Finanza,
Revenue Police, Italy

Lieutenant-
General
Italo PAPPA

is Head of the Training
Institutions and
Schools for the Italian
Guardia di Finanza.
This upper division
coordinates all training
activities in the various
senior operational
and teaching fields
of the Italian financial
and economic police
force. General Pappa
has held important
leading roles in the
Guardia di Finanza,
such as the Chief of
the Italian Central
Inter-regional Division,
which encompasses
all the middle regions
of Italy. Aside from
his military position,
he is also Head of
the Investigative
Office of the Italian
Football Association
(FIGC) which deals
with all irregularities
committed against
fair play, ranging from
disregard for the
rules, to more serious
problems in the world
of Italian football.

'On the side of the honest: how informing and communicating can help to fight and prevent fraud'

My contribution to this interesting round table is based on more than 40 years' experience as an officer of the revenue police. Now at the highest rank in the force, I am responsible for all of the schools and training departments for the more than 70 000 staff, from basic college up to specialised and vocational qualifications [92]. At the end of the 1980s, I was for a few years director of the fifth branch of central headquarters, which at the time included the legislation office and the press and public relations office.

My varied experience has made me an out-and-out supporter of the view that law enforcement authorities need to have their own communication strategies. A strategy of this kind means not just developing ideas but providing resources. It means serving the public. It means guaranteeing the independence, subject of course to the legal framework in force, of the investigative function that forms part of any system founded on the values of democracy and the rule of law.

I would like to thank OLAF for this exemplary initiative, and for embarking on a strategy of communication and information which is intended to help prevent fraud affecting the Community budget, and which can only benefit the process of European integration. A recent opinion poll carried out by the European Commission [93] has made it clear that OLAF is on the right track here: the public need to be aware of the effort being made by their domestic investigation services and by OLAF to protect their finances from criminal attack. They need to be informed using the channels and methods of the media society in which all of us, like it or not, have been living for some time [94]. Voter turnout at the recent European elections has made it plain enough, I think, that government has to grow closer to the citizens and to make itself more comprehensible. The quality and the great authority of the contributions to the seminar on communication as a tool in the fight against fraud, organised by OLAF last year in Romania, are only one example [95]. The fact that a head of State, a head of government and the most senior representatives of the Community anti-fraud bodies should decide to take part in a seminar of that kind merely confirms that OLAF has taken the right course.

So let me begin by saying, without hesitation, that I am convinced of the importance of communication and information as a tool for the prevention of fraud affecting the Community's financial interests, even before measures are taken to detect and punish it. But of course this work has to be conducted within the inviolable boundaries laid down by the law, that is to say the domestic and the Community legal order ([96]).

Let me try to justify this position from my own experience.

When I took up the post that made me responsible for the press office at the central headquarters of the revenue police, communication and public information were not among the great traditions of the illustrious force on which I have the honour to serve. The watchword was to appear and talk in public as little as possible. But the policy of keeping one's own counsel, taking the part of the *grande muette* ([97]), was no longer suited to the times.

The citizens needed to know what the State was doing for them despite all the difficulties. This included the work being done by the revenue police, quietly, with many a sacrifice, 24 hours a day, 365 days a year. We had to overcome the sense of resignation to the worst that some news reports could so easily induce, and indeed often still can induce ([98]), and to raise the level of information among the public, who were entitled to know what the law enforcement authorities were doing, often in silence, on their behalf. In 1988 I decided that for the first time in its centuries-long history the revenue police too would mount a publicity campaign.

Our own very sound staff were highly competent and no less enthusiastic, though by comparison with what the force has now the resources we had available then can only be described as rough and ready. We used the same advertising agency that handled the image of the *Carabinieri* police force: while in substance the *Carabinieri* continued to observe the motto 'obey in silence and in silence die' (*usi obbedir tacendo e tacendo morire*), they had nevertheless adapted to the times and had already achieved a high degree of professionalism in information and institutional communication. We launched a campaign that ran in the main national weeklies until the end of the year. The themes were drug trafficking and tax evasion ([99]).

I do not think it is immodest to say that that was the starting point for a new era in the strategy of communication and public information pursued by the revenue police. It amounted to a cultural revolution, and since then the new course has enjoyed steadily growing resources — though of course it could do with more — and has performed an important service to the force itself and to the country.

Faced with continuous growth in the number of drug users, the country seemed to be inherently helpless. But this was a serious problem that affected all layers of society without exception, from the best-off classes to the poorest, whatever their cultural level and wherever they lived.

If it had not been for the forces of law and order, with the revenue police in the frontline, who did regularly announce drug seizures and arrests, the people of Italy would have had the strong impression that they had been abandoned to their own devices.

But these news items still came over to the public as one-off events, strokes of luck rather than the result of long and meticulous preparation.

Not everyone realised then the scale of the work being undertaken by the revenue police to confront this danger, which threatened, and still threatens, not just the health and the lives of young people but also the stability of society and the democratic system.

The drugs campaign sought to address the millions of readers of the main national weeklies, in order to reassure the public that the revenue police were working to reduce the danger posed by criminal organisations, though without self-congratulation and without cherishing any illusion that they might be able to do the job alone and without the support of the population.

A similar line was taken on tax evasion, which is closer to the subject of this round table: the figures, although they were regularly published in the mass media, often gave the impression that government did not have the tools it needed to be able at least to contain the problem within limits. The number of tax dodgers was high then and it is so now, but without proper information it might have grown even more gigantic, suggesting that the taxman could be evaded in Italy without any real risk. That has not in fact been true for some time, but potential dodgers might have been encouraged to make the leap from legality into illegality, believing that in any event they would never be detected and would have proved themselves shrewder than those who paid their taxes properly.

Nor did everyone realise that by taking action against tax dodgers the Revenue Police was acting in the interests of those who did pay their taxes.

The concept that the Revenue Police tried to get across in this first use of advertising and mass communication was that those who avoided contributing to the revenues of the State were depriving the country of the resources it needed to progress, or in other words stealing from all their fellow citizens ('With you, against the people who want to make you pay their taxes too').

This basic concept, associated with the emotive image of a man in a white collar being arrested, clearly also set out to deter potential tax dodgers by drawing attention, especially in the case of large-scale evasion, to the seriousness of the crime, something most people often underestimate.

The approaches to the two problems, tax evasion and drugs, were intended to involve the reader. The two advertisements began 'With you, against the people who want to make you pay their taxes too' and 'With you, against the people who want to gamble with the lives of your children', and both ended 'The Revenue Police. On the side of the honest'. They tried in a very simple and direct way to show who were the real enemies that the Revenue Police wanted to confront, with the support of the healthy section of the public.

In direct, dramatic images based on journalistic reporting, the force presented itself as one of the main allies of the 'honest', with them in the frontline against the destructive forces that stood in the way of the free development and growth of the country.

Hard images of a boy helping a girl to inject herself with heroin, or an arrested white-collar worker between two police officers ([100]), appeared to be taken from newspaper reports (appeared to be, because for obvious reasons of privacy the photographs were reconstructed using actors). They were accompanied by the following texts: 'With you, against the people who want to gamble with the lives of your children'.

The revenue police are locked in close combat with the merchants of death who gamble with people's lives, and especially the lives of young people. Against the powerful and battle-hardened drug organisations, the revenue police are fighting back with skilled men and modern technology, and they are getting results. To win a war where the victims may be our own children, the revenue police are hitting the drug traffic where it is most intense, at border crossings and on the seas. Along the 8 500 kilometres of the country's coastline, the men with the yellow flame badge stand guard day and night in a spirit of self-sacrifice and dedication, combining efficiency and competence with military discipline and devotion to duty. The revenue police are building a steadily more effective wall of checks and inspections against the entry of drugs, so that all those who fear this threat to their own children — and they make up the vast majority of the Italian people — will be able to feel safer.

'The revenue police. On the side of the honest'.

'With you, against the people who want you to pay their taxes too'.

The revenue police are defending your interests against those who try to escape the taxman and offload their own tax burden onto you. To do the work to supply the public services that everyone expects, the State needs revenue, and the State's revenue comes from taxation. Anyone who does not contribute in proportion to their own income is depriving the State of part of the wealth that belongs to everyone. It's a bit like stealing from all your fellow citizens. The men in the yellow flame badge are acting against the dodgers every day, more and more, and by doing so they are promoting social justice and fairness for everyone. So that all those who pay their proper share of taxation — and they make up the vast majority of the Italian people — will be able to pay a bit less.

'The revenue police. On the side of the honest'.

The campaign was presented to the media in August 1988, before it appeared in the main national weeklies, at a press conference held for the first time at central headquarters.

Reaction in the press and on radio and television was lively: there was favourable coverage for the two themes, which were of great current interest, and special and positive emphasis on the initiative taken by the revenue police to enlist the public in its own battles in defence of the values of our society ([101]).

In the October 1988 issue of *Salve*, the monthly health supplement of *Corriere della Sera*, there was a full feature on the drug campaign, under the headline 'The Yellow Telephones'.

The magazine had grasped the social significance of the campaign, over and above the publicity message, and tried to provide a practical contribution to the fight against the spread of drug addiction by itself publishing the telephone numbers of the Drug Field Units (GOAs) of the revenue police, asking anyone who might have information that might be useful for the launch of investigations into large-scale 'death trafficking' to contact the specialised revenue police departments (the writer correctly pointed out that small-scale drug dealing could be better dealt with by other police departments).

From a survey of a sample of people interviewed by a market research company after the campaign was over, it emerged that although the themes chosen, tax evasion and drugs, were unappealing, the campaign was more 'interesting', 'clear and comprehensible', 'credible and convincing' than the average for advertising in Italy that year, 'giving a good impression of the revenue police and sound information on its activities'.

That result, taken together with the gap between the results of the enquiry into the awareness of the revenue police and the approval rating given to the revenue police by the citizens for its role in society, disproved an old myth that my staff and myself had refused to believe, namely that the tasks performed by the revenue police, especially in tax matters, meant that the officers of the revenue police, like all tax investigators, would innately and necessarily be disliked by citizens and taxpayers. We refused to believe it, and the facts proved us right, because over time we succeeded in demonstrating the high social content of the difficult daily work done by the revenue police in the sole interest not of a tyrannical State but rather of a State that existed to manage and protect the well-being of the community.

Even more solid evidence of the results of the revenue police communication strategy in the second half of the 1980s came when *Corriere della Sera*, on the basis of a survey it had had carried out, awarded its 'Likeability Prize' (*Premio simpatia*) to the revenue police, something that would have seemed incredible only a few years earlier.

'The force, which was incorporated into the armed forces by Giolitti in 1906', wrote the author, Costantino Muscau ('Carabinieri overtaken', *Corriere della Sera*, 12 June 1990, p. 11), 'is nevertheless the one preferred by families and friends advising young people on a choice of career, because "it is a fine force, less dangerous (than the other two), pays well, does a good job"', and the members 'do a responsible job, are intelligent and well-trained'. 'One big danger: being vulnerable to corruption'.

'Of the negative factors indicated for the three forces,' writes Muscau, '63 % of the 1 280 respondents indicated corruption as the great danger facing the revenue police'.

A few years before, this finding would have made the revenue police stiffen into an embarrassed and offended silence; but this time the force, quoted by Muscau, provided the illuminating comment that 'this is only natural. A coalminer runs the risk of contracting silicosis, and in the same way it is fairly probable that a revenue police officer may be tempted by corruption. The people we deal with are entrepreneurs, business people — money, to put it in a nutshell; so the temptation is constant, in the nature of things. But when there has been corruption we have been the first to denounce it publicly: look at the oil scandal eight years ago'.

Muscau goes on, 'At headquarters they add jokingly — though maybe not entirely jokingly — "When will there be a book written telling the story of all the daily acts of heroism of our officers in their dealings with certain bewitching charmers?"'.

The spontaneity of this answer from the revenue police illustrates the character of the new way of standing calmly and confidently before public opinion, in an authority which has never had anything to hide but which has not always been able to make the broader public aware of its worth. The campaign around the slogan 'The revenue police. On the side of the honest' came a few years before the historic period known as 'Clean Hands'. This is certainly a coincidence. But it is no coincidence that in that period as always the revenue police played their role as guarantors of the rule of law, even though, like many other authorities, they too paid their tribute in terms of people who had succumbed to temptation. True to its traditions, the force succeeded in fighting the disease of corruption in its own ranks. The disease is one that can never be eradicated, anywhere in the world, but the revenue police have always combated it and always will combat it with all the resources at their disposal.

That, then, is what I wanted to say about an aspect of my experience in a force that has made a major contribution to the fight against fraud affecting the Community budget. The revenue police have also made a huge contribution to the building of the Community anti-fraud structures, often forgoing some of their best officers to put them at the disposal of the Community institutions. Among their many tasks the revenue police guard one of the longest of the Community's frontiers. It is to be hoped that this contribution will serve as strong and determined encouragement for the continued development of the OLAF Anti-Fraud Communicators Network; I myself will lend every possible personal and official support to this policy of bringing the public and European Union investigators closer together.

I am pleased that the key words associated with such a communication and information policy should be 'openness, service to citizens and prevention'. The only limit to such openness should be, let me say it again, strict respect for investigations in progress, for the Community and domestic rules on the confidentiality of enquiries, and last but not least for the inviolable fundamental rights of individuals.

But the principle that our conduct must be strictly in accordance with the law does not mean we have to accept the view put forward by those who would have us believe, or who perhaps naively believe themselves, that in an age of globalisation of information as of other areas investigators should continue to play the *grande muette*: keeping silent, deprived of any channel for communicating and providing information to the public that would enable them where necessary to offset or respond to the wave of information or disinformation that sometimes submerges and interferes with the proper conduct of the most delicate operations and investigations.

To be quite honest, on the basis of my own experience, which for my sins now extends over nearly half a century, I do not believe that this view is put forward in good faith. Nor do I believe it is merely a matter of naivety. With the sharpness of an old investigator, I am more inclined to think that those who advance this argument want to prevent any sort of communication on the part of investigation services, domestic or Community, not so much in order to protect noble and indisputable principles, but instead for the rather less noble reason that they hope this will leave the field clear for others to talk about the work of the investigation services and law enforcement, if necessary via the 'leaks' that are always going to remain possible, and often in ways that are not completely disinterested.

That is not a service to the public. It is not a tool for preventing fraud. And it is not a method of upholding the law.

---

(92) http://www.gdf.it/

(93) http://europa.eu.int/comm/anti_fraud/press_room/eurobar/en.html

(94) A. Butticé, 'Strategia della comunicazione e comunicazione strategica', in 'La pubblica informazione militare nei 12 Paesi della CE', Rivista Militare, 1992.

(95) http://europa.eu.int/comm/anti_fraud/olaf-oafcn/seminars/bu_en.html

National institutions, investigative and judicial services

(⁹⁶) See A. Butticé, 'Forze dell'ordine e mass media: il limite del segreto al diritto di informazione dell'opinione pubblica', in *Rivista della Guardia di Finanza*, No 6/1989.

(⁹⁷) The 'great mute', as the French army was described — but in the time of Napoleon!

(⁹⁸) Eurobarometer survey, 'Attitudes related to defrauding the European Union and its budget: public opinion in the Member States' and 'Public opinion in the acceding and candidate countries' (Brussels, European Commission, 2003), http://europa.eu.int/comm/anti_fraud/press_room/eurobar/en.html

(⁹⁹) A. Butticé, *Forze dell'Ordine e comunicazione: Polizia di Stato, Carabinieri, Guardia di Finanza, Opinione Pubblica e Mass-Media* (Rome, Bariletti, 1990).

(¹⁰⁰) Of course the arrested man was an actor.

(¹⁰¹) Headlines of the main reports, 'First publicity campaign at end of month — Revenue police step into limelight — Like other State bodies, the revenue police have decided to promote their image. They have taken on the Ayer agency for the job. The slogan of the two advertisements will be "On the side of the honest"' (*Italia Oggi*); 'Revenue police advertise: "Allies of the honest" Against drugs and tax evasion' (*Il Giornale*); 'Campaign on drugs and tax — New "image" for revenue' (*Il Messaggero*); 'Fight against drugs and tax evasion. Revenue police use advertising — Advertisement against drugs' (*Il Mattino*); 'Revenue, advertisements against dodgers and drugs' (*La Stampa*); 'Advertising campaign on tax and drugs to be launched — Revenue police identified 1 378 all-out tax dodgers last year' (*La Gazzetta del Mezzogiorno*); 'Image campaign to be launched — Revenue police use advertising against dodgers and drugs — Bringing the force closer to the public' (*Il Popolo*); 'Revenue police launch "poster campaign" to make themselves better known' (*Il Gazzettino*); 'Tax evasion — the force of advertising' (*Il Piccolo*); 'Revenue police seek coooperation and advertise for themselves' (*Messaggero Veneto*); 'Revenue police campaign to draw attention to their activities — Revenue police on the side of the honest' (*La Sicilia*); 'Prestige security force seeks new "image" — Revenue police intensify fight against drugs and tax evasion — Following example of *Carabinieri* and Navy — To draw attention to work that most often goes unacknowledged — Main areas covered — Two messages to newspaper readers' (*Giornale di Brescia*); 'Advertisements to beat pushers and tax dodgers' (*Il Giornale di Napoli*); 'Revenue police: Campaign to combat drugs and dodgers' (*Ore 12*); 'Slogan designed to publicise revenue police — Revenue police on the side of the honest' (*Il Tempo*); 'Revenue police advertisement: united against tax dodgers' (*Il Sole 24 Ore*); 'Revenue police on the side of the honest' (*Patria*); 'Revenue police advertising campaign — The real image — Public participation and involvement among objectives of image campaign launched by revenue police as part of war on drugs and tax evasion' (*Ordine Pubblico*).

Lieve PELLENS,

Spokesman,
Federal Prosecutor's Office, Belgium

'The press magistrate'

Lieve PELLENS

has been working as a Federal Magistrate at the office of the Belgian Federal Prosecutor since January 2003, in the International Cooperation in Criminal Matters Unit.

From 1993 until 2003 she was a prosecutor in Brussels and specialised in prosecuting cases of sexual delinquency and trafficking of human beings.

After obtaining a law degree in 1990 she worked for a couple of years as a lawyer. She was designated spokesperson for the Prosecutor's Office in Brussels in 1998 and now for the Federal Prosecutor's office.

Introduction

Clear communication with citizens through the press is essential in our democratic system. Justice can no longer remain deaf and dumb or be perceived as being in an ivory tower. Information must be provided on legal procedures to ensure that those involved are informed of all aspects of the administration of justice. The press judges, together with the spokesmen of the public prosecution service and the courts, therefore play a key role. Precise and accurate information and a simple, clear explanation of how justice is administered are in everyone's interests.

The term 'press magistrate' covers both the spokesmen for the public prosecution service and the press judges. Unlike the prosecution service spokesmen, press judges do not have any legal status.

1. Historical background

Since 1953, the procedure for providing information on court cases has been regulated by three circulars issued by the Ministers for Justice.

A circular issued on 24 July 1953 by Justice Minister Du Bus de Warnaffe set out, for the first time, the conditions under which 'passive information' can be provided by the public prosecution service. 'Passive information' is information supplied at the request of the press and press releases issued to provide information on and explanations of criminal cases that arouse strong public interest.

This circular stipulated that both the police and the public prosecution service were authorised to provide information to the press subject to certain conditions, except in cases in which professional secrecy in the strict sense of the term was required: defence rights had to be respected, no personal opinion could be given, and information on a case currently being examined could only be provided if authorised by the magistrate in charge of the case, and then only if justified on the grounds of the public interest.

A circular issued on 9 April 1965 by Justice Minister Vermeylen sought to create a climate of mutual trust between the press and the courts and introduced public prosecution spokesmen.

A circular issued on 15 June 1984 by Justice Minister Gol once again underlined the need for both judges and prosecutors to exercise caution and discretion. No statement of any kind could be made to the press without first being expressly approved by the officer's superior and/or the examining magistrate in a legal proceeding.

Without prejudice to the circulars applicable at the time, in March 1993 the presiding judges issued a common circular containing guidelines for 'active information', that is, participating in a radio or television debate or granting interviews to the press. 'Active information' could not be given without the approval of the officer's superior, who had a right of veto.

A change was introduced when legal practitioners signed a declaration of intent on 29 February 1996. The then Minister for Justice, Stefaan De Clerck, gave priority to improving communication and the public perception of the administration of justice. The task force set up for this purpose drew up a consensual text establishing the function of press judge in addition to press magistrate for the public prosecution and spokesman for the bar. This text was submitted to the presiding judges of the courts of appeal at the beginning of August 1996 with a request to them to seek judges to perform this function on a 'voluntary' basis in order to 'specifically implement the initiative' from September 1996.

'Press judge' meant a judge acting as the press spokesman, preferably on a voluntary basis and preferably someone with several years' experience in different fields of law, willing to perform additional duties 'not within fixed working hours' and in a position of authority (preferably not the presiding judge himself), assisted by an administrative assistant (a post that has not yet been created) and a court press clerk.

Apart from passive information provided at the request and on the initiative of the media (information on the progress of hearings of certain cases, communication of decisions consisting simply of the necessary objective information (such as possible means of appeal) without additional comment, communication of certain actions taken by magistrates while safeguarding the privacy of the parties concerned and observing all the relevant legal provisions, and the entering into of agreements regarding photos and/or recordings in the courtrooms), scope is also left for own initiative.

'Own initiative' meant providing general information on the court (such as on the roles of the different players and on court procedures and rules), rectifying incorrect, inaccurate or incomplete information, liaising with other press spokesmen and protecting the magistrates in charge of a particular case.

The function of press judge was to be introduced 'spontaneously and gradually'.

With the passing of the Franchimont law on 12 March 1998 on the improvement of the investigation and examination stages of criminal proceedings, public prosecutors were required to provide information to the press during preliminary investigations, enquiries or examinations. A legal status was immediately established for public prosecution spokesmen.

The legal framework, nature, content and form of the communications to be provided by the press spokesmen of both the public prosecution service and the police were stipulated in joint circular 7/99 issued by the Minister for Justice and the Public Prosecutors' Association on 30 April 1999.

2. The Belgian legal framework for the function of press magistrate

These guidelines apply to preliminary investigations, held as part of a judicial enquiry or examination, conducted to investigate infringements and the perpetrators thereof, gather evidence and do everything necessary to initiate criminal proceedings.

In accordance with Articles 28(d)(3) and 57(3) of the criminal procedure code, the public prosecution service is responsible for providing information on criminal investigations. However, subject to certain conditions, it can delegate the function of spokesman to the police. In certain cases, particularly sex cases, in principle this function cannot be delegated. In judicial examinations, the authorisation of the examining magistrate is always required.

Under Belgian law, during a judicial examination the task of providing information falls not to the examining magistrate himself, but to the public prosecutor subject to the approval of the examining magistrate.

The examining magistrate is in charge of the investigation, which means that no information can be divulged on the investigation without his agreement.

The public prosecutor can designate one or more members of the public prosecution service as substitutes to act as permanent or temporary press spokesmen. These spokesmen are press magistrates, as are the magistrates in charge of relations with the press during legal proceedings. Nowadays all public prosecution services in Belgium have spokesmen. Some of them also hold daily press conferences.

Public prosecutors on duty at night or at the weekend may also brief the press, as may those who are personally in charge of an investigation that is being covered in the media. The criminal procedure code stipulates that the public prosecution service or, if duly authorised, the police, can brief the press on criminal investigations 'if it is in the public interest'. In doing so, the spokesman must ensure that 'the presumption of innocence, the defence rights of the defendant, the suspect, the victims and third parties, privacy and human dignity are respected. As far as possible, the identity of the persons named in the case must not be revealed.'

The circular of 30 April 1999 describes these obligations in more detail. Some of the main stipulations are set out below.

'2.2.1.   The spokesman must ensure that the interests of the investigation are not damaged. He must also ensure that the rights of the suspects, the victims and the witnesses are respected in any communication to the press.

2.2.2.   The spokesman must ensure that the right to information is respected subject to the limitations stipulated in point 2.2.1. Correct observance of the procedure for providing information may also be in the interests of the investigation.

2.2.3. Appropriate communication of information increases citizens' confidence in the legal institutions.'

'7.1. Basic principles

The task of the public prosecutor and of the duly authorised police spokesman is to provide the press with correct and objective information, taking into account the nature of the medium in question. A refusal to provide information may lead to the publication of false information which is difficult to correct. Also, the investigation may be weakened by the publication of erroneous information. In view of the legal requirements mentioned in point 6, when providing any information on court proceedings it is advisable to exercise discretion and reserve, to be careful as to the exact language used and to avoid making personal judgments.

As regards the victim and their family, no details may be provided that might lead to secondary victimisation. In the spirit of Article 3 of the law on the function of the police referred to in point 6.4, their right to privacy must be guaranteed.

As far as possible, care should be taken to prevent them from learning directly from the press certain sensitive facts or matters relating to the case in which they are involved. If the press appears to know the victim's identity, it can be asked not to reveal it until the immediate family members are informed by the court or administrative authorities.

The only information that can be provided to the press without authorisation is the sex, age and, in some cases, the place of residence of the persons involved in the case (see point 7.2), bearing in mind that no information should be provided that could enable them to be identified. Personal data such as ethnic origin, nationality and sexual orientation may not be provided unless they are relevant.

(…)

Comments on Article 7

To ensure that the presumption of innocence is respected, it is advisable always to state that the person concerned is only suspected of committing a particular act. If the accused denies the charge or puts forward grounds for excuse or justification, this should be specified.

Article 3a of the preliminary title of the criminal procedure code requires the legal authorities to 'treat victims of infringements and their families properly and conscientiously, in particular by providing them with the necessary information'. If those involved in a case learn important information (not protected by the secrecy requirements for investigations) through the press, this may do additional harm and lead to an irreparable breakdown of trust. A good way of avoiding this can be to impose an information embargo or black-out. It is not always possible to guarantee the anonymity of those involved in a case, particularly if the person in question plays an important part in society or is a public figure. However, as far as possible identity should remain secret.'

The 1999 circular also provides guidelines on whether or not the press should be briefed on criminal investigations. Thus, the public prosecutor 'may decide to make statements if a particular criminal offence has aroused strong public interest and/or if it is preferable to inform the public of the policy adopted in such cases' (point 7.2).

3. Who information can be given to

In principle, information on court proceedings is provided only to professional journalists and trainee journalists recognised by the Belgian journalists' union (AGJPB). Only information on cases relating to driving, housebreaking, the discovery of illegal immigrants and any other case that does not fall within the province of the specialised criminal investigation police may be given to non-professional journalists provided they are associated with one of the media. Foreign journalists can only be given this information if they hold an official press card.

In their general relations with the press, however, spokesmen treat all journalists on an equal footing. Exceptions to this are, for example, where a particular journalist claims exclusive rights, provided the general right to information is respected.

4. The ways in which information is provided

It is up to the public prosecutor or the authorised police spokesman to decide which communication technique it is appropriate to use, depending on the case in question and the different interests to be taken into account.

The communication techniques used can be classified as follows:

- 'on the record' communication: the spokesman can be officially cited;

- 'off the record' communication: the information can be used but the spokesman cannot be cited; the information provided must enable the journalist to correctly reproduce the information provided on the record;

- background information: this concerns information which cannot be published by the journalist and is given to him solely in order to extend his frame of reference and understanding of the case;

- embargo: a temporary silence regarding certain information, that is, an agreement to postpone making it public; the public prosecutor or spokesman can, in exceptional circumstances and on reasoned grounds, specify the conditions for an embargo, either on an individual basis with a particular journalist in possession of exclusive information or collectively with all the media;

- black-out: temporary silence on all information; in very exceptional cases, the public prosecutor or police spokesman may announce a temporary complete black-out.

The circular stipulates that if a journalist fails to respect these conventions, the public prosecutor or police spokesman may report this fact to the Belgian journalists' union (AGJPB) so that the case can be examined by its ethics committee and by the editor of the press organisation concerned.

5. The public's right to information

The question arises whether journalists can publish information at any time on the progress of a legal investigation or court case, that is, whether the public has the right to be informed at all times, at the risk of influencing the investigation or the court case if the information published has any bearings on them.

Since the *Sunday Times* v *the United Kingdom* judgment handed down by the European Court of Human Rights (ECHR) on 26 April 1979, it has been accepted that the press can and indeed should disclose information on court cases subject to certain conditions, in particular respect for the presumption of innocence.

The ECHR judgment states that 'There is general recognition of the fact that the courts cannot operate in a vacuum. Whilst they are the forum for the settlement of disputes, this does not mean that there can be no prior discussion of disputes elsewhere, be it in specialised journals, in the general press or amongst the public at large. Furthermore, whilst the mass media must not overstep the bounds imposed in the interests of the proper administration of justice, it is incumbent on them to impart information and ideas concerning matters that come before the courts just as in other areas of public interest. Not only do the media have the task of imparting such information and ideas: the public also has a right to receive them.' In this judgment, the ECHR states that Article 10 of the European Convention on Human Rights and Fundamental Freedoms guarantees not only the right to inform the public but also the right of the public to be properly informed. It would not be realistic to expect the media to wait for the outcome of a court case that is arousing strong public feeling before reporting on it. It therefore seems disproportionate to apply to the press the concept of 'contempt of court' existing in English law, aimed at protecting the administration of justice when articles are published on a court case.

But the judicial authorities sometimes ask the media temporarily to refrain from publishing certain information in order to protect the interests of an investigation or of one or more persons. This is known as an embargo.

This concept is defined in the joint circular issued by the Minister for Justice and the chief public prosecutors on 30 April 1999 as 'a temporary silence, that is, an agreement to postpone publication of certain information'.

According to the AGJPB's Ethics Committee, a request for an embargo must be respected provided that:

- it has been made in the appropriate way;

- the request is a reasoned one with precise content;

- it applies to the media as a whole, that is editors have reached agreement on the request for an embargo;

- it is for a limited time period.

6. The right to anonymity

Certain categories of person are protected by the right to anonymity; in particular victims of sex scandals, minors under youth protection rules and persons involved in divorce or legal separation proceedings.

7. Specific precautions regarding certain persons

Certain persons, while not protected by the right to anonymity, should nevertheless be treated with some discretion by the press. They are victims of crime, accidents or catastrophes, parties to civil proceedings, suicides, foreigners, suspects, accused persons and convicted persons.

8. Suspects and accused persons

With some exceptions, legal proceedings are public, meaning that in principle the names of accused persons are made public. Usually the media cite in full the names of accused persons, except for minors and victims of sex crimes, while procedures vary for suspects waiting to appear in court.

Both suspects and accused persons have the right to be presumed innocent.

9. Presumption of innocence

Strictly speaking, there is no legislation requiring the press to respect the presumption of innocence principle for accused or convicted persons. Only public authorities are subject to this obligation. Magistrates and the police, in particular, must consider an indicted or accused person to be innocent until convicted.

However, case-law requires the media to observe the presumption of innocence principle. In the landmark *Worm* v *Austria* judgment of 29 August 1997, the European Court of Human Rights confirmed that journalists must also respect the presumption of innocence, as defined in Article 6 of the European Convention on Human Rights, even for public figures and politicians. In this case, an Austrian journalist had published articles attacking a former finance minister who was tried by a magistrates' court comprised of two lay and two professional judges. By doing so, the journalist considerably reduced the politician's chances of having a fair trial and conducted a kind of pseudo-trial in the media, which, according to the ECHR, threatened to undermine public trust in the role of the courts in administering justice in criminal law cases.

The civil courts require the press to respect the presumption of innocence as required by Article 1382 of the Belgian civil code. A charge that is dismissed as unfounded may be considered an injury for which damages can be claimed. In cases of this kind, judges therefore take into account the tone of the information, any confusion between facts and comments, the headlines and sub-headlines used and the illustrations published.

10. Slander, defamation, insults and other similar accusations

Articles 443 et seq. of the Belgian criminal code define certain specific offences against a person's reputation or honour which violate the right to privacy. The said offences are slander, defamation, insults, malicious prosecution and malicious disclosure.

(a) Slander

Slander means maliciously imputing to a particular person a precise fact that is of a nature to undermine that person's honour or to expose them to public contempt, in cases in which evidence can legally be provided, for example, a person is accused of having committed a tax fraud but no evidence is provided to back this up.

(b) Defamation

Defamation means maliciously imputing to a particular person a precise fact that is of a nature to damage that person's honour or expose them to public contempt, in cases in which evidence cannot legally be provided. For example, someone is accused of having committed an offence but legal evidence cannot be supplied because the statute of limitations period has expired.

(c) Insult

An insult is the disclosure of an imprecise fact damaging to another person's honour.

(d) Malicious prosecution

Malicious prosecution is slander in the form of a statement made to the authorities.

(e) Malicious disclosure

Malicious disclosure means making a true fact known to the public at large solely with the aim of damaging another person.

When the press is guilty of such offences, they are said to constitute criminal declarations of opinion by the press or, more simply, press offences. Article 150 of the Belgian Constitution provides for a privilege of jurisdiction for these press offences. They can only be tried in an assize court, except for press offences of a racist or xenophobic nature, which come under the jurisdiction of the magistrates' courts. Under current case-law, only criminal declarations of opinion in the press in the strict sense of the word, rather than in the audio-visual media, fall within this category.

Press offences coming under the jurisdiction of the assize courts are rarely, if ever, tried. However, legal proceedings based on Articles 1382 and 1383 of the Belgian civil code can be brought against journalists who have committed such infringements.

Conclusion

Belgian legislation on the function of the press magistrate seeks to establish a harmonious relationship between the Belgian judiciary authorities and the press as regards the communication of information on court cases. The advisability of providing such information and the content of the information given must in all cases be assessed in the light of the public interest. And the public interest in this context must be the result of a balance, necessarily established by the public prosecutor, between ensuring that justice is properly administered and that accurate and reliable information is transmitted.

National institutions, investigative and judicial services

Victor PONTA,

Doctor (PhD), Chief of Prime Minister's Control Department, April 2001–March 2003, Chief of Government's Control Department, March 2003–December 2004, Minister Delegate for the Control of the International Grant Programmes' Implementation and for Monitoring the Application of the *Acquis Communautaire*, 2004
Speech — Training seminar for OLAF communicators — Bucharest, 22 October 2003

'Information and communication: why an investigative service should have the powers and the duty to communicate its work and what its limits are'

Ensuring transparency in decision-making and information at public administration level, as well as at the control and audit establishment level, is handled in Romania, at national level, by the constitution. The free access to information of public interest that deals with transparency in public administration, of conflict of interests and control of the dignitaries' fortune law is also addressed through the constitution. At an international level, transparency is dealt with through the pacts which Romania has adhered to.

At the present time, Romania has set up audit and control procedures, such as the prime ministerial inspection and follow-up to the transparent use of Community funds department, the anti-corruption national prosecutor's office or the national control authority which looks after the correct use of European funds.

The activity of the Transparency Committee, established this year and coordinated by the European Integration Ministry, meets every three months to find efficient solutions regarding the administration of Community funds, and follows and disseminates information about the administration of these funds in the context of an 'international market'.

The problems related to transparency that appear during an inquiry in investigative services of these establishments are obviously questioned, because the information, through its own character, is split into three segments: confidential information, restrictive information and public information.

The transparency of an inquiry made by investigative services relates to information, and information means communication.

The communication process is related in the first place to image, because image is the first aspect which we come in contact with. Then the other factors interfere: hearing, taste, touch, temperature and pain.

The communication process is a complex process based on codes: culture, education, society, geographical space, history, religion and individual perception of values.

If we take from management and marketing two basic rules, the SWOT analysis and the 20–80 % rule over information, we will see that the communication report is based on a realistic formulated vision being projected to produce communication results not immediately but after a significant time after the information investment effort. The existence of a good vision is an intrinsic condition for the development of any organisation; it is the rational result of the development for successful information.

The information is emphasised for a certain inquiry, and the information need is enough to serve freedom of expression.

Freedom of expression involves various environments, social conflicts and antagonistic concepts, while the importance of freedom of expression as a modality to develop and reflect a tolerant society involves a communication law which is regulated by a series of procedures, traditions and values that ensure unifying themes, not by a substantial theory.

The belief that freedom of expression hastens the truth-search process is expressed through the 'ideas market' metaphor. The best test for truth is to be accepted in market competition. The ideas market participants look for the most original, truthful or useful information. Consumers have to be very careful not to accept inferior information from a qualitative and quantitative point of view.

Information changes constantly during its transmission through communication channels. These changes start when the person who transmits the information does so by coding it. When he broadcasts this information he is obligated to code it taking into account the receiver. On the way, the information flows through the communication channel, while modifying factors intervene that can change its form or content, and when the information reaches the receiver he will decode it using his own value system. That is why it is very important for the person who transmits to get feedback from the person receiving the information, positive or negative, so that he can then verify it himself. Communication in essence means information exchange within time and space, which produces predictable or unforeseeable effects and results. Communication involves change, and could cause or affect changes in social structure.

People lose sight of the dynamics of truth because it intersects with error. Information exchanges do not always take place under the sign of a perfect reciprocity. History abounds with cases in which truth was reduced to silence through persecution and censorship. It is important that truth wins for the auto-rule purpose, but truth is not our biggest need, because people are their own masters. This way, the awareness of different principles which can guide conducts and opposite interests is imposed, depending on the professional or social role played by each individual.

The press is an institutionalised counterweight of government. It has two important functions: information and information control.

Freedom of speech and the right to publish do not mean anything without the right to listen and to obtain information. This involves the existence of an audience which listens, reads and answers.

In regard to mass media and the public, information in investigations made by control institutions investigative services has three specific characteristics: confidentiality, restrictiveness and a public facet. One main aspect of confidentiality is represented in large part by information with an internal institutional circuit and with a high-risk level that can cause unforeseeable effects and results, which are difficult to control and improve. This type of information will never be made public, because it can provoke important damages, obstruct and burden the investigative services' inquiry at an individual and general level, and at an institutional, national and international level.

The Supreme Court recognised the limited constitutional right to receive information, just by its nature and character.

The person who uses confidential information with the intent of damaging an institution encroaches upon the law. The Supreme Court stipulated that an establishment has the right of property over confidential information which it can settle independently and that this information is for the exclusive use of the establishment.

Information of a restricted nature circulates at the communication level between establishments, and internally at the level of administration departments, research and execution, the information being selected and orientated to qualified persons who can hold and use it to solve investigations. These information networks, within establishments, are relatively closed, meaning that they function according to certain rules regarding who should participate, which effects are expected and which information is relevant for the system. Between public and private establishments there is a special coordination structure that leaves nothing to chance.

Collaboration between establishments and authorities of European States ensures information support: the knowhow, as well as the technical support necessary to fight financial embezzlement, corruption, encroaching upon legislation and individual rights. The mission of investigative services is the fight against corruption, information transparency and the need to always operate in the citizens' interests, thereby serving community interests. Information which benefits citizens can be made public. So this transparency is not total; it is limited by the law regarding the character and nature of information, the effects and results which information has and can cause. Communication has to be programmed and conducted according to the information that consumers need. To reach the final decision to buy or exchange information, the individual passes through several stages: awareness of the need, the search for connected or supplementary information, the assessment of alternatives, information purchase or exchange, and post-purchase or post-exchange assessment, concerning the material and functional character of information. The analysis of communication effects represents the key to public communication. Communication serves four types of needs: recreation, personal relationships, interpersonal identity, and factual information. 'The use of communicational resources can be well characterised as an interactive process between mass-media content, needs, individual perceptions and values, as well as the social context the person belongs to', said Denis Mcquail, one of the most important public communication researchers.

Public information is framed by a few secondary principles, such as the circular and complex principle in which transmitted information functions and returns as a boomerang; the interactive principle which has at its basis mutual action; the assembling principle and context which involves the idea of organisation, of relationships connected to obtain certain characteristics.

Written press is the most intrusive and it is open to all compared with audiovisual media. In regard to audiovisual media we can say that: 'visual denotes and verbal connotes, and in other cases visual connotes and verbal denotes'.

The Internet has the biggest possibilities as far as freedom of expression is concerned; it cannot be considered limited because it offers a relatively unlimited communication capacity (virtual space) at a low price.

The level of freedom of every media channel depends on a few factors: channel availability for communication, media coverage and intrusion, and the historical relationship between media and government.

The lack of efficient communication leads to communication crisis situations inside establishments as well as in external reports.

The principles which the establishments and investigative services should look for in their relations with the mass media, in my opinion, should be as follows: to be competent, not to do anything that could damage citizens' trust, to have a large and profound vision about the report, to offer an exact image, which is complete and intangible about the present (topical interest), to serve all social groups, to stimulate communication, to protect and promote human rights and democracy, to contribute to the harmony of society. 'Not finding a solution is an impediment, but the problem identification', said G. K. Chesterson.

Any citizen has the right to a fair trial, without the judge or juries being influenced by the press. The press's obligation is to explain the circumstances, not to interpret them, influencing the nature of the inquiry and the citizens' opinion. Every individual has the right to protect his reputation, so that he can sue those that harm him in such a way. Through its informative context, the press can reach two important aspects, namely the reputation and emotional intelligence of every individual. That is why information is framed within well-fixed limits of emotional, psychological, sociological and cultural values. Terms such as embezzlement, deception or corruption must be used with great care because these kinds of charges can lead to a loss of customers, establishments and organisations especially for banks and insurance houses, while statements about financial instability or the impossibility of payment lead to the diminution of establishments' credit and also to losing customers.

The communication of results, by investigative services, during the inquiry is like a sword and, unless you know how to handle it, you can neither defend nor attack; worse, you could injure yourself and become the victim of an accident. That is why the information that has to be revealed to the public during an inquiry only represents general aspects of the embezzlement that cannot affect the inquiry as a whole; the establishment assuming the responsibility of a possible risk, estimated and calculated which it can afford. The investigative service of every control establishment, by means of its specialised departments in mass media and citizens' relationships, must not yield to pressures from the press or to public opinion, if a resistance to protect the interest of the inquiry and citizens implicitly comes out. The limits in which the investigative service can give inquiry details are given by the particularities of every case. In a fraud case communicating this to public opinion, even if the message is general and addressed to a large audience, the message may also be addressed to possible future defrauders.

Starting from the statement of J. F. Kennedy that 'if a free society cannot help the many and poor, it cannot save the few and rich either', we can say that the law deals with economic–financial offences at all social levels, and, at the time they are made, the investigative service is obligated to inform public opinion about them, as well as about the consequent lies that result from deception and reflect upon perpetrators and upon society. By showing public opinion the offences and their effects, as well as their results, the message transmitted by the investigative service is twofold: over public opinion consciousness by opening the issue to a collective outlook and secondly, for preventing possible offences, by increasing awareness of the dangers that perpetrators face, of a psychological and social nature.

The investigative service has the duty to supply public opinion, during the embezzlement inquiry, only with the information that does not affect the inquiry's progress, the limits being different for each case. After the inquiry is finished and the perpetrators have been punished, only the information that the control and investigation establishments consider that can be made public is revealed.

The press has to ask the authorities to demonstrate that the information is relevant to a certain inquiry and that the need for information is enough to serve the citizens' interests.

The art of an intelligent conversation is to encourage the other to talk. The decisive factor is how well you know how to listen to others, and then to understand them so that you can reply.

The way in which the information is presented depends not on what it does in particular, but on its socio-cultural influence. 'We cannot become what we have to become, remaining what we are', said Max De Pree.

Francesca RUGGIERI,

Lawyer, Academic Project Manager,
Centre for European Criminal Law, Como, Italy

Francesca RUGGIERI

is currently Professor
in Criminal Procedure,
Faculty of Law,
University of Insubria
(Como) and Scientific
Supervisor of the
Centro Studi di diritto
penale europeo.
She also works as
a criminal lawyer in
Milan. Before teaching
she worked as a judge
(magistrate in Turin
and public prosecutor
in Milan).

'Information and fraud prevention in the European Union: the viewpoint of a criminal procedure lawyer'

Information and fraud prevention in the European Union: the viewpoint of a criminal procedure lawyer

1. At the end of the last century a well-known German scholar 'read', reconstructed and probed criminal procedure from the point of view of information in ('input', evidence) and data out ('output', decisions by the judicial authorities). Nowadays there is probably no aspect of society or the law that escapes this kind of scrutiny. The questions OLAF wishes to discuss not only highlight the growing importance of information flows, but are being looked at, understandably, in the context of the more or less confidential and quasi-judicial investigations carried out by the European Anti-Fraud Office.

At first sight, the discourse clearly has different aspects:

(a) investigative and information services: here a balance must be found between the need for confidentiality, to avoid compromising the outcome of investigations, and the public's right to be informed. The problem is akin to the old question of 'publicity' in criminal procedure;

(b) methods of information: thought must be given to the use of news, both from the point of view of technology (media or otherwise) and forms of dissemination. This second aspect obviously presupposes a very flexible response to the first.

2. On the first point, there is one thing I think must be stressed: the right of citizens to be informed of the investigations carried out by OLAF. To reverse the order of points for discussion somewhat, I believe we must ask why and to what extent the right to information (see also Article 10 of the ECHR) should not be satisfied.

It is worth pointing out how useful it is to disseminate news about OLAF activities. Making public OLAF's findings and its attempts to uncover fraud against the Community's financial interests may serve two purposes: it gives people the sense that the Union's assets belong to all the citizens of the Member States, and, as well as this awareness of the common good, it spreads the sense that any offence against those assets is unlawful. This is the only way to make people aware of the importance of the resources that are essential to the Union. We should remember how often we have heard the complaint that the European Community is too 'remote' from ordinary people.

Now the question has been rephrased, it is easy to acknowledge that the right to information may be sacrificed if the essential requirements of the investigation so dictate. It may be sufficient to give reports that conceal references making it possible to identify persons or companies. The need for confidentiality in investigations is subordinate to the right of information, if confidentiality is not absolutely essential to the effectiveness of the investigations.

3. It is a simple matter, even in the short time allowed here, to look at the second aspect, in other words, the methods of information. Once we agree on the absolute need to inform Union citizens about what is being done to prevent fraud against the Community, it is obvious that such information must be broadcast via the medium that reaches most people, television. More complicated is the control over the accuracy of the news to be broadcast: to this end it would be appropriate for OLAF, not least in order to balance the right to information and the need for confidentiality, to check the information via its own press office.

Mihai TANASESCU,

Minister for Finance, Romanian Government,
December 2000–December 2004
Speech — Training seminar for OLAF communicators
Bucharest, 22 October 2003

'Information and communication: improving transparency and the procedures for spending public funds'

It is a pleasure for me to be here this morning with you and to present a few ideas about communication but also to see exactly how the Romanian Finance Ministry is seeking to improve transparency and the procedures for spending public monies. Public control here plays a very important role.

I have some figures available but it would be preferable if I were to say exactly what I think about these issues. Everyone knows, and we have seen here too, that communication signifies prevention. That is the situation. It is of the utmost importance that, when dealing with large amounts of money in the form of a budget (which in all countries is financed out of public money), we need to have a very clear idea about how the budget is to be allocated and spent. Preventing fraud is the prime objective of the process. When the budget is discussed with ministers, transparency is important. In our case, transparency means programmes and projects, and a few weeks ago we began implementing the budget by way of programmes and projects. What does this mean? It means that we know very well how the money is to be spent. We know, for example, that the Education Minister will be running 25 programmes next year and will be monitoring on a monthly basis how the money is being spent. It is extremely important to know and to discuss with it how the money will be spent and how we are thus going to prevent widespread abuse.

We attach great importance to this since the Finance Ministry is responsible for European funds. We have a special department entrusted with this task and with liaising closely with the other ministries and with all those involved in the movement of these funds.

This year, 2003, we have adopted some very important legislation concerning the monitoring of EU funds. In my opinion, this legislation can set an example in the fight against fraud and for the disbursement of EU funds. The legislation is very clear and we have begun to implement it. The Finance Ministry has the special task of monitoring and controlling these funds, and this is a crucial role it plays. We have three programmes of this kind with the EU. We have Phare, Sapard (a new programme providing funds for agriculture and the development of rural infrastructures) and ISPA. These funds must be spent in a very transparent manner. We have very clear rules and procedures for this. All these measures to control public monies are hugely important.

At the same time, however, prevention is also very important. In my opinion, prevention is the key issue in ensuring that financial resources are used properly in all countries.

What does prevention mean in our case? It means that you see how the legislation is being implemented since I am convinced that we have very good legislation but an important problem in Romania is its implementation.

How is the legislation being applied? I believe here that we must be well equipped for this task since, in our case, implementation is key. Both prevention and strong, clear legislation as well as transparency are very important in the fight against fraud.

What does transparency mean? It means that the legislation must be unequivocal so that there is no possibility of interpreting it, as this is how some people are able to evade controls and to commit fraud. Transparency not only means very meticulous work but, at the same time, enables us to prevent fraud involving public funds.

Like the other candidate countries, Romania has embarked on a complex process of transforming everything: legislation and its implementation, institutions, and the setting up of new bodies and instruments for handling European resources. In this essential transformation process, monitoring and control will, in my opinion, play a very important role. We need here to have well-educated individuals who put into practice what has been decided and approved.

Eliminating fraud involving public funds means communicating since communication involves not only discussions but also explaining to people many times over what is necessary, how European funds are to be handled, the fact that financial rules must be complied with and how the legislation is to be applied. In our case, communication is a key aspect of eliminating fraud and, at the same time, I believe that these three aspects, namely transparency, prevention and communication, are the principal elements of the proper implementation of legislation and will ensure proper utilisation of European funds and public money.

National institutions, investigative and judicial services

Juha VILKKO,

Senior Customs Inspector,
National Board of Customs, Finland
Speech — OLAF training seminar, Finland, 2002

Juha VILKKO

Senior Inspector, LLM, Enforcement Department, National Board of Customs, has worked since 1984 as Senior Inspector and Head of Investigation in the southern customs district in Helsinki and at present works as a legal expert in the National Board of Customs.

'The role of mass media in the fight against fraud'

Almost totally opposed as their starting points may be, authorities and the media lead an interesting coexistence or even live in a kind of symbiosis. Authorities, of course, are solely interested in combating fraud, investigating fraud cases, and preventing fraudulent action. The media for their part are keen on publishing news dealing with fraud. Depending on the type of media, the publishing of a fraud case may also aim at attracting the widest possible circle of readers, hoping to increase the turnover. It is characteristic of the so-called tabloid papers sold as single copies to pounce even on unimportant and unintentional errors made by authorities. On the other hand, the media may support and give credit to authorities for the protection of society when writing on their accomplishments on the fight against fraud.

Needless fear of booze rally

Yet the media's publishing policy may also support the authorities' efforts to combat fraud. A recent example thereof is the threat of the so-called 'booze rally' from Estonia to Finland expected to start in the beginning of May 2004, when 10 countries including Estonia access the EU as Member States.

This threat was not diminished by the fact that at the very beginning of 2004, when the quantity restrictions were abolished on alcohol allowances between the EU Member States, several major lots of alcohol had been imported to Finland from Germany and declared to be intended for its own use. The media reported that these lots, which comprised several hundred litres of alcohol, had been withheld by customs, and commented on the pertinence of the action taken by the authorities.

Time and money required to cross the sea between Finland and Estonia are only a fraction of the cost for a return trip to Germany. Thus it was well founded to expect that alcohol would now be imported from Estonia in massive quantities.

The expectations concerning an alcohol import rush were reflected in the media as never before. Experts on customs and alcohol policy were interviewed in direct programmes dealing with current affairs. It could not possibly remain unclear to anybody that despite the abolishment of exact quantity restrictions, customs would still be able to seize major import lots likely to be intended for commercial distribution.

Alcohol tax had been cut well in advance before the H hour in order for alcohol purchases to take place at home instead of Estonia. Yet both authorities and press were on the alert, meeting the first alcohol lots acquired in EU Estonia at the port of arrival during the first few hours of 1 May 2004. It was the authorities' task to prevent or impose taxes on excessive import lots likely to be commercial. The media for their part were on the look-out for strikingly large alcohol lots.

What a great surprise it was for all parties that not a single import lot from Estonia came up to the volumes expected! However, the journalists' professional skill turned this 'non-news' into a sensation. The alcohol quantities which failed to materialise got larger headlines than the very effects brought about by the accession of the new Member State.

This matter is also linked with OLAF's field of responsibilities: A large quantity of alcohol imported for purposes other than for own use would have implied a violation of the harmonised tax on alcoholic beverages to be collected by Finland.

The media are partly to thank for the no-show of those expected large import lots of alcohol. The publicising by the media of the authorities' powers to control excessive alcohol lots reached a considerably wider circle of readers than would have been the case if the information were to have been distributed by the authorities themselves. The press also acts in this way regarding fraud cases having a considerable news value. The reaction of enlightened media usually supports the goals of authorities.

Blue Spirits case

There are cases where the interest expressed by the media in criminal action which is being committed may have prevented either the fraud itself or its possible impact. One such example is the so-called Blue Spirits case.

A few years ago Finnish authorities were informed that a batch of spirits would be imported in transit containers from the Far East to Finland, for selling on the black market. According to this intelligence, the containers would be addressed to a Russian consignee and declared to contain anti-freeze solution. Authorities were astonished to see the number of containers which actually arrived: they were more than 10, which meant almost a quarter of a million litres! Yet more surprising was the blue colour of the substance, which really did not look anything like a drink. Maybe the substance really was alcohol to be used as anti-freeze as stated by the documents? For various reasons, it was not possible to arrange thorough laboratory examinations. Neither would the methods then available have enabled the trailing of each container from Helsinki all the way to the Russian border.

It would no doubt have been possible to ensure the exit of the containers, but despite sealing them, their contents might have been substituted secretly. It was also possible that the substance now located in Finland was just legal transit traffic. Authorities were unable to interfere, unless fraud relating to the cargo was to be committed in Finland such as its removal from under customs surveillance.

From an anti-fraud viewpoint, the authorities would certainly have followed another line of action than what actually happened. But in this special case still another possibility had to be considered seriously: that the substance would contain poisonous methanol. If so, it would lead to a great number of deaths and cause serious damage to persons drinking it.

The press were tipped off about a large obscure transit lot. National television channels and major Finnish newspapers made a sensation of it. The news was also noted abroad. The publicity gained by the container lots would have been the main reason for the fact that they were never fetched from the port. This confirmed that they had not come to Finland as normal transit traffic but were presumably being imported for the illicit market, just as claimed by the information obtained.

This publicity also had the effect that not all the information on those involved in the fraudulent project could be disclosed and that the fraud may never be completely solved. Yet the correctly timed media publicity worked as the authorities had wished: the forbidden, possibly even dangerous substance was prevented from entering the illicit market without any proper measures taken by the authorities.

In the opposite case, if the substance had reached the market, the media of course would have had something very exciting to tell: failure of authority control, possible methanol poisoning in the worst case, and so on. Luckily, there was no news like that to publish. The chosen strategy seems to have been the only correct one.

Maintenance of a 'working in peace' environment

The above examples describe how publicity by the media, when professionally applied, can promote fraud combat and thereby crime investigation. Yet crime investigation shall strictly adhere to the principle that unfounded publicity be avoided, thus securing its possibility to work in peace until all evidence has been obtained that is required for the case to be solved.

If the media so desires, it can indeed seriously disturb the anti-fraud efforts of the authorities. This could happen, say, by publishing received confidential information at a much too early stage of the investigation. In Finland the entire media exert exemplary self-discipline in this respect. Authorities can rest assured that information that is sensitive in terms of investigation is not being published prematurely. This by no means implies, however, that authorities would somehow be trying to infringe one of the very basic principles of society: the freedom of the press to decide on the subjects and contents of what is published.

1.5. TRANSPARENCY INTERNATIONAL

Transparency international

Jeff LOVITT,

Former Director of Communications,
Transparency International, Germany
Speech — Seminar on anti-fraud communication — 'Deterring
fraud by informing the public' — 24–26 November 2004

Jeff LOVITT

is the Executive
Director of PASOS
(Policy Association
for an Open Society),
a not-for-profit
network of 23 public
policy centres in
central and east
Europe and Central
Asia, committed to
democracy, good
governance, and
the promotion of
economic and social
development. (http://
www.pasos.org).
Until launching the
PASOS Secretariat
in Prague in March
2005, he was Director
of Communications
at the international
secretariat of
Transparency
International (TI), the
international anti-
corruption network.
Prior to that he was
a journalist, editor
and communications
professional, and
from 1995 to 1998
worked for The
European newspaper
as central Europe
correspondent.

'The information challenge: Transparency International and combating corruption'

Thank you, Mr Chairman, for inviting me to speak here today, not least because I am sure that a number of the economic crime offices and customs offices in the various countries have come across the work of Transparency International (TI) at the national level, but this is my first direct contact with OLAF, yet alone the OLAF communicators' network. I very much hope that it will be the beginning of a fruitful cooperation.

But first I should tell you something about TI. It was founded in 1993, which makes it a fairly young organisation, albeit not quite as young as OLAF. It was founded by a group of people from many different countries who were angry at the way corruption was strangling development in developing countries, or perhaps, because of corruption, I would say in non-developing countries.

Corruption does not only line the pockets of corrupt politicians and public officials. It prevents money flowing to those who need it, depriving hospitals of vital medicines, leaving schools without schoolbooks.

The development focus has always been very strong at TI, and one of the early figures in TI's history was a former Director-General of Development at the European Commission, Dieter Frisch, who remains very active in our Transparency International Brussels office today. The relationship between TI and the EU actually goes back quite a long way.

Transparency International does not investigate cases: we leave that to investigators and, of course, to investigative journalists. TI's approach is to propose systemic reform. We try to see institutional change come about, and to make sure that corruption becomes a high-risk activity instead of a low-risk activity, to make sure that the laws are in place, that the laws are enforced, and that offenders are put behind bars.

We define corruption as the abuse of entrusted power for private gain. Now, a lot of people used to define corruption as the abuse of public power for private gain, but the private sector is so enormous now that it is impossible not to include private sector corruption in any definition.

Now, to be transparent about Transparency International, I should explain our governance structure. A few people have already asked me: where does the money come from? TI has national chapters in 92 countries plus contact organisations in another 25. Every year we have an annual meeting, where the national chapters elect the International Board. The International Secretariat in Berlin, where I am Director of Communications, reports to the International Board.

Our funding: TI tries to have as diverse a funding structure as possible, so TI takes funding from governments, the private sector and foundations. Very little actually comes from the private sector; the primary source of funding is governments. But TI is not dependent on any one government — it comes mainly from development agencies — ranging from Norway, the Netherlands, Germany, the United Kingdom, the USA, Sweden, Denmark, Switzerland and Canada.

It is essential that civil society organisations engage with governments in both the developed and developing world. The role of civil society is crucial, not just in raising awareness and making lots of noise in the media, but also by working with governments, lobbying politicians and confronting international institutions. Just as laws to clamp down on bribery require teeth, namely prosecutors with the resources to enforce the law, so civil society must be more than just angry crowds throwing stones on the sidelines. Civil society organisations need to engage with each other, but also with governments, and also with the private sector, so that their voice is heard and taken seriously by policy-makers.

So Transparency International is an international non-governmental, not-for-profit organisation.

More than one third of TI's national chapters are in Europe, so the EU is a major focus of TI's work. Our national chapters determine their own priorities. For instance, in Latvia, Transparency International often focuses on political party finance or access to information. In fact, Delna, TI's national chapter in Latvia, provides an example of where TI was a bit more public in its advocacy work recently with the European Commission. Ingrida Udre, the proposed European Commissioner from Latvia, was accused of party political funding irregularities, and vociferous protests by Transparency International and other civil society organisations met with success. That Commissioner was one of those dropped from the new line-up of EU Commission President José Manuel Barroso earlier this month.

So, one of the key plans of the work of TI is the spreading of greater access to information and a greater understanding of the need for greater transparency in government. This is where TI has a natural alliance with the media.

The key question for us, and even more so for the media is: Who holds the power? And how can we check the abuse of power? This is of course a question that is central to the role of the investigative journalist, who has to follow the trail of power. When corruption takes place, it is invariably the powerful that set arbitrary rules allowing too much discretion to public officials, who benefit by ensuring, for instance, that key tenders or privatisations go to the cronies of the powerful.

The whole notion of transparency and public accountability stands and falls with our own ability to organise and publish the right information.

On the discussion under way here today on when to say 'No comment', well I would say: use it very sparingly. On the whole, it is much better to tell journalists that you will ascertain the facts or a response and get back to them. But then make sure you do get back to them, and promptly. That is far better than ad-libbing with a vague answer. And where a more precise answer can be formulated it is also better than 'No comment', and the interpretations that can be drawn from that phrase. But what I think might be interesting from the perspective of this network is really: 'What is your message, what are your goals and what is your audience?'

I have a feeling that your audience is not on the whole going to be investigative journalists. It may be professionals such as lawyers, prosecutors and public officials. So you might want to develop close relationships with specialist media. To give an extreme example, China has a newspaper called the *Daily Prosecutor*. With about 250 000 prosecutors, China is probably the only country in the world that could possibly justify, from a readership size, a *Daily Prosecutor*. But there are weeklies and monthlies for the legal profession and for the civil service, which might be very important target audiences for you. Although you are selling a product in the way that a commercial organisation would be, you do have a goal, namely to further the aims of the office, which could be to clamp down on abuse of the customs services, loopholes in taxation or fraud generally. That very often means seeking to do more than just improving the public image of your office.

The goal is often to inform key audiences, which include not just the general public, but more targeted audiences such as the business community and the financial community, about the importance of the subject matter of fraud, and that will sometimes require a more proactive approach.

It is important that you do not just wait for a scandal to break out before you talk to journalists. Fraud is a very complex problem, and you should as a matter of course regularly meet with key journalists from your target media, because when a scandal breaks you will complain the next day that they have all their facts wrong, because you have not kept up contact on a regular basis so that they understand the issue.

As well as a regular briefing with journalists, I would also suggest, perhaps every year, an open day. It would be a very good idea, showing them how you operate, giving them just a better feeling for what your work is. Although you are not selling a product, the relationship between a spokesperson and a journalist must be mutually beneficial. And I think you will find that that comes quite naturally. You want to make sure they get their facts right; so do they.

You want to make it clear what your office does and what the role of your office is; and they want access to the information that you can provide. So it should be a win–win situation from that point of view. But that does require building up and maintaining good relations. Now, the chairman talked yesterday about crisis communications — how to deal with an aeroplane crash and the importance of having plans already hatched beforehand.

That is very important, but in any public office, particularly one dealing with economic crime, clear codes of conduct and policies are even more important. Do not wait for a crisis to implement a crisis communications plan. Institute and implement a compliance policy, so that the scope for criminal or serious unethical conduct is specifically condemned and punished — and provide and publish a regular annual report outlining how cases that have arisen under the codes and policies have been handled, and monitor and review the effectiveness of those policies.

With a name like Transparency International, reputation is vital. So we have a code of conduct, we have a conflict of interest policy, we have a clear donations policy, and we have now instituted for our national chapters around the world a reaccreditation process, so that one bad apple cannot bring down the whole organisation, so that there are clear financial reporting lines and clear governance criteria. If at the end of the three-year cycle a national chapter fails to live up to those requirements, it will cease to be a member of the Transparency International family.

This is an approach TI is also taking towards corporate governance in the private sector. When the Enron, Global Crossing, WorldCom and Parmalat scandals broke out, shareholders and pension fund managers were jolted into reality. The public no longer has any confidence that a given corporation's books show a true and fair statement of its finances. The implications for the efficient operation of capital markets are far-reaching. That is why companies must establish codes of conduct, including detailed rules designed to combat bribery at home but also in their subsidiaries abroad. TI has developed, together with leading companies and Social Accountability International a set of business principles for countering bribery, because the only way you are going to implement a change of practice is by pre-empting national laws. It is essential to work with the business sector to effect change, to secure their buy-in to ensure that the scope for bribery is minimised.

In terms of how an NGO like TI can make an impact, can effect change, we do not always do it by calling a press conference. We do not see the media always as the first point-of-call. Instead, we need to target our message by working with and influencing governments, private companies, other civil society organisations, and of course the media. From the start, TI took a very non-confrontational approach towards governments. That does not always work. In Zimbabwe, our chapter is very confrontational because in Zimbabwe there is no way to talk to Robert Mugabe.

Another example was perhaps Delna, our chapter in Latvia, with their protests at the choice of an EU Commissioner. TI also works with other NGOs, for instance in the 'Publish what you pay' campaign, which brings together TI, Global Witness, Oxfam and a range of other NGOs, calling for international companies in the extractive industries to disclose what they pay to the host government and State-owned companies, for instance in Angola.

Another important area where TI has combined advocacy work with carefully targeted media work is in engaging with international institutions, particularly on international legal instruments and conventions. One is the OECD Convention on Combating Bribery of Foreign Public Officials in International Business Transactions, which aims to curtail bribery of foreign public officials by OECD exporters. Until 1999 it was tax-deductible in countries such as France, Germany, and other OECD members to pay bribes abroad. But the key to securing support for the convention actually was the support of big European companies. TI secured the support of the International Chamber of Commerce, and 20 European companies signed letters to their ministers to encourage them to sign the OECD convention.

That is an example of where an NGO does not need to shout on the streets, nor go to the media. Instead, it is often more effective to try to influence policy-makers directly. It is all the more important now, therefore, that each country that has signed the OECD convention, feels confident that the other signatories have not only introduced the appropriate legislation, but also that they are now effectively enforcing that legislation. A follow-up process is under way at the OECD to translate this into law and practice, and this is where the monitoring role of NGOs is crucial. Civil society organisations led by TI are providing input and monitoring the follow-up to the effective implementation of the convention. I have to say that there have so far been no successful prosecutions under the OECD convention. Luckily there are now cases going through the courts, but we are still waiting for the first successful prosecutions (excluding cases brought in the USA under the already existing US foreign corrupt practices act, which predates the OECD convention).

In November 2002 there was a big problem. It was clear that the governments were not putting the resources into place to make it even possible to bring cases to trial under the OECD convention. In this instance, TI deployed a dual strategy. We not only made sure that our national chapters pressured their governments to vote for real budgets to enforce a peer review process; we also made sure there were letters in front of everybody at a key OECD meeting. We placed op-eds and letters in the *Financial Times* and *The International Herald Tribune*, and encouraged our national chapters in OECD countries to write letters to the editors of key newspapers in their respective countries.

Now, another important partner of course is the EU. TI has been engaging with the EU for many years and, as with our approach to the OECD, it has been an example of bringing about change through direct advocacy work rather than high-profile media campaigns. As in the case of the OECD, in the case of the EU, the European Commission has produced two comprehensive papers on corruption.

The Commission issued an EU policy against corruption in May 1997, which was significantly influenced by a memorandum from TI dating from 1995. In November 1999, TI issued a second memorandum to the Commission urging for a comprehensive EU strategy to fight corruption, and that paper fed into a second EU communication in 2003. TI has also been actively working at the EU level to see the development of the blacklisting of companies bidding for EU tenders, so that any company that has been found guilty of paying bribes will be excluded from future bidding for a prescribed period of time.

Another area is export credit insurance. Export credit agencies have been prone to underwriting contracts, where as much as 20 % of the total sum involved can be taken up by bribe payments. The relationship between TI and the EU — despite being very low key — has resulted in a very welcome change of heart in the EU, which is excellent news.

One very important development has been the adoption of blacklisting, but there are also further actions that need to be taken. One is to make realistic the new European arrest warrant, which probably requires really the establishment of a European prosecutor. In addition, conflict-of-interest regulations for EU staff are urgently needed as are the protection of whistleblowers and the introduction of anti-corruption provisions in foreign aid programmes.

TI has also worked with the EU in the accession process by making sure that the issue of corruption in the candidate countries has been placed very high on the EU's agenda. While new members have put in place a wide-ranging body of legislation, implementation does require effective prosecution services with sufficient resources and an effective independent judiciary, which is sadly one of the institutions most prone to bribery in many countries. In fact, one of the biggest areas of corruption in accession countries has been the distribution of PHARE funds, although it is important to note that in a more longstanding EU member, Greece, regional Structural Funds have also been a major area of corruption. So membership of the EU certainly does not preclude the problem of corruption. In fact, in TI's annual corruption perceptions index some of the new EU members, particularly Slovenia and Estonia, have scored consistently higher than countries such as Greece and Italy.

The media's success in exposing corruption does not depend so much on the quality of journalism as on other external factors, from press freedom laws, freedom of information acts, to fair, strong and independent judges, as well as courageous public prosecutors, and the development of an environment that permits the media to serve as an effective public watchdog. The media love TI's corruption perceptions index, because it is a league table ranking more than 140 countries, so it is a very sexy headline grabber. But what we find very difficult is to engage the media into a more thoughtful debate about how to tackle corruption. For all forms of media, it is essential to relate news through human interest stories.

One way is by showing the impact of corruption on ordinary people who cannot afford to pay bribes, and therefore cannot, for instance, receive urgent medical attention. One way that TI tries to do that is that every year we have an Integrity Awards ceremony where we recognise the bravery of individuals or groups who have taken courage into their own hands by taking a stand against corruption. These courageous figures have demonstrated great courage despite very often facing death threats to themselves or to their families. A couple of examples that are particularly relevant to economic crime officers are the cases of two public officials, namely a TI Integrity Award winner from 2002, a Slovak judge, Jana Dubovcova, and a TI Integrity Award winner from 2003, Dora Akunyili, Head of the Nigerian Drug and Food Inspectorate.

Ms Dubovcova took on the judicial establishment by conducting a survey of bribery in her own court in Banska Bystrica in Central Slovakia. Her actions drew the wrath of the judicial establishment when she did this, but luckily the then Justice Minister, Ján Carnogurský, supported her fight, and she made a lot of headway in implementing a new system designed to randomise the allocation of court cases in Slovakia, so as to reduce the scope for corruption and bribe-taking on the part of judges.

Dr Dora Akunyili, a pharmacologist and university lecturer in her field, was called upon to become the new Director of Nafdac, the National Agency for Food and Drug Administration and Control in Nigeria two years ago. In Nigeria, the high level of corruption has led to thousands of deaths. But, Dr Akunyili was not afraid to indict those responsible, even taking on multinational companies in the international food sector. She also took on the powerful drug cartels, confiscating products worth millions of dollars and destroying them in public. Her brave actions have saved countless lives, preventing Nigerian citizens from consuming drugs and food harmful to their health. But her brave stand against corruption has come with a price. Her own life has been threatened.

Her successful prosecution of some of the big multinational companies, as well as her own campaign against corruption, has restored the credibility and the integrity of Nafdac, a government institution. In a society where up to 65 % of all drugs on the market are fakes, commanding respect is crucial for the director of the national control organisation, and concrete anti-corruption tools such as her telephone hotline, where people can report cases of corruption anonymously, will help her in her fight against corruption. TI Nigeria was convinced that awarding Dr Akunyili the TI Integrity Award would help the fight against corruption in Nigeria.

TI Integrity Awards include posthumous tributes, and one of them went in 2001 to Georgy Gongadze from Ukraine. He was an investigative journalist who had an anti-corruption website, and as you have seen from recent events, corruption remains very much at the top of the agenda in Ukraine. Corruption, combined with concern about a lack of democracy, underpinned the protests on the streets at the falsification of Ukraine's presidential election; very much like we saw in Georgia just a year ago. Georgy Gongadze's brutal death is a tragic reminder that investigative journalism is a very dangerous trade, and the killing unfortunately has not stopped.

According to the Committee to Protect Journalists, it was possible to identify 36 journalists who had been killed because of their work as journalists in 2003. Thirteen of those deaths were in the war in Iraq, and another six in conflict zones. But of the remaining 17 journalists killed, seven are believed to have been killed due to the fact that they were investigating cases of corruption. So it is a very dangerous profession. When it comes to investigative journalism of government corruption, the best stories would actually never emerge if it were not for the cooperation of honest public officials, which is why I chose two examples here of public officials who had been awarded TI Integrity Awards.

The linkage between honest public officials and journalists needs to be more widely appreciated, because they really can work in harmony, and we all have to work to strengthen laws and systems in countries to protect whistleblowers and to encourage whistleblowing.

Next 9 December is the first ever UN International Anti-Corruption Day, and it is to mark the day that the UN Convention against Corruption was signed in December 2003 in Merida, Mexico. So from 2004 onwards, 9 December is International Anti-Corruption Day, and one of the things TI will be doing this year is to pressure governments around the world not just to sign the convention, which they did in rather a hurry, but also to ratify it, because only about a dozen have ratified it a year after it was signed. Thirty ratifications are required before the convention actually comes into force. So a lot of TI's national chapters will be making some noise on 9 December to make that happen.

The World Bank has put an estimate on the cost of bribery annually at USD 1 trillion. It does not take much to think how many hospitals could be built in sub-Saharan Africa with that money, or how many medicines could be provided for HIV sufferers, or how many people could be provided with clean water supplies and clean sewers.

So it is not so challenging to make clear the importance of the fight against corruption, and what would be very encouraging to me is if some of your offices might also make use of 9 December. It might be a bit early for this year, but if you have any ideas, still try, or perhaps contact TI's national chapters in your countries, just to see what they are doing, to see to what extent you can work together, and perhaps this will open up possibilities for cooperation in the future.

The impact of corruption, and the impact of fraud, can make for compelling television and —hugely important — television reporting. To help things along, TI on a miniscule budget has just created a television spot, which is already in English, French, Spanish, German, Russian and Arabic. It will be running on Deutsche Welle, and we have heard very positive noises from CNN International that they will be running it. We decided to launch the spot in time for 9 December, but it can run all year round, and as you know, it is important to have short messages in the television era. So we have a 30-second version and also a 15-second version. When you see the spot, I hope it leaves a very clear message and one I would like to end on — namely that corruption is a disease that kills — but it is preventable.

So thank you very much, and remember 9 December.

Transparency international

Anke MARTINY,

Board Member of Transparency International,
Germany

Dr Anke MARTINY

born in Dortmund,
Germany, is a
member of the board
of Transparency
International,
Germany. Prior
to that, she was
a member of the
Federal Parliament
Deutscher Bundestag
between 1972 and
1989, belonging to
the Committees for
Economy, Economic
Aid, Health and
Environmental
Questions. She
has also dealt with
consumer affairs.
She was Senator
for Cultural Affairs
in Berlin for two
years and headed
the Office of the
Friedrich-Ebert-
Stiftung in Tel Aviv for
five years. She has
worked as a freelance
journalist since 1997.

'Communication — Key to flushing out corruption'

I

Of all the white-collar offences, corruption must be the crime that has the greatest need for discretion, cover-ups and secrecy. No one boasts about bribery or venality, the giving or receiving of money or financial advantages; they are not the right subjects for bar-room chat, or even the sort of subject to be mentioned to 'good friends'.

Moonlighting, tax evasion, fiddling travel expenses or faking attendance during core time are all venial sins, peccadilloes as some might say. No one pays that much attention because, as a rule, everyone has some little skeleton in their cupboard. But corruption shuns the spotlight like vampires avoid daylight.

This is why it is no coincidence that the majority of corruption cases come to light as the result of acts of revenge. The secretary who feels undervalued, the colleague passed over for promotion, the cheated wife, the competitor who always thought that something was not right; they all take their revenge on those guilty of corruption if they know about it. They spill the beans anonymously or openly to their superiors or to the public prosecutor; they phone an anonymous hotline and ultimately set corruption proceedings in motion. This is at least what the investigating authorities have found: corruption is often reported by people working in the same environment.

II

Corruption benefits both givers and takers. It is a third party that is left to count the cost: usually a company, local authorities, an association or an organisation, all of which are fairly abstract impersonal structures. As giver and taker both have the feeling that they are doing no harm to anyone they know, they have comparatively few scruples about breaking the rules. No one would defraud their next-door neighbour, whom they see every day, but the health insurance system, the household insurance system or the public works department of a large town or city authority is different.

It often takes a great deal of effort on the part of the criminal to breach the walls set up to protect the system from the self-service of corruption. Accounts are doctored, secret commissions are concealed in invoices and orders, double invoices are produced, receipts are forged, distribution channels are fiddled with, packaging is opened, consignment papers are 'replaced', money is shipped abroad. Contracts are awarded for overpriced and useless studies. Procurement procedures are disregarded; the goods delivered are not of the promised quality; deals are struck 'between friends'. The range of corruption offences is wide and varied.

III

If there is one thing that is anathema to all the crooked dealings, it is the spotlight of publicity. This is why the key to preventing corruption is communication. The wrongdoers must live in fear that it could all come out because A tells B, or C tells boss D about their suspicions, or because Y might ask X a follow-up question but, because X is not there, Z gets asked and starts wondering what is going on.

Most corruption offences are discovered by chance. That is something of which the investigating authorities are fairly sure. They also know that every case they investigate is connected to a further five cases at least. This is why it takes a lot of staff to investigate suspected corruption. Authorities are reluctant to look into suspicious circumstances because they do not want to launch complex investigations for which they do not have the staff. This is ultimately why less corruption is brought to light than could be the case.

Communication can take a variety of forms. Private conversations or recordings are the simplest form. But checks along the chain of events are also a method of communication. Internal audits also communicate with departments and other structures within the organisation. External auditing, in other words, checking annual accounts and the annual report, also shines the spotlight. Reports in the company paper and public relations work by companies or authorities open up further channels. Lastly, it is possible to talk to similar or comparable organisations to influence structures. Transparency International, Germany, benefits from these ideas.

IV

Transparency International was founded in Berlin and The Hague in 1993 with the aim of combating corruption. The idea was to build coalitions within civil society to prevent corruption and create structures within which corruption would find it less easy to flourish. Such structures are created by calling for them and lobbying until they are finally set up. The first step towards achieving Transparency International's goals was the signing in 1997 of the OECD Convention on Combating Bribery of Foreign Public Officials in International Business Transactions. The second step was getting the convention ratified by most of the OECD Member States. What is needed for the third step is a broad-based campaign to make as many people in the OECD as possible aware of the aims of the convention. Regrettably, that this is not happening; business organisations persist in the belief that there are just a few black sheep engaging in corruption, that the few have no impact on the market and that therefore this convention is ineffectual and unnecessary. A glance through the daily papers, however, is enough to realise that this is not the case.

Transparency International's work would be impossible without extensive communication between all members of society. TI's work therefore depends on the media. It is generally the case that the media play a key role in uncovering and analysing corruption cases, and then of disseminating their findings. As Transparency International does not conduct any investigations of its own or monitor individual cases, without media input its work would soon grind to a halt.

Both Transparency International and the media are not even indirectly involved in prosecutions. But by adopting a clear line, by lobbying and by working to keep public interest alive they can make a considerable contribution to the prosecution of corruption cases.

Every year Transparency International gives Integrity Awards to honour the heroes of the fight against corruption. This is another way of reaching out to a wider public. The public are interested in the heroes' life stories and at the same time learn about the corrupt environment that has made them into heroes. Often these heroes are journalists and often they are honoured post-humously, as reporting corruption is almost as dangerous as being a war correspondent, and can sometimes be even more perilous.

A few weeks ago Transparency International, Germany, made a further attempt to reach a wider audience. 'Im Schatten der Öffentlichkeit' (In the shadows of the spotlight) was the title of a conference that focused on the media and media corruption. It was concluded that the greatest possible professionalism and economic independence were the most effective weapons available to journalists in the fight against corruption. The view was also taken that guidelines for conduct with regard to the objects of reports and the marketplace were necessary and would be useful.

2. FIGHT AGAINST FRAUD ON VISION:
Television drama as a means of fighting fraud and corruption affecting EU financial interests*

* Based mainly on the contributions for the round table on anti-fraud communication during the seventh training seminar of the OLAF Anti-Fraud Communicators' Network (OAFCN), Vienna and Bratislava, 23 to 26 September 2007, concerning 'Deterring fraud by informing the public — Fight against fraud on vision: television drama as a means of fighting fraud and corruption affecting the EU's financial interests'.

2.1 ACADEMICS

Milly BUONANNO

Professor of Theory of Television in the Faculty of Sciences of Communication — University of Rome 'La Sapienza', Director of Osservatorio sulla Fiction Italiana

Developing trust in institutions — The contribution of television drama

In drama which takes place in a professional or institutional setting, where the characters are individuals or groups of people belonging to specific professions or institutions, we can begin to understand why this medium can assume a symbolic role of some importance. This role basically reflects one fundamental aspect of modernity — the individual and collective trust placed in 'abstract systems' through the personal relationship of trust established with the 'concrete agents' of those systems. In social theory, abstract systems or expert systems are defined as structured groups of professional competences and technical machinery which govern the organisation of many aspects of contemporary life; medicine and surgery, for example, or the legal profession, investigators or judges and many others are all examples of expert systems made up of codified knowledge, skills and techniques unknown to the uninitiated, which are practised (more or less properly and effectively) by members of those professions.

Expert systems are the basis of virtually all modern institutions, and rely to a very large extent on the trust placed in them by the public. It is important to emphasise that, in principle, trust is placed in the abstract capability of the systems without necessarily presupposing or requiring any direct contact or personal relationship with their agents or representatives. We trust the expert knowledge of medicine even if none of our friends are doctors whom we would trust on a personal level, and even if the relationship with the doctor treating us is sporadic and formal; the same applies to trust in the technique of flying an aircraft, or organising a postal service, which normally exists regardless of whether or not we know the pilot or postman.

However, in large numbers of everyday situations, members of the public come into contact with the concrete agents, the experts and representatives of the abstract systems; these occasions, referred to as 'access nodes', constitute points of particular vulnerability for the systems because the proper exercise and effectiveness of their competences are put to the test and, if the experience is unsatisfactory, the trust placed can be entirely or partially withdrawn. Alternatively, it can be confirmed and reinforced.

Milly BUONANNO

Professor of 'Television studies' at the University of Roma 'La Sapienza'.

Director of the School of Television Scriptwriting (Centro Sperimentale di Cinematografia).

Founder and Director of Osservatorio sulla Fiction Italiana, since 1988.

Coordinator of the Eurofiction project, 1996–2005.

As the author and editor of more than 50 books and 100 essays, she has widely published in different languages on issues related to:

• television theory, television story-telling: recent works in this field are *L'età della televisione* (The age of television, Laterza, 2006, and Intellect Books/ University of Chicago Press, 2007); *Realtà multiple* (Multiple realities, Liguori, 2004); *Le formule del racconto televisivo* (The formulae of television story-telling, Sansoni, 2002);

Hence, the numerous contacts which take place in drama with individuals and environments belonging to the security institutions can be considered as forms of transposition through indirect experience of direct contacts with the 'access nodes' of the institution.

The point at issue here is whether the leading characters of fictional drama can inspire that particular trust which arises from contact with the concrete agents and is potentially able to evolve into a general trust in the abstract system of the institution.

The reply — which we should probably say at the outset is in the affirmative — firstly requires reliance to be placed on two levels of trustworthiness: personal and professional. The former is based, logically, on requisites, attitudes and behaviour which form part of the characters as human beings with their own personality and individuality; the second on the requisites, attitudes and behaviour which define the characters as members of the institution, required to behave in accordance with its rules and aims. Naturally, personal and professional trustworthiness often go hand in hand and serve to reinforce and guarantee one another.

Security officers (members of the police, *carabinieri*, *guardia di finanza*, etc.) in Italian drama, with their affable manner, ability to listen, and sensitivity which, together with their other personal qualities, become a professional resource deployed to help, and above all support, the victims of crime, show they can inspire confidence, thanks, first and foremost, to their exceptional and well-developed 'human qualities'. These gifts, also deployed or at least contributing positively on a professional level, are mainly revealed in the numerous private-life situations in which Italian television fiction — which is incidentally extremely popular with Italian audiences — traditionally places the leading characters of detective drama (and other genres as well). It is here, in the vast background of their private lives (often and deliberately superimposed on or colliding with the foreground of their investigative work) that these characters, as they strive to cope with the cataclysms and minutiae of everyday life and with their relationships with family, friends or lovers, display their most authentic and human face.

Normally, and perhaps invariably, the face is that of an individual with nothing special about him, indeed one who is preferably simple, down-to-earth, and not without his faults. But, at the same time, these are individuals worthy of esteem because they show that they have a heart ('you have a heart, that's what makes you special' is a comment made to Inspector Rocca), they know the value of friendship (Captain Anceschi and Marshall Cecchini repeatedly prove this in *Don Matteo*), they know how to fight for a just cause (Lieutenant Martinelli of 'RIS' successfully launches a difficult legal action against the factory responsible for his father's illness, while Captain Venturi goes to great lengths to enable the daughter of his colleague and friend Marshall De Biase, handicapped after an accident, to undergo expensive surgery in the USA), and — at the very lowest common denominator — they can be summed up as 'good guys'. In the universe of Italian drama, there is no central character in the police, *carabinieri* or *guardia di finanza* to whom a similar description could not be applied — and much more besides in the case of more substantial characters.

Although, on a personal level, the characters can be said to be worthy of trust, in terms of professional trustworthiness — the proven ability to fulfil the responsibilities of a security institution competently and efficiently — the situation is more complex. Clearly, all crimes are solved and all criminals are brought to book — something which the conventions of thrillers and public expectations demand. Clearly, the protagonists never, or hardly ever, appear less than worthy of trust in their professional role. From this point of view, however, some particularly successful characters have managed more effectively to gain audience esteem and respect. This applies to Marshall Rocca, the eponymous hero of a long-running and highly popular series.

Certainly no leading character in uniform is such a strong catalyst for trust as Marshall Rocca. While he clearly matches his 'colleagues' in other series for honesty and respectability, his stature propels him above this basic level of trustworthiness. The character of Rocca is a successful and unique blend (at least in drama) of human and moral qualities, vital components for the image of a member of the *carabinieri* — even more rich and complex thanks to the artistic depth and appealing portrayal of the actor Gigi Proietti — and the professional qualities of a vastly experienced investigator, an authoritative leader and point of reference in his unit ('you are my role model', admits the younger Marshall Banti).

Unlike the RIS [scientific investigations unit], but like traditional professional or amateur detectives, Rocca shuns investigations based mainly on scientific evidence — but not because he prefers to use his undoubted intuition: his best professional resources are more carefully woven, more deeply ingrained — his propensity for reflection and logical thought, often in a harmonious duet with his closest colleague, the wise Sergeant Cacciapuoti — his well-developed understanding of the world and of people — 'if he's guilty, then I don't understand people and it's time I changed job' — the systematic doubt he applies to the evidence — the subject of ceaseless and ritual clashes with Prosecutor Mannino to whose hasty conclusions he responds by stressing 'this annoying fault of mine of always trying to understand' — the dogged determination, almost echoed in his very name, to 'try to get to the truth wherever the truth lies'.

Marshall Rocca is indeed a role model — not to be confused with a model of perfection — an exemplary person in many ways in his public and private life, in which he tackles with commendable flexibility the 'ordinary' trials and tribulations of a man of mature years dealing with children, grandchildren and girlfriends. The fact that this exemplary and hence highly trustworthy character, who on top of everything else is a likeable individual, is an officer of the *carabinieri* makes him the catalyst for a huge wave of individual trust, from which there is little doubt that the institution to which he belongs also derives a reflected benefit.

Thus, through stories and fictional characters with the ability to develop and cement the bond of trust between citizens and institutions, television drama makes an influential contribution to the workings of contemporary society.

Academics

Michael LEVI

Professor of Criminology and ESRC Professorial Fellow — Cardiff University, UK Academia Fraud Prevention and Organised Crime

Michael LEVI

Professor of Criminology and ESRC Professorial Fellow — Cardiff University, UK Academia Fraud Prevention and Organised Crime

He has degrees from Oxford, Cambridge, Southampton and Cardiff universities; Professor of Criminology at Cardiff University School of Social Sciences; editor-in-chief of *Criminology and Criminal Justice*. Elected to the Academy of Social Sciences and granted a DSc (Econ) from Cardiff University; awarded Professorial Fellowship by the UK Economic and Social Research Council to research transnational economic and organised crime.

He has carried out research for the UK Government Fraud Review, the Council of Europe, the ASEM countries, the Association of Chief Police Officers, the UK Prime Minister's Strategy Unit, the UK FSA.

He wrote: *The phantom capitalists: the organisation and control of long-firm fraud*,

The media and white-collar crimes: the communicative act

Historically, there has been a shift from seeing the public as 'black boxes' who passively record the messages sent by them (whether by OLAF, the SFO or any other body) towards a more proactive model in which consumers actively interpret 'the evidence' through pre-existing lenses. The reactions of the British public towards the crisis at the somewhat porous Northern Rock bank in 2007 are an excellent illustration of the refusal of the public to accept the official version of their financial 'safety'. (The queues also generated a wonderful supply of stock film to use in future financial crises.)

But, as I see it, the task facing OLAF is a different one. In my perspective, OLAF's objectives are:

• to reduce objective levels of fraud;

• to encourage Member States to prosecute and to deal competently with crimes against the financial interests of the EU;

• to return proceeds of EU fraud to us, the taxpayers of Europe;

• to encourage the legitimacy of the EU by getting the public:
  — to see EU fraud as harmful rather than as OK (or a national sport), and
  — to view OLAF and national bodies as doing a good job in fighting fraud.

One of the key problems in this respect is that the media are largely uninterested in institutional victims. They *are* interested in what they see as institutional incompetence either in prevention or prosecution, and it is fashionable to criticise such bodies. The only fraud victims who regularly receive positive publicity are 'widows and orphans' or those who are defrauded by particularly evil people. In principle, a focus on the 'opportunity costs' of fraud — i.e. what could have been done for the public if fraud had not happened — *might* work. One of the reasons for the media success of the costs of fraud report I headed for the UK Association of Chief Police Officers (2007) was that we could have two Olympic Games annually if we saved the costs of fraud: however, what was the longer term impact of this report?

But given OLAF's objectives, what are our target populations? A key problem is to determine the relevant audiences for different programmes, depending on the kind of messages we are trying to get out. These are:

- actual offenders;

- potential offenders;

- guardians (e.g. law enforcement, private sector compliance officers, regulators);

- potential informants;

- the general public/voters (for legitimacy purposes).

Unfortunately, what *we* think matters most to 'people like us' is only a very limited guide to the effectiveness of communication to some of these populations. What, for example, do we know about what might deter people who are currently serious offenders? Alas, there is very little in the way of debriefing EU fraudsters. People may not be the best judges of what has motivated them but, in essence, they may be subdivided into:

- those who are committed to a criminal way of life, at least until they have enough money to afford to be honest;

- people who fear the bad opinion of others around them, but believe (rightly or wrongly) that EU fraud is not viewed very negatively;

- those who may have a large stake in legitimate business that might be harmed by publicised raids and/or by conviction.

How are we to get messages of the right sort to people like that? Are we actually more interested in a sympathetic portrait of those of us who are fighting fraud, so that we are seen as doing a good job? We need not always think of television but also of radio, whose listening figures post-digital and Internet have been rising. There are also channels such as You Tube, which one could use as a free mechanism for getting messages across. Cartoons are a good method, especially but not exclusively for younger and for less articulate people. One has to avoid, however, the austere 'socialist realism' model since one cannot get people to listen to or view such didactic material.

Whistleblower stories are popular as images of heroic sacrifice, but the EC must get its own house in order in tolerating or praising such revelations before encouraging such behaviour in others if it is not to be seen as hypocritical. In short, there are many forms through which anti-fraud messages can be communicated, but we must be clear about our objectives, our target audiences and our monitoring of impact if we are to deal with these issues in a rational way.

Academics

Drugs and money, The investigation, prosecution and trial of serious fraud, Regulating fraud, a special issue of *Criminology and Criminal Justice* on 'The organisation of serious crimes: developments in research and theory', 'Organised crime and terrorism' and 'Violent crime' in *The Oxford Handbook of Criminology*. He has published in the *British Journal of Criminology, Crime and Justice* and in *Crime, Law and Social Change*.

2.2 EUROPEAN INSTITUTIONS

European institutions

Alessandro BUTTICÉ

Head of Unit 'Spokesman, Communication, Public Relations' — Spokesman of OLAF

Outline and objectives of the seventh seminar of the OLAF Anti-Fraud Communicators' Network (OAFCN), Vienna and Bratislava, 23–26 September 2007

Alessandro BUTTICÉ

Head of the Spokesman, Communication, Public Relations Unit within the European Anti-Fraud Office (OLAF) of the European Commission. He created and coordinates the OLAF Anti-Fraud Communicators' Network (OAFCN). Before joining the European Commission, Mr Butticé served as Colonel in the Italian *Guardia di Finanza* where he held several managerial positions, which included leading the operational unit of investigators into financial and economic crimes and drug cases, as Deputy Head of Communication and Spokesperson in the Guardia's headquarters. He has also worked as a freelance journalist and a part-time professor at the University of Bari, in Italy.

The initial presentations for this seminar have already identified our core objectives for these three days of discussion.

We shall spend these three days in Vienna and Bratislava, this duration including the journey between Austria and Slovakia. This is a journey that will not only be an enjoyable opportunity for further discussion and to cement the personal relationships that have underpinned the highly positive work done by OAFCN for over seven years; it will also be a journey across a symbolic bridge, sailing that immense and magical waterway which crosses so much of Europe: the Danube.

A river which is now much more of an artery and much less of a border in the now-enlarged Europe; an artery which is also a bridge of civilisation, and between civilisations, for those values and that wealth which have formed the basis for the wealth and greatness of this continent and which, under the flag of the European Union, now unquestionably represent a beacon and a unique point of reference throughout the world for freedom, justice, peace and democracy.

The Danube: more of an artery, less of a border. The Danube, where in less happy times in our history bridges have been destroyed, is now the river which enables us to move freely between the old and new Member States of the Union; it unites, it does not divide; it is the symbolic bridge linking that diversity which is the heritage of Europe.

And what better and more symbolic way to organise a seminar of the OLAF Anti-Fraud Communicators' Network than on the banks of this great river, between two very different Member States?

What better way than this journey, this symbolic bridge, this seminar devoted to exploring the possibility of using a tool — television — which itself represents the world's greatest bridge for knowledge, information and training?

And within television, the unchallenged king of the media, despite the remorseless advance of the communicating power of the Internet, it is the power of 'fiction' to use the continental or American term, or 'drama' to use the British one, which today represents the language of communication and education, as well as entertainment, able to touch countless millions of citizens in Europe and across the world.

The national experience of televised fiction or drama — thrillers as well as other genres — will be the subject of the first part of our seminar today.

The second part, based on the findings of the first, will be devoted to a discussion of the feasibility of applying this extraordinary medium for entertainment, training, education and awareness to the combat against fraud and corruption, which damage the vital interests of citizens in ways they often fail to realise.

But also, and above all, we shall be discussing the wider issues of European construction, and the extent to which Europe is closer and more integral to the real interests of European citizens than many of them — due to poor communication and the lack of a language accessible to all, not just to the cultural, financial, political or economic elites — can imagine. A tool to foster closer contact with them, but also, and above all, to support the activity of this organisation: the prevention of fraud and corruption. A development which, as Vice-President Kallas has clearly said, would certainly be highly innovative and, I would suggest, perhaps even unprecedented on an international level.

I believe we are all fully aware of the risks we must be ready to face whenever we set out to do something really innovative. The OLAF Anti-Fraud Communicators' Network is a clear example of this. In 2001, when it was set up, it was the target of scepticism and criticism from people who (whatever their reasons or interests) were ready to bet that it would never succeed and would prove to be a pointless waste of time and resources.

Thanks to the courage of the Director-General of OLAF, Dr Brüner, in defending it, and to the commitment of all its members then and now, the results are now plain for all to see, recognised at the highest political levels in the Commission and Member States ([102]), and appreciated by the International Federation of Journalists and its national and regional associations which have formed part of the network for a number of years.

Even this seminar did not come about without a degree of scepticism from people who perhaps cling to the belief that Europe or the fight against fraud are issues too 'serious' or 'complicated' to be 'trivialised' — although I would prefer the term 'decoded' — by the use of a tool which even raised some eyebrows in Brussels, a reaction that has certainly not discouraged us. Maybe the sceptics will be proved right. And they will certainly be right if the outcome of this seminar is to show that it is impossible for us to use this tool to focus on issues of Europe and the combat against fraud. Whatever the outcome, this seminar will have had the merit of being the first platform for a discussion and debate on this topic at a European level, and will perhaps avoid further wasted effort in this area.

However, it is also perfectly possible — and this is our second working assumption — that this seminar, thanks to our discussions and the national experiences recounted by leading investigators, academics and television producers, will conclude that it is perhaps not such an eccentric idea after all, and that perhaps, within a few years, it may enable us to demonstrate to millions of Europeans and millions of viewers outside Europe — without the technocratic or Eurocratic language familiar and irritating to so many — the potential of Europe, which includes all of us, and its present and future contribution to the wellbeing of all.

If this seminar, with our discussions and pooled experiences, does no more than sow the seed of a future European television production, one not merely comprising news or documentaries, able to help reduce the still-gaping divide between Europe and its citizens, or between the fight against economic and financial fraud and corruption and the citizen-taxpayer, then I believe we could all be satisfied with the result. If our efforts ever come to fruition on the television screens, wherever we are or whatever we are doing at the time, we shall all be entitled to say: I was there in September 2007, in Vienna and Bratislava!

That is the primary goal of this seminar, as well as responding to the great curiosity and expectations of Vice-President Kallas, to whom we shall not fail to reply and whom we shall seek not to disappoint.

My thanks go to all those who have contributed to the organisation of this event, and above all to our Austrian and Slovak colleagues and friends. I would also like to thank the speakers who, at considerable personal inconvenience to themselves, will be with us over the next three days, leading and guiding our discussions.

Thank you and I wish you all a successful seminar.

---

(102) In a report of the Council of the European Union concerning the 'customs cooperation' working party of 10 May 2007 on a work plan (2004–06) for the 'strategy for customs cooperation' project group — Action 6.8 (Evaluate and report on cooperation between Member States' competent authorities in customs and the Commission — OLAF), there is, for example, the following comment under point 5 'Information and communication — Public relations' that 'the cooperation between OLAF and its communication network OAFCN has been assessed by the MS as being an excellent and efficient instrument of communication. OLAF's actions in publicising the MS efforts to combat fraud and protect the Community interests are considered to be adequate in the field of information distribution and communication to the public.'

Karl DOUTLIK

Head of European Commission Representation in Austria

**Karl Georg
DOUTLIK**
Leiter, Dipl.-Ing.

Head of the Repre-
sentation of the Euro-
pean Commission in
Austria, Vienna

Born in 1945, he
graduated from the
Universität für Bod-
enkultur, Vienna, and
obtained a Master of
Science from Lehigh
University, worked
as a project engineer
(environmental tech-
nology, water supply,
wastewater disposal)
at G. Edwin Pidcock
Consulting Engineers,
as Manager for Tech-
nical Development,
Sales Manager and
Division Manager at
ETERNIT-Werke L.
Hatschek AG and
as General Manager
at ETERNIT Tiefbau
GmbH. He then
worked for the
European Commis-
sion as Enterprise
DG Head of Unit
for 'Environmental
aspects of enterprise
policy', as Head of
Unit for 'Improv-
ing framework
conditions for SMEs'
and as Head of the
Representation of
the European Com-
mission in Austria,
Information broker-
ing and commenta-
torship, Communica-
tion DG.

Fight against fraud on vision

Vice-President Siim Kallas has nicely presented the essence in a nutshell. At European level, we are achieving great successes in combating fraud. In the EU institutions, we have sound systems to detect and combat fraud. We should make use of every tool to make this known to our European citizens.

So why not use the power of imagination — combine reality with fiction — and take advantage of the good practice examples at national level and elsewhere in the world to demonstrate that, in combating fraud too, cooperation at European level provides for added value and is highly effective?

Again in a nutshell (now in a German nutshell): *Tue Gutes und rede darüber!* This German proverb could be translated as: 'Do good and make it known!' Being deeply engaged in communication for several years, it is frustrating — even frightening! — how little our fellow citizens (even educated ones) know about European cooperation and the function-ing of its institutions and programmes.

The knowledge gap is tremendous. It leads to a widespread credibility gap and to a danger-ous confidence gap. This fact and the widespread habit of actors on the national level shoving responsibility for inconvenient decisions to Brussels (widely known as 'Brussels bashing') leads large communities to feel that they are determined by Brussels, that 'the EU is deciding'. We need urgently to demonstrate the reality: 'We are jointly deciding at European level' (decisions are taken by the European Parliament and the national minis-ters in Council — not by the Commission).

We need to demonstrate — clearly and with concrete examples — the added value of co-operation at European level, and combating crime and fraud is an excellent example to visualise the positive effects of this cooperation. The Commission, and in particular the Communication DG under the political leadership of Vice-President Wallström, has shown the way to concise and professional communication on the benefits of acting at European level: Plan D and the forthcoming White Paper on partnership in communication are the two lead strategies of EU communication. The latter in particular will pinpoint the use of modern communication tools such as audiovisual media and the Internet.

Let me not forget: Networking and partnership are two 'musts' in problem-solving as well as in modern communication. So why not accentuate the fruitful European cooperation in combating fraud by using existing networks like yours to inspire authors and providers of audiovisual programmes. Dramas on TV, at the cinema, etc. have the ability to capture the public imagination and make people find out that reality is often not too far away from vision. In this sense, I am already eager to watch 'Inspector Olaf' as the hero in a forthcoming drama!

Thank you for your attention.

Memberships

Austrian Water and Waste Management Association: Steering Committee member, until 1997; Association of Graduate Engineers for Water Management: Member of the Board, until 1997; Austrian Standardization Institute: cooperation and committee management ONI, CEN, ISO

Siim KALLAS

Commissioner in charge of Administrative Affairs,
Audit and Anti-Fraud

Siim KALLAS

Vice-President
of the European
Commission,
Commissioner
in charge of
Administrative
Affairs, Audit and
Anti-Fraud. Before
joining the European
Commission in
November 2004,
he served in Estonia
as Prime Minister,
Minister for Foreign
Affairs and Minister
for Finance where he
was closely involved
in the EU accession
negotiations of his
country. Mr Kallas has
also been President
of the Estonian
Central Bank and has
been elected three
times to the Estonian
Parliament.

Fraud with the EU budget: facts and fictions

First of all, I would like to express my regret at not being able to attend the conference in person, which was made impossible by my busy agenda. It is my pleasure to be able to address some thoughts to the participants of this seminar 'Fight against fraud on vision'.

To many citizens, what happens in Brussels sometimes seems unreal. Accordingly, myths and stories abound. This is in particular the case in the area of fraud and corruption, where the interesting combination of money and crime always is a powerful mixture to send the fantasy spinning.

Brussels, the swamp of corruption; the EU, the gravy train for greedy fraudsters of all kinds. Non-existing olive trees, and milk powder that is imported and exported for years on end. Who has not seen those headlines!

We at the European Commission are constantly fighting to prevent any fraud and irregularity, but also to convince the public that our systems are reliable and sound. It is crucial to gain the citizens' trust for the European project.

The Commission is in charge of spending the more than EUR 120 billion annually of the EU's budget. We constantly adjust controls, investigate thoroughly and cooperate in this with the national finance and fraud services — you are all involved each day in this joint commitment.

The Commission makes a great effort to be fully transparent on what is done with the European taxpayers' money and what is achieved. For instance, from next year on, the beneficiaries of EU funds will be published on the Internet.

In the prevention and fight against fraud, communication and awareness are central tools. Because it is the money of all citizens and because it is spent across the Union and the globe, fighting fraud needs to go beyond Brussels and the national administration.

And indeed, this seminar has set out to discuss how the ingredients of money and crime could be packaged into fictional television products to bring the EU's anti-fraud efforts closer to citizens. Television is the most powerful media in our present society. TV drama productions have the ability to capture the imagination of millions, often more so if the drama is a series and is therefore regular viewing. Though the stories are fiction, the dramatisation is drawn from real experiences, making use of the guidance of the investigating agency. It therefore becomes a collaborative project where both parties can benefit.

It is very innovative to explore whether the existing good national experiences can be replicated in the wider EU context to prevent fraud and to reduce the distance between Europe and citizens, communicating to an audience of some millions the effort made by the European institutions and EU Member States to fight against EU fraud.

To this end, this seminar brings together experts from all sides, to share and learn from the experiences which some national television and national anti-fraud agencies already have in this field. It will be very important for the Commission to know what the challenges have been, the difficulties, and the practical solutions.

This could be a good contribution of ideas and experience to see how the complex technicalities of EU spending can be explained to a broad public and how the joint efforts of European and national fraud busters can be made more visible. There is, I am sure, no shortage of material and true stories that would be truly incredible if they hadn't actually happened!

With this I would like to thank the OLAF Anti-Fraud Communicators' Network and its members and our Austrian and Slovak hosts for making this event happen. The network has often proved a very useful multiplier, for our annual reports or customs operations, and this seminar is exploring new ways of cooperation.

I wish you success and am looking forward with great curiosity and expectation to the outcome.

Elisabeth WERNER

Member of Cabinet in charge of OLAF and anti-fraud

'The European Commission needs to fight not only fraud and corruption but also the suspicion of corruption'

Ladies and gentlemen, it is a pleasure for me to be here in Vienna.

I would like to pick up and elaborate on two statements made by Vice-President Kallas and in particular what he said on the benefits of information and communication and about the possibility of using true fraud stories for fiction TV.

Mr Doutlik set out Commission communication efforts. The two quotes are:

1. 'In the prevention and fight against fraud, communication and awareness are central tools.'

2. 'Money and crime make fantastic fiction stuff. There is … no shortage of material and true stories that would be truly incredible if they hadn't actually happened!'

Why does the Commission believe that more information on fraud is good?

The institutional position of the Commission is the conviction that a maximum of transparency and accountability are the best measure to gain the public trust and are best to dispel any suspicions and misperceptions.

The European Commission needs to fight not only fraud and corruption but also the suspicion of corruption. It needs to dispel rumours and show it is serious in addressing the issue. In this regard, transparency is a win–win for the administrations and the public alike.

Whilst the consequences of transparency can be highly political, transparency itself is not a judgement. It is an instrument, empowering the public — the European citizen — to exercise their own judgement. As such, the Commission firmly believes that the EU's policies and institutions will benefit from this scrutiny; not least because it helps in fighting real fraud as well as the suspicion of it.

The Commission is fully aware that this is a large task.

- We need to demonstrate how the EU money is used, who gets what and what impact is achieved.

- We need to explain how decisions are made; Europe is not full of hidden plots; from next year lobbyists should register.

- Citizens must be able to inform themselves about the controls, the governance system and the checks and balances in place. Our systems are reliable and sound.

- It must be made clear that the protection of the EU taxpayers' money is a joint responsibility of the EU administration and authorities and the national bodies. At least, when the citizen doesn't trust Brussels, he would tend to trust his own police, customs and financial crime departments.

The Commission takes accountability seriously and wants to be an open institution. Fraud cases are not swept under the carpet, these cases happen, but they are not endemic and every time the Commission tries to give as much information as possible under the limitations of the secrecy of investigation, presumption of innocence and protection of personal data.

With regard in particular to the protection of financial interests and fight against fraud, in addition to the 200 or so pages published by the Court of Auditors, the Commission publishes an annual report describing national and Community efforts, as well as statistics, and OLAF publishes an activity report, which also contains anonymous case studies.

This leads me to the second part. Mr Kallas also said that 'Money and crime make fantastic fiction stuff. There is … no shortage of material and true stories that would be truly incredible if they hadn't actually happened!'

Thanks to the transparency and reporting of the EU, as part of our accountability efforts, there is a wealth of anonymous cases that could serve for inspiration. There is material for suspense plus thrill. Let's look at a few.

- Smuggling with health aspects — Cigarettes are legend by now. But our joint customs operations have unveiled amazing products being faked and smuggled. Some of them only present a commercial and copyright loss; others are outright dangerous for public health and safety. The range extends from fashion items with designer logos but in poor quality to dangerous medical products or explosive lighters. After the recent scare about children's toys with toxic paint, these topics figure high in the public's awareness!

- VAT carrousel, where high-value, low-volume items are imported and exported and traders that have claimed a VAT reimbursement suddenly go missing in the area of agricultural products. There are at least two famous cases, one of adulterated butter, where additional ingredients were mixed into butter to stretch it, and the product then sold to make cheese and to various bakeries. Luckily, health effects were excluded in this case. It became prominent because it involved at least four Member States, Belgium, Italy, Germany and France, and because one MEP, Paolo Casaca from Portugal, was very actively interested. The second agricultural case goes back a few years already and is related to preferential trade agreements which the EU had with Balkan countries. Suddenly, sugar imports increased substantially, which arose suspicion. When it appeared that the sugar was cane sugar, which does not normally grow in the region, it was clear that some sort of fraud was going on.

- Structural Funds: The ESF is vulnerable; it finances many smaller-sized projects for instance to retrain and increase employment opportunities.

Some of the stories involve really big money and serious, internationally organised crime. This shows that not all fraud is simply down to the corruption of EU officials!

All of them are about familiar products that everybody uses in daily life. In each of these areas, the European bodies and OLAF work with national counterparts to establish the facts, so that both European and national services are involved. The cases go across borders.

These examples could be turned into very entertaining stories that capture and absorb the imagination: the right mixture of money and crime; and hopefully commercially interesting. And for the Commission as an institution, a divulgation of such stories would also have the benefit of sending the following message:

- initial objective and purpose of the project;

- sophistication and 'professionalism' of fraudsters involved/perpetrators and victims;

- seriousness about dealing with irregularities found;

- benefits of cooperation — faced with cross-border issues and organised crime, law enforcement today also needs to operate at international level;

- damage to general society because of the fraud since objectives of the project are not met, fraud with EU money is not a victimless crime;

- recoveries and sanctions as a deterrence.

Finally, it would make the European Anti-Fraud Office (OLAF) better known, so that when citizens hear the name they would not primarily think of a young Swede or an Ikea shelf, but of European efforts to fight fraud.

Thank you very much for your attention.

European institutions

Rosalind WRIGHT
Chairman, OLAF Supervisory Committee

Rosalind WRIGHT

Rosalind Wright is a member of and past Chair of the Supervisory Committee of OLAF, the European Anti-Fraud Office.

She has been Chair of the Fraud Advisory Panel since 2003. She is also an independent member of the Insolvency Service Steering Board. Rosalind was Director of the Serious Fraud Office, from 1997 to April 2003. She was also previously General Counsel and an Executive Director for 10 years at the Securities and Futures Authority, one of the principal City financial services regulators. Prior to taking up that appointment, she was an Assistant Director of Public Prosecutions at the DPP's department, where she worked for 18 years, after five years in practice at the Bar. She is a QC (senior counsel) and a Companion of the Order of the Bath.

Presentation to the 'Fighting fraud on vision' conference, organised by the OAFCN

The fight against fraud is an international problem and one which crosses all boundaries. The fight against fraud on the European budget is a continuing one, which affects us all. OLAF's role in this is pivotal and absolutely vital. We, the Supervisory Committee of OLAF, support OLAF's work and work with them to reinforce the message that fraud and corruption to the prejudice of EU funds will be thoroughly and professionally investigated. Where fraud is identified, it will be stopped and the proceeds, as far as possible, recovered.

This crucial work must have the support of all EU citizens. Unfortunately, to very many within the Member States, both private citizens and indeed politicians, too little is known about OLAF and its successes. Where the fight against fraud is mentioned, the contribution made by OLAF teams, working with national enforcement agencies, is not brought to the fore as much as it deserves to be.

How can we, as communicators, address this problem? One way is to marshal the mass broadcast media to get the message across. Virtually everybody in the EU and outside has access to television and the graphic crime dramas on the screens of every network throughout Europe and beyond are popular and compelling viewing.

The great fictional detective series, made by the BBC and independent television in the UK, based on Sherlock Holmes, Miss Marple and Hercule Poirot are syndicated worldwide and have been seen by millions of people. But how many of the programmes and instalments concern financial or commercial fraud, rather than the juicier and more immediately dramatic murder, or better still, multiple murders, to be solved by the fictional sleuths?

The trouble is that financial crime doesn't make for easy or comprehensible viewing. It requires a degree of sophistication to understand what has happened in a fraud.

How the transactions were put together, the structures of the markets in which they took place or the mechanism for reclaiming funds from public sector agencies are all difficult for the uninitiated to grasp and, truth to tell, not very riveting for the ordinary lay viewer. We here today all find fraud fascinating. I certainly do, and have devoted the greater part of my professional life to combating it. It's not everybody's idea of excitement, however. Those of us who have been concerned in a fraud investigation know the months, even years, it can take to follow the audit trails, investigate company accounts and obtain orders worldwide to examine banking transactions in many different jurisdictions. All this is bread and butter to the fraud investigator, but it doesn't make for the most exciting television viewing.

There has been, of course, the odd exception. Spectacular company failures, including Enron, BCCI and Maxwell have caught the public imagination. And where colourful characters are involved — usually the crooks rather than the investigators — such as Maxwell himself (and you today in Bratislava are close to Robert Maxwell (né Jan Hoch)'s birthplace) the press and the broadcasters have been quick off the mark to plaster their names and faces across news and factual programmes. But a fictional series about a fraudster? We were recently treated to a docudrama, featuring David Suchet, the well-known British actor, who plays Poirot on television, as Robert Maxwell in *The Last Days of Maxwell*. The BBC billed it as follows:

> Maxwell's world is collapsing. Cracks are appearing in his multi-billion business empire, his marriage is in difficulties and his weight has ballooned dangerously.
>
> He owns some of the world's best-known media companies — Macmillan Publishing, the *New York Daily News* and the *Daily Mirror*.
>
> But his obsession with both power and his great rival, Rupert Murdoch, is causing his downfall.
>
> With time running out he retreats to the heart of his web and sets about saving his skin. He is trapped and paranoid.
>
> His attempts to stem the tide of debts culminate in him stealing a billion pounds from his companies and their pension funds.
>
> But he is still hurtling towards disaster and, ultimately, death.
>
> *Maxwell* is a gripping account of how greed and ambition destroyed a man and led him to commit one of the world's biggest ever frauds.

The point of the drama was not the fraud itself, or the investigation into it, but the psychological makeup of Maxwell himself and the way he manipulated his staff, his colleagues and his family and mistresses. So the fraud wasn't the central point of the programme, much as we would perhaps have preferred it to be.

Likewise, and incidentally made by the same director, some time ago the BBC produced programmes on two other fraud cases, again featuring the extraordinary personalities of the crooks although their modus operandi was central to the films and could hardly be left out of the programmes. One, *The Secretary Who Stole £4million,* featured Joyti de Lauri, who stole from her two bosses, senior executives of Goldman Sachs in London to fund a lavish lifestyle of exotic holidays, jewellery and clothes. The other featured two middle-aged Australian former prostitutes, Evelyn Frances Burton and Lyla André, who were convicted of conspiring to defraud investors. Clients, many of whom were found by the two women at race meetings, were offered investment opportunities in an American company, with claims that the company would be able to invest the money in bank trading programmes generating spectacular profits. They managed to fleece investors of many millions of pounds. They were highly colourful characters, who dressed flamboyantly, and, again, being women, unusual defendants in this sort of crime, made for compelling viewing. The work of the Serious Fraud Office which investigated the Maxwell and the Burton and André cases did not feature in the programmes and indeed in the latter case wasn't mentioned at all, even though our investigators spent years on the case and in extraditing the two women from New Zealand to face trial in the UK.

This is the drawback in seeking to persuade the broadcast media to feature financial crime. Because the crime itself is not that camera-friendly, the producers look for a feature which will attract viewers: in these real-life cases, as opposed to the crimes investigated by Holmes and Poirot, it is the lifestyle of the criminals that they centre on, rather than the skill of the investigators, or indeed, the danger to the public of the crimes they commit as a warning to others.

The only programme that I know of in the UK that portrays fraud and financial trickery in a very entertaining and graphic way is *The Real Hustle*, now in its fourth series, broadcast on the satellite channel, BBC Three. In this programme, three actors take the part of 'hustlers', confidence tricksters, to demonstrate some common frauds and scams, which they perpetrate on innocent members of the public while they are being filmed. Of course, in the end, they refund any monies taken, but the programmes, which are compelling viewing, are intended to serve as a public warning to show people what to look out for and how to avoid being scammed. In the programmes, they pass off counterfeit cash, sell some very pretty but completely worthless gems, and get punters to pay for non-existent debts — all whilst helping themselves to a constant supply of other people's cameras, passports, cash and bags.

One couple has the entire contents of their living room stolen in less than 20 minutes; one actor, Alex, passes himself off as a peer of the realm; another, Jess, makes GBP 200 by convincing someone she's just been run over; and Paul makes a mint by inventing a machine that is just as useless as it is desirable.

In seeking to persuade programme-makers to feature OLAF and frauds against the EU budget in fictional television series, we want to make quite sure what we want to achieve. Is it simply to warn people of the extent of fraud on the EU budget? Is it to let the public know what OLAF is there to do and what its job consists of? Or is it to warn the public that if they get involved in fraudulent or corrupt activities, OLAF is going to crack down on them and bring them to justice?

We have to be very careful that we understand the purpose of drawing attention to OLAF in the broadcast media. Things have a tendency to backfire, if one isn't very careful. The fact of massive fraud on the EU budget in itself is the stuff of current events or business news factual programmes, with limited interest for the general viewer. That there is a European office charged with the investigation of fraud and corruption to the prejudice of European finances is of little interest to the general public unless there is some other factor — a huge and immense fraud on an international scale or colourful characters involved. And, dare one say it, some ineptitude on the part of the investigator, on the lines of Inspector Clouseau, will probably be of more immediate interest to programme-makers than showing OLAF to be the tough and effective investigator we all know and fondly hope the programmers will portray.

It will be very important to maintain some kind of control over the content and the focus of the programmes. We can't allow a programme-maker to fictionalise OLAF and its work to portray it in a totally unfavourable light. At the same time, programme-makers, as I am sure some of them at this seminar will tell you, are jealous of their independence and will brook no outside interference. So we may be taking a dangerous step in the dark by suggesting OLAF as a theme for a fictional television series.

Some years ago, when I took over as Director of the Serious Fraud Office in London, the BBC decided to make three films for *Panorama*, a documentary programme, on the work of the Office. My predecessor had signed a contract with them. They enlisted our cooperation and made the three films, over a year, which were broadcast in 1998/99. To an extent, they put the SFO on the map. However, all our shortcomings and faults were exposed, as much as our strengths and achievements. One of our senior managers, noted for his enjoyment of good food and wine, was innocently portrayed constantly referring to lavish meals he had been partaking of when the call came through to take on a new and important case. The programme-makers, who, after all, are in the entertainment industry and seek to put on interesting and diverting programmes, are not interested in worthy but dull themes. They want excitement, glamour and a fast-moving plotline, none of which are usually provided in fraud investigation. Hence the *Panorama* programmes tended to concentrate on the 'human interest' angles, the pretty secretaries, the failures of the SFO to get a conviction (this seemed to feature more frequently in the series than the SFO's successes) and the rueful explanations by successive directors of why things had gone wrong. Is this really what we want for OLAF?

In a farce (*In the Club*) recently put on at the Hampstead Theatre in London, which took as its theme the travails of a hapless and corrupt UK MEP and his domestic entanglements in Strasbourg, a central heating engineer, apparently innocently involved in checking the water supply, turns out to be an undercover OLAF investigator. He spends most of the play concealed in a cupboard, wired up for sound, while he spies on the MEP and his wife and colleagues confessing to frauds relating to their secretarial and travel expenses. He is a much-feared character and causes alarm when his presence in the cupboard is revealed. This may be as good as we can get with dramatic fiction featuring OLAF.

2.3 MEDIA

Martin AMBROSCH

Soko Kitzbüel — Beo film ZDK/ORF

Martin AMBROSCH

Born 1964 in Vienna

Studies in economic science

1999 training as screenplay consultant through the Filmboard Berlin-Brandenburg, Drehbuchforum and FOCAL

Screenplays for feature films:

Scripts for feature films:

Heile Welt (Allegro Film, Florian Flicker)

Stille Wasser (Allegro Film, Max Linder), 1995

Nachtfalter, Franz Novotny (Novotny Film/Franz Novotny), 2000

Kaltfront, Valentin Hitz (Coop 99), 2001/02

Spiele Leben, Antonin Svoboda (Coop 99), 2005

Screenplays for TV:

Soko Kitzbühel (Beo Film) for ZDF/ORF, TV series 2001/02/03/04/06/07/08

Martin Ambrosch, Scriptwriter of Soko Kitzbüel — Beo film ZDK/ORF

Well, if I can briefly introduce myself. I am the scriptwriter of a very successful series in Germany and Austria. We have done more than 100 episodes which are going to be broadcast in the near future. We have got some good and bad news. The good news is that a 90-minute special that I wrote was very successfully broadcast, and there was an OLAF official in it who was put across as a very good upright person, but the bad news is that he was murdered! I think we can have a quick look at that, the end of an OLAF official.

Now, obviously we are trying to produce things which will go down well with the public and we are looking into this at the moment, as we want people to react positively to a given taste. Our hero, the OLAF official, was taken on board because it was a question of European food safety, and there was some blackmail going on. I had a problem with my research in this area because I have never asked a genuine OLAF official how work is really carried out there. We are a bit afraid that the EU might not be very happy if one of their officials is shown as being a blackmailer from the food safety authorities! The OLAF person comes across as squeaky clean.

This is one of the areas where we think cooperation could be improved to take our fears away and at the same time be a bit more specifically rooted in practice. This could happen through communication with OLAF or the whole of the EU.

Now what that means is that I should not just be faced with concrete figures, I need to face concrete examples. I am going to go into a little bit more detail here. For example, we may have a forensic judge in front of me and they would help me to plan a perfect murder, and at the same time they build in a little mistake somewhere so that we cannot have a copycat murder from the public or somebody who might be interested.

So it is very interesting for me to hear about very interesting examples, specific examples, from the organisations, in which we can integrate little mistakes which the OLAF official can then have slapped on to them, showing him as a hero. They can help me in specific

Since 2004 head
writer, many episodes,
including 90-minute
specials

Screenplay and
Director:

Im Auftrag Seiner
Majestät, 50 min.,
Aichholzer Film for
ORF/ARTE, 2005

Under preparation:

Das Verhör (Aich-
holzer Film) ZDF/
ORF

Zielfahnder (Beo Film)
ZDF/ORF

Das Glück dieser Erde
(Satel Film) ARD/
ORF

Awards:

Grand Award Screen-
play/feature films of
the City Salzburg
for Heile Welt at the
'Diagonale 1994'
festival

terms. I think that I cannot come up with ideas myself which you have never had. You have probably had the same ideas a very long time ago.

For example, I have asked a forensic expert what a perfect murder is. Well there is a plant, and if you press it you can come up with a transparent liquid which is very poisonous. You can add it to other liquids, schnapps for example. He gave us an example of a tax adviser in Vienna having offered a client a bottle of vodka. This is a real case. The customer drank from this and died. The tax adviser got this drink from a patient, a doctor, and there were an awful lot of other bottles around in Vienna that the police could not find, although they knew they were there.

So they were looking for these bottles, spending months doing so, and they finally found them. Now these are ideas that I could never come up with. It is only an expert who deals with this sort of thing on a daily basis who can come up with this and then put it to me and tell me where I could slip in my little mistake. That is something which can be done in terms of the cooperation between us and you. You can provide us with the stories, either through the press or on a one-to-one basis. You could tell us what cigarettes are being smuggled and where.

It does not help us to just get those figures. We need these interesting stories which we can slip something into so we can make sure that you, the OLAF officials, are heroes while at the same time twisting it in such a way that the public cannot pick up on it and then actually commit the same sort of crime.

A speaker

Now, Mr Ambrosch, I have a question for you. Since you talked about OLAF in one of your episodes, why did you not get in touch with OLAF? I mean, we have a whole series of cases and we could have sent you some judgment, some sentences, and that might have been of some use to you.

My question is, maybe you did get in touch with us but we did not get back to you or we did not cooperate. I hope that was not the case.

Martin Ambrosch

It is really a matter of being very cautious, when you work in the creative industry, vis-à-vis the authorities. I put the question of whether there are any exciting cases in your department, and it can get an exciting answer. The official would then say to be careful and we are only in front of a computer. I say I would like to turn it into a drama and then the answer is no, and it is not reality. I would say sorry, as my job is to come up with exciting material.

So you start getting cautious, as there are officials that want to cooperate and are more than helpful. Others are not that helpful. When I am dealing with the institutions, or institutions new to me, I send out a feeler. If I get the right feedback, then there can be good cooperation, as long as it is based on mutual understanding. If you understand that I have got to turn all this into drama, and every once in a while people leave their computers, pull out a gun and fire the darn thing, then maybe it is not quite reality.

Media

Christina CHRISTOVA

Legal advisor to the producer of 'Action',
BNT-Bulgaria

Police work — live on television 'Action' television broadcast on Bulgarian national television

'Action' started two years ago, in 2005, and its first broadcast on Bulgarian national television was in the autumn of the same year. This is the first broadcast that recreates live police work — aspects from the different kinds of activity of the particular services and directorates in the system of the Ministry of the Interior.

After assessment of the audience and a series of analyses of interests and existing programmes, it turned out that up until then there had been no such production recreating the different aspects of the Bulgarian police services' work in an authentic way. Different types of television movies were broadcast — serials, criminal serials, actions, thrillers and so on — but there was no television broadcast on State public television, presenting the diversity of activities and particular facets of the work of the policeman, the fireman, the preliminary investigator, the juvenile officer, the officer from the service combating organised crime or countering corruption, etc.

The aims of 'Action', set out at the beginning, were as follows:

- to publicise activities of the different services in the Ministry of the Interior and its structures;

- to satisfy the audience's interest and to make up for certain omissions in relation to particular details in the prevention and fight against crime;

- to inform the audience about the operative laws and the changes in the normative order, regulating the actions of the law enforcement authorities in Bulgaria;

- to inform the audience about EU requirements — after the accession of Bulgaria to the European Union, at the moment and for the past two years — regarding some special features of European legislation on law enforcement and differences from the Bulgarian one;

- to acquaint the public with the newest work strategies of the police services;

- to create new knowledge in the public sense of the necessity of civil society's participation in the fight against crime and thus encouraging non-profit organisations and citizens to cooperate with police authorities. At this point we should say that 'Action' works in close collaboration and interaction with the Ministry of the Interior, as well as with the Prosecutor's Office of the Republic of Bulgaria.

The television broadcast is an external television production, negotiated with Bulgarian national television, expenses being covered by sponsors and advertising time.

What is the structure of 'Action'?

'Action' is a 30-minute block with several permanent rubrics: 'Fraud', 'In action'/'Operations — live'/, 'Wanted', 'Security' and 'Hero of the week'. There is also an occasional rubric about different international events, meetings, conferences, etc. in the country or abroad. The production is broadcast every Monday, at prime time just before the news edition — from 18.30 to 19.00 — on Channel 1 of Bulgarian national television.

(1) The 'Fraud' rubric shows cases of victims of different types of fraud — frauds with counterfeit money, documents, credit cards, etc.

(2) 'In action' is of great interest to the audience, since the cases presented are shot in real time. The production team patrols with police officers on duty on the streets of different towns of the country. Rough material from the police surveillance cameras is shown as well, which is interesting to the audience since it cannot be seen anywhere else. That opportunity — at least for our country, but as experience shows for other countries as well — is a unique chance for ordinary people to 'look through' the eyes of the police officers who watch over the streets. 'In action' also shows different police operations of the Ministry of the Interior's directorates and services.

(3) The 'Wanted' rubric displays people reported for a national investigation during the previous week, by showing pictures, contact addresses and telephone numbers in case people have any information about them. There is a compulsory announcement that 'anonymity is guaranteed'.

(4) 'Security' is another permanent rubric of the production, where people are given instructions on what to do if they become a victim or a witness of a crime. In each case presented every week — crime reconstruction (except for presenting the offence itself), theft, sexual abuse, robbery, car accident and so on — conclusions are drawn, with the aid of an expert opinion from an officer of the Ministry of the Interior or a lawyer, and tips are given about how to avoid the incident happening again.

(5) 'Hero of the week' is also a permanent rubric showing a distinguished officer from the Ministry of the Interior — a police officer, fireman or other agent from the different

police services — someone who has taken part in life-saving actions or in an important case where the officer has helped people in various serious and difficult situations.

All the stories presented are based on real cases and most of the material — information about different incidents — is provided by the Press Office of the Ministry of the Interior. Some of the plots are also taken from the information databases of the Ministry of the Interior and Prosecutor's Office. They can be defined as reconstructions of real cases from the police's daily routine by means of artistic recreation. 'The actors' are police officers or employees of the other services in the Ministry of the Interior, but some of them are real actors, for example the ones playing the crime victims.

The Ministry of the Interior is the institution committed to guaranteeing the security and peace of citizens, to help people. That is only possible if the laws are observed and if there is a firm will to work on prevention of and counter measures to the different kinds of crimes — juvenile crime, organised crime, traffic in human beings and drug traffic, corruptive behaviour and so on. Only on that basis can the police do its duty and protect people. On the other hand, the public, ordinary people, should be fully aware that if they cooperate with the police, they help the whole society. This becomes quite possible when people also get a visual notion about the activity of the police authorities. We all know how powerful the influence of television is.

To conclude, I would like to say some words about future ideas for the programme. We would like to show the Bulgarian public how police structures work in other countries. In relation to this, we are currently having talks with Greece, Turkey and Romania for closer cooperation — bilateral in the beginning and multilateral later on. The idea is that teams from the Balkan region pay visits on an exchange basis and shoot television broadcasts. Later on, our intention will be to try to cooperate not only with Balkan countries, but also with the central European EU Member States, as well as with international organisations. We would highly appreciate your assistance in this.

Thank you.

Media

Media

Cecilia COPE DI VALROMITA

Senior producer
RAI Fiction Department

RAI Fiction Department

Well, as others have already done, I am going to speak in my own mother tongue. I thank everyone for the invitation, which is particularly interesting for people like us from the fiction world. I work for RAI Fiction, which is RAI's department responsible for producing fiction for RAI 1, RAI 2 and RAI 3. We read about 1 500 scripts per year and we produce 750 hours or thereabouts for daytime and prime-time TV.

This seminar gives me, by explaining the work of RAI Fiction, the possibility of sharing a unique experience, and it is the first time we have been in such a highly specialised and well-represented group. So for us as producers, the storytellers, the narrators if you like, the people who tell the fairy tales, we are here with our ears flapping. We are trying to draw out some ideas so that we can then include those within possible productions or co-productions.

Police fiction — from the word 'go' when it comes to television — is the most highly attractive genre, if you like, with *Sheridan* and *Maigret*, and then we had *Octopus*, which presented the break between the first stage and the second. It allowed us not only to work through the newspapers and the television news, but to find out more about the Sicilian mafia situation. This has helped bring about, I think, a growth in the public's perception of and attitudes towards civil issues. (I apologise as I get lost in my notes every now and again.)

These programmes, in terms of quantity and quality, are one of the strong points for us. They go down very well with the public and critics. We produce excellent products which reach out to a very broad public and tell the tale of modern-day Italy. We have produced some major serials, as speakers beforehand were telling us. We had the *Carabinieri*, *Maresciallo Rocca*. Sometimes, when you have a major success, people pick up on that and we moved on to *Commissario Montalbano*, another policeman of a different type. That is drawn from an Italian writer's books, who worked for many years producing *Maigret* for RAI. Those books are based in Sicily. Then we produced *The Coast Guard* and *The Capitano*, with the *Guarda di Finanza*.

We want to have a broad range of products to put to our public. We are a public broadcasting service, and so we have to cover the whole scope from comedy and drama right through to police series. That is our job. What is very interesting, and something the public can identify with in these people, is their human nature. We have got people who are not untouchable superheroes. It is the man on the street, someone who has got their own family, their weak and strong points. And it is indeed that which makes them very attractive for a broad-ranging audience.

In other words, any Tom, Dick or Harry could be a hero. As has been said already on various occasions during the course of this meeting, television is able to reach the broadest audience and through narrating, through the series form, obviously these programmes are really one of the ways of reaching out *par excellence*, towards the public.

RAI 3 broadcasts another product of ours as well. RAI 3 is not the big target channel but it has a production called *La Squadra* which is pretty low-budget, costing EUR 600 000 per broadcast — a low budget compared with other productions. It is based in the centre of Naples and deals with a group of police officers facing up to the tough reality which is Naples.

As Mr Butticé was saying this morning, a book called *Gomorrah* has recently been published. I do not know if it is going to be or has already been translated into other languages, but it relates the dreadfully difficult situation which exists in Naples. An awful lot of the episodes of this programme, *La Squadra*, have been shot in the port of Naples.

What makes a show attractive is its national nature. *Commissioner Rex* and *Derek* are typically German series but they are very successful in Italy as well. There are constant re-runs. Our type of production, as we heard from Mr Corsetti this morning, is like *Maresciallo Rocca*, which has been sold across the boards. He told us once that apparently he speaks Chinese as well and the series has been translated into Chinese. *Commissario Montalbano* has been bought in Russian as well. They are typically national products but they are so attractive that they are capable of putting across these universal values and crossing the borders of different countries. These are values which we all share.

I do not know if there are any questions, but I can answer them if you have any. I would like to show a short video of about three minutes and then hand over to Professor Buonanno, who has done some great research into our products.

Rainer Newald

Thank you very much indeed for that very impressive presentation. I did actually want to raise a couple of additional questions and maybe some additional points for discussion in so doing.

Personally, the way I see this is, I think that themes such as the ones we are seeing now, which come from daily life, should be put across. I do not know about Maresciallo Rocca *and to what extent it deals with this type of thing, but our experience, and this is where I want to pick up on the previous discussion, is that cases of fraud are largely related to questions of illegal employment and things like this. It does not have to be death and murder and things like this. This type of thing can also be dealt with by a good producer so that the argument can be put across that must have some sort of affinity for this sort of issue that comes down in the public.*

Cecilia Cope

I think it is possible. I think you have to look at the idea and then try to get together and work on it with the scriptwriter because, yes, these are problems of everyday life, problems that all Europeans are having to face. So I think it can be done, if you have a good scriptwriter. It takes a bit of time, because from the idea through to production and broadcasting, the timing, it takes about two years. It is tough work. You know, until the scenario is going to work, it is re-worked again and again. So it is highly-skilled work which is put in. It is not something which is just cooked up overnight and that is it.

Rocca, for example, is very attractive because it is a product which appeals to the entire family, from children right through to grandparents. The Italians love it and I think it is loved abroad as well. As I say, it has been sold all over the place, so, yes, I think it is quite possible.

You just have to check out the idea, you have to see what it is going to give us in reality. You have to try to inform and you have to make it possible to bring about this social growth, put across values to your audience, universal values. I think that is all quite feasible, what you were suggesting.

You just have to try not to be frightened to stick your neck out and do something which has never been done before there, basically.

Peter HAJEK

Film producer, Mungo-film, Film- und Fernsehproduktion GmbH,
producer of *Commissioner Rex*

Peter HAJEK

Author, director,
film producer

Born in 1941 in
Vienna. As a jour-
nalist, he worked
from 1959 for the
Austrian newspa-
per *Kurier* and for
German magazines
including *Twen*,
pardon and *Der
Spiegel*.

Together with
Helmuth Dimko he
created the award-
winning TV pro-
gramme *Apropos
Film* (ORF/ZDF) in
1967 (broadcast
until 2002) and in
1976 they founded
Mungo-film. He
gained reputation
as a script-writer
for the TV show
Wünsch Dir Was
(ORF/ZDF) and
created and direct-
ed the acclaimed
TV portraits *Wer
war André Heller*,
Margot Werner
and, in 1983/84,
Helnwein (Berlin
film festival 1984,
Grimme and Rhein-
Preis Awards). His
portrait of the
Austrian illustra-
tor and cartoonist
Manfred Deix, *Küss
die Hand, Österreich*
(1987/88), also
premiered at the
Berlin film festival.

Peter Hajek, film producer, Mungo-film, Film- und Fernsehproduktion GmbH, producer of *Commissioner Rex*

I am going to be very brief in what I have to say here. I think my colleague Mr Ambrosch has already made most of the points. They are responsible for this and questions such as television series, writers and producers, etc. They want to be able to cooperate with the EU. We have had an example of this which boiled down to a question of trust.

A few years ago, in Vienna, we found out that there was a possibility of undermining the State so that, within six or seven days, basically the town would become uninhabitable... I am not going to say what it is or whether it still exists, or whether it concerned weapons or anything else. We went to the police and people responsible for this and we discussed it with them. They said, well, if you include it in your series, then all hell will break loose, and we should not give anybody the idea of doing whatever it was. You know, it is actually a great story in itself, but to put it in a nutshell, we agreed with the authorities that we would not run the story but that they should give us the possibility of working in an area that they are responsible for, shooting there while making sure it would not give anybody any wrong or bad ideas.

So, the point I am making here is that we must be able to discuss with OLAF and find out what it is really up to and doing. Then maybe we can tell the story afterwards, without actually hampering them in the work that they are going to be called upon to carry out thereafter.

Let me just pick up straight away on what you have said here. I mean, I do not know about any studies or anything, but your work has become globally known, worldwide, and how can you be sure that it has changed your access to an authority? I am talking about the police, of course here.

What lies behind this, the basis, is that you have a man and a dog who are the main figures. Rather, it is the dog and then the man. When we started to write this, 12 years ago, we discovered that all Commissioners in Europe were pretty old. As far as the dog is concerned, dogs are nice, are they not? That is not really the point, more that the dog is the only living being which has attached itself to man. It is a very different relationship to, for example, what exists between man and horse. We have this long-established relationship between man and dog and that is the background to all of it. That is why we have been so successful, as that is a relationship which is understood around the world, I think.

As far as the police are concerned, I will have to pick up on what previous speakers have said as well. What we have tried to do is show people as human beings, to show that these are people who exist, normal people. We have sat down with the police before the episodes to discuss how to go about it and, with the dog, it is the same thing. We discuss how they work with the dogs. I do not want to have a dialogue here, so can I just ask whether there are any questions from the floor or from anybody else?

A speaker

I have got a comment and a question. You are talking about OLAF, and that applies to all of us, I think. You were talking about establishing confidence. We are there. We are not an independent body. We have got to be seen in conjunction with others. And so, I think we can actually work better across the face of Europe.

We have to show that there is this cooperation and that we are not all enclosed within our own little national borders. What struck me is when I compare this with the clip shown by our Italian colleagues, where you saw the uniformed police officer. I think that in middle Europe, it is basically only the criminal police who play a role there, whether we are talking about Germany or Austria or whatever, and you do not see very much of these uniformed officers. It is not the service element that is coming to the fore, but rather the individual. You know, you have got the dog here and the Commissioner. You see the team.

Peter Hajek

What comes through from the Italians is the competent police authority. Does that depend on the audience or the story? Well, basically, we wanted to show this cooperation, this link between the human being and the dog in this environment. This has been copied on many occasions since but it did not exist when we started. And, you know, that is the way we were trying to tell our crime story.

When I was researching, we were in contact with the genuine authorities, the genuine officials. None of them wore uniforms, but were 'in civvies'. You know, they basically hid the weapons in the waistband or something. It is counter-productive in terms of identification, with the hero or main protagonist, if you show people too much in uniform. I think you have to have a balance and let the team work in the background. Otherwise it is not possible to identify them. I mean, you cannot hugely identify with a team, it happens with an individual.

A speaker

I have got a couple of comments I would like to add. The different way of showing these people shows that you have a diversification within European public opinion. You have this middle

European awareness and then you have a southern European one, and that is Europe. I think Commissioner Rex *has had a major role to play and has done a great service not only for the Austrian police but in Europe in general. It has given a very different image of what was coming across, for example, from Germany. We have seen a very different image coming through, particularly looking back at the German and Austrian police when they were being shown in a very different light to what we have now with Rex.*

Now I do not know whether this just happened or if it was intentional. It has done a major service not only for Austria but for Europe as well, as it is made up of young people, democracy and the image that Rex gives to the Austrian police. I think that is the real image, which is a very good one, and it has been exported beyond your own country. That is the first comment.

I have a question I would like to raise.

Peter Hajek

I just wanted to react to that. In *Commissioner Rex*, the police officer is the sort we would like to have, and I hope we will have it. As far as Vienna is concerned, we have seen a tripling of the number of Italians coming here on holiday compared with what we used to get, probably as a result of this.

A speaker

Well just let me add communication with the outside world. I do not know if this is intentional, but I would like you to tell me how much you cooperated with the Austrian police. I am convinced that communication with the outside world can be very positive in terms of internal communication within the institution as well. I hope that the Austrian police does live up to the image provided by Commissioner Rex, *but if it did not, I am sure that* Commissioner Rex, *if it is watched by the Austrian police officers, would probably have helped them as well to identify there. So it is good in terms of internal communication as well. That is an additional comment I wanted to make.*

I have a question for Mr Ambrosch.

Peter Hajek

Can I just answer that one? There is no doubt that an awful lot of the police officers I know have actually started enjoying their job more since *Commissioner Rex*. It has improved their professional life. And also, a very important point is that, as we have heard in Italy, they sit down with the police and discuss the scenario with them. Now we haven't done that, but have tried to do it time and again. We have discussed at great length on many occasions with the homicide division what we could do, what was possible and they turned around very often and said, well please do not do this or that because it will trigger new crimes.

We have been doing this sort of thing for 14 years now and we have built up a very good friendship. We mutually assist each other and certain things that we did find out about we have not actually used in order to avoid problems. You know, we know an awful lot. We do not want to create social disturbance or upset anything and so we are careful about what we use so that we can respect that.

A speaker

Thank you. What you have just said goes to show that Commissioner Rex *is a very good example of a television drama. There is the freedom of the author, and the author at the same time is providing a public service and informing people. So I think that is very good on your part. It is not only a matter of being successful but it bears in mind the interest of the community.*

As Dr Brüner said, when it comes to OLAF, we are just a coordinator. I think that all of those here would be more than happy, and hundreds of cases could be put forward. When it comes to investigative efforts, I do not think there is any risk of giving anybody wrong ideas.

Media

Heinrich MIS

Head of ORF — TV film production, Austrian Broadcasting Association

Heinrich MIS

Born 1953

Academic record:

Mass communications, political science and philosophy (PhD Vienna University), post-graduate: international affairs (UN headquarters, Geneva, Switzerland, diploma), international relations (Johns Hopkins University, Bologna Center, Italy, diploma),

Professional record:

1974–79: IBM Austria: public relations

1980–82: OPEC Secretariat, Vienna: public liasion

1983–87: ORF Austrian Radio and Television: radio and TV reporter

1987–92: ORF director of TV documentaries, daily radio show

1992–98: ORF in charge of TV avant-garde programme Kunst-Stücke, a weekly four-hour slot for art house, creative documentary and shorts; production, acquisition, commis-

Heinrich Mis, Österreichischer Rundfunk (ORF)

Ladies and gentlemen,

Capital crimes as mass entertainment is our business.

Murder mysteries must have deaths, otherwise they would not be murder mysteries. If murder is committed in the context of white-collar crime, it falls within the ambit of your profession. I shall return to that point later. Let me first make a few observations on reality and fiction.

Crime has served as a source of entertainment for thousands of years, the only difference now being the medium of television. It began in the Bible. Greek drama was not essentially different from today's detective novels or crime films.

Whether it is Medea killing her Jason, Oedipus hopping into bed with Mum (with fatal consequences), Macbeth having his rival slain or a private banker eliminating a competitor is ultimately immaterial. It is all about love, money and power, about the Seven Deadly Sins or the Ten Commandments — nothing more and nothing less.

Although everything is based on reality, because such things do happen in real life, it is also dreadfully imaginary. I assume that you professionals often shake your heads in despair in front of the television of an evening when you see how the greenhorns from the television studios envisage the work of criminologists trying to solve crimes.

The King of England would have reacted just like that in the theatre when watching *Macbeth*. But things work differently in our trade.

The main difference between television crime drama and real life is that the culprits are apprehended and brought to justice within 45 or 90 minutes on TV. In your case it takes longer, and sometimes no one is arrested and convicted. In ancient Greek tragedies, the bolt of lightning was delivered by Zeus, ruler of the Gods. In our case, it is delivered by the likeable and attractive female Commissioner in the television series. There is no such thing as an unsolved case.

sioning editor.

1999–2002: ORF,
Head of Department,
Fernsehfilm/Kultur
(TV film), commis-
sioning editor.

Since 2003: ORF,
Senior Vice-President,
TV film and series
(production)

Other functions and
activities:

1993–95: Adviser to
the Austrian Minister
for Cultural Affairs

1995: Artistic director
of Diagonale Salzburg,
Festival of Austrian
Film

Media

And if it gets too realistic, viewers start to complain.

Let me focus now on reality.

In all the new dramas and repeats shown on German television last week, a total of some 380 persons met with violent deaths. About 20 of them were murdered in connection with white-collar crimes. In real life there are never any more than three or four cases a year that would make suitable material for television. All the other murders are committed within families or are utterly unspectacular.

What this means is that writers up and down the country are paid to work day and night to dream up the most sordid crimes and heinous atrocities or the most credible reconstructions of criminal behaviour.

I invite you to join me in a bit of make-believe. Imagine you are an alien from another planet who tries to form an image of life on earth with the aid of European television. You see people either singing, trying to win millions on quiz shows or killing each other. Life is deadly dangerous and evil lurks around every corner. Most problems at work and in the family are resolved with an axe, a pistol, poison or a knife. And nice criminologists arrest the baddies, who are then led away, downcast. Our alien would not wish to venture onto the streets of our planet, for it is no consolation to potential victims to know for sure that the murderer will be caught.

Our visitor from outer space would regard life on earth as a sequence of horrors, ranging from the news to murder mysteries.

That, of course, is not the true picture. The world is not so dangerous and evil as television portrays it.

So what social purpose is served by all of this? Why do people like to spend their evenings wallowing in horror, murder and manslaughter? The same phenomenon can be observed in Greek drama. It is instructive and didactic; it is cathartic, in other words it releases most people from their darkest fantasies. For a tiny minority of the public it has a hypnotic effect, inciting them to commit either the perfect crime or an act of mindless bloodshed. That, however, is sidetracking us somewhat into the debate on television violence, and I have no desire to subject you to that.

Nor is there any end in sight. Germany is our main co-production and funding partner. Talks with our German counterparts have revealed a lack of public interest in portrayals of an ideal world and an insatiable appetite for corpses on television. Subtle plots are not wanted, partly because they are not appreciated in a competitive context.

If one channel is showing a realistic and somewhat complex crime drama and another is offering an extravaganza of light entertainment in the same time slot, the bulk of viewers will opt for the latter.

At the same time, the public broadcasters — and the ORF is one of these — do set themselves higher standards. In our films we try to impart a sense of right and wrong too, a moral code based on the values of the Christian West, and to feature socially relevant issues in our programme content. That can be done more or less effectively. In the worst case, the outcome is easily identifiable as a goody-goody film, and the result will generally fall far short of the intention.

Portrayals of white-collar crime are complex, difficult and complicated. This is why they are mostly avoided. They are not spectacular either. Moreover, portraying the world of finance poses a plausibility problem.

Let me cite an example. We recently had a major mini-series in our schedules, a joint venture with the German channel Sat. 1. Shown in four parts, *Shame and Scandal* was set in the world of high finance, in a private bank. In Germany, the series had a bit of a plausibility problem, which could be discerned from viewers' reactions. Germans found it hard to believe in power politics and tax evasion behind padded doors in wood-panelled offices. The institution of the private bank was an alien concept to them.

The same would presumably have happened in Austria if the real-estate company Meinl European Land had not almost crashed at the same time as we were transmitting the mini-series. And suddenly we had a real private bank on the scene — Meinl Bank, headed by a magnate who looked and acted exactly like the main characters in our film. Our thanks, of course, are due to that bank and to its owner, Julius Meinl, for giving our film a link with reality and lending it public credibility. At least the setting of the series was being featured as a piece of the real world in the press and as a fictional nest of intrigue on television, for nobody died, of course, in the Meinl case.

Nevertheless, the general public did not understand the precise transactions that were taking place, either in our film or in the Meinl Bank. All we were able to offer the public was a courageous, likeable and efficient detective, who used to be a financial investigator, and shady criminals in designer suits.

And that, ultimately, is what television can do for you: it can make people aware of the existence of good, competent and hard-working individuals who detect and fight crime.

You can also help to ensure that the cases we portray are less hair-raisingly divorced from reality by giving writers an insight into your working methods.

Let me make one final request: do not take television and cinema as seriously as you take your profession.

When all is said and done, it is an entertainment medium, although I do hope that we entertain responsibly.

Television film

ORF is a public service broadcaster with three television channels, a comprehensive website, 12 radio channels and a range of supplementary services providing information and entertainment. My department is responsible for producing, meaning that we develop materials ourselves or together with producers, and produce them for third parties or with other legal structures. Series have episodes lasting 25–45 minutes, and so-called television films are around 90 minutes long, the established cinema format.

Media

Media

Cristian UNTEANU

Journalist, European Correspondent for *ZIUA*, Romania

Cristian UNTEANU

was born on 14 July 1950, in Bucharest. In 1973 he started working as a reporter for Romanian radio and television, specialising in international relations and defence and security issues. Since 1996 he has worked as a journalist in Brussels for PRIMA TV.

Possible interaction between television fiction and media reports

Films and television productions can, and do, play an important role in influencing public perception not only of the reality of crime, corruption and fraud but also of the capacity and effectiveness of the systems developed by society. Fiction can also help build new relationships between society and individuals, who are finding themselves increasingly surrounded by a climate of violence and uncertainty.

In our view, it is crucial to know whether directors are pursuing a purely professional line or whether they are working to someone's agenda. In other words, does the programme tell a story, irrespective of whether it is based on fact or not, or does it reflect an order handed down directly or indirectly to a director to create a favourable image of the organisation financing the programme, which wishes to improve its image or project a public image it does not really have?

We would also like to introduce into the debate the ethical dimension, which interests us both as journalists and as an international organisation for, I would remind you, it was our federation which launched the idea of ethical journalism. Why would this bring value added to the debate?

Quite simply, because the best-selling productions on the audiovisual market are those based on, or inspired by, real facts. Heroic films which depict the world in black and white with the good and valiant James Bond employing the sophisticated technology of the free world against the brute force of the criminal barbarians from the frozen wastes of the Communist East are passé and sometimes even ridiculous. Although this type of scenario will continue to be screened, its ideology and message are becoming increasingly visible and, consequently, making less and less credible its primary aim: to influence public opinion and to mobilise it around one idea or to generate patriotism.

These Rambo-type films give a hyped view of the physical and technological capacities which enable the hero to confront a cohort of agents of evil whom he has to vanquish spectacularly and irreversibly in less than one and a half hours. The implacable logic of this heroic hype has given us films such as *Mission Impossible* or *Die Hard* which are saved from degenerating into a totally fictitious mythological universe along the lines of that of *Bat-*

man only by their humour. But the message is loud and clear: the public perceives such fiction simply as successful or less successful heroic fiction with a declining social impact because of the discrepancy between the exemplary fiction they are intended to project on the screen and the reality of daily life.

This is perhaps the explanation for the continuing success of productions which are based on real facts and/or which present, even in a technical form, the procedures used by investigation agencies. The public is tired of contrived mythology, which is clearly motivated by a desire for propaganda and is turning to another type of fiction where it has to follow the facts using expert logic and techniques rather than to judge or condemn or to form an ideological opinion. The public is invited to participate in the investigation itself, to form part of the investigation team and to follow a complex process of doubts, certainties, defeats and victories. In doing so, the public does exactly, at the virtual and symbolic level, what investigative journalists do when they begin work on such a case.

There are a huge number of examples which show that many scenarios are based on an accumulation of facts or even corroborate the media coverage of an actual event. In one way or another, the professionalism of investigative journalists has perhaps been the source(s) of a director's inspiration. Clearly, the ethical dimension of the journalistic product is extremely important because it concerns fiction based on real facts, and the public has already been able to form its own opinion from the media coverage of events.

There is also another dimension to this discussion: the initial credibility of the investigation agency. This problem arises when a scenario is based on a real event rather than on one involving a fictional investigation team, particularly where this involves an official investigation. Consequently, and I return here to a topic discussed at another of the network's seminars, it is essential to pay attention to the institution's degree of credibility with public opinion. It is investigative journalists and the media in general who build or destroy this credibility. This is why your communications department plays such a huge role and why your perception of communication and the way you work with investigative journalists are so important.

If you treat them as enemies or, at the very least, as a necessary nuisance in a democratic system and close all doors and stifle communication, a good detective film scenario is not going to save the image of your institution or investigative team. If, on the other hand, you adopt a policy of normality towards communication and, dare I say it, follow the spirit of the memorandum between the IFJ and OLAF with mutual respect for professional and ethical rules, this can be a powerful argument for the credibility of your message. If you want to build up your credibility over the years through an intelligent policy of openness, a scenario based on one of your successes is not going to surprise anyone. And nobody will say that you have a hidden agenda. You can make documentaries in the knowledge that you will always have difficulties in getting them screened on the major television channels or that they might be used only for picture libraries.

As journalists, it is our objective to provide the public with correct information that is as comprehensive as possible. It is up to you to facilitate access to events. We all have the duty to combat, with the arms at our disposal, corruption, fraud and crime and trafficking of all kinds. We are witness to your successes and failures. We are neither your public information office nor your propaganda tool. We are the interface with public opinion, which, ultimately, will draw its own conclusions regarding our work as well as yours. But there can be common ground between us where ethical journalism meets ethical investigation.

And if such a meeting is successful, this type of seminar will be of added value.

Media

Jonathan YOUNG

Executive Producer, *The Bill*
Talkback Thames TV Studios

Jackie MALTON

Advisor to Talkback Thames
TV, former Senior Officer of
the Metropolitan Police

Jonathan YOUNG

He took up the
post of Head of
Drama for Thames
Television in May
2005. He is Executive
Producer of *The Bill*
and responsible for
the Talkback Thames
drama development
slate.

He produced on
Eastenders, Casualty
and was Executive
Producer on the
first series of *Holby
City* before joining
Channel 4 in 1999.
At Channel 4 he
looked after *Brookside*
and *Hollyoaks* and
commissioned *North
Square* and *Teachers*.

He joined BoxTV in
2001. His Executive
Producer credits
include *SUNDAY* for
Channel 4 and and
Trust for BBC1.

He joined Talkback
Thames in November
2003 to produce the
second series of *Mur-
der investigation team*.
He developed and
was Series Producer
on *The golden hour*, a
4 × 90-minute drama
series for ITV1.

He became Head of
Drama and Executive
Producer of *The Bill*
and *Family affairs* in

Jonathan Young, Executive Producer, *The Bill*, Talkback Thames Television Studios UK

Good afternoon. As with the other speakers I would like to start off by thanking you all very much for inviting us here. Talkback Thames is owned by Freemantle Media and we have a number of conferences that we go to within Freemantle Media to try to encourage cooperation within our company. We make a number of the Soko brand shows in Germany and we make *La Squadra* in Italy.

I have been with the company for three years and we are just beginning to communicate with each other on a regular basis. Although I can see a myriad of problems with working together within Europe, I feel very strongly that it is something that we should be looking to do. I also think there is a real future in it.

I think a lot of what Jackie and I are going to say will have been covered earlier on. We have prepared a presentation which I am going to go through and, as I do so, I hope I can refer-ence some of the notes I have been making as we have been going through to try to pool some of these ideas together.

It is important, before we talk about fraud from our point of view, that we talk a little bit about *The Bill*. *The Bill* has been going for 24 years and is the longest-running UK cop show. We do two one-hour episodes a week and we transmit at 8 p.m., so it is a prime-time show, and we currently average a 25 % share. The share has been going up this year but, as with all terrestrial broadcasters in the UK, the share is generally on the slide. We will talk a little bit about that later.

It is very important for us to be mainstream and we need a popular audience. Longevity for the show is really important for us, so we are constantly discussing ways of reinventing the show but remaining true to our core audience.

It is clearly a successful show. Let us look at why cop shows work. We have talked a little bit about this today already. Cops are heroes and television viewers want to identify with characters who can do heroic things. Cops are heroes because if anybody is in trouble, the first person they want on their side is a cop. For cops, the stakes are high, partly for themselves as police officers, they get into dangerous situations. The stakes are very high for the members of the public that they deal with as well.

Cops interact with everybody in society. In London, where our show is set, it is absolutely credible for one of our cops to go from an MP or a lord to a homeless person on the street within one day, and I think that people understand that cops can reach every person in society.

Cops face human dilemmas in every decision that they make. Of course, cops have protocols, within which they operate, but the decisions they actually make when they are facing members of the public define what kind of society we live in. By that I mean that issues like racism and sexism are to do with how the cops interact directly with members of the public. This is drama and conflict. Detection is storytelling. The police process absolutely mirrors the narrative process that we go through when we are looking at a story. Quite often, our lead cop will walk into a situation and say 'What is the story?' That is because he wants to know who the characters are, what has happened, why it has happened and who it has happened to. Where did this story start, where is it going, where is it going to end?

It is really interesting. When I first started working with Jackie on the first cop show I did, I realised that the process of an investigation that cops go through when they are breaking down a crime absolutely mirrors the process of storytelling that we go through when we break down a story.

So cop shows work, but all of us in broadcasting are facing a very difficult and changing climate. When *The Bill* started there were four channels, and there are now 250 channels available to the audience in the UK. From the work I have done with our European partners, I think Britain is slightly closer to the American model, but undoubtedly Europe will start to get more and more channels. This really puts the squeeze on the mainstream channels.

That has led to a lot more cop shows. One of our script editors did an exercise going through the listings on Saturday at 8 p.m. and he counted 20 cop shows available at one time for the audience in a multi-channel environment. So that puts a lot of pressure on us, understanding what our show is.

The terrestrial audience shares are declining. There is nothing we can do about this as the Internet penetrates more and DVD sales penetrate more and as digital accounts for a bigger share of the viewers. It is a bigger share of the really attractive viewers to advertisers as well. The squeeze is put on us but the pressure on us is not only to not slide but to see how we can recapture some of that lost ground. We are spending a lot of time looking at how the marketplace works and budgets are being driven down because the advertising pound or euro is being more thinly spread, and we have less money year on year to make the show. In an inflationary environment we have to look for clever ways of doing that.

I wanted to mention that one of the clever ways of doing that might well be co-production. I think that is one of the things that make me feel that we have got to find a way of making these co-productions work. If we can double the money we can make better shows.

What do we need to do? We need to work harder to grab the audience. There is a lot of work that we do now on *The Bill* to make sure that our show is exciting and right up on the pace

May 2005. In addition to the long runners he has been Executive Producer on *Little devil* a 3 × 60-minute drama for ITV1, two series of *As the bell rings* for Disney, and *Up close and personal*, a pilot for ITV2. He currently has *Minder* in production for Channel 5 and *Laconia*, a co-production with Teamworx for BBC2/ARD, in the very early stages of pre-production. TalkbackThames drama continues to nurture a healthy development slate and is working with all major commissioners.

Jackie MALTON

Story consultant to *The Bill*

It was watching television shows such as *Dixon of Dock Green* and *No hiding place* that inspired Jackie to become a police officer in 1970.

Fifteen years later, in 1985, Jackie, whilst working as a detective inspector in the West End was asked to advise *The Bill* regarding an episode involving the rape of a young girl. Jackie continued to advise the programme and on leaving the Metropolitan Police in 1997 has been employed at *The Bill* as a story consultant.

Jackie was also the inspiration for the

Media

with the audience. You have to shout louder. By this I mean I, as a producer, am encouraging writers, storyliners, publicity, casting and everybody on the team to think of what we
can do to make the show bigger and make it have more impact.

You have to be distinctive. It is a very crowded marketplace out there. One of the criteria we
use when we are looking at the show, and I think anybody who has a flipper in a multi-
channel environment will understand what I am saying, is that as you flip through the
channels and land on our show, you need to know it is our show. We reckon the audience
probably samples shows, giving it two or three seconds before they flip on. In those two or
three seconds, any two or three seconds out of our show, how do you make the audience
know that they are watching *The Bill* and getting them to stick with you?

I think a lot of that is to do with understanding the format, the thing that makes your format distinctive. So for us, that is a very clear proposition. Our show is about ordinary cops
on the beat in London, ordinary people doing extraordinary things. The other thing that
distinguishes our show from most other shows in the UK is that it is from the police point
of view. We never let the audience see anything that our police do not see.

These are rules that were established when the show started. We have discussed endlessly
whether we should bend these rules, but every time we start to nudge towards that, we realise we are destroying the central proposition.

We need to work really hard to make an emotional connection. The audience needs to care
about what they are watching. I am pretty sure this does not necessarily mean a high body
count, but life and death is the biggest emotional stake. If it is not life and death, how are
you going to get the audience to care in this crowded marketplace?

You have to have a universal experience. If your ideas are too niche, it is going to alienate
the mainstream audience. There is a role in broadcasting for very niche ideas on niche
channels, but on mainstream channels you need mainstream ideas. We need to work hard
to keep the detection exciting.

I had a discussion with a broadcaster when he was defining what he felt the channel was.
He said to look at what sells newspapers, and if you look at the newspapers in Britain, the
headlines, it is the stories like murder, rape, bullying in schools, infidelity and sex which
sell. There are custody battles, kidnap. It is not all life and death but these are things which
really affect the audience. They are subjects where you know you have an emotional charge
when you see these words.

This is going to be a problem with fraud. Fraud is deliberately not on that list. If we are
looking at how we do stories about fraud, we absolutely have to find a way of giving it that
electric emotional charge that you see, that you get, when you see those words on screen.
Newspapers grab attention and they are sensational. The one thing they have that I think
the public recognises, by and large, is that they are believable, based on real events.

The real challenge for us at *The Bill* is that we are a drama which has been going for 24 years.
We need to keep our feet on the ground. We need to be real and we need the audience to
believe us. We have to come up with new ideas the whole time.

The way we do that is by talking to the police. We have got three retired police officers with
us at *The Bill* all the time, a full-time researcher and a full-time medical adviser, and then
we bring in experts as and when we need them for stories.

I asked a researcher just the other day to list some people she was talking to at the moment. They include: the head of a child abuse investigation; a child exploitation and protection centre; scene of crime officers (whom we talk to on a regular basis); explosive experts; criminal barristers.

This is a listing of people involved in the stories that we have got on at the moment, but we talk all the time to experts and we listen to our audience.

I think the audience is the best way of us judging whether we are on message or not. We go out twice a week and get pretty instant feedback. We get feedback on the Internet, we get feedback through broadcasters' duty logs and we have a mailbag. If the audience finds what we are doing unbelievable, you think you are probably in trouble and you need to rein in your melodramatic impulses.

This is not a limitation for us. Truth is stranger than fiction. The experts will give you something that is more interesting than you can invent. I was talking about this during the break, as writers like to think that their imagination is unfettered, and if they were free they could go into exciting and new places. Some can but the truth is, when you analyse what writers come up with, if they have not talked to the experts you will very quickly find that it is actually an idea they have got from another television show.

If your television show is going to have authenticity and feel real, you really need to talk to the experts, which is why we have Jackie Malton with us full-time on *The Bill* and in development. Jackie is going to talk a little bit about herself and her background. She is a retired police officer.

Jackie Malton, Advisor to Talkback Thames TV, former Senior Officer of the Metropolitan Police

Thank you very much indeed, Jonathan. My name is Jackie and I was, in a previous life, a detective chief inspector in the Metropolitan Police. I also say that what I loved about being a police officer was that I was a voyeur. What was fantastic about being a police officer is witnessing the messiness of the human condition.

The messiness of the human condition is what storytelling is all about. Way back in 1991, I was one of three female detective chief inspectors in the Metropolitan Police, a very male-dominated culture. There was a well-known writer in England called Lynda La Plante who wanted to write a drama about a female detective chief inspector, and that drama was called *Prime Suspect*. It starred Helen Mirren and the programme has gone on to be very powerful in terms of television fiction globally. Lynda La Plante did all the research with me for that character.

It was a little bit like a catharsis, a little bit like going to therapy every week, to tell her what it was like to be in a male institution and being a very lone female voice. I also say that I was one of the first officers, I think, to be in the Serious Fraud Office when I was a detective inspector. I was in the Metropolitan fraud squad, which I must say I did not like at all.

The reason I did not like it was that there was this attitude that people who committed fraud had that they were not really a thief. My experience of people who commit fraud and economic crime is that they are thieves. They thought it was a little bit of a grey area and I found that very interesting. The people I arrested were fascinating in themselves and, by being a voyeur, I was interested in that kind of person who committed that kind of crime.

A lot of those people were professional and male. Very few who committed the crime were professional and female. When I left the police service, doing *Prime Suspect* and subsequent television shows gave me that appetite for creative storytelling. In my short presentation today, I would hope that my purpose of talking to you is to appeal to the creators within you. You need to have somebody who will kind of spill the beans.

Jonathan mentioned that there is a detective principle in the storytelling of the drama and the process and the logic. Basically, what you do need to make the character authentic is someone who is willing to spill the beans. That is, in OLAF, you don't just sell the good things about yourselves. You have to tell some of the darker things about yourselves and be open. One of those things about being open is talking to the scriptwriters. They are the ones who will make that process, if you like, and turn it into drama.

We are not a police documentary. It is not a documentary about OLAF. It is fiction and it will be appealing to the audience. We have already spoken today about emotion, about identification, about how the audience will deal or identify with the hero, the protagonist, and of course our antagonist. One of the things I have learned in drama is to make your antagonist likable as well as your protagonist is likable. My favourite word is 'verisimilitude' (which I cannot even say now!), and this applies to the protagonist, a core sense of truth and belief about the character, and of course their vulnerability, which is very important.

Often this character is complex, as with Tennyson, and at war within themselves. They are consistent, as the previous speakers spoke of, but there is a heart within the range of emotions. They are surprising, fresh and authentic in the moment. Define who the character is and do not let the character bleed into something else. Go to the edge of the abyss with your character, let them fly close to the sun.

In drama we expose and tolerate the messiness of the human condition. Humans in a constant changing flux, and change is what we know best about ourselves. We have to appeal to the human-ness within all of us. Make friends with your shadow, own the dark side of yourselves. Our inner conflicts drive our relationships, our relationships' conflicts drive our external conflicts. We must look at all of those issues about ourselves.

The world at work is a family. When I was a police officer in the Metropolitan Police, when I joined in 1970, obviously most of you were not born then, but in 1970 it was perceived to be, and my experience was, that it was a dysfunctional family trying to get better. In 1985, when I was in the fraud squad, and 1992 talking to Lynda La Plante, I had that whole sense of betrayal about talking to a writer about the Metropolitan Police and my experience within that Metropolitan Police, the feeling I had that I was disloyal to the organisation but loyal to my own soul. Little did I know that there would be a conference here in 2007 talking about fraud and television fiction, which is absolutely fantastic. I was a lone voice.

I would like to show you a little video, and in it there are a number of things. One of them is about using your city as a character. This city we are in now is absolutely beautiful. I have never been to Vienna before but for all the countries that you come from, use your city as one of the characters, especially in economic crime. The city of London is beautiful, so use it.

Also in this video, what it will show you is what we have done from *The Bill*, taking clips from *The Bill* to show the city of London. I am also showing you a little clip from a documentary when an undercover police officer works as a fraudster, and he identified himself with a fraudster. It is a little interview with him, and it is interesting about his observation. There is also a little bit of *Prime Suspect*. Thank you very much.

[Video clip played]

Jonathan Young

I just wanted to round this off by talking specifically about fraud. We make drama and we have a lot of advantages over documentaries. We have to be believable but we do not have to be literally truthful. Dramas tend to rate higher than documentaries, dramas can create big characters and we can be really bold with the literal truth. We can pull together strands from different real stories to create 'what if?' scenarios, such as what if this were to happen? We can really appeal to a big broad audience.

Fraud is complex. It is outside the headline titles I put there. Clearly if we were literally going to do something about fraud, you have to look at how you package it so you get it within a world where there are emotional connections. Almost certainly it would involve some of those other headline cases, there is bound to be some kidnapping or murder along the line.

How would we approach a show, specifically? What would we need to have as well as the drama? We would have to care about the perpetrator, who is doing the fraud, and why they are doing it. Are they in debt, are they being blackmailed? We would have to care about the victim. Jackie talked about fraud as a victimless crime. A victimless crime really is a hard sell for a television production company and for a broadcaster. We need to find out who the victims are and to breathe life into those victims.

There is a third person we need to care about. We need to care about the cop who is doing the investigating. The cop is going to be our way into this story and we need to create a character who is really, really compelling.

So how would I approach it? I think the first thing I would need would be a writer who is passionate about the subject. I am sure it is true of television throughout Europe — it is particularly true, I think, in England — that the writer is the character that sells the show. The broadcasters believe that if you have the right writer, you can attract the right talent. An exciting writer is the first thing, and, to excite the writer, you would need some way into the story. We will talk about that.

You need to be confident that you could create a character that could become iconic. This may also be part and parcel of casting. You would have to create a character that really could attract heavyweight casting. You need a unique point of view. That goes back to the thing that Jackie and others have mentioned. With the unique point of view into fraud, you have to tell us that it is going to shock, surprise or entertain the audience.

If we are going to put fraud on television and make it seem good and rosy, it is not going to be that exciting to the audience and it is going to look a little bit like propaganda. It would just encourage you to say that you talked about the truth that was in the public interest and the truth that, by implication, was not. Really, all truth should be in the public interest, as far as we as broadcasters are concerned, even if it looks like it is getting you into trouble. Surely that is a good thing to do. You need to provoke a response, you need to provoke a debate and you need to put something in front of the public that is really going to excite them.

Media

That is what we need to do as entertainers. If you want to get broadcasters on-side, between us we are going to have to find a story that is fresh, original and surprising. Thank you very much indeed for your time, we have really enjoyed being here. I hope some of this will be useful and lead to cooperation between yourselves and various broadcasters.

Jackie Malton

Way back in 1985, I was part of the Serious Fraud Office. Since then, organised crime has grown and grown, and organised criminals have grown and grown. It is much more interesting, with these type of people, in 2007, since I dealt with organised crime. The criminals seem to be much more colourful and richer.

The other thing that is quite interesting about organised criminals today is that they are coming from a level where they are putting themselves in academia. They are going to university, learning about marketing, learning about the financial side of it and then going into criminality intentionally. I find that in itself fascinating.

I would agree that if I went to the Serious Fraud Office today, I would probably find it much more interesting than I did in 1985.

A speaker

Do you think it can always be translated into good films? I think it has enough for a good story.

Jackie Malton

It does have enough for good stories. That is why we are trying to appeal to the creators that are within you to be voyeurs, to make those detailed observations. It has been said today that some people will talk and just say how it is, but not particularly with much detail or observation. There are other people who will talk within any organisation, who will tell you much more.

We spoke to two police officers two weeks ago. One gave the party line and the other one gave the richness. That is the one you want, that is the person you need to talk to. The more that you observe about the people that you deal with, not just as investigators, the more detail that you get, the more you give out which is colourful and adds texture.

You will always find those people within an organisation who are passionate about what they do but also passionate about the characters they observe. That is fascinating and that makes rich television. The people who want to make rich television about fraud are you guys. You are the ones who will create it, not us, because you live and breathe it every day. Therefore, if you want to make it then you have to do your parts in the process, and your parts in the process are to observe, be a voyeur yourself, be passionate about it and tell us. We will do the rest.

2.4 NATIONAL INSTITUTIONS, INVESTIGATIVE AND JUDICIAL SERVICES

Gilbert BELTRAN

Chief Inspector and Deputy Head of Information and
Communication — Directorate-General of Customs and Excise

Gilbert BELTRAN

Born 28 September
1965 in Lavelanet
(Ariège), France.

Entrance in customs
in 1985 as field agent.

On duty at the com-
munication desk since
July 2006.

Address delivered
by Gilbert Beltran

After viewing the extract from the television film *La taupe* ('The mole'), which was broadcast in the spring on the French television channel TF1 and attracted more than nine million viewers, one starts to think about the limitations of such a series for the purposes of an authority like the French customs administration.

This is because there is a definite risk of confusing some of the roles of the different authorities. As we have just seen in this extract, the operating conditions of the customs service could easily be confused with those of the police, in terms of both the characters' attitude and equipment. This confusion arises from the necessity of simplifying the production and because the messages have to be adapted to production constraints.

The result can therefore be detrimental to understanding the role of an authority or an organisation and how it operates. It is also very difficult to interest television drama production companies in certain aspects of our work that are neither visual nor easy to explain. As Dr Brüner said yesterday, it is impossible to do justice to an investigation lasting four and a half years in an audiovisual format lasting 45 minutes. The production companies are therefore tempted to confine themselves to the sensational aspect of the assignments.

The film *Anthony Zimmer*, which tells the story of the manhunt for an international drugs trafficker by the customs administration using an undercover agent, gives the impression that the customs administration employs extremely sophisticated investigation methods.

Despite these limitations, it may be in the interests of some authorities, such as the customs administration, to take part in television drama productions as an authority's image can become well established in public opinion through this medium.

The fact that the public identifies with the fictional characters and that messages are repeated in the series means that exposure in a television series is a better way of improving the image of a service than an item in the television news or a report in a current affairs programme.

Thus, for example, French customs officials carrying out inspections at the suspect's place of residence are sometimes asked to produce a search warrant, as is often done in American police series, even though this is not required by French law.

In the same way, the repetition of simplified messages and the image of the character delivering the message serve to develop awareness among the general public of the social desirability of an authority.

Nevertheless, the authority should take precautions when participating in television drama projects.

Firstly, it is essential to set down in writing the conditions for collaborating with production companies, which, in some cases, ask if they can use materials (signs, documents, logos), premises (warehouses for storing confiscated goods) and equipment (aircraft) or if the authority can provide them with a list of its suppliers, for example.

It is important that the general message to be conveyed by the television drama is put across clearly. Thus, it is necessary to read the screenplay so as to correct the most blatant mistakes. It is not necessary to have technical experts read through the screenplay as well, since their point of view is too literal for making the events into a screenplay. In addition, an attempt must be made to respect professional secrecy with regard to the cases portrayed or to certain working or investigative methods.

Finally, the impact of such television dramas on internal communication and on how our own agents feel should be assessed since this kind of television drama inevitably gives rise to reactions in agents who cannot watch it in the same way as the rest of the public.

All the more care must be taken if the television drama leads to confusion with another authority or if the message has been oversimplified to the extent that it is no longer convincing.

Dušan ČAPLOVIČ

Deputy Prime Minister of the Government of the Slovak Republic
for Knowledge-Based Society, European Affairs,
Human Rights and Minorities

Address delivered by the Deputy Chairman of the Slovak Government for an Aware Society, European Affairs, Human Rights and Minorities

Ladies and gentleman,

It is an honour for me to be able to welcome you to the second, Slovak, part of the seventh training seminar for communicators of the European Anti-Fraud Office (OLAF), which is an expression of cooperation between two Member States of the European Union — Austria and the Slovak Republic. This honour is both for me and Slovakia greater since the OLAF communicator training seminar is taking place — for only the second time in its history — in two countries simultaneously.

The problem of the fight against fraud and other illegal activities which damage the interests of the European Community is always very current. For Slovakia even more so since, in this programming period, bodies of the Slovak Republic will directly manage implementation of significant financial resources from European Community funds. We are aware of our obligation in the area of protecting the financial interests of the European Community.

For this purpose, the Government of the Slovak Republic has adopted a national strategy for the protection of the financial interests of the European Community in the Slovak Republic, which was prepared with the professional and financial assistance of the European Union. This forms a basic framework for the development of all our policies in this area. The objective of the strategy is to ensure thorough protection as required from a Member

State by Article 280 of the Treaty on European Union. To achieve this objective it was necessary to select a strategic approach based on three mainstays:

• prevention;

• detection and investigation of irregularities;

• corrective activities and prosecution.

All measures focused on protection of the financial interests of the European Community, implemented in the process of handling European Community resources and resources of the State budget of the Slovak Republic, are intended to prevent illegal acts and should act as a deterrent to potential wrongdoers.

However, our objective cannot be only repression, detection of illegal actions, fraud and prosecution of their culprits. Our objective must be to create public awareness which views illegal behaviour in relation to public resources as absolutely unacceptable. Therefore it is important to inform the wider public of the measures introduced focused on preventing and detecting all forms of irregularities, and measures for recovery of misused resources and prosecution of illegal activity.

The public has a right to be informed and we have an obligation to inform them of the protection of the financial interests of the European Community. It chiefly concerns information about to whom and the way in which the public can address requests for information on measures adopted for protection of the financial interests of the European Community, but also about to whom and the way in which the public can notify a suspicion of irregularity. The general public should be encouraged into active participation in the notification of suspicions and irregularities. Such participation should be facilitated through simple telephone and e-mail contact.

In terms of the participation of the public in detection of damage to the financial interests of the European Community, as well as the endeavour to prevent them, the theme of this training seminar is also important — television dramatisation as a means for fighting against fraud and corruption affecting the financial interests of the European Union. Precisely this form of presentation can stimulate the public imagination much more than regulations, manuals or commercials.

Ladies and gentlemen, in conclusion, allow me to express the belief that this seminar will bring new knowledge and impulses for our further work. Once again I welcome you to Bratislava and hope that, despite your workload, you find a little time to take a walk around our capital city.

Thank you for your attention.

National institutions, investigative and judicial services

Carlo Felice CORSETTI

Head of Press Office and Public Information,
Carabinieri National Headquarters

The CC Force in television drama

Carlo Felice CORSETTI

Born in 1947, Carlo Felice Corsetti is a General of the Arma dei Carabinieri, graduated in the Science of Security at the University of Rome 'Tor Vergata', admitted to the National Order of Journalists.

He has performed important tasks at various commands of the *Carabinieri* and the Anti-Mafia Investigative Directorate. He was praised for investigations in Europe, America and Australia.

He worked in institutional information: Head of the press office of the *Carabinieri*; Head of the press and public relations of DIA; Head of Public Information at General Headquarters of the *Carabinieri* and editorial director of the *Carabinieri*'s online magazine.

A teacher in a European project 'The operator of police between the needs of the press and protection of victims of crime', arranged by the University of Rome 'La Sapienza', he also

The CC Force, with its nationwide distribution of over 4 600 police stations and 19-year history, occupies an important position in the Italian general public's imagination. It is an institution of notable prestige for public opinion as regularly shown by public opinion polls.

The CC Force's deep integration within society is especially felt in rural and suburban areas (in Italy, 65 % of the population lives in towns that count fewer than 50 000 citizens). Films and television series enhance this important societal element, turning it into a 'key figure' for narrating Italy and the Italians.

The first memorable encounter between cinema and the CC Force goes back to the 1950s and the lucky series *Pane, amore e fantasia* starring Gina Lollobrigida and Vittorio De Sica. As the neo-realist age drew to an end, it gave life to the unforgettable role of Maresciallo Carotenuto, on duty in a small rural community.

Clip — *Pane, amore e fantasia*

There are two moments where the CC Force come into play: the arrival of the Maresciallo at the CC police station to which he has been assigned and the participation of the CC Force in local festivities.

In past years, film-making has continued to contribute to this vast public success by offering two Italian comedy films on life within the CC Force and the activity it performs. They managed to show, with irony and affection, the true potentials of the Force, when in action repressing crime. The film was *I due carabineri* starring popular actors Enrico Montesano and Carlo Verdone (1984).

Clip — *I due carabineri*

We can see the two main actors in two short episodes which recall the typical irony that is so dear to Italian comedy. In the first scene a 'unique' approach during searching activities; in the second the jokey simulation of an arrest between the two actors that ends with them losing the keys of the handcuffs.

The sequel, entitled in English 'The lieutenant of the CC Force' (1986), starred Enrico Montesano, who played the role of an officer, and the late Nino Manfredi.

Clip — *Il tenente dei carabinieri*

We can also see in these scenes how irony is always present in the adventures of the main actors.

During the 1990s, television began to show repeated interest in the CC Force. In 1995, the CC Force started to cooperate with television fiction-making with *Il Maresciallo Rocca* (we will deal with this later on) which obtained wide public approval thanks to the brilliant performance of actor Gigi Proietti. The success was such that film-making went on to release a number of sequels in 1999, 2000, 2002 and 2004, with the sixth in 2007. *Il Maresciallo Rocca* went on to achieve worldwide public approval with sales of the programme in Latin America and eastern Europe, in Japan, in the USA and in several Asian countries.

Clip — *Il Maresciallo Rocca*

The scene illustrates, giving particular attention to the operational aspects, the phase of an arrest and of searching activities performed by personnel of the CC police station of *Il Maresciallo Rocca*.

Other television series that represented the CC Force's activity in its usual characteristic 'habitat', that is to say, of a police station in a small town of an Italian province, are *Don Matteo* and *Carabinieri*. They have been of great pleasure to the Italian public and have given rise to numerous sequels.

Clip — *Don Matteo*

These scenes show two encounters between the priest who is the main actor and the commander of the CC police station in two typical everyday contexts of a small town: the CC police station and a café.

In *Don Matteo*, the CC Force cooperates with a parish priest called Don Matteo, who is interested in resolving minor detective cases of various types. The CC Force helped in producing the many sequels that followed in 2001, 2002, 2003, 2005 and 2007 (sixth edition).

In *Carabinieri*, the film shows daily life inside a police station located in a small township in central Italy. The CC Force assisted here as well in producing this television success that began in 2000 and is still running today.

Clip — *Carabinieri*

The female element is emphasised. In these scenes, the commander of the CC police station talks with one of his female collaborators. There is also a scene showing operational activities and a car chase.

There have been other television fictions that have given importance to specific fields of the CC Force, such as the strong investigative skills.

RIS Delitti Imperfetti, which we will deal with later on, appropriately represents the extraordinary level that the institution has reached in scientific investigation: the General Headquarters of the CC Force assisted in making the first three television series in 2003, 2005 and 2006 and is helping in the production of the fourth edition in 2007.

Clip — *RIS*

In these scenes the main actors are shown while they are using sophisticated laboratory equipment.

The three parts of the television drama *Ultimo* which the CC Force helped to make in 1998, 1999 and 2003 show the effectiveness of contrasting organised crime through its protagonist — a CC officer who took part in capturing Totò Riina in 1993, boss of Cosa Nostra in Sicily at that time.

Clip — *Ultimo*

We can see the phases leading to the arrest of a criminal in the streets of a Sicilian city by ROS personnel (Special Operations Group), elite of the CC Force active in the fight against organised crime.

In recent years there have been many tributes to servicemen of the CC Force who have fallen while on duty. The institution was called upon to cooperate in producing two television dramas dedicated to very important figures well known to the public:

• Vice Brigadiere (Sgt) Salvo D'Aquisto, who is undergoing the process of beatification, heroically sacrificed his life in September 1943 in order to avoid the killing of numerous civilians, due to Nazi retaliation;

• the 19 Italian victims (12 of whom CC servicemen) who were killed by a terrorist attack against the Italian peace mission contingent deployed in Iraq in November 2003.

The television dramas *Salvo d'acquisto* (2002) and *Nassiriya* (2006) narrate the dedication to duty of a few servicemen that ended with the extreme sacrifice of their lives. These films are intended to honour all the CC servicemen, of all times, who have silently fallen, while performing their duties for the community.

Clip — *Salvo d'acquisto*

Clip — *Nassiriya*

The scenes of the hero Salvo D'Acquisto, from his noble act of responsibility to his execution, and the attack of Nassiriya in Iraq, are shown in their full drama.

Within the path of silent devotion and the extreme sacrifice, we also find the television drama *Il Generale Dalla Chiesa*, recently shown on TV. It is inspired by the life of CC General Carlo Alberto Dalla Chiesa, a key figure during the 1970s in the fight against terrorism, who was designated Prefect of Palermo in order to oppose the Mafia but who was murdered by them in an ambush in Palermo, in September 1982.

Clip — *General Carlo Alberto Dalla Chiesa*

The General is shown during his fight against terrorism and during his tragic end in Palermo.

We can also mention the contribution that the CC Force made to other successful television dramas such as *Amanti e segreti* (2003), *Amanti e segreti 2* (2004) and *Cefalonia* (2004).

The daily picture of the CC Force is made up of little daily events, sacrifices, abnegation, and at times by heroic acts but continuously characterised by the contact it has with the population.

The concept of 'being in contact' with the population is part of the 'genetic inheritance' of the CC Force. This is shown in the ability of creating true harmony with the local community. The skill of listening to the citizens' daily problems also contributes to 'reassuring society' which is guaranteed by the presence of the CC police stations.

The objective of 'community policing', is surely strategic in the security system of our country because it is capable of increasing the level of security perceived. It may be achieved naturally by the traditional means of controlling the territory, of preventing and repressing crime, and by safeguarding public order as well but also as a way of mediation. This is why television dramas are so successful. TV has become, in fact, the ideal way of showing the general public various issues. Programmes concerning such issues are spread out and perceived by the public (often in moments of privacy, together with family members, after a working day, while eating or during a family reunion) and enables the message sent out to be very convincing.

In this way, the CC Force uses television fiction as an instrument of communication on one hand, in order to increase a feeling of security, while on the other hand it addresses information to the community. This helps people to become more aware of common crimes and increase trust in institutions.

In order to achieve this goal, television dramas (which the CC Force has helped to make possible) usually unveil the 'private side' of the actors wearing a uniform, favouring the 'humanising process' that touches the audience. In this way, the CC serviceman — who is also from time to time, a solicitous husband, a protective father, a jealous boyfriend, a heartbreaker or a shy lover, according to the script — the image of the institution is strengthened and the citizen becomes very familiar with the modus operandi of criminals and learns how to defend his/her self. So the message conveyed is 'we are not only near you, but we are also like you'.

In the background of the plot, which is obviously based on narrative demands, we are always able to find such values as integrity, humanity, dedication to duty and the willingness to sacrifice oneself, that, together with a qualified and updated professionalism, have always characterised the CC Force, making it a true synonym of State and justice for many Italians. The message sent out in that way helps to eliminate or at least diminish eventual suspicion caused by the so-called 'fear of public authority' that can still be found today, especially among the less fortunate and less educated population. This helps to spread (in a more incisive way) the concept of 'law'.

At this point, it is clear that the role of fiction, illustrated here, gives an immediate advantage to the audience and to the institution: major trust means major cooperation on behalf of the citizen this brings to better duty and, above all, more efficiency towards every form of crime. The CC Force therefore uses television drama as a means of communication to produce security and stimulate the audience to cooperate with the institutions in the fight against crime. However, the potentials of such a modern way of communication do not finish here. Other important aspects that bring the institutions to use such forms of communication can be found in the narrative sequences, so common with fiction.

Let's see how. The drama is usually divided into three parts: the opening, the unfolding of the plot with its climax (the peak of the drama that is anticipated by growing emotions) and the ending of the story.

The opening is the beginning of the story and introduces the spectator to the context where the events will happen. Normally it is used to describe the preparation and the perpetration of a crime. This type of circumstance surely has an important descriptive aim because it makes the viewer more aware of how criminals behave.

The unfolding of the plot with its climax is the central part of the story. This is the stage in which the investigative activity, usually done by the CC Force, is illustrated.

Even here, we find a special kind of service done for the citizen because he/she is put in the best conditions, as a potential victim of the crime, to discover the most important elements used by the investigators to identify the criminals.

Such elements may give the spectator, on the one hand, the possibility to learn about the potentials of investigative activities and the elements necessary to perform them; on the other hand, they allow the institution to compare itself with the citizen, who is already aware of the situation in which he/she has become the victim and turns to the CC Force with more confidence and full knowledge of the facts, providing in this way a qualified type of cooperation.

The ending of the story usually identifies the author of the crime. It strengthens public imagination on the importance of a sure punishment which is the basis of prevention. Even in this case, however, punishment is emphasised as a re-educational aim, instead of underlining the true meaning of it according to the constitutional laws.

The *carabiniere* serviceman shows great respect for human dignity under every circumstance and the author of the crime is always shown to be a human being who committed mistakes but may redeem himself. The *carabiniere* serviceman always deals the delinquent with manners and never judges him but only his behaviour.

The CC Force stands out for its devotion to its history and traditions. This love for the past does not prevent it from having a modern spirit that looks towards the future. It is always in search of new and technologically advanced solutions to resolve problems and to improve its efficiency. The union of these two spirits — one that bases its roots in the past and its traditions and the other in technology which launches it towards the future — has given an important response even to the image of the institution used in the fiction. Two of the best and most successful television series, which lead to the production of sequels, are in fact *Il Maresciallo Rocca* and *RIS Delitti Imperfetti*.

These are two rather different types of drama which have the CC Force in common but the detective plot varies somewhat, not only in style but also because of the diversity of the institutional aspects they represent.

In the first case, we have a description of a typical Italian province with its traditional values, its reference points and its community, where the figure of the CC police station commander stands out, brilliantly performed by the actor Gigi Proietti. In the background of the events that are narrated, we find the CC police station which resembles the state, law and justice for the small community that it serves. Within the CC police station there is a family atmosphere, based on shared values and strengthened by the spirit of duty and sacrifice of its personnel.

Clip — *Maresciallo Rocca*

It is the conclusion of an investigation: Maresciallo Rocca follows the magistrate, with whom he has cooperated in concluding the case, outside the courthouse. The fiction represents the diversity of the institution and draws its best part from its traditional heritage, that is still present today in over 4 600 CC police stations spread nationwide.

On the occasion of the 10th anniversary of the first series, on 27 September 2005, the General Commander of the CC Force underlined that *Maresciallo Rocca* 'gives a real picture of everyday life in the CC police stations, in which the servicemen work close to the needs of the community and with which they establish a tie of confidence' and he wished that the series could continue 'within the path of tradition, giving Italians that positive message that they need, that feeling of security that so many times we look for' (ANSA).

The CC police station is considered by the population as a 'heritage' of each community, capable of directly affecting the individual feeling of security, as demonstrated by the numerous requests of the local communities to build or strengthen CC commands.

The second successful drama is *RIS Delitti Imperfetti*. This is based on scientific investigations that the CC Force carries out with instruments and highly advanced technology that help resolve, even in true life, many cases that appear impossible.

Here too the human and professional values of the actors wearing a uniform are somewhat similar to those already described in *Il Maresciallo Rocca*: comradeship and a spirit of duty, humanity and devotion to justice and the truth.

But the central point of this scenery is scientific technology. With an original narrative style that is not traditional but dynamic, the spectator becomes involved in a plot that, with a continuous turn of events, will be resolved by the actors wearing a uniform with the most modern scientific investigation techniques and a good amount of sagacity.

In this fiction, the teaching aspect is a key element because it shows how crimes are performed and how important each element found, even those that are apparently meaningless, may have on the scene of the crime, in order to resolve the case.

Clip — *RIS*

In this scene we can see the activities carried out by the main actors on the crime scene.

Both dramas became popular and successful thanks to the variety of its audience. *Il Maresciallo Rocca* was particularly appreciated by a mixed audience where the families and elders were predominant. *RIS Delitti Imperfetti* was liked by young people thanks to the innovative style introduced by its production.

The public success achieved by these fictions has determined a growth in the number of enlistment applications and has increased the general interest of young people with a scientific high school diploma in the career opportunities the RIS offers.

With regard to public response, a general audience survey has shown how drama concerning the CC Force has a strong media appeal, with percentages reaching some 41 %.

An example for all is the enormous success of the series *Il Maresciallo Rocca*: On the occasion of the 10th anniversary of the fiction (2005) it was remembered thus: 'with 22 episodes and with an average peak of 10 800 000 viewers per episode it is one of the most successful and biggest drama productions…' (ANSA).

The constant share rate (25 % and 30 %) obtained for the main fictions on which the CC Force cooperated (besides the two already mentioned, *Don Matteo* and *Carabinieri*, etc.) shows the strong appeal that the actors wearing a uniform have on the general public.

According to regulations, the use of uniforms and equipment — similar to those assigned to the CC Force — in film-making and the examination of the narrative issues are governed by rules in force which provide that the CC general headquarters be responsible for authorising or denying its cooperation to public or private agencies.

The Ceremony and Promotional Activity Office of the CC General Command is responsible for examining the preliminary documentation that precedes an eventual collaboration. This office examines the applications forwarded by the film-making agencies, analyses the script and the professionalism of the agency, by carefully evaluating if the product is compatible with the institutional objects mentioned so far, while keeping the target and the format of collaboration in view.

Once the cooperation with the CC Force has been established, it is important that personnel are limited to their daily working schedule and essential needs.

The CC servicemen never appear as extras in film-making except for those circumstances that refer to specific activities that are highly spectacular and aimed at putting into evidence the participation of special units (scuba divers, helicopter personnel, k-9 experts, RIS, etc.) while remaining as close as possible to reality.

The participation of CC specialists are, however, a part of the activities already programmed and the related expenses (petrol, insurance, etc.) are paid by the film-makers. The equipment assigned individually or belonging to a unit are paid for or are free of charge but must be returned once no longer necessary.

In order to be able to represent, as closely as possible, the reality of the institution, actors who wear a uniform are initially informed as to how to properly use the uniform and how to behave as a *carabiniere*.

Finally, the CC Force will continue to pay great attention to and make itself available for television drama, an instrument which not only entertains but brings citizens closer to the institution and increases their confidence, while improving the inclination towards cooperation of the spectators and, as a consequence, the efficiency of duty provided to the community.

The dramas have become a true means of information by which citizens can receive information on the potential and professionalism of each law enforcement agency.

But, above all, they affect citizens' feeling of security, while giving value to the link of trust with the institution.

Thanks to the confidence inspired by the realistic representation of the operational potentials of the law enforcement agencies, a dialogue is stimulated and the feeling of separation, which at times the institutions experience, is overcome. This is beneficial for the community and the police forces.

The topic that we are dealing with today seems more or less appropriate, because as we have seen so far, drama — with due tactics — may become a learning tool, as indicated by the seminar. It must be a winning product that nevertheless pursues a teaching goal, showing the citizen the damage that fraud can cause to the community and, at the same time, the behaviour that the citizen must adopt in order to prevent such crimes happening.

National institutions, investigative and judicial services

Tibor GAŠPAR

Director of the Office for the Fight against Corruption,
Police headquarters, Slovakia

Address delivered by Tibor Gašpar

Ladies and gentlemen,

It is a great pleasure for me and an honour that, at the close of a seminar with the title 'Television drama as a tool in the fight against fraud and corruption affecting EU financial interests', I can appear before people whose everyday work is the fight against criminality. Before people who, in the time of digitisation, the Internet and thousands of cable television programmes, are trying to inform the viewer in an arresting form about clientelism, corruption and any other kind of activity against the public interest, about preventative or repressive activities against these problems faced by every society.

I want to use my participation in your discussions today, since the contributions which I have been able to hear affect what I want to say now.

As director of a police unit involved in the fight against corruption, I can state that even a short report on the radio on one of our successful cases struck a note in the consciousness of another offender who had been intending to commit the criminal act of corruption, who then stopped his actions for fear of discovery. We discovered this immediately after broadcasting the radio report from the tapped telephone of our offender, where he mentioned that fear of detection. I would like to assure you, however, that the offender was already being prosecuted for his actions on the basis of evidence already acquired.

In a second case in my practice, I met with a situation where an older lady who had been robbed asked us whether we could ask our colleagues in Austria to bring their famous television serial dog Rex to catch the criminal, because he alone could do it. Her thinking was greatly affected by that television serial.

I would like to remark that the point of communication between us as a punitive body against corruption and the media and television producers is not only to increase the viewing figures of programmes, but to act preventatively, possibly even repressively, to bring a message, information or request and not simply work them into a specific television format without secondary effects.

As part of that communication, it is necessary to balance positive and negative information provided by the media on our activity in view of the indisputable effect of the media on public opinion and trust in the activities of the police or other punitive bodies in either a negative or positive direction.

Cooperation with the media brings not only positive and negative opinions of this work, but particularly the risk of forming subjective opinions and views of activities of detection and investigation by the receiver of the information.

Furthermore, I would like to emphasise that all forms of media communication have their importance and they are an inseparable part of the process of prevention of criminality. As the director of a modern punitive police unit — the Bureau of the Fight against Corruption of the Police Presidium — I welcome every form of informing the ordinary public on the damage caused by corruption and its negative impact on the economy and morality of society, whether it is a newspaper interview, investigative report, action film or television drama.

Television is just the medium which can address most people without difference of age and education. That is why we, the police, turn to that medium when we need help in finding missing persons, dangerous criminals or when we want to calm the public after scaremongering. Many police officers would certainly say I was right when I say that, thanks to television and citizens addressed by it, we have unravelled and investigated complex criminal cases where we would otherwise have come to a dead end.

We don't want the public just to view us as men and women in uniform who collect fines for illegal parking. We want people to see our everyday work and to understand that a policeman or policewoman is a person who protects their life, health and property and of course we welcome when television brings our occupation, albeit in the form of a television drama, closer to the viewer and that young educated people who care about upholding the laws of society will join us.

Ladies and gentlemen, I want to assure you that we perform our work responsibly and seriously, and since the establishment of our authority in 2004, we have done a great deal of work in the fight against corruption and other serious criminal acts, which is incomparable with the previous period. Thanks to the work of our authority today, corrupt doctors, public officials and so-called white-collar criminals committing the most serious economic crimes stand before court or have been convicted. We have done great work in the fight with corruption in healthcare, sport and public administration, and, at the current time, we are aware of threats in the form of sophisticated criminal attacks on resources of the European Communities.

That is why I personally made sure that our authority — which enjoys a good reputation — became the coordinator of detection and investigation of damage to the financial interests of the European Communities from this April. I really believe that in the future we will increase our cooperation with OLAF and other renowned European institutions fighting against corruption and fraud affecting the European Communities' financial resources.

Once again, I would like to thank the organisers of this unique seminar which has taken place here and in neighbouring Austria. I would also like to thank all the participants for their work and express the conviction that the conference has fulfilled its expectations and, last but not least, I hope that you have enjoyed your stay in Bratislava — a large and small capital city. We look forward to seeing you again.

National institutions, investigative and judicial services

Herwig HELLER

Head of Enforcement, Ministry of Finance

Herwig HELLER

Head of Enforcement, Ministry of Finance

Born in 1956, joined the Tax and Customs Administration after obtaining a Doctorate of Law from the University of Vienna in 1981. From 1985 he worked for 10 years in the Ministry of Finance in the customs organisation dealing with the opening of the border to the former communist countries and the preparation of the accession to the EU. In 1995 he became head of the anti-fraud division with competences for customs and excise fraud, mutual assistance and the EU third pillar. Since 2002 the controls of illegal employment and since 2004 tax fraud issues fall within the competence of the enforcement division due to the merger of tax and customs at the level of the Ministry of Finance.

Address delivered by Herwig Heller

Deputy Prime Minister, ladies and gentlemen,

I have been asked to provide an Austrian contribution on the subject of how to incorporate tax fraud into television crime dramas. In my view, the most important thing is that we — and by 'we' I mean the customs and tax authorities — should feature in these programmes. Yesterday and today we have heard and seen several kinds of portrayal on television, and we agree that there is probably no single correct method but many different methods, the suitability of which depends in part on the country and the cultural practices of its people.

As we have heard, my fellow Austrians from the realm of television crime-series production cannot imagine responsibility for the content of television scripts being entrusted to us. I likewise believe that the appearance and personality of the central character, his or her behaviour, predilections, sexual orientation and sex life, and indeed his or her sex and age, should be left to the television people. It is the task of those responsible for television production to draft a screenplay which will be funded and produced and which will culminate in a series that attracts the highest possible number of viewers. The plot should also be left to the producers, for — as we heard yesterday — there are formats that the public want and that therefore determine the success of television series.

What we can contribute are stories. Television also seeks to tell stories, and that is where our paths meet.

From my own experience of tax fraud, customs fraud and illegal employment, I have compiled a few examples of potential storylines, beginning with carousel tax frauds and moving on to smuggling and then to more specialised swindles.

The first case is a carousel fraud with mobile phones, which circulate until their batteries run out and which are never intended to be sold but only to earn VAT refunds from tax authorities. The supply chain stretches from Britain to Dubai and Hong Kong. Some of the criminals, so my British counterparts have told me, are of Pakistani origin. The high profits that come in have to be laundered. The forms of international cooperation I can cite in this case are the cooperation between national tax authorities and the Eurocanet (European Carousel Network) information system, which operates with the support of the European Commission.

The Austrian director of the *Sonderkommission Kitzbühel* series said that the first seven minutes of a television crime mystery provide points of reference such as the portrayal of the characters and of the detective in a more private setting and the presentation of a murder. In this first case, I could envisage a link with an Islamist organisation. That would suggest an explosives attack in which 50 people are killed, though it could be as many as 100.

The second case relates to motor vehicles that are sold illegally throughout the EU. This is another carousel fraud, involving the use of numerous small businesses to camouflage the supply chain. Intervening VAT refunds and non-payment of VAT in southern Europe make many German cars about 10 % cheaper than the factory-gate price in Germany. Here too, there is cooperation between tax administrations and occasional assistance from OLAF. Yesterday, to the surprise of the OLAF representatives present, we saw an excerpt from an Austrian crime drama in which an OLAF official was shot. That could be made to happen in this case too.

Another problem we have in Austria is fraud relating to the national registration of cars. In 2006, a Mr Uzelac collected vehicles in Austria for a German company with the authority of that company. Under the VAT directive, these were sold to him VAT-free after the seller had checked the validity of the German company's VAT number. Two days later, one of the cars was offered for sale in a newspaper advertisement and was sold at a price that not even vehicle wholesalers could match — for they, of course, would have to pay VAT. By cooperating with their German counterparts, the Austrian authorities discovered that the German company had never bought a car in Austria. A web search revealed that this Mr Uzelac had been shot in Bosnia back in 1991 during the wars in Yugoslavia. This gives us a corpse before the story begins. Someone is using the dead man's identity to engage in criminal activity. There are numerous other tales involving cars, but for reasons of time I shall confine myself to these two scenarios.

Another rich source of storylines is fraud relating to customs duties, which traditionally form part of the Community's own resources. All customs authorities in the EU are currently being confronted with under-invoiced imports of textiles and trainers from China. According to the invoice, a training shoe costs only EUR 1.17, and this happens with countless container loads throughout the EU. These loads are often delivered by small transport businesses, which are immediately wound up if the fraud is discovered. This is the domain of European triads with links to the Far East. In one of the cases we solved, Austrians, Hungarians and Chinese were involved. OLAF is particularly keen to coordinate the activities of all Member States. Rosalind Wright, Chair of the OLAF Supervisory Committee, has stressed the need to present viewers with a favourable image of OLAF as an institution. I would therefore advise against having yet another OLAF official shot dead. In this episode, the owner of a small transport business could be eliminated because he knows too much, or else it could turn out at the end of the episode that he committed suicide.

The best-known stories concerning customs are, of course, the cases of cigarette-smuggling. The tracked delivery of container loads of cigarettes to England would surely have dramatic potential, as would the deployment of our dogs that are trained to sniff out cigarettes, playing a role like that of the police-dog hero of the *Commissioner Rex* series. The discovery of illegal cigarette factories has aroused a particularly high level of media interest. In the most recent case in Austria, which came to light in July 2007, an illegal factory had been set up in a warehouse near Vienna airport; fortunately, it was discovered while trial production runs were still taking place. The production machinery came from China and was a counterfeit version of a European model that has been on the market for about 10 years. The customs administrations are cooperating with each other with assistance from OLAF. Europol is also investigating cigarette counterfeiting in the framework of an analytical database known, hardly surprisingly, as 'Smoke'. We could thus vary the scenario by having a Europol official come to Vienna and being shot here.

One broad area of activity is the imitation and counterfeiting of products of all kinds, from vehicle spares to medicines. These crimes can also be combined with murder. One possible fictional tale is that a husband who is on Viagra drives to his girlfriend's flat and collapses and dies on arrival. Laboratory tests show that the medication is Chinese counterfeit Viagra but that it does not pose a health hazard. It ultimately emerges that the man's wife has found out about the girlfriend and has poisoned his Viagra. Another possible variation on the same theme would be the wife's death in a car crash after her husband had tampered with an Asian counterfeit brake lining.

Ladies and gentlemen, I wanted to give you a few examples of stories that could be set in the context of a customs or tax administration. The purpose of this event is to find ways of telling these stories on television. During yesterday's break, we Austrians agreed that we would have a meeting with the director of the *Sonderkommission Kitzbühel* series and tell him some of our stories. He can then select material that he will be able to use in television crime dramas. For detailed information on the cases that interest him, we can put him in touch with the investigators. If we bring only a few stories into crime dramas, by way of a 'product placement', as it were, that will represent a great public-relations success for the customs and tax authorities, making people more aware of the purpose of our work.

The stories I have just related contain rather a lot of murder and manslaughter. It is possible, of course, to develop ways of making television dramas that do not involve murders, but I believe that is a matter for those in the television industry who are responsible for funding and transmitting programmes. Films with minimal viewer ratings will do nothing to raise our profile. Allow me to conclude by quoting Umberto Eco, who wrote the book *The Name of the Rose*, in which he tells of life in an early mediaeval monastery and a great deal more besides. He was asked how he had hit on the idea for his best seller, which all of us have read. His answer, recorded in his little book *Reflections on the Name of the Rose*, was that he had felt the urge to poison a monk. It seems that even such wonderful stories generally need a murder as a focal point, both in literature and on television.

Thank you for your attention.

Milan JEŽO (opening address)

General Director, Section of Control and Fight against Corruption
Government Office of the Slovak Republic (SRGO)

Milan JEŽO

General Director, Section for Control and Fight against Corruption, Government Office of the Slovak Republic (SRGO)

He studied in the Faculty of Economics and Industrial Management at Bratislava's Economic University. He worked in the credit business, retail and wholesale banking, currency and finance policy, the control sphere and has knowledge of insurance products, and as lecturer and consultant in diverse marketing strategies (public relations, media collaboration and advertising). He was, initially, Head of Section at the State Bank of Czechoslovakia and then Head of the financial division at the District National Committee in Bratislava. He was a specialist at the Ministry of Finance of the Slovak Republic and the Director of the Bratislavan branch of the Istrobanka bank. Following this, he was appointed Director of Strategy, Marketing and Advertisement at the Headquarters of Istrobanka. He spent time in the private

Address delivered by Milan Ježo

Ladies and gentlemen,

In order to open bridges between European countries I'm going to talk in Slovak.

Dear Mr Wolfgang Nolz, Mr Franz-Hermann Brünner, Mr Alessandro Butticé, Mr Rainer Newald, and Ms Elisabeth Werner, please allow me to say a few words on the occasion of the opening of this seminar.

It is a great honour that we, as representatives of the Government Office of the Slovak Republic, may participate in the preparation and organisation of the seventh training seminar for communicators of the European Anti-Fraud Office (OLAF). At the same time, I would like to express thanks for the invitation to these beautiful representative rooms of the Royal Hofburg, seat of the President of the Austrian Republic.

In Bratislava, we will also be meeting not far from a place which was the seat of kings. I'm sure that this seminar will be full of interesting and informative contributions which will lead to fruitful discussions and therefore to fulfilling the objectives and purpose of this seminar, as introduced by Mr Butticé, spokesperson for the European Anti-Fraud Office.

The content and focus of the seminar should help us find other forms of activity directed at eliminating problems of fraud and other illegal activities damaging the financial interests of the European Community. One of these forms is the use of a fictional dramatised story as a medium by which we can provide information on this problem and on the ways and possibilities of preventing it to a wide spectrum of the inhabitants of the European continent in a compelling form. It should help create public awareness of the unacceptability of illegal acts in relation to public resources.

Ladies and gentlemen, at the end of my short speech please allow me to express the conviction that this seminar will bring many new inspiring suggestions and impulses, not least with the contribution of Slovak representatives.

It is a great honour to invite you all to the second part of the seminar, which will take place in Bratislava. I look forward to inviting you to our beautiful city on the Danube and

Milan JEŽO

General Director,
Section for Control
and Fight against Cor-
ruption, Government
Office of the Slovak
Republic (SRGO)

He studied in the
Faculty of Econom-
ics and Industrial
Management at Brati-
slava's Economic Uni-
versity. He worked in
the credit business,
retail and wholesale
banking, currency and
finance policy, the
control sphere and
has knowledge of
insurance products,
and as lecturer and
consultant in diverse
marketing strategies
(public relations,
media collaboration
and advertising). He
was, initially, Head of
Section at the State
Bank of Czecho-
slovakia and then
Head of the financial
division at the District
National Committee
in Bratislava. He was a
specialist at the Min-
istry of Finance of the
Slovak Republic and
the Director of the
Bratislavan branch of
the Istrobanka bank.
Following this, he was
appointed Director
of Strategy, Marketing
and Advertisement at
the Headquarters of
Istrobanka. He spent
time in the private

Address delivered by Milan Ježo

Ladies and gentlemen,

In order to open bridges between European countries I'm going to talk in Slovak.

Dear Mr Wolfgang Nolz, Mr Franz-Hermann Brünner, Mr Alessandro Butticé, Mr Rainer Newald, and Ms Elisabeth Werner, please allow me to say a few words on the occasion of the opening of this seminar.

It is a great honour that we, as representatives of the Government Office of the Slovak Republic, may participate in the preparation and organisation of the seventh training seminar for communicators of the European Anti-Fraud Office (OLAF). At the same time, I would like to express thanks for the invitation to these beautiful representative rooms of the Royal Hofburg, seat of the President of the Austrian Republic.

In Bratislava, we will also be meeting not far from a place which was the seat of kings. I'm sure that this seminar will be full of interesting and informative contributions which will lead to fruitful discussions and therefore to fulfilling the objectives and purpose of this seminar, as introduced by Mr Butticé, spokesperson for the European Anti-Fraud Office.

The content and focus of the seminar should help us find other forms of activity directed at eliminating problems of fraud and other illegal activities damaging the financial interests of the European Community. One of these forms is the use of a fictional dramatised story as a medium by which we can provide information on this problem and on the ways and possibilities of preventing it to a wide spectrum of the inhabitants of the European continent in a compelling form. It should help create public awareness of the unacceptability of illegal acts in relation to public resources.

Ladies and gentlemen, at the end of my short speech please allow me to express the conviction that this seminar will bring many new inspiring suggestions and impulses, not least with the contribution of Slovak representatives.

It is a great honour to invite you all to the second part of the seminar, which will take place in Bratislava. I look forward to inviting you to our beautiful city on the Danube and

that, despite the short time you will have to get to know it, it will leave you with pleasant memories.

I wish the seminar a great success and wish you all a pleasant and successful day.

Thank you for your attention.

sector as a financial products manager before accepting a position as Deputy Director-General in the Department of Control, Complaints and Petitions at the Slovak Ministry of Defence. He is currently working in the Government Office of the Slovak Republic where he is General Director of the Section for Control and Fight against Corruption.

Martin KREUTNER

Head of the Austrian Government Anti-Corruption Office (BIA)
Federal Ministry of Interior of Austria

Martin KREUTNER

Director of the Federal Bureau for Internal Affairs, Federal Ministry of the Interior of the Republic of Austria

Born in 1964; studied law at the University of Innsbruck. Commissioned officer in the Austrian Armed Forces; served with UN and NATO missions in Syria, Israel, Lebanon and Albania. Transferred to the Austrian Federal Ministry of the Interior; commissioned to build up an anti-corruption service unit (BIA); heads the Austrian Federal Bureau for Internal Affairs (BIA). Obtained a Master of Science in Policing and Public Order Studies (University of Leicester); guest-lectured on international humanitarian law at the German Red Cross and the Ruhr University in Bochum; lectured on security and anti-corruption topics at European security and military academies and universities and at international conferences.

Member of Interpol's International Group

Martin Kreutner, Head of the Federal Bureau for Internal Affairs
Fraud on vision

D ear ladies and gentlemen, colleagues and friends,

It is a great pleasure for us to welcome you here in Vienna for your seventh OAFCN training seminar. We wish you all the best and all the success for this important gathering. As our common goal is to fight fraud and corruption and to promote this essential endeavour to the general public, let me share just a few brief thoughts with you.

From a theoretical point of view, a product or service should be the basis for the development of marketing concepts and communication strategies. In today's world, it sometimes seems to be the other way around: communication is the basis for the product or service. The European Court of Human Rights in Strasbourg classified the media as a fourth source of power in the res publica, the society. Most people with a legal background will certainly agree that the media have to be key players in modern societies.

In my opinion, a one-way street with demands on one side and no obligations or responsibilities on the other side has to be avoided. It can be witnessed in a number of areas that fighting corruption and fraud will necessarily have repercussions in the media. Corruption is not only perceived by the media but also exists within them. This fact has already been explored in detail on numerous occasions.

Sometimes, opposing forces are at work. We all agree that the free flow of information is indispensable; however, this involves the tendency to scandalise or to exploit cases. Two cases we dealt with in the past few years will illustrate this trend.

We are a relatively young organisation. Set up in 2001 in Vienna on the basis of international models, we published our first annual report in 2002. Although we had been warned and informed on how to convey the report, its publication became an example of backfiring.

It was not a matter of how many people had been caught, for the headlines said, 'My goodness, look how corrupt the Austrian authorities are!' and 'Look how corrupt Austrian police officers are!' That was a tough time for us because we were the ones delivering the message, and, of course, it is easier to hang the messenger than the perpetrators of the crimes in question.

Corruption issues always have a great impact on the media. The second case I would like to point out is that of an investigation against a very senior official of the ministry, which led to an interesting situation: the media were split into two camps; practically no medium was balanced, unbiased or neutral. The majority of the media were very much in favour of the investigative work we were undertaking, whereas other media took the opposite tack: all kinds of pot shots were taken at the investigators and numerous articles were published trying to defend the person in question. One of the offences that the individual was charged with was to have unlawfully passed on information to the media. And it was exactly the media having illegally received information by this individual that reported against our investigations. Thus, as one of our investigators put it, it would have been fair to say thank you for this kind of confession on the part of the media. They came out loud and clear on the wrong side.

This example demonstrates that facts served up are often not treated as such, due to the tendency to scandalise and to exploit information. On this score, I might usefully quote Heidenheimer's *Political corruption*, Professor Blankenburg's reference work, 'If ever you want to damage a competitor in politics, if you think that a generation of politicians has been in office for too long, or if you want to set the agenda for politics anew, look for corruption as an instrument for political scandal'.

So also in the scientific world, as it were, it is quite clear that scandalisation is an instrument applied against competitors and to drive your own agenda. It has also to be taken into account that entities, organisations or States investing in fighting corruption must live with the fact that, in the short and medium terms, they will be perceived as worse than before they invested. At the risk of oversimplifying, it can be said that when it comes to politicians, CEOs of companies or heads of units, the obvious thing to do is to regret having invested in fighting corruption. The idea is to forget, sweep it all under the carpet and pretend that the problem is solved.

Fighting corruption and fraud has been considered, until recently, to be a national issue. It was only about a decade ago that, thanks to (among others) Transparency International and the conventions of the Council of Europe and the OECD, the issue was started to be dealt with on a transnational and international basis, which I believe is essential. Conferences, or get-togethers, are of the utmost importance for looking beyond borders and seeing what is happening elsewhere.

We all know that prophets are never listened to at home and that our findings are uncomfortable for a number of people. This OLAF Anti-Fraud Communicators' Network is a means of providing us with a mutual back-up in order to avoid things being swept under the carpet and anti-fraud units being extinguished.

Over the past years, a lot has been happening. Three years ago, we had the opportunity and honour to bring together police oversight bodies and anti-corruption authorities of the EU Member States here in Vienna, and that bore fruit. At present, a Council decision is in the works, which is to carry the EPAC network forward by giving it an official status.

of Experts on Corruption; Chair of the EU network European Partners Against Corruption; member of the Advisory Board to Transparency International; a court expert on criminology and VIP protection; Chairman of the Supreme Disciplinary Commission of the Federal Ministry of the Interior and member of the Federal Appeals Tribunal; author of papers on security issues, editor of a book on corruption and co-author of a legal commentary.

National institutions, investigative and judicial services

A current example of cross-border prevention in Austria is the first International Anti-Corruption Summer School (IACSS) organised with the support of OLAF. Investigators, prosecutors, customs officers, journalists, etc. from some 25 countries, including countries of the European neighbourhood policy and the western Balkans, participated in the IACSS. The summer school is a symbol of the importance we attach to the prevention of corruption.

Dear colleagues and friends, I would like to conclude with one of my favourite quotations. It is by Milton Friedman, who passed away in 2006. In 2001, the Nobel laureate said that if he had been asked a decade earlier what his advice would be to countries in transition, he would have told them to privatise, privatise, privatise. Five years later, he acknowledged that he had been wrong, and said that the rule of law, apparently, was of more importance than privatisation.

Our (net)working for the fight against fraud and corruption is extremely important, not only for our organisations or our countries. It is important for Europe as a whole, and for sending a clear message even to the rest of the world. All the best to you for this common challenge.

Rainer NEWALD

Head of Communication Division
Austrian Federal Ministry of Finance (BMF)

Rainer Newald, Head of Communication Division, Austrian Ministry of Finance

Rainer NEWALD

Rainer Newald was born in Austria in 1970. Subsequent to a Masters degree in Business Administration, Rainer became involved with information activities for the euro introduction in Austria on behalf of the Chamber of Commerce and the Federal Ministry of Finance. In 2000 he was appointed Head of the Governmental Information Office at the Federal Chancellery on European information campaigns. He held this position until 2003 when he began a two-year position as Head of Public Affairs at TBWA/Vienna marketing agency.

From 2005 until 2008 he worked as Head of Communication at the Federal Ministry of Finance before embarking on his current role as Head of Corporate Affairs and Communications at JTI Austria.

Fraud is damaging to Austria as a business location and hence to Europe. It is important to fight fraud in order to create confidence in an economic area and to preserve it in the long term for honest traders.

Efforts to combat fraud are imperative for international investors and companies, since they operate only in reliable markets, but also for the self-esteem of the people of Europe and their economy. Europe-wide cooperation in the fight against fraud is essential — particularly in the light of new circumstances in Europe, namely open borders and freedom of movement.

We cannot deal efficiently with organised crime unless we tackle it together. Close cooperation with the customs and tax administrations of other EU Member States and non-EU countries as well as with the European Anti-Fraud Office (OLAF) is essential to protect both companies and consumers.

Combating fraud is a task that serves the interests of taxpayers, because it also puts a stop to the evasion of taxes and other public levies. All exchanges on the subject of best practices and on ways of intensifying cooperation, such as those taking place at this workshop, are therefore to be welcomed.

One serious issue concerns the choice of methods: it would be valuable to include innovative ways of communicating the necessity and importance of anti-fraud work to the public at large.

An innovative subject has been chosen for this meeting, namely the visualisation of the fight against fraud in film and television. Action builds confidence, and the use of popular television programmes to impart information about the measures that are being taken provides people with easier access to knowledge about these matters.

In Austria, people talk a lot about television programmes like *Commissioner Rex*. This helps to create a sustainable preventive effect.

Information must be credible, so no propaganda!

Cross-border cooperation in the fight against organised crime

Effective judicial action against many categories of fraud can be taken by means of coordinated cross-border checks in several Member States of the European Union.

The success of this action does not depend solely on cooperation between national authorities. OLAF also continuously assists national authorities with their investigations; time and again it assigns officers to obtain an overview of cases on the spot.

One point which keeps emerging clearly is that only by thinking European and looking beyond our own backyard can we take timely and successful action to combat cross-border fraud.

In the fight against cigarette-smuggling, the Austrian tax and customs administration cooperates very closely with OLAF and with other customs administrations, both inside and outside the EU, as well as with the World Customs Organisation and Europol in order to wage a robust struggle at the international level too against a problem that does not stop at national boundaries.

New modern anti-fraud structures have been created in Austria. A new system of tax investigation has been introduced, and the customs and tax authority now has its own risk-assessment, information and analysis centre, providing regular customs updates for travellers and setting priorities in the fight against product piracy.

In the realm of e-government, Austria is using the latest technology to combat fraud. The entire tax and customs authority is extremely well equipped. The flagship E-zoll project links the customs offices together into a network in order to simplify the processing of data for public authorities and for businesses.

Modern communication methods are important when it comes to disseminating information. Combating fraud and communication must go hand in hand, and such communication also helps to improve the image of the EU — a difficult task in Austria, given the great volume of criticism of the EU that appears in the media. Efforts and successes need to be highlighted, the message being 'Do good things and talk about them'.

Austria's exceptional successes over the past year

Through cooperation involving the Anti-Fraud Directorate at the Federal Ministry of Finance in Vienna, the competent fiscal enforcement authorities at the customs offices and OLAF, an internationally active gang comprising Hungarian, Chinese and Austrian nationals was uncovered. The gang had been running a large-scale operation in which textiles and footwear were brought into the Community with vastly understated invoices. Checks conducted by sworn experts revealed that the prices stated on the invoices were up to 15 times lower than the market prices of the goods.

In July 2007, a police patrol discovered an illegal cigarette factory and informed the local customs investigation team. Eight persons — Bulgarian and Polish nationals — were arrested, and 21.5 tonnes of tobacco as well as machinery components for the production of some 20 million cigarettes were seized. Thanks to this timely discovery, serious harm to Austrian consumers, the Austrian economy and the national and EU budgets was averted.

Outlook

Past events have shown how important professional and transparent information flows are in combating cross-border fraud and protecting the financial interests of the European Union.

This seminar, which has been organised jointly with Slovakia and is the first such seminar to be staged in cross-border cooperation, is an important means to this end.

My thanks go to the organisers from the Federal Ministry of Finance, the Slovakian Government Office and OLAF.

The presentations and discussions at this seminar have shown that OLAF and its network of partner organisations are not standing still but are receptive to up-to-date, creative approaches.

Wolfgang NOLZ

Head of Tax Department, Austrian Federal Ministry of Finance (BMF)

Wolfgang NOLZ

Director-General of Tax Department, Austrian Federal Ministry of Finance (BMF)

He was born on 17 March 1943, in Bruck/ Leitha, Lower Austria. After his school-leaving examination (Matura) in 1961 he studied law at the University of Vienna, then passed his military service and after training in court proceedings joined the Austrian Tax Administration in 1969.

There he was first assigned to the local revenue office for the 12th, 13th, 14th and 23rd district of Vienna (1150 Vienna) and subsequently became an officer in the appeal division of the Regional Finance Directorate (Finanzlandesdirektion) in Vienna.

In mid-1974 he was called to the Ministry of Finance and assigned to the income tax division.

At the beginning of 1983 he became head of the tax policy division and in 1988 he was appointed Director-General.

Dr Wolfgang Nolz, Head of Tax Department, Austrian Federal Ministry of Finance

My speech will be in German in general. Ladies and gentlemen, on behalf of the Federal Ministry, I would like to welcome you very warmly to today's conference. You will be aware that the Vice-Chancellor was supposed to be speaking but unfortunately that is not going to be possible and so I have been invited to welcome you here and wish you a very successful seminar.

Mr Newald has also already mentioned the weather god and I am sure he is going to grace us tomorrow as well because, according to the weather forecast at least, you are going to have a wonderful trip up the Danube from Vienna to Bratislava on the river which links Europe. For Wednesday, I am not sure, but for two days out of three you have guaranteed fine weather, which is a pretty good mark of success for this conference.

We have experts together to discuss the subject before us but we should start by seeing what we can do using the modern media to fight fraud. I think we must start by looking at the slightly broader picture. Tax fraud is Europe-wide, I would say, and there is no European State that can escape this phenomenon. No European State can stand up and say it does not really affect it.

There is a holy person within the Catholic Church, Florian as we say in Austria, and there is a bit of a cynical saying here. We talk about houses burning down with St Florian, and you know people ask him to protect their own houses and burn somebody else's. I am sure that does not work in other languages they way it does in Austrian German. Anyway, we cannot stand up and say cigarettes are smuggled elsewhere and people just drive through Austria with them because they cost more in the UK, so they are shoved up there instead of here. That is not the case.

We want to provide the necessary training to fight all of this but we are not going to learn from the cigarettes which are being sent to Austria. We are going to learn from what is going on elsewhere as well. Let me pick up on an example we saw quite recently, which I think has already been documented as well. I am speaking about a Europe-wide phenomenon here. Is there a clear distribution of roles here between the hunter on the one hand and the hunted? I am not convinced.

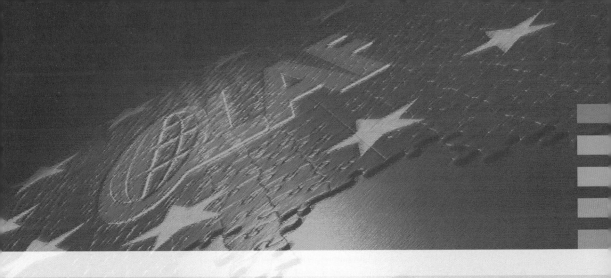

3. ANTI-FRAUD COMMUNICATION AND WEB 2.0:

New technologies, new tools, new audiences

* Based mainly on the contributions for the round table on anti-fraud communication during the eighth training seminar of the OLAF Anti-Fraud Communicators' Network (OAFCN), Nicosia, Cyprus, 12 to 14 October 2008, concerning 'Deterring fraud by informing the public — Anti-fraud communication and Web 2.0: new technologies, new tools, new audiences'.

3.1 EUROPEAN INSTITUTIONS

European institutions

Alessandro BUTTICÉ

Head of Unit 'Spokesman, Communication, Public Relations' — Spokesman of OLAF

Alessandro BUTTICÉ

Head of the Communication, Public Relations and Spokesman Unit within the European Anti-Fraud Office (OLAF) of the European Commission. He has created and coordinates the OLAF Anti-Fraud Communicators' Network (OAFCN). Before joining the European Commission, Mr Butticé served as Colonel in the Italian *Guardia di Finanza* where he held several managerial positions, which included leading the operational unit of investigators into financial and economic crimes and drug cases, as Deputy Head of Communication and Spokesperson in the *Guardia's* Headquarters. He has also worked as a freelance journalist and a part-time professor at the University of Bari, in Italy.

Outline and objectives of the eighth seminar of the OLAF Anti-Fraud Communicators' Network (OAFCN)

The introductory speakers for this seminar have already identified our core objectives for this two-day seminar which is being held on this island and Member State of the European Union, and which, according to legend, was the birthplace of Aphrodite, the goddess of love and beauty, a logical choice given its great charm.

I should like to remind you that the programme for these two days grew out of a request by members of the OAFCN to devote our annual seminar, the eighth since the network was established, to new technologies, new means of communication and new audiences which are developing in this new millennium — technology, communication tools and audiences which appear to be radically changing the already-revolutionary scenario seen at the end of the 20th century.

I would also remind attendees and non-attendees of last year's seminar that we had an original idea — one of such originality that it was initially met with scepticism — of organising a seminar on the use of television series (TV fiction, or 'drama' to use the British term) as a vehicle of preventing fraud by increasing awareness in the general public, represented by the millions of viewers who follow the most popular television series broadcast in Europe and throughout the world.

In my introduction to the Vienna and Bratislava seminar last year, I pointed out that if that seminar, with its discussions and pooling of experience, did no more than sow the seed of a future European television production, one not merely consisting of news or documentaries, and if it could help reduce the still-gaping divide between Europe and its citizens, or between the fight against economic and financial fraud and corruption and the citizen-taxpayer, then I believed that we could all be satisfied with the result.

I ended my speech by saying that if the results of our efforts ever came to fruition on the television screens, wherever we were or whatever we were doing at the time, we should all be entitled to say: I was there in September 2007, in Vienna and Bratislava!

I am therefore very pleased to announce today that, thanks to this seed planted last year by those of you who were present in Vienna and Bratislava, at least two major television producers are already working to deliver what less than a year ago appeared to be an over-ambitious or visionary project: the plan to encourage major television producers, without the promise of any subsidy, to produce a Europe-wide television series about the transnational collaboration of the national anti-fraud services and their work with OLAF.

I have just received a communication 'hot off the press' from Peter Hajek, the creator and father of the television series *Commissioner Rex*, that his production company, Mungo Film of Vienna, has begun work, in collaboration with major German and Austrian television companies, on a television series about the work of OLAF with its partners in the Member States. A first draft of the script has already been produced. We shall present it and discuss it with members of the network during the next meeting in Brussels and, if everything goes smoothly, the first episodes will be recorded in the spring.

I believe that this result, as well as other separate projects of the same sort which appear likely to come to fruition in Germany and Italy in the near future, is the best possible recognition for the joint efforts and work of our network. I believe it is a moment of great satisfaction for all of us.

The seminar beginning today, following that of last year which raised the possibility of using a medium with a huge impact on public opinion to reduce the gulf still separating Europe (and the process of combating those out to defraud European financial interests) from its citizens, now sets out to go beyond television — still the leading means of communication today.

The aim is to make an ever-increasing use of new communication technologies, with which our children or grandchildren are undoubtedly more familiar than the majority of my generation or the previous one. Television, which is still the king of the media, appears likely to be overtaken by other new means of communication in the near future. For the youngest generations, tomorrow's adults, television even seems to have lost its appeal. Young people appear to be watching less and less television. The television audience now mainly consists of adults, or indeed senior citizens.

Web TV and second life communications systems which contact their users by GSM rather than by satellite, and others which may still seem to be science fiction but which are increasingly filling the market for contemporary communications, are all tools which appear likely, if not to replace, at least to compete fiercely in the immediate future with what have hitherto been the most modern means of communication.

We are talking about Web 2.0, but we are already moving into the era of Web 3.0.

The global village is increasingly becoming a virtual village.

Up to now, there has been a saying: 'If a tree falls in the forest and is not filmed by television, did it really fall?'

Tomorrow's version of the same saying will be: 'If a tree falls in the forest and is not on Web 2.0, MySpace, Web 3.0, or in real time on my GSM screen, did it really fall?'

In other words, all communications managers, regardless of the type of communication, must and will increasingly have to cope with these technological changes, as well as generational shifts which alter the audience at the speed of new technological inventions and applications.

This also applies, and must apply, in the field of combating fraud and defending the rule of law.

We have also seen confirmation of this in the last few days from the results of the latest OLAF survey into the perceptions of fraud and the fight against it, a survey conducted in the 27 Member States of the Union on the Commission's behalf.

The full results of this Eurobarometer (the name given to the European Commission's surveys) will be published by us in the next few days, but members of the network will today receive a preview of these results with some of the documents distributed.

However, I want to draw your attention in advance to the fact that the results show clearly that European citizens are demanding far closer collaboration among individual Member States and between the Member States and the European institutions, in the combating of fraud and corruption.

Another very important finding of the survey, and one that affects us directly, is that 67 % of people interviewed claimed to prefer radio and television as sources of information about the results of anti-fraud activity, although a substantial number, between 37 % and 25 % (hardly a small minority), indicated that they preferred the Internet, other web sources such as YouTube and — primarily in the United Kingdom — television fiction or drama as preferred channels of communication for information about these issues.

These findings encourage us to make further progress along our chosen path — the work we have been doing for eight years within our network, based on maximum cooperation and participation.

In line with the principle of subsidiarity and the aim of adding value to the efforts of Member States, a characteristic of OAFCN's activity, this seminar, after a general introduction on new technologies, and particularly Web 2.0, which will follow these remarks, will aim to be a forum for discussion and ideas about what is already being done or what should be done by the heads of communication in the national anti-fraud services.

For this reason, the eminent speakers invited to this seminar include not only prominent representatives of the scientific world, of the International Federation of Journalists and the world of communications, but also representatives of some of the leading national investigations services, some of them of international importance, such as the FBI and the Hong Kong Anti-corruption Authority, whom I would like to thank for accepting our invitation to be here with us today.

In three separate sessions on 'Public relations and new technologies', 'New technologies and the media', and the 'Experience of the investigation services with Web point 2', we shall seek subjects for discussion and stimuli to a further adaptation of our communications efforts to make them increasingly modern and consistent with the reality of the media and their new and constantly-changing audiences in our increasingly global and ever more virtual village.

I end by saying that these are the primary objectives of this seminar, together with the goal of meeting the expectations expressed, among others, by Vice-President Kallas and by Mr Lopes, Chairman of the Supervisory Committee of OLAF — expectations to which we shall not fail to respond and which we shall seek not to disappoint.

I therefore thank all those who have contributed to the organisation of this event, and, first and foremost, the Cypriot authorities and all our Cypriot colleagues and friends.

My thanks also go to the speakers and the leaders of the three panels who, at considerable personal inconvenience, will be with us over the next two days leading and guiding the discussions.

Thank you all for your attention and your contributions to the discussions.

Keir FITCH

Member of Cabinet of Siim Kallas in charge of Administrative Affairs, Audit and Anti-Fraud — Speech on behalf of European Commission Vice-President Siim Kallas

Keir FITCH

Member of Cabinet of Vice-President Siim Kallas (responsible for Administrative Affairs, Audit and Anti-Fraud), European Commission in Brussels.

Mr Fitch worked in the Cabinet of Vice-President Kinnock (2002–04) and before that in the Agricultural Section of the European Commission's Legal Service (1999–2002).

In the Cabinet, Mr Fitch's main tasks involve the consolidation of administrative reform, simplification and regulatory aspects of personnel policy, and policy aspects of OLAF's work. He deals, inter alia, with security, health and safety, social dialogue and relations with the staff unions and equal opportunities. He is also responsible for OLAF 'internal' investigations, OLAF staff matters and OLAF legal issues.

Mr Fitch, a British Maths and Law graduate of Gonville & Caius College, University of Cambridge, worked

Opening message delivered by Keir Fitch on behalf of Vice-President Siim Kallas

Conference participants, members of the OAFCN,

On behalf of European Commission Vice-President Siim Kallas, I am very pleased to welcome you to this seminar, which continues a series of ambitious events exploring new paths to better informing the public about the fight against fraud and about your and our work. Let me also convey Siim Kallas' thanks to our Cypriot hosts for their cooperation in organising the event, and to our colleagues in OLAF for their enthusiastic work in bringing us all together.

Last year's successful seminar on the possibilities of using television fiction was a great example of what can be achieved if we are prepared to take a step back and reflect about your work beyond the usual way of doing things.

This year's topic — looking into the possibilities offered by the new web-based technologies — is a logical, but rather ambitious continuation of that earlier work. For Vice-President Kallas and my other Estonian colleagues, it is particularly interesting, since Estonia has developed into a very active and efficient 'web-based' society, where a great deal of public services can be done and are, very naturally done, over the Internet.

Using Web-2 in anti-fraud communication is also fully consistent with Mr Kallas' work — via the transparency initiative — to make the inner workings of the European Commission more accessible to the outside world. In particular, we are encouraging the thousands of lobbyists who work in Brussels to register, acknowledge who they are working for, and accept a code of conduct — and we are using new web tools to make publicly available details both of the lobbyists, and of the end recipients of EU funds.

Of course, transmitting Mr Kallas' greetings to you by sending me as his representative does not, at first sight, really look like 'Web 2.0 best practice'. Indeed, apart from the fact that the journey's got a bit quicker, we could have done it like this at any time in history. Yet, on closer consideration, this way of presentation has several features dear to the Web 2.0 discussion. Like an experienced speaker, Web 2.0 offers individual feel and approach, adaptable interactive modes and good responsiveness to client needs and you can run it (almost) everywhere. Of course, technology can fail — but speakers can have off days too.

Web 2.0's adaptable approach is vital if we are to communicate effectively on fraud and corruption — and, more importantly, on what we are doing to combat it and how our citizens can help. Too often today, fraud is something which the public know is there, but feel powerless to deal with. And this vague, pervasive sense of wrongdoing can then be used to discredit systems and institutions, which, though imperfect, have a vital role to play. Think of the UN and the oil for food scandal, for example.

Traditional communication from the authorities appears to many as worthy exhortations to deal with the problems. Worthy, but remote from the problems as experienced by the people at the grass roots. Not only does this failure to communicate leave people cynical about our anti-fraud efforts, it also means that we cannot build the trust that is vital if they are to work with us, confident to pass on the information necessary to our anti-fraud efforts.

Web 2.0 is clearly not a panacea. But it offers a new approach breaking out of bland 'top down' messages — static one-way information flows — to actual 'communication' between and within groups; from generalised standard content to individualised messages, adapted to the needs of particular audiences. Instead of short, one-off contacts we can now offer possibilities for extended exchanges. Instead of slow and lengthy information updating cycles, quick responses to current, possibly rapidly evolving information needs should become the norm. Web 2.0 also offers a chance to reach new groups — particularly the young — who have largely abandoned traditional media.

Of course, new communication tools present new challenges. How can we keep public credibility and trust when, for legal reasons, we cannot say much about ongoing investigations? Or how to explain when a lack of sufficient admissible evidence means that apparently serious cases go unpunished? Many recent cases have shown the tensions between the demands of globalised, 24-hour, media, and the legal controls applied to protect the integrity of ongoing investigations, and the presumption of innocence. Certainly our experiences in OLAF and the European Commission suggest that the European courts, at least, do not give effective communication on anti-fraud work the highest priority. Considerable ingenuity will be needed to satisfactorily reconcile these requirements.

Equally, it is a big commitment of resources to promise ever more tailored communications tools. We need to ensure that we do not damage our credibility by making promises on which we cannot deliver.

Thus there are many important issues for us to look at over the next two days, and I look forward to some lively discussions.

Let me also use this occasion to convey Vice-President Kallas' appreciation to OAFCN members for your daily efforts in communicating to the public and the media and in maintaining collegial cooperation amongst yourself. We are deeply convinced that transparency, honesty and personal integrity, together with partnership, are the key ingredients if we want to successfully engage the public in our work. Being open about the possible extent of a problem, but without unnecessary alarm or premature judgement, and constantly stressing the consequences of fraud and irregular activities for society, will helps us win and maintain the credibility that is central for making our efforts last.

Thank you all for your commitment to this cause.

European institutions

Luis LÓPEZ SANZ-ARANGUEZ

President of the OLAF Supervisory Committee,
Public Prosecutor at Supreme Court, Spain

Luis LÓPEZ SANZ-ARANGUEZ

President of
the Supervisory
Committee of OLAF

Public Prosecutor at
Supreme Court, Spain

Born in Madrid, Spain
1957

Graduated in Law
from the Universidad
Autónoma de Madrid
in 1979

Elected Prosecutor
attached to the
Offices of the Public
Prosecutors of
Barcelona (1982–84)
and Madrid
(1984–95)

1995–2002: Deputy
Chief Prosecutor
of the Special Anti-
Corruption and
Economic Crime
Prosecutor's office

Since 2002:
Prosecutor at the
Supreme Court of
Spain

1995-2005: Associate
Professor in the
Department of
Procedural Law at
the Universidad
Autónoma de Madrid

'The purpose of this seminar should be to discuss the numerous means of fraud prevention offered by Web 2.0 as well as any resulting problems and their possible solutions.'

*K*alimera, Good morning everyone,

First of all I wish to thank OLAF (both Mr Brüner, the Director-General, and Mr Butticé, the OLAF spokesman and Head of the Information Unit) for asking me, as the Chairman of the OLAF Supervisory Committee, to speak at the opening session of this seminar.

Secondly, I would like to apologise for not being able to join you in person and for being obliged to speak to you by video. Agenda problems which proved impossible to resolve have prevented me from speaking to you in person today and also from participating in the seminar sessions, as I would have liked to do.

I am speaking to all of you as the Chairman of the OLAF Supervisory Committee. This Committee's core task is to reinforce OLAF's independence through regular monitoring of its investigations. Undoubtedly, an effective prevention policy is important with regard to this independence.

The fight against fraud and corruption, which are OLAF's core aims, must play a part in preventing these practices. OLAF's day-to-day experience of conducting and drawing conclusions from investigations place it in a privileged position to provide concrete data that can be used to establish strategic policies and specific initiatives for prevention.

In order to prevent a problem it is necessary to anticipate it. To this end, we must adapt to an increasingly complex situation and use all the means at our disposal, particularly in the field of communication and information.

Since 2005:
Associate Professor
of Procedural Law
at the Universidad
Nacional de
Educación a Distancia
responsible for
courses at masters
level in the field of
penal procedures

Since November
2005: Member of
the Supervisory
Committee of OLAF
(European Anti-Fraud
Office)

2007: Elected
President of
the Supervisory
Committee of OLAF

2008: Re-elected
President of
the Supervisory
Committee of OLAF

In a global society, communication and information are increasingly accessible to everyone, and this has both advantages and disadvantages. Those of us who are engaged in the task of combating fraud and corruption must recognise this situation and endeavour to use all the means at our disposal. I therefore believe that the initiative behind this seminar is an excellent one, namely to discuss how the most advanced versions of the Internet can be used to help prevent fraud against the financial interests of the European Union.

The new possibilities offered by Web 2.0, the new Internet technology, which is regarded by experts as the best, represent an evolution from traditional applications used merely to obtain facts and data towards a model for exchanging information which enables active participation.

While the highly sensitive nature of fraud prevention must not deter us from applying the possibilities of Internet Web 2.0, we must act with caution to ensure that this tool does not turn against us. We must therefore establish security systems capable of detecting suspicious or malicious actions. The dangers lie in the general access to sensitive information and also in the risk that attempts will be made to share and alter this information for illegal purposes. We must respond to this danger.

This is not only common sense, it is in fact our legal requirement in accordance with the secrecy and confidentiality obligation stipulated in Article 287 of the EC Treaty, Article 17 of the Staff Regulations for officials and Article 8 of Regulation (EC) No 1073/1999. This obligation is also laid down in the data protection rules deriving from Article 8 of the EU Charter of Fundamental Rights, Article 8 of the European Convention for the Protection of Human Rights and Fundamental Freedoms and Article 6 of the present Treaty on European Union.

In this regard, I would like to point out that if these new-generation Internet applications are used incorrectly or for the wrong purposes in the area of prevention of fraud and corruption, this may be seriously detrimental to the efficient conduct of future or current investigations, which would be unacceptable. In addition, it would mean that those acting negligently by sharing such highly sensitive information could incur serious liabilities.

These security measures and precautions, which are already in place for the exchange of information between directorates, units or staff of OLAF itself, must be subject to more rigorous control and compliance when this information is shared with third parties.

Despite these essential precautions, we must all be committed to using all the technologies available to us in the field of information and communication. In the past, all advances made in means of disseminating knowledge, such as the invention of printing, the radio, telephone or television, caused concern and uncertainty, but the passing of time has shown that these advances have been crucial for human progress.

The purpose of this seminar must be not only to discuss, based on our experience, the numerous possibilities for fraud prevention offered by this new generation of the Internet, but also to assess the problems that may arise and provide possible solutions.

The OLAF Supervisory Committee is willing to collaborate and provide constructive opinions that will help in the task of preventing fraud against the budget of the European Union.

Thank you very much for your attention. I am sure that the debates and conclusions of this seminar will be fruitful.

3.2 MEDIA

Petros PETRIDES

Secretary, Cyprus Media Complaints Commission
on behalf of the Union of Cyprus Journalists

**Petros
PETRIDES**

Born in 1941, a
graduate in Law from
Aristotelian University
of Thessaloniki
and in Journalism
from Thomson
Foundation College,
Cardiff, he worked
as a reporter for
several newspapers
including the *Ethniki*
newspaper and the
Cyprus Mail; then as
Editor-in-Chief for the
AGON newspaper;
and for the Cyprus
Broadcasting
Corporation. He
was also a teacher in
journalism.

His research and
publications include a
*Historic Encyclopaedia
of Cyprus 1881–
1981* (a 16-volume,
detailed history of
Cyprus) and his
journalism teaching
notes.

The new-generation Internet: challenge and opportunity for journalists

The subject of my presentation is 'The new-generation Internet: challenge and opportunity for journalists', but I hope you will indulge me if I go back a little farther in time to find my starting point.

Time magazine has often dedicated special features to new technologies — the automobile, the plane, radio, television and — later, around the end of the 1980s — the personal computer. Although I've always been interested in technology, when I read about this new invention which promised so much — making life easier, making work faster and more efficient — I decided that this latest technological advance would have no effect on me. Given the snail's pace at which new technologies made their way into life in Cyprus, I would have retired long before I was required to use this new technology.

But precisely then, in 1990, CNN gave me and 12 colleagues from various countries the chance to learn at first hand about its brave new world of communications, to work for three months in the World Report section, broadcasting news sent in by television stations all over the world.

CNN was the first channel to use the newsroom computer system — in fact, it was really this system which made CNN, and the crazy vision of its founder Ted Turner, a reality. As you can imagine, from the moment I set foot in the southern wing of the CNN complex in Atlanta I found myself face-to-face with that personal hate-object: the computer. The next three nights were spent poring over the user's manual — and the next five years writing letters and memos to my employers urging the necessity of installing a similar system in our own workplace!

Finally, the system came to us in 1995 — confirming my original fears over the tardy introduction of new technology into certain organisations in Cyprus.

I remembered this story when I read the title of our seminar, which lays emphasis on Web 2.0, and I was reminded that John Markoff of the *New York Times* has been writing since 2006 about Web 3.0 — basically a new, smart Internet based on artificial intelligence. Obviously if this version of the Internet was possible today, then the seminar itself might not be necessary. So I shall confine myself here to journalism 2.0.

Each of you can draw your own conclusions from what I have said so far, but I believe there are two basic points. Firstly, that technology in the areas of information science and the Internet is evolving so rapidly that today's technology is superannuated tomorrow. This means that people need to think and make plans, always bearing this rate of progress in mind. Secondly, that no one can ignore technology, because ignoring it will mean being trampled underfoot by its implacable progress or, at the very least, finding oneself side-lined. So those of us who wish to remain in the mainstream, journalists included, must accept technological advances and proceed in step with them.

The new Internet offers numerous opportunities and challenges to journalists — young and old alike. I shall speak of the most important of them below. The opportunities and chal-lenges do not come only from so-called globalisation. This has been around ever since Reuter used carrier pigeons to send financial news from the Continent to Britain — and we all witnessed globalisation at work when we watched the so-called Gulf War live on CNN.

The great challenge and opportunity for journalism in general is whether it can respond to the wishes of a globalised audience. One example: If someone logs on to YouTube he will notice two things — the sheer number of people with broadband connections, and, above all, the way in which they now want to get their news. This latter is without any doubt quite different from the way familiar to traditional journalism. I cannot say with certainty how far this is the best way of practising our profession, but it is certainly an alternative way with all sorts of possibilities.

The fact is that the new Internet has created a new culture, new attitudes towards the me-dia, which the journalist must at least try to understand even if he cannot share them. Generally speaking, understanding the new culture is easier for younger people — pre-cisely those people who are the future readers of the news.

The journalist's mission is to inform through communication. In this respect, it is to some extent identical with the mission or purpose of Web 2.0, since one of its basic functions is communication among users and reciprocal provision of information through sharing of the data which each user has processed.

Of course, in traditional printed or electronic journalism, via radio or TV, the communica-tion is one-way. Journalism via the Internet allows the opportunity for two-way communi-cation, in the sense that the recipient of the information has the opportunity to intervene, add, correct, contradict or even provide new information. This will occur, obviously, only to the extent that the owner or operator of a journalistic website allows it. The opportuni-ties and challenges for journalism do not spring only from the possibilities inherent in the new Internet. They also arise from the fact that, according to research, a significant propor-tion of young people take their information only or largely from the Internet — and they expect it to be different.

The opportunities for journalists, especially the more youthful among them, are obvious. Young people who know what other young people want to learn can create their own jour-nalistic organisation on the Internet, in one form or another.

The opportunities the Internet offers to journalists are varied. They involve both the finding and the communication of information. They also involve the provision of journalistic education and the receiving of education by young people who want to enter the profession. Finally, they involve the participation of the public in the process of informing.

Each of these areas offers its own opportunities and challenges — but also problems which must not be overlooked.

Finding information

Not so many years ago, a journalist would look for information on a subject he was working on in encyclopaedias, books of facts and figures and statistics, or the cuttings archive of a newspaper, the archives of broadcasting media or his own personal records and files. This kind of research was never absolutely satisfactory. It tended to be a slow and painstaking process.

But today, all a journalist has to do is log on to a reputable journalistic site or type a few key words into a search engine — and like magic he will find hundreds or thousands of entries, in almost real time.

This is the positive side of collecting information via the Internet.

The negative side is that if information is not gathered from known and reliable sites, the result will resemble a form of Internet fraud — the subject of our seminar. The journalist has to teach himself to tell the reliable from the suspect, because nobody would easily admit passing on propaganda or conveying inaccurate information. Unfortunately, however, there are individuals who have no scruples in this area. One or two years ago, I received an e-mail with a message along these lines: 'Dear Sir, I am a fraudster who has managed to embezzle millions of dollars from the company X. My problem is that I can't get the money out of the country and I need your help … etc.'.

On the other hand, the Internet can serve as a tool for obfuscation and for preventing the work of journalists and the dissemination of the truth. More and more governments, agencies and businesses are now shunning direct contact with journalists and referring them to their websites instead. A good example would be the way journalists were treated at the last Commonwealth Summit in Australia. The accredited journalists were kept locked in an air-conditioned tent, denied any direct contact with the leaders and Heads of State and unable to put questions or verify the information they were fed over the Internet.

Communicating information

The opportunities to convey information over the Internet are unlimited, for all journalists, young and old. There is no need for imposing office premises and equipment, just the essential computers, some software and a good designer to set up a website. I am sure you all know that there are thousands of sites on the Internet offering information in various guises. Let me just offer a brief overview of the situation here in Cyprus. Most of the Cypriot journalism websites that are not an extension of some existing newspaper or media organisation have been slow to develop and are, at present, few in number. But I am confident that more and more journalists will eventually come to appreciate the new opportunities available.

The same opportunities are available to others outside our profession, and this is no bad thing — a plurality of voices never did any harm. What can cause problems and should concern a journalistic organisation like ours is the quality of the information provided. Let me cite a few grounds for concern. Since the financial viability of these sites depends on advertising, and the volume of advertising on the number of hits, there is always the temptation to be led astray into the area of scandal, cheap gossip and interference in the private lives of celebrities and ordinary people alike. We saw something of the sort when private radio and television made their appearance in Cyprus. It has been observed that information will be published on the Internet which printed or electronic media will avoid or shy away from publishing.

There are other aspects of the Internet which give rise to concern, such as copyright issues, morality and ethics, and the right to privacy. But who is responsible for regulating the Internet?

The Cyprus Journalists Union was set up mainly to protect and promote the interests of journalists. But it also takes an interest in the professional conduct of journalists and the media. This is why it became one of the founding members of the Journalistic Ethics Committee, whose mission is to scrutinise journalists' conduct and protect members of the public from journalistic excess and invasions of privacy, or other violations of the Code of Journalistic Ethics.

Here the question arises of the impossibility of finding who is responsible. As you know, the Internet is simultaneously everywhere and nowhere. Just remind yourselves that even the United States haven't managed to work out who runs the Al Qaeda websites or where they are based.

Even in the case of websites belonging to well-known organisations, staffed by individuals whose identity is known, it can sometimes be impossible to gather the necessary evidence of wrongdoing. A controversial article on a website can be made to vanish at the click of a mouse.

On the other hand, there are complaints that, in some countries, journalists are not granted protection of their right to freedom of expression in cases of libel.

We don't have a problem of this kind in Cyprus, Here the law on libel is a replica of the British legislation dating from the early 20th century. It has remained unchanged despite the fact that the law in Britain has been amended and updated repeatedly. I hope someone in authority is listening.

Another form of discrimination against Internet journalists is the failure to provide amenities and facilities comparable to those available to their colleagues in more conventional media. This is alarming.

A journalistic organisation like the Journalists Union would be concerned if competition from the Internet led to redundancies among colleagues. We haven't yet seen this in Cyprus, but in other countries, newspapers have shed employees. Some of the victims took advantage of the possibilities created by the Internet and set up their own sites. Some did not.

Providing and receiving education

The Internet and the many opportunities offered by information technology together provide almost infinite opportunities in the area of journalistic education. Many schools and teachers have already seized these opportunities, presenting their educational material via blogs. Journalism students, too, can benefit, submitting their work through blogs so that it will be available to other students for comments and observations. The Journalists Union is intending to use this method in its plans for a programme of ongoing education for journalists.

Finally, let me refer to another aspect of Internet journalism — the involvement of the public in the exercise of our profession. This is a practice which has been employed in the past in the form of live interviews or discussions, in which the public had the chance to pose questions — sometimes live by telephone, sometimes in written form.

Many channels in the USA have already started to use the practice known as 'twitter' to take questions from the public. The practice has been used successfully in live broadcasts on the current global financial crisis.

Before I finish, allow me to refer to the subject of your seminar — the prevention of fraud by provision of information. What you are looking at is the use of the new Internet to provide this kind of information. You must not overlook the importance of the provision of information by journalists — information which will never be effective if journalists are compelled to reveal their sources. This is why our own Journalists Union, in association with the European Federation of Journalists and the International Federation of Journalists, will continue to resist any attempt to oblige colleagues to reveal their sources.

Ladies and gentlemen, the subject of this presentation could easily provide enough material to fill a whole book. I hope I have at least been able to use this brief time available to me to give you some valuable information and views.

Thank you very much for listening so attentively, and I wish you every success in the proceedings of your seminar.

3.3 NATIONAL INSTITUTIONS, INVESTIGATIVE AND JUDICIAL SERVICES

National institutions, investigative and judicial services

Zeta EMILIANIDOU

Director-General, Department of Customs and Excise
of the Republic of Cyprus
Welcome address

Zeta EMILIANIDOU

Director-General
of the Cyprus
Department of
Customs and
Excise and VAT
Commissioner

Born on 2 September
1954 in Nicosia.
A graduate in law
from the Aristotelion
University of
Thessaloniki and
with a Diploma
in Marketing
Management from
the Cyprus Institute
of Marketing, she
succeeded in
the Cyprus Bar
Examinations and
was registered as
a lawyer in 1978.
First appointed
in the Cyprus
Department of
Customs and Excise,
she participated in
drafting the legislation
for VAT and was
then appointed
as a Senior VAT
Officer. She has been
Director-General
of the Department
of Customs and
Excise as well as
VAT Commissioner
since 15 August
2001, prior to which
she was Acting
Director-General
of the Department
of Customs and
Excise and VAT
Commissioner from

Address by Director of Customs Department

Dear colleagues, representatives of the Commission, ladies and gentlemen,

I am both honoured and delighted to welcome you today to Cyprus and to the city of Nicosia, on the occasion of the eighth seminar of the OLAF Anti-Fraud Office Communicators' Network. I wish to extend particular thanks to the representatives of OLAF, who have chosen Cyprus as the location for this very important seminar. It is my belief that the work being done through the OLAF Anti-Fraud Communicators' Network is of vital importance in preventing irregularities and fraud from threatening the economic interests of the European Union. The network is performing an essential service in keeping the public informed of the work of the Office in combating corruption and fraud.

During its long collaboration with OLAF and, by extension, with the Communicators' Network, the Cyprus Customs Department has established the necessary infrastructure to promote the work being done in the area of the prevention and elimination of smuggling. The purpose of this promotion is to update and add value not only to the work and achievements of the national services engaged in the prevention and combating of fraud, but at the same time to promote the general image of the battle against fraud at the Community level.

The agenda for this seminar covers a great deal of important ground, and our discussion of the issues involved — such as new technology for communication with the public — will be vital in allowing real promotion and provision of information on the work being done by our various services. The intention is to convey the right message on the real danger

2 May 2000 and Chief Customs Officer from 15 July 1996. She was also an ex officio member on the Board of Directors of the Ports Authority of Cyprus, from 2001. She was responsible for the implementation of the acquis communautaire with regard to Customs and Excise during the Cyprus–EU negotiations that resulted in Cyprus's accession to the European Union on 1 May 2004. She participated in drafting the current legislation of the Customs and Excise. She wrote a book The value added tax in Cyprus, published in 1992, when the first law on value added tax was enacted in Cyprus.

represented by fraud to the economic interests of the European Union and on the work of our services in combating it.

I look forward to a very successful seminar, confident that the way has been paved for a fascinating and constructive dialogue leading to important results in respect of the key challenges we face: allowing us to develop more effective channels of communication with the public, so that they can appreciate what exactly we mean by fraud, what dangers it poses and what is being done by our services to combat it.

Finally, I should like to congratulate the organisers of the seminar. I am sure its proceedings will be successful and I wish you all a happy stay in Cyprus.

National institutions, investigative and judicial services

Charilaos STAVRAKIS

Minister for Finance
Ministry for Finance of the Republic of Cyprus

**Charilaos
G. STAVRAKIS**

Minister for Finance

Republic of Cyprus

Born in 1956, graduated in Economics from the University of Cambridge, with an MBA in Business Administration, Harvard. He was a member of the Chartered Institute of Bankers (ACIB); a consultant in the World Bank; a Head of Strategic Planning and Business Development, a Senior Manager of Treasury and International Services at the Bank of Cyprus; a General Manager of the Cyprus Investment & Securities Corporation Limited (CISCO), the investment banking arm of the group and on the Board of Directors of the Cyprus Oil Refinery; a member of the Board of the Bank of Cyprus Australia, the Bank of Cyprus (Channel Islands) Ltd, the Bank of Cyprus (AEDAK), the Bank of Cyprus Mutual Funds Ltd and BOC Ventures Ltd; a Chief Executive Officer — Cyprus and Deputy Group Chief Executive Officer with the management of the

Address by the Minister for Finance

I am both honoured and delighted to welcome you to Cyprus today, on behalf of the Republic of Cyprus, on the occasion of the eighth seminar of the OLAF Anti-Fraud Communicators' Network. We are greatly honoured that the representatives of OLAF have chosen our island as the venue for this very important seminar, and I offer them my especially heartfelt thanks.

The Republic of Cyprus is a vital partner in the common struggle for security and the protection of society, the environment and the economic interests of the European Union. Key to this struggle are the elimination of smuggling, fraud and all related criminal activity.

In this context I must congratulate the Cyprus Customs Department for its massive and effective contribution to attaining these objectives.

As Minister for Finance, I appreciate the importance and significance of the work undertaken by the OLAF Anti-Fraud Communicators' Network.

The complexity and difficulties which stand in the way of public appreciation of the issues of irregularity and fraud against the economic interests of the European Union require ongoing cooperation and exchange of information among all competent departments. The existence of the appropriate technological support is a vital condition of success if the public are to receive the right message, delivered quickly and effectively, and to understand better the nature and importance of these issues.

I have been informed of the very interesting agenda for your seminar and it is my belief that information on new media technology and collective initiatives can make a vital contribution to the goals you have set — sending the right message to the public on the dangers subsidiary companies of the group and the setting up of banks in Russia and Ukraine; an appointed Chairman of the Electricity Authority Cyprus Board of Directors; an elected Chairman of the Cyprus Bankers Employers Association and re-elected in June 2006 for another year.

presented by fraud and irregularities that menace the economic interests of the European Union.

Finally, I should like to congratulate the organisers of the seminar. I am sure its proceedings will be successful and I wish you all a happy stay in Cyprus.

National institutions, investigative and judicial services

4. ANNEXES

4.1 The European Anti-fraud Office (OLAF)

The European Anti-Fraud Office (OLAF) came into being on 1 June 1999. By creating OLAF, the European institutions provided themselves with a mechanism to combat transnational economic and financial crime, fraud and corruption against Community interests, in particular Europe's public finances. OLAF is independent in its operational activity, as the legislator wanted to give OLAF full legitimacy and guarantee the independence and impartiality of its investigative work. It translates into practice the determination of the Community and the institutions to protect and defend the interests of the European taxpayer. In order to strengthen the fight against fraud, corruption and any illegal activity affecting the EU, OLAF exercises the power to investigate, conferred on the Commission by the EU Community Regulation and the cooperation agreements in force.

OLAF's powers extend to all the activities relating to the protection of the Community's financial interests against irregular behaviour and/or illegal acts liable to administrative or criminal proceedings. OLAF thus has the power to conduct external administrative investigations in the Member States of the Union and in third countries, but also internal administrative investigations within the Community institutions, bodies, offices or agencies.

Beyond the protection of Europe's public finances, OLAF also has responsibility for combating counterfeiting, piracy and forgery of the euro.

Within the institutions, bodies, offices and agencies established by, or on the basis of, the Treaties (hereinafter `the institutions, bodies, offices and agencies©), the Office shall conduct administrative investigations for the purpose of:

- fighting fraud, corruption and any other illegal activity affecting the financial interests of the European Atomic Energy Community,

- investigating to that end serious matters relating to the discharge of professional duties such as to constitute a dereliction of the obligations of officials and other servants of the Communities. This could result in disciplinary or, as the case may be, criminal proceedings, or an equivalent failure to discharge obligations on the part of members of institutions and bodies, heads of offices and agencies or members of the staff of institutions, bodies, offices or agencies not subject to the Staff Regulations of Officials and the Conditions of Employment of Other Servants of the European Communities (the Staff Regulations©).

As part of its investigative function, OLAF shall exercise the power conferred on the Commission by Council Regulation (Euratom, EC) No 2185/96 and by Article 9(1) and in the sectoral rules referred to in Article 9(2) of Regulation (EC, Euratom) No 2988/95 to carry out on-the-spot inspections and checks in the Member States and, in accordance with the cooperation agreements in force, in third countries.

OLAF protects taxpayers' money, then, by making sure that EU funds are properly spent, that the EU is not being deprived of its due revenues and that EU staff behave according to the rules.

Lastly, OLAF defines the overall anti-fraud strategy, draws up the necessary legal instruments and helps to make legislative texts fraud-proof.

4.2 OLAF's anti-fraud communication and public relations strategy

The anti-fraud communication strategy under discussion in this note considers the anti-fraud "communication and information activities" as dealt with by the communication strategy for the European Commission([103]), in strong co-operation with DG Communication and the spokesperson of the Commissioner.

1. Basis of OLAF's independent communication policy

While following the guidelines of the communication strategy for the European Commission, the statutory independence of OLAF, set up as an autonomous investigative body, requires its own external communication policy.

Therefore, only the Office itself has the right and the duty to report on its operational activities and dispose of resources of its own for this aim. The communication and information actions are exercised in the light of the Office's obligation to protect investigations and to respect the fundamental rights of the individual, within the constraints prescribed by international, Community and national law.

2. Main objectives of OLAF's anti-fraud communication strategy

- to prevent fraud through the "free-flow" of information ("prevention is better than cure").
- to satisfy the citizens' right to know about what is being achieved to protect their interests; ([104])
- to support OLAF's operational independence;

One of the main tools of this policy has been the creation of the OLAF Anti-Fraud Communicators' Network (OAFCN) in 2001 ([105]).

3. OLAF organisation for external communication activities

Contrary to what some people may think and considering the sizeable output from its motivated staff, OLAF's Unit "Spokesman, Communication and Public Relations" is one of the smallest information-communication units of all the Directorates General of the Commission, and it is the only one having a spokesman function.

In addition to being responsible for communication and external information it is also responsible for external visits to the Office ([106]), in the framework of public relations, and for the management of the OLAF website ([107]).

([103]) "Implementing the information and communication strategy for the European Union" of 20 April 2004

([104]) According to a recent study, made within the framework of Euro barometer, a Flash Euro barometer carried out between 26th and 30th June 2008, a majority of European citizens consider themselves poorly informed about the fight against fraud affecting the EU financial interest and request the European Institutions to inform them better, especially through television, daily newspapers, and radio. http://ec.europa.eu /anti_fraud/press_room/eurobar/en.html

([105]) http://ec.europa.eu/anti_fraud/olaf-oafcn/en.html

([106]) During the last year 71 visits to the Office have been organised, involving some 900 persons in total, mainly from customs, investigation services and public prosecutors offices from Member States and other countries. Additionally, prominent delegations were welcomed to OLAF from a variety of public offices.

([107]) The OLAF Website, http://olaf.europa.eu, continued to be the basic tool of the communication and information policy of the Office. The number of hits has constantly risen since its first installation, demonstrating the increasing interest of the public into the work of the Office. In 2008, the pages which received most hits were those of the "Press Room" followed by the "Reports" and the "Partners" pages.

4. Anti-Fraud information and Communication policy as a means of fraud prevention — the OLAF Anti-Fraud Communicators' Network (OAFCN)

All forms of fraud against the Community's financial interests, from evasion of the taxes and duties which produce revenue for the European budget, to abuse of the financial assistance granted by the Community, involve a real, substantial loss for European taxpayers

Taxpayers must be informed of cases of fraud, but also of what is being done, at national and Community level, to ensure that their money is being put to best use and that the fight against fraud is as effective as possible.

The OLAF Anti-Fraud Communicators' Network (OAFCN) ([108]), which was set up in 2001, groups together OLAF's spokesman and those responsible for public relations and communication in the national investigation services with which OLAF collaborates — in both the Member States and the candidate countries.

The network strives to raise awareness among the European public of the need for an anti-fraud programme which is comprehensive, balanced and effective throughout the territory of the European Union.

The objectives of the anti-fraud communication policy of OLAF, through this network are to:

- prevent fraud through the 'free flow' of information: *Prevention is better than cure*;
- create a permanent dialogue between OLAF's external communication service and its counterparts in the national investigation services;
- inform European citizens on what OLAF and its partners in the Member States do, both jointly and individually, in order to protect its financial interests;
- provide information to the general public (in particular through the media) regarding the fight against fraud and irregularities affecting the financial interests of the European Union.

OAFCN tries to add value to the work of the national investigation services and to highlight not only the work done in individual Member States, but also the overall Community aspect of the fight against fraud.

As far as it is legally and operationally possible, the members of the network keep each other up-to-date on issues involving press releases of mutual interest.

They also help the media to evaluate the information sent to them by other members of the network, whatever their nationality. As a rule, national investigation services are more effective and more comfortable with their national media than with foreign media.

However, one of OAFCN's purposes is to ensure that the door of each national investigation service which cooperates with OLAF is open to all the international media. The members of the network provide joint media coverage (videos, photos, press releases, publications([109])) to illustrate OLAF's operational activities in the fight against fraud.

Seminars and training sessions for communicators and journalists are being organised in the new MS and in the Candidates Countries ([110])

([108]) http://ec.europa.eu/anti_fraud/olaf-oafcn/en.html
([109]) http://ec.europa.eu/anti_fraud/publications/index_en.html
([110]) http://ec.europa.eu anti_fraud/olaf-oafcn/seminars/en.html

5. Communication activities to stress the cooperation with the operational partners in the Member States

Responding to the European citizens' demand for more information on the fight against fraud ([111]), OLAF, in its information and communication policy, has emphasized the existing close co-operation between the Office and its operational partners in the Member States (investigative services, police, judicial and administrative authorities).

In this context, OLAF has given them the opportunity to describe their tasks in OLAF's videos and in brochures. ([112])

6. OLAF's media relations

Notwithstanding the fact that media relations comprise only a part of this communication strategy, if OLAF cannot speak to the media concerning aspects of its operational independence without reference to the Commission then the independence of OLAF in its investigative function, and therefore its *raison d'être,* would be severely compromised.

Media relations of the Office are handled professionally on a centralised basis, to avoid misunderstandings that may arise through interpretation of information given by different persons. Rules and modalities of operation have been put in place in the OLAF Manual of Procedure to set out how information is passed within OLAF and how it can then be passed on to members of the press.

Due to its operational independence, OLAF is the only service of the Commission that has a spokesman function. ([113])

As events (e.g. leaks of confidential information) have shown, nothing can be more damaging in media terms than silence. A committed journalist, if he can't get the information he needs from the official source, will find other ways of investigating the subject.

Acting as an interlocutor with the media means talking to the media, being open, responsive and concerned.

The Office however has adopted a very cautious approach in its relations with the media and in general says very little or nothing about ongoing investigations. This is in order to be as open as possible within the constraints prescribed by national and Community law, the need to protect investigations, and respect for the fundamental rights of the suspect. In any event, any decision to make any operational information public is authorized by the Director-General, only after discussion in detail within OLAF. Of course, there is always a

---

([111]) see Flash Euro Barometer 2008: 'Citizens' perceptions of fraud and the fight against fraud in the EU27: http://ec.europa.eu /anti_fraud/press_room/eurobar/en.html

([112]) http://ec.europa.eu /anti_fraud/publications/index_en.html

([113]) The Spokesman function has been created in order to:

provide a counterpart for the media, acquainted with established practice in public relations and prepared to provide accurate information in an accessible format at any time,

protect OLAF investigators and other OLAF staff from media intrusions in sensitive areas of their work;

ensure that the Office as such rather than the individuals working on particular cases or issues is seen to act, thus protecting the personal identity of the officials and avoiding the risk of personal recognition in the media;

reduce the risk that the media may seek information on the Office's operational activities through inappropriate channels.

push-pull effect in the way that media relations activities are implemented: journalists want the maximum information on a given case while the Office must protect fundamental rights, legal norms and the integrity of its investigations.

7. OLAF's relations with journalist' associations

OLAF and representatives of the associations of journalists have been engaged, for many years, in exchanging ideas on anti-fraud communication. Two seminars, jointly hosted by OLAF and the International Federation of Journalists for members of OLAF's Anti-fraud Communicators' Network, have already taken place (Brussels 2005 ([114]), Sofia 2006 ([115])). The debates relating to them are included in this Round Table «Preventing fraud by informing the public ([116])», which gathered together journalists, representatives of the International Federation of Journalists (FIJ ([117])) and the International Press Association (IPA-API ([118])), as well as correspondents in Brussels.

Furthermore, various seminars, aimed at journalists, have been organised by OLAF on the investigative powers of the European Anti-fraud Office (OLAF), the EU budget and EU protection in general.

Mr. Siim Kallas, Vice-president of the European Commission, praised this initiative: "dialogue between services involved in the fight against fraud and journalists is an example of transparency and openness on a practical level. Communication can help discourage and prevent fraud and irregularities by strengthening awareness-raising and by informing citizens of the risks that economic crime represents to them".

Mr. Franz Hermann Brüner, OLAF's Director-General, moreover said: "the work of journalists can help uncover cases of fraud, corruption and other illegal activities detrimental to the financial interests of the European communities, about which EU citizens have the right to be informed".

For his part, at one of these seminars, the Secretary-General of the International Federation of Journalists, Mr Aidan White, emphasised that: "journalists and investigators work better when both groups have professional relations based on mutual respect, without ever forgetting the importance of public interest. This seminar will allow journalists to better understand the challenges they face when they present cases of crime and measures taken to combat fraud and corruption. It will consolidate their role as "public wardens". He added: "this seminar will serve to increase professionalism both on a journalistic and an investigative level. Criminals and offenders are the only ones to lose out when journalists do their work well".

Several investigative journalists also took part in the OLAF-FIJ seminars, during which they were told about the work of law enforcement bodies investigating cases of fraud, corruption and other illegal activities detrimental to the financial interests of the EU.

([114]) http://ec.europa.eu/anti_fraud/olaf-oafcn/s/5th/i_en.html
([115]) http://ec.europa.eu/anti_fraud/olaf-oafcn/s/6th/i_en.html
([116]) http://ec.europa.eu/anti_fraud/olaf-oafcn/rt/4thts/i_en.html
([117]) http://www.ifj.org/en
([118]) http://www.api-ipa.eu/

4.3 Conclusions of the Fourth Training Seminar of the OLAF Anti-Fraud Communicators' Network (OAFCN)

Brussels, 24–26 November 2004
Deterring fraud by informing the public: Round Table on Anti-Fraud Communication
Conference chairman: Alessandro Butticé, OLAF spokesman

The following is a summary of the three-day seminar organised by OLAF and designed for spokespersons and other communications specialists from governmental anti-fraud agencies ('agencies') throughout the EU Member States and the candidate countries. It outlines the key issues discussed and the suggestions that were made by delegates and speakers.

This summary does not attempt to record in the form of minutes the full discourse of the seminar or attribute specific comments or ideas to particular speakers or delegates.

Instead it attempts to distil the event into its core themes and discussion points.

Key senior message

The event opened with keynote addresses from Mr Siim Kallas, Vice-President of the EC designated (Administrative Affairs, Audit and Finance), Mr Szabolcs Fazakas, Chairman of the Budgetary Control Committee of the European Parliament, Mr Raymond Kendall, President of the OLAF Supervisory Committee and Mr Franz-Herman Brüner, Director-General of OLAF.

The senior speakers reiterated the continued need to develop closer and stronger public messages throughout the European Union. The seminars of the OLAF Anti-Fraud Communicators' Network (OAFCN) and the underlying 'virtual round table' demonstrated a wide interest throughout the agencies to debate the role of media communication and public information. The senior speakers confirmed the need for agencies to create effective communication policies in order to maximise public awareness that fraud is a serious crime that debilitates economic activity and can affect confidence in business, commerce, investment and individual financial security. It was stressed that the governments of the EU Member States and the EC executive, through their anti-fraud agencies, must communicate to citizens what is being done to protect their interests.

The main points

After the keynote addresses, Mr Butticé (OLAF) introduced the guest speakers who throughout the three days introduced specialist topics which were debated in open forum with the delegates. The main features were agencies must adopt communications policies and practices that have proper observation of law and without jeopardising operational imperatives of investigation and prosecution. It is a fundamental requirement that spokespersons have a duty to protect the case.

'No comment!' Despite the obvious unhelpfulness of this answer, there are many occasions when it is proper for a spokesperson to use it. A responsible media should respect that in some situations it is not practical, legal or operationally safe for a spokesperson to give a detailed answer to a specific question. Any attempt to mask a 'no comment' with a complicated, confusing and possibly misleading reply is likely to discredit the spokesperson in the eyes of the journalist.

Spokespersons in agencies must set ethical standards when dealing with the media. To manipulate or to mislead the media are potentially dangerous tactics which will soon be seen by a journalist and will damage personal relations and could be exposed publicly in the media report. The best media relations are built on trust and mutual respect not on suspicion or a 'siege mentality'. The point was made that a deep understanding by both the journalist and the spokesperson of each other's roles was a necessity. This required a two-way effort. Journalists must understand the legal limitations that affect what can be disclosed by the spokesperson publicly and when it can be disclosed; in other words protecting the case. Similarly, journalists have a fundamental responsibility to protect their sources of information. Investigating agencies must accept this principle and also respect the fact that journalists can expect discretion and confidentiality from a spokesperson about discussions they have.

The best story is told when the agency and the media try to find a way of cooperation in a kind of 'information partnership'. Based on (selective) trust, the media can be given an advance embargoed briefing by the spokesperson or operational specialist and given some access to inside details about the case many days before the matter can be reported.

Sometimes events in cases are quickly triggered and publicity becomes possible or desirable. Consequently, if a journalist has no previous information from the agency, he will use what information he has got from his own research which might include information from those persons being investigated or prosecuted who will have their own communication agenda.

The resulting media report will not fully represent all that the agency has achieved. If it is about a success for the agency, a pre-briefing can make the report bigger and better and include more details that will be a graphic illustration of the agency's work. A pre-briefing can be especially helpful if the particular circumstance is an investigation that has run into problems or a prosecution that has failed. In a disaster or failure scenario, there will be little time for an agency to tell its side of the story and, once the negative report has appeared in the media, it is extremely difficult — usually impossible — to get any counterbalancing or redeeming media reports at a later date to have the same impact.

To consolidate the OAFCN's efforts it could be beneficial to develop a 'common language' (meaning adoption of basic guidelines for the structure, drafting and presentation of press releases). However, the variation in the different legal systems as they affect communication policies and practices in each country does pose a challenge. It was commented that this concept was an ambitious notion and a topic to be further explored at a future OAFCN meeting to identify its purpose and practicality.

There was an unchallenged argument that the media is the main platform for communicating to the public. A number of delegates echoed this. The media platform was not only for informing the public about case-related events but also for educating the public about the risks and threat to them of economic crime and for informing them of the legal and structural developments that help to create and evolve the agencies. Delegates were invited to think about their own agency's ability to directly communicate, such as through publications and news items to a mailing list or by speaking at public seminars or through the 'hits' on their websites and then to contrast that with the indirect communication mass circulation power of the media. The underlying message here for spokespersons is that every effort should be made to cultivate relations with the media because of its wide reach.

The above principle was developed further with the idea of giving structure to the dialogue; specifically by using primary and secondary channels for the dispersal of information. This is about selective focus; adjusting the message to meet the attention level of a particular audience and delivering the message through a suitable channel.

It was said that OLAF has a media management situation quite different to the national agencies and that structure of dialogue is especially relevant for OLAF which has to consider a public audience of many millions across at least 25 countries in its communications strategy. Even so, for OLAF, Brussels is like a 'village' where a false message spreads like a 'virus'. Viruses grow in the dark. Consequently, the greater the openness with the media, the less likely is the chance of damage to reputation or inaccurate messages taking hold through such a 'virus'.

Media relations are an organic/dynamic synergy and very difficult to write an exact manual about. It is not quite the same as drafting a step-by-step instruction in order to create a mechanical masterpiece. Media relations were described in discussion as 'not an exact science but an imprecise art'.

The chairman summarised the session by saying that fraud and the activities of the agencies that fight fraud are of great interest to the press. Consequently anti-fraud agencies need well defined policy for media relations, a shared philosophy throughout the organisation and spokespersons who are natural and comfortable communicators willing to be proactive in balance with the circumstances. It is also important to have a clearly understood media policy and ethos when looking inwards within the organisation. Colleagues in other parts of anti-fraud agencies must appreciate how important the role of media relations is and the role of those who work for the organisation.

Anti-fraud agencies throughout the EU are important bodies with crucial roles to play to deter economic crime and to track it down and bring fraudsters to justice; and in larger EU countries like Italy or the United Kingdom or in smaller members like Cyprus or Estonia the principles of the threat of economic crime are the same. Consequently, though some agencies are larger than others, though budgets will create different pressures on priorities for different organisations, the principle is that press and public relations should not be a part-time job for doing from the corner of the desk. It is a mind-set.

Workshops

The workshops were delivered on different topics by (1) Mr Richard Linning and Mr Johannes von Dohnanyi, (2) Mr David Jones and Mr Mark Killick and, (3) Ms Lieve Pellens and Mr Oscar Bartolli. (See programme for details of workshop speakers and workshop topics.) These workshops reinforced some of the communication messages discussed during the seminar and were regarded to have added value to the event and the workshop principle should be adopted for further training seminars. One idea raised was the topic 'Communication or propaganda: Where does one end and the other start?'

Finally

The oral version of this summary was delivered at the seminar by Mr David Jones. He made a general observation about the event. He said that the fourth training seminar of the OAFCN represented a massive collective commitment involving four quarters.

The first is the strategic commitment by the EC and its anti-fraud office — OLAF. This commitment was represented at the seminar in the form of opening presentations by the senior speakers mentioned at the beginning of this note. These persons are 'big guns' in the EC framework. Their presence was an encouragement for others to participate.

Secondly, the tactical commitment by Alessandro Butticé of OLAF and his staff who through good organisation and planning, hard work and attention to detail brought together almost 100 representatives from the Member States, the candidate countries, the European Parliament and the Commission and selected media to participate in the event.

The seminar programme, the delegates' and speakers' travel and accommodation arrangements were no small task. The names of the individual OLAF staff who worked tirelessly 'behind the scenes' to make the event an organisational success were read out.

The third aspect of commitment was shown by the delegates who took time off from their particular jobs and professional responsibilities and also time away from their private lives in order to participate. This represented commitment at national organisational level.

Fourthly, there was the contribution by specialists who attended as seminar speakers and workshop presenters who through their commitment brought their experience and perspectives to enrich the event.

Yet despite these four categories of commitment, it is worth noting from the presentation made by Mr Alain Dumort of the EC Press and Communication Unit (which included an audiovisual survey of perspectives of ordinary people in various EU States) that there apparently remains a high degree of ignorance about the EU throughout Europe. If communicating the meaning of the EU to the many millions of EU citizens remains an uphill task, so there remains a similar challenge to communicate the anti-fraud message.

David Jones, Serious Fraud Office, London
6 December 2004

4.4   Memorandum of Understanding

between

the OLAF Anti-Fraud Communicators' Network (OAFCN)

and

the International Federation of Journalists (IFJ)

Brussels, 28 October 2005

The seminar 'Building mutual trust between anti-fraud services and journalists', jointly organised in Brussels by the European Anti-Fraud Office (OLAF) and the International Federation of Journalists (IFJ) for the OLAF Anti-Fraud Communicators' Network (OAFCN) on 28 October 2005, has led to the following conclusions:

1. OAFCN-members and the IFJ and its regional organisation, the European Federation of Journalists (EFJ), agreed that they should promote close and regular cooperation in the field of anti-fraud information and communication, without prejudice to any legal provisions or to the right of journalists to report freely and the defence of the social and professional interests of journalists.

2. During their discussions OAFCN-members and the IFJ/EFJ expressed their belief that transparency, openness and good communications can help deter and prevent fraud, corruption and any other illegal activity by raising awareness and promoting public debate.

3. They also underlined the fact that independent and professional journalism and free media not only play a pivotal role in contributing to raising awareness about anti-corruption activities within the European Union, but that they also act as public watchdog.

4. OAFCN-members and the IFJ/EFJ noted that in the context of their responsibilities and obligations under European law, national law and the European Convention for the Protection of Human Rights and Fundamental freedoms national law enforcement agencies strive for effective and comfortable relations with all media, both national and foreign. In this context they also pointed out that t OLAF and its partners in the Member States as the services in charge of investigating cases of fraud, corruption and any other illegal activity affecting the financial interests of the European Community, are key interlocutors for media professionals.

5. At the seminar the role of the IFJ/EFJ in working for improvements in levels of protection of working journalists and their right to report freely and to work ethically and professionally, including in the protection of confidential sources of information was particularly emphasized. Participants expressed there conviction that a good working relationship is in the mutual interest of both OAFCN-members and the IFJ/EFJ and is in the public interest, too.

6. The IFJ/EFJ believes that the balancing of rights, for instance on whether to publish or not to publish, is a matter for the judgement of journalists aware of the cardinal principles of their profession: respect for the truth, the need for independence and impartiality, and an acute awareness of the consequences of a publication.

7. The anti-fraud service and OAFCN-members for their part, need to communicate truthfully and respond as soon as possible to journalists' questions, including those coming from foreign media. In order to guarantee a free flow of information they should be as transparent and as explicit as possible with the information they hold.

8. OAFCN-members and the IFJ/EFJ agreed on the usefulness of seminars and awareness raising activities between journalists, their associations and OAFCN-members in order to ensure up to date information on latest developments, to promote relations are based upon mutual professional respect, and to generally improve the flow of information about anti-fraud and anti-corruption work.

9. OAFCN-members and the IFJ/EFJ further noted that, within its competencies and constitution in co-operation with its national member organisations, the IFJ/EFJ supports the right of all journalists to report freely and to seek out relevant sources of information.

10. Participants took note that the IFJ/EFJ is willing to consider, where all parties are in agreement, to encourage discussions between journalists and their representatives and OAFCN-members or any national law enforcement agency to resolve problems that may arise.

11. OAFCN-members and the IFJ/EFJ called for the continuation of the common dialogue, not only on European but also on national level. They also agreed that meetings like the present one should be repeated at least once a year.

Aidan White

General Secretary of the IFJ
Tel. +32 22352200
Fax +32 22352219
http://www.ifj.org

Alessandro Butticé

OLAF Head of Communication,
Public Relations and Spokesman Unit
Tel. +32 22965425
Fax +32 22998101
http://olaf.europa.eu

4.5 Conclusions of the Sixth Training Seminar of the OLAF Anti-Fraud Communicators' Network (OAFCN)

By John Powell, HM Revenue & Customs, United Kingdom, OAFCN Member
Transparency and media relations as a means of fighting fraud and corruption affecting EU financial interests
Sofia, Bulgaria, 8 to 11 October 2006

Distinguished guests, fellow delegates,

In delivering the summary and conclusions of this seminar, I have a very difficult task. Because this has been an event at which we have given the topic — 'Transparency and media relations as a means of fighting fraud and corruption affecting EU financial interests' — a very careful and comprehensive examination. We have heard from a series of eminent speakers, who have delivered stimulating and thought-provoking presentations, and prompted lively and informed discussion.

Firstly, by way of personal introduction, my name is John Powell and I am the representative of Her Majesty's Revenue & Customs Department in the UK. I have been part of the network for two years, and find this membership to be valuable and developmental. Many other delegates at this conference are experiencing great change in their countries and their national organisations, and there is a great deal that we can and do learn from each other. At home in the UK we have brought together two large government departments, and merged them into one *very* large organisation responsible for taxation and customs law enforcement. The two former departments: Customs & Excise and the Inland Revenue had a long and rich heritage, dating back hundreds of years. And it is easy to become comfortable and complacent, thinking you know all the answers, in such circumstances. When we merged and changed the organisation drastically, we all had a lot to learn, and we never stop learning.

The opening session of the conference was given great prestige with the presence of His Excellency Mr Sergei Stanishev, the Bulgarian Prime Minister, and his senior ministers, to open the event. Delegates certainly got the clear sense that we were attending a very important and significant seminar, at a historic time for our Bulgarian hosts. Mr Stanishev's opening remarks set a very high standard. In welcoming delegates, he expressed the excitement among the Bulgarian people on the eve of their full membership of the EU, and acknowledged the challenges they face, not least those of anti-fraud and corruption issues. He outlined just a few of the measures they already have in place to tackle fraud issues, adding that it is better to prevent fraud happening, than having to chase its effects afterwards. He explained that his government has set up a register of the assets of high-ranking political figures, which is published for all to see, in a move to ensure transparency. A range of anti-fraud activities is also being coordinated by AFCOS.

The presence of our journalist colleagues certainly enriched this seminar and provided a fascinating perspective. We have had a frank exchange and a mature debate, providing an insight into each other's worlds. We have been challenged to look at ourselves. We have looked at some differences we have, but also at the similarities, and agreed that we are in this together. Aiden certainly challenged us in his early session. He outlined the many difficulties that committed journalists face in different parts of the world. He talked about journalists' right to protect their sources and the implications of this not happening. He also said that good journalism will always expose lawlessness. Other contributors from the journalist community pointed to the way that world media is changing, citing a worrying trend in some areas for journalists to move from freedom to security, and the effect that can have on investigative techniques.

We gained a valuable insight into the world of investigative journalism from those who do it well, and robustly debated points and issues. As communicators and press officers we were urged not to be frightened of probing questions from journalists but to see them as an opportunity for us. A reality check, if you like, to hear what public opinion is saying. Grasping opportunities was also urged by Rosalind as she stressed the importance of providing background briefing and detail, wherever possible, to fully explain what can often be very complex fraud scenarios. Alessandro added the point that communicators need to be well acquainted with the investigative process and full details of the cases they are dealing with, to serve our journalist customers well — to put ourselves in the shoes of the journalist.

We heard details of the Bulgarian money laundering and terrorist financing agency, which, despite dealing with very highly sensitive information, has successfully built a communications strategy to assist transparency.

We also heard from Christian about the interesting initiative being built in mutual cooperation to run a programme of training courses for new young investigative journalists in Romania. This is a practical demonstration of the benefits of our close collaboration.

In Thierry's presentation, we were reminded that OLAF exists to provide added value — a real theme of this seminar — and OLAF is not here to intrude into the work being performed at national level.

David gave us an appraisal of his experience of dealing with the media in different parts of Europe. Is there an East–West or North–South divide? Although a clear conclusion was difficult to draw, it was a timely reminder that our audience is potentially global, and we should be aware of this, and not domestically blinkered.

Jorg's presentation of case studies proved that we are brave enough to expose examples of both good and bad practice. We must critically evaluate what we do and look for ways to do it better. The Operation Fake exercise in 2005 demonstrated the first collaboration for this group, in which every Member State contributed to a concerted media campaign to demonstrate mutual cooperation in a European anti-fraud operation.

Two input sessions provided comprehensive insight into the European lobbying process, from Paolo, and a detailed description of the European transparency initiative from Elisabeth, the latter providing details of the latest announcement from Siim Kallas on contracts and subsidies information recently published.

Claudio graphically illustrated building and maintaining bridges, as he took us on a world tour of magnificent structures, drawing the analogy that we must develop and foster an atmosphere of mutual trust and cooperation to achieve what is right. Investigators must not compromise in their task, and committed journalists must do likewise.

As I said, this has been a highly professional and productive event, organised to the very highest professional standards, and I congratulate Alessandro and his team, our Bulgarian hosts, and fellow delegates for the energy and enthusiasm they have brought. I have really enjoyed taking part. I feel that I have enhanced my personal professionalism as a result. And professionalism is actually what this is all about: our professionalism as communicators, as investigators, as journalists; to be the best we can; to make a difference. After all, we are all in the same business, the anti-fraud business. And the key word is professionalism.

4.6 Conclusions of the Seventh Training Seminar of the OLAF Anti-Fraud Communicators' Network (OAFCN)

By David Jones, Head of Communications, Serious Fraud Office, OAFCN Member
Fight against fraud on vision: Television drama as a means of fighting fraud and corruption affecting EU financial interests
Vienna and Bratislava, 23 to 26 September 2007

On Monday morning, Mr Newald welcomed us to Vienna. Did he or any of us fully realise what a fascinating and stimulating event this would be? He pushed the button that launched the rocket of the 'fight against fraud on vision' into the sky. The question was: where will the rocket land?

The plans for that rocket were hatched in discussions many months ago. Many of us here were part of those earlier discussions. Many, including me, were sceptic at that time. Where would that rocket land? Disappear into space? Not to be seen again? Would the effort produce results? However, I was fully supportive of that proposal that this 2007 seminar should be devoted to this topic. It deserved to be considered fully and seriously.

My task now is to summarise the key conclusions of the seminar. Not an easy task, but I hope that the panel of chairmen might embellish where necessary if I have missed anything important.

Firstly, we cannot ignore television drama as a communication medium. We all here might be involved in television news and documentaries but working with television drama is a new idea for many of us, including me. We have seen some impressive, explosive, exciting crime dramas on show at this seminar and not forgetting examples of portraying the police characters as trusted, honest and brave members of society. We can relate to them as human beings with strengths and weaknesses of character just like the rest of us.

But can it work for fraud drama? Whatever we think about that, we cannot let the doubt or the unknown make us ignore its possibilities.

We all agreed that, in a sense, it would be a crime by us if we anti-fraud communicators were to ignore considering the possibility to use television drama, as another tool in our bag. It must be explored.

So, what is the aim? Mr Kallas referred to perception of Brussels as being a swamp of corruption. So, are we all here to help pull the EC and OLAF out of that perceived swamp? Are we here to make heroes out of OLAF and its officials? Both Mr Brüner and Alessandro Butticé were quick and unequivocal in saying 'No', it is not the aim. Such an aim would result in early failure. The launched rocket would not reach much of an altitude.

There was a common recognition amongst us that it was absolutely vital that 'shared glory' was the only way to proceed. It is clear that the national television producers will want to deliver local heroes to their audiences and the audiences will want to identify with those local heroes, which will also be a shaping factor. Though it amazes me how the UK audience has embraced the fictional character of a Belgian private detective, Hercule Poirot. Even so, there were opinions expressed that cross-border collaboration against crime has some television drama merit. It does seem to me though that the aim and objectives need to be fully understood by all involved. For example, what message are we trying to get across? Fraud prevention? Profile of the institutions? European cooperation? Protection of citizens' wealth? The fight against harm to the European economy? This may depend from country to country. The objectives that might apply to Bulgaria might not be the same as the UK.

It is, by the way, worth noting in this summary the by-products of television crime drama. For example, the French customs recruitment and internal morale or pride in the institutions themselves. Also, Mr Corsetti of the Italian *carabinieri* is visibly and rightly proud of the way his institution is portrayed on Italian television. It gives prestige to the institution.

What did the television producers say?

With all due respect to all institutional communicators here, the stars of this seminar have been the television drama companies. It's been said that they turn a photograph, a picture of reality into a painting, a work of art, where some deviation from reality is necessary to make it attractive.

Well, we said that not all television productions are of the best artistic merit but with good storylines, quality scripts, good acting and state of the art production, you can achieve the excellent examples we have seen here. We asked the television people if fraud was interesting as a drama possibility. They said, cautiously, it could be. Fraud fiction would have to be dressed up with human interest elements such as domestic situations of the characters, romance, tragedies, etc. Fraud on its own is very dry material so it might need an injection of 'sex, drugs and rock and roll'. However they did offer us some hope. RAI put their hand up and said let's talk some more! I was also pleasantly surprised by the British television people who said something similar, as did the Austrian television *Commissioner Rex* producer. So clearly, our seminar has stimulated something. RAI looks the initial promise now. But turning these lukewarm possibilities into something more concrete will be a real challenge. Will tomorrow bring a cooling as we get on with our other jobs?

There are two faces of risk here; one for the institutions and one for the television companies. For the institutions, it is the risk of how the television production turns their story into drama and what the resulting impact is on public perception. There was the Austrian example of a drama about a corrupt official. Therefore does that mean that corruption is widespread in Austrian government institutions? The risk is that a commitment to work with television drama, by briefing them on fraud crime, might be counterproductive.

We have heard of different examples. The *carabinieri* seem to have a closer involvement with the drama producer. They work in collaboration with scriptwriting, for example, which is not conventional in the UK. Perhaps the *carabinieri* can, in that way, help paint a more positive picture, yet without compromising the media's independence.

The second risk is financial. What commercially is in it for the television producer? There will always be an audience for crime dramas involving guns, helicopters, car-chases and so on. But could fraud fiction, for the television companies, prove to be a money spinner? This may well be the fly in the ointment, the loose screw in the rocket that sends it spiralling earthwards.

So, what 'action' now? All this debate, exchange of ideas and experiences during this seminar has brought us to this morning's summary. We have benefited here from the intellectual and analytical insights of our academic guests as well as our television specialists. A lot of interest has been created and Alessandro Butticé has asked us to consider which of our cases might be good drama material.

The test now is to take this forward and give it a go. Wolfgang Schmitz of the ZKA has made an eloquent case to do so.

For my part, I have learned quite a lot, but, to use an English expression, my feet remain firmly on the ground. The challenge is not a walk in the park. We said it will require commitment, time and energy. But the rocket we launched on the opening day of this seminar seems to be soaring skyward. Let's keep it on course is the ultimate summary I have noted, and I look forward to being part of the review in the future.

Conclusions of the Eighth Training Seminar of the OLAF Anti-Fraud Communicators' Network (OAFCN)

By Michael Cassar, Assistant Commissioner of Police, Malta, OAFCN Member
Anti-fraud communication and Web 2.0: New technologies, new tools, new audiences
Nicosia, 12 to 14 October 2008

The eighth training seminar of the OLAF Anti-Fraud Communicators' Network that we have just attended provided much food for thought: an illustration of both the new challenges and additional tools we can use to confront fraud. It has provided a framework, and now it is for us to exploit these ideas and put them into practice in order to consolidate the fight against fraud.

This year's seminar continued on the same path as its predecessors, that is, to deter fraud by informing the public. On this occasion, however, we have moved forward a step in to the future. Without doubt, the scope of this seminar was to make us proactive in achieving our goal. This was revealed by our discussion regarding anti-fraud communication and Web 2.0.

The very carefully selected experts each made presentations on new technologies, new tools and new audiences. These speeches took us on a virtual voyage that illustrated and guided us through the tools available to continue this fight in combating fraud.

In his opening speech, Mr Butticé set the scene by explaining that the aim of the seminar was to promote ideas and discussions on what should be done at both EU and national levels with respect to the prevention of fraud by using the media and the new tools and technologies available. As the Eurobarometer survey's results will show in the next few days when its results are made public, EU citizens expect enhanced cooperation between Member States and the EU in combating fraud, the adoption of new means of informing the public and actions against fraud which bridge the gap between Member States, the EU institutions and EU citizens.

Mrs Bernice Germain made an excellent presentation in which she gave a detailed overview of almost all the various tools currently available on the Internet. She explained the basic differences between Web 1.0 and Web 2.0: in Web 1.0, communication remained relatively limited and top-down in its approach; whereas with the advent of Web 2.0, communication expanded drastically with Internet surfers feeding back their information. Thus, in Web 2.0, ideal information is generated by the users themselves.

She explained the various main Web 2.0-based applications, namely social networking sites, social book-marking, wikis, blogs, rich Internet applications, Vod cast, Pod cast, RSS, Ezines, mini-sites and online games. The expert concluded by saying that Web 2.0 is a citizen-oriented communication tool and leads to an increased focus on individualities rather than audiences as a whole and to the listener increasingly getting their voice heard.

Mr Christos Ellinidis made a presentation on using web technologies to communicate with administrations, businesses and citizens. He described how the European perspective shows that the web has moved from being purely a source of information to a tool of multi-channel interactive communication between citizens, businesses and administrations.

Web 2.0 impacts the European Commission because it communicates with citizens wherever they are, listens to what citizens say, increases participation in government, expands the reach of the European Commission and makes it transparent. This, in turn, increases trust in the European Commission, fosters collaboration and builds communities.

The European Commission is moving dynamically and effectively towards this modern and synchronous method of communication. At the same time, the Commission realises that there is also great potential for the usage of these technologies in the various Member States. It is for this reason that the European Commission recognises the need to balance the web-based channels of communication with traditional ones.

Another interesting topic was presented by Mr Nick Jones who spoke about government public relations in the age of Web 2.0. He provided us with an overview of the challenge of transforming public services, turning the citizen and government relationship around, giving the citizen greater control over the way in which they interact with public information and public services. The expert concluded that our plan should be:

• to deliver information and services to citizens and businesses in a 'joined-up' way;
• to use a limited number of websites, TV or mobile routes;
• to create a consistently high-quality experience through higher standards;
• to share and re-use public sector information, people and infrastructure.

In the face of Web 2.0, we have to start by understanding the spectrum of engagement, moving from passive monitoring to active promotion of discussion.

Mr Christof Hammerschmid's presentation entitled 'Austria in cyberspace: getting the government's message across', portrayed the developments that have taken place in recent years in Austrian cyberspace. He explained the strategy of having one platform for the outside world, and the ground rule of one face to the customer, a tightly organised writing team, a managing editor who ensures compliance with the style guide and writing guidelines and the Internet, as well as external coordination in developing new media.

He also encouraged us to consider some issues in the ambit of the units in which we work, such as:

• What communication strategy does our unit pursue?

• Who are our readers and how do we address them?

• Which topics and content are suitable for delivery by Web 2.0 technologies?

• How do we want to organise it all?

• Do we have adequate staffing to achieve this?

That morning's session was followed by a panel discussion that was chaired by Mr Alessandro Butticé. The panelists Mr Ellinidies, Mr Jones and Mr Hammerscmid were bombarded with numerous intelligent and interesting interventions from the floor. This was a very interactive discussion.

The afternoon session was opened with the presentation by Mr Lutz Deckwerth and Mr Matthias Engels who gave an overview of the web TV and video blogs which constitute journalism's new approach. They said that for those who work as communication officers, information is becoming faster and more volatile, and, consequently, it is becoming increasingly difficult for viewers and listeners to absorb all the information available to them. Communications thus need to be focused on core information.

They then went on to explain that, in the current climate, users own more personal computers than televisions and are therefore more likely to get information from the Internet than TV and other traditional means of communication, such as newspapers and radios. This trend is obviously heightened by a decline in advertising via traditional means of communication and an increase in advertising on the Internet. Accordingly, communicators have to be aware of this shift so that we can channel our information accordingly.

Another interesting presentation, by Mr Oscar Bartoli, followed immediately after. He spoke on communication without frontiers: public relations and cyberspace from a European and transatlantic perspective. Mr Bartoli explained how economic globalisation results from the globalisation of information and person-to-person communication. Frontiers are constantly being pushed forward and distinct technological fields no longer exist.

The expert said that we have reached the point where even politicians are obliged to maintain a regular and consistent presence on Internet sites. This trend reiterates how far communications should strive to exploit and maximise to the full their use of modern means of communication, particularly the Internet.

Mr Peterides spoke on behalf of the president of the Cypriot Press Association in his presentation entitled 'The new-generation Internet: challenge and opportunity for journalists'. He emphasised two important points:

- Technology in the field of computers and the Internet is developing quickly. If this is not kept in mind in the context of planning within your organisation, then your technology would become obsolete within a few days.

- One should work together with the developments in technology rather than trying to avoid them. Failure to do so could mean one is left at the margins.

The greatest challenge (or opportunity) for communicators and journalists is whether they would be able to respond to the desires of the currently globalised public, in particular, the young people who resort more to the Internet for news than to other traditional media forms such as television.

Mr Peterides' presentation also explored the ethical standards that communicators and journalists should uphold in disseminating information.

The last presentation of the day was delivered by Mr Christian Untenanu, a journalist who spoke about 'information, misinformation, disinformation: new technologies and the risks for communication in a democracy'. He explained how one can render information credible to the public. He described how on the Internet one can find all types of information and answers, but one should distinguish between those which are good, those which are bad and propaganda. The problem is that one cannot inhibit all this information being uploaded on the Internet for all to see. Therefore, verifications should be made when getting information from such sources, apart from ensuring that Internet sources are reliable.

The first day ended with another panel discussion that was chaired by Mr Jorg Wojabn, whilst the panelists were Mr Deckwerth, Mr Engels, Mr Bartoli, Mr Kannaouross and Mr Unteanu. Again, like the previous day, this was a very active discussion in which the participation of the floor was high.

The second day began with a presentation delivered by Mr Richard Kolko from the FBI. In his presentation, he proposed that new media has created new rules. Particularly in recent times, the public is no longer content to be merely a consumer of content and it is now a content provider.

Communicators must be aware of the changes taking place. Mobile devices mean that people are omnipresent — sources for information as well as consumers. Some 62% of all Americans are part of a wireless, mobile population that participates in digital activities away from home or work. In this situation, we have to instil the perception of our organisation that our viewers and listeners have and build a good reputation through our use of media.

Ms Rebecca Li informed us of the efforts made by the Community Relations Department of the Independent Commission Against Corruption (ICAC) in Hong Kong to combat corruption. The ICAC promotes public awareness of the anti-corruption cause, disseminates anti-corruption methods through mass media and promotes positive values through schools, etc.

She also presented the main challenges of the Internet to investigators, namely that the Internet:

• enables criminals' involvement in multiple crimes simultaneously;

• facilitates their involvement in cross-border crime;

• poses difficulties to investigators in establishing the true identity of users and in preserving the evidence ;

• poses difficulties in overcoming anti-forensic tactics.

Nonetheless, threats and challenges can be viewed as opportunities. The communicators can look at the above developments as an opportunity to spread anti-corruption and anti-fraud messages in a borderless cyber world.

Miss Rikke Medson explained how 'Second Life', launched in 2003, is a privately owned Internet 3D virtual world. Second Life provides an advanced-level social network service. The Danish Customs and Tax Administration (SKAT) has established a presence in Second Life, the first Danish authority to do so. The SKAT approach was two-fold: information and adventure. Users are diverse, ranging in age from 18 to 54 years, and some 10 % of them spend more than 40 hours per week on Second Life. The platform has to be developed further and Second Life can only be seen as a supplement rather than a substitute for existing guidance channels.

A final panel discussion followed with the input of the three preceding speakers.

Ultimately, two broad conclusions emerged from this seminar:

• Modern technical equipment: New and modern technologies make it possible to communicate very fast and coordinate between more than two communication units. The use of modern audiovisual communication equipment is very helpful in conveying positive messages to the public. The use of modern video blogs facilitates the installation of video messages into the OAFCN Network. The use of modern camera systems can be very helpful in creating these new and modern kinds of communication.

- TV drama/TV series: In spite of the possibilities of new and modern technologies today, television is the most important medium for the citizens of the European Union.

In conclusion, the members of the network are convinced that the creation of a fictional TV drama or a TV series about the work of the investigative authorities at international level would be very helpful in raising awareness of the fight against fraud for the benefit of the European citizens and might be an important means of deterring fraud by informing the public. The members of the network, including OLAF, will give as much support as possible to this project.

Thank you.

4.8 The OLAF Anti-Fraud Communicators' Network (OAFCN)

OFFICE EUROPÉEN DE LUTTE ANTIFRAUDE

EUROPEAN COMMISSION
EUROPEAN
ANTI-FRAUD
OFFICE

Referat D.1 Pressesprecher, Kommunikation, Öffentlichkeitsarbeit
Unit D.1 Spokesman, Communication and PR
Unidad D.1 Portavoz, Comunicación y Relaciones Públicas
Unité D.1 Porte-parole, Communication and Relation publiques
Unità D.1 Portavoce, comunicazione e pubbliche relazioni

Le réseau de communicateurs
antifraude de l'OLAF (OAFCN)

■

Das OLAF-Netz der Betrugsbekämpfungskommunikatoren

■

La Rete OLAF dei comunicatori
antifrode (OAFCN)

■

La Red de Comunicadores
Antifraude de la OLAF (OAFCN)

Information as a means of fraud prevention,
a service for the citizens
■
L'information comme moyen de prévention contre la fraude,
un service pour les citoyens
■
Information als Mittel zur Prävention von Betrug,
ein Dienst für die Bürger
■
L'informazione come strumento di prevenzione della frode,
un servizio per i cittadini
■
La información como medio para evitar el fraude,
un servicio para los ciudadanos

■ **http://ec.europa.eu/anti_fraud/olaf-oafcn/en.html**

An ambitious objective

The OAFCN has an ambitious objective: it aims to be an information and communication link for the major players involved in the fight against fraud and irregularities affecting the Community financial interests.

Un objectif ambitieux

L'OAFCN poursuit un objectif ambitieux: servir de passerelle d'information et d'échanges entre les principaux acteurs impliqués dans la lutte contre la fraude et les irrégularités portant atteinte aux intérêts financiers de la Communauté.

Ein ehrgeiziges Ziel

Das OAFCN hat sich ein ehrgeiziges Ziel gesetzt: Es möchte als Informations- und Kommunikationsverbindung für die Hauptakteure der Bekämpfung von gegen die finanziellen Interessen der Gemeinschaft gerichteten Betrugsdelikten und Unregelmäßigkeiten agieren.

Un obiettivo ambizioso

L'OAFCN si pone un obiettivo ambizioso. Vuole costituire infatti un nodo di comunicazione e informazione fra i principali operatori coinvolti nella lotta contro la frode e le irregolarità a danno degli interessi finanziari comunitari.

Un objetivo ambicioso

La OAFCN persigue un objetivo ambicioso: ser un canal de comunicación e información al servicio de los protagonistas de la lucha contra el fraude y las irregularidades que afectan a los intereses financieros de la Comunidad.

OAFCN origins

The OLAF Anti-Fraud Communicators' Network (OAFCN) includes the OLAF spokesman, spokespersons, public relations and information officers in the national investigation services with which OLAF cooperates in the Member States. It forms a part of the external independent communication strategy of OLAF.

Origine de l'OAFCN

Le réseau de communicateurs antifraude de l'OLAF (OAFCN) regroupe le porte-parole de l'OLAF, les porte-parole, les responsables des relations publiques et les responsables de l'information dans les services d'enquête nationaux avec lesquels l'OLAF collabore dans les États membres. Il s'inscrit dans le cadre de la stratégie de communication externe indépendante de l'OLAF.

Die Entstehung des OAFCN

Das OLAF-Netz der Betrugsbekämpfungskommunikatoren (OAFCN) setzt sich zusammen aus dem Sprecher des OLAF und den mit der Öffentlichkeitsarbeit befassten Sprechern und Informationsbeauftragten der nationalen Ermittlungsdienste, mit denen das OLAF in den Mitgliedstaaten zusammenarbeitet. Es ist Teil der unabhängigen externen Kommunikationsstrategie des OLAF.

L'origine dell'OAFCN

La Rete OLAF dei comunicatori antifrode (OAFCN) è composta dal portavoce dell'OLAF e dai portavoce dei servizi investigativi nazionali con cui l'OLAF coopera negli Stati membri, nonché dai responsabili per le relazioni pubbliche e dai funzionari responsabili dell'informazione di questi ultimi. Si inserisce nella strategia di comunicazione esterna indipendente dell'OLAF.

Origen de la OAFCN

La Red de Comunicadores Antifraude de la OLAF (OAFCN) incluye al Portavoz de la OLAF, portavoces, relaciones públicas y responsables de información de los servicios de investigación nacionales con los que la OLAF coopera en los Estados miembros. La OAFCN constituye un elemento de la estrategia de comunicación independiente externa de la OLAF.

OAFCN objectives

The OAFCN was created in 2001 to:

1 prevent fraud through the 'free flow' of information: 'prevention is better than cure';
2 create a permanent dialogue between OLAF's External Communication Unit and its counterparts in the national investigation services;
3 inform the European citizen of what OLAF and its partners in the Member States are doing both jointly and individually in order to protect their financial interests. This includes making all concerned aware of the need for an anti-fraud programme that is global, balanced and effective throughout the territory of the European Union;
4 give information to the general public (in particular through the media) relating to the fight against fraud and irregularities to the detriment of the European Union's financial interests.

Objectifs de l'OAFCN

L'OAFCN a été créé en 2001. Ses objectifs sont les suivants:

1 prévenir la fraude grâce au «libre flux» de l'information: «il vaut mieux prévenir que guérir».

2   créer un dialogue permanent entre le service de communication externe de l'OLAF et ses homologues dans les services d'enquête nationaux.

3   informer le citoyen européen sur ce que l'OLAF et ses partenaires font dans les États membres tant conjointement qu'individuellement afin de protéger ses intérêts financiers. L'OAFCN s'efforce de sensibiliser toutes les personnes concernées à la nécessité d'un programme antifraude qui soit global, équilibré et efficace sur l'ensemble du territoire de l'Union européenne.

4   fournir des informations au grand public (en particulier par le biais des médias) en ce qui concerne la lutte contre la fraude et les irrégularités au détriment des intérêts financiers de l'Union européenne.

Die Ziele des OAFCN

1   Prävention von Betrug durch einen freien Informationsfluss: „Vorbeugen ist besser als heilen";

2   Schaffung eines ständigen Dialogs zwischen dem OLAF-Referat für Öffentlichkeitsarbeit und seinen Partnern in den Ermittlungsdiensten;

3   Aufklärung der EU-Bürger über die gemeinsamen und individuellen Betrugsbekämpfungs-maßnahmen des OLAF und seiner Partner in den Mitgliedstaaten. Dies bedeutet u.a., dass allen Betroffenen die Notwendigkeit eines Be trugsbekämpfungsprogramms vor Augen geführt werden muss, das umfassend, ausgewogen und in allen EU-Ländern wirksam ist;

4   Aufklärung der Öffentlichkeit (insbesondere über die Medien) über die Bekämpfung von gegen die finanziellen Interessen der EU gerichteten Betrugsdelikten und Unregelmäßigkeiten.

Gli obiettivi dell'OAFCN

L'OAFCN è stata creata nel 2001 con i seguenti obiettivi:

1   Prevenire la frode tramite il «libero flusso» delle informazioni: «prevenire è meglio che curare».

2   Avviare un dialogo permanente fra l'unità di comunicazione esterna dell'OLAF e i suoi omologhi nei servizi investigativi nazionali.

3   Informare i cittadini europei sulle attività condotte dall'OLAF e dai suoi partner negli Stati membri, a livello sia individuale che congiunto, a tutela dei propri interessi finanziari. A tal fine è necessario sensibilizzare tutti gli interessati sull'esigenza di un programma antifrode globale, equilibrato ed efficace in tutto il territorio dell'Unione europea.

4   Fornire al pubblico informazioni (specialmente tramite i media) relative alla lotta contro la frode e le irregolarità a danno degli interessi finanziari dell'Unione europea.

Objetivos de la OAFCN

La OAFCN se creó en el año 2001 para:

1   Evitar el fraude a través de un flujo libre de información: «más vale prevenir que curar».

2   Mantener un diálogo permanente entre la Unidad de Comunicación Externa de la OLAF y sus homólogas en los servicios de investigación nacionales.

3 Informar a los ciudadanos europeos de lo que la OLAF y sus socios en los Estados miembros hacen conjunta e individualmente para proteger sus intereses financieros. Esto incluye concienciar a todos los interesados de la necesidad de un programa de lucha contra el fraude global, equilibrado y eficaz en todo el territorio de la Unión Europea.

4 Facilitar información al gran público (en especial a través de los medios de comunicación) sobre la lucha contra el fraude y las irregularidades que afectan a los intereses financieros de la Unión Europea.

OAFCN actions

The OAFCN tries to add value to the work of the national investigation services and to highlight not only the work done in individual Member States, but also the global Community aspect of the fight against fraud.

As far as is legally and operationally possible, OAFCN members keep each other up to date on issues involving press releases of mutual interest. Equally, it assists journalists in evaluating information forwarded to them by other OAFCN members regardless of their nationality. Normally, national law enforcement agencies are more effective and more comfortable with their national media than with foreign media. However, one of the OAFCN's purposes is to ensure that the door of each national investigation service with which OLAF cooperates is open to all the international media.

OAFCN members provide joint media coverage (videos, photos and press releases) to illustrate OLAF operational activities with national investigation services.

In the candidate countries

There is also a need to educate public opinion in the candidate countries with regard to what constitutes the types of criminal activities we are all trying to combat, and their potential risk for taxpayers. Actions are ongoing aimed at extending membership of the OAFCN to the AFCOS (Anti-Fraud Coordination Structures) in the candidate countries. Seminars and training sessions for communicators and journalists will be launched in the countries in question.

Actions de l'OAFCN

L'OAFCN tente d'apporter une valeur ajoutée au travail des services d'enquête nationaux et de souligner non seulement le travail réalisé individuellement par chaque État membre, mais aussi l'aspect communautaire global de la lutte contre la fraude.

Dans la mesure des possibilités légales et opérationnelles, les membres de l'OAFCN s'informent mutuellement des questions impliquant des communiqués de presse d'intérêt réciproque. De même, ils assistent les journalistes dans l'évaluation des informations qui leur sont transmises par d'autres membres de l'OAFCN, indépendamment de leur nationalité. Normalement, les administrations répressives nationales sont plus efficaces et plus à l'aise avec leurs médias nationaux qu'avec les médias étrangers. Toutefois, un des objectifs de l'OAFCN est de veiller à ce que la porte de chaque service d'enquête national coopérant avec l'OLAF soit ouverte à l'ensemble des médias internationaux.

Les membres de l'OAFCN assurent une couverture médiatique conjointe (vidéos, photos et communiqués de presse) destinée à illustrer les activités opérationnelles de l'OLAF avec les services d'enquête nationaux.

Dans les pays candidats

Il est également indispensable d'informer l'opinion publique des pays candidats sur les types d'activités criminelles que nous tentons de combattre et les risques potentiels que celles-ci représentent pour les contribuables. Des mesures visent actuellement à étendre l'adhésion de l'OAFCN aux AFCOS (structures de coordination antifraude) dans les pays candidats. Des séminaires et des sessions de formation pour les communicateurs et les journalistes seront organisés dans les pays en question.

Maßnahmen des OAFCN

Das OAFCN möchte die nationalen Ermittlungsdienste bei ihrer Arbeit unterstützen und sowohl die Betrugsbekämpfungsmaßnahmen in den Mitgliedstaaten als auch die Gemeinschaftsdimension der Betrugsbekämpfung herausstellen.

Soweit in rechtlicher und operativer Hinsicht möglich, halten sich die Mitglieder gegenseitig auf dem Laufenden über Fragen, zu denen Pressemitteilungen von gegenseitigem Interesse veröffentlicht werden. Ferner unterstützt das OAFCN Journalisten aller Nationalitäten bei der Auswertung der ihnen von OAFCN-Mitgliedern übermittelten Informationen. In der Regel ist es für die nationalen Ermittlungsdienste effizienter und einfacher, nur mit ihren landeseigenen Medien zusammenzuarbeiten. Eine der Aufgaben des OAFCN besteht darin, dafür Sorge zu tragen, daß die Tür zu den nationalen Ermittlungsdiensten, mit denen das OLAF zusammenarbeitet, allen internationalen Medien offen steht.

Die Mitglieder des OAFCN erstellen gemeinsam Pressematerial (Videokassetten, Fotos und Pressemitteilungen) über die operative Zusammenarbeit des OLAF mit den nationalen Ermittlungsdiensten.

In den Kandidatenländern

Auch in den Kandidatenländern besteht die Notwendigkeit, die Öffentlichkeit über die von der EU bekämpften Kriminalitätsformen und die von ihnen ausgehenden Gefahren für den Steuerzahler zu informieren. Daher laufen derzeit Bemühungen, das OAFCN um Mitglieder der Betrugsbekämpfungskoordinierungsstrukturen in den Kandidaten-ländern zu erweitern. In diesen Ländern werden Seminare und Schulungen für Kommunikationsbeauftragte und Journalisten durchgeführt werden.

Azioni dell'OAFCN

L'OAFCN cerca di apportare un valore aggiunto all'operato dei servizi investigativi nazionali, dando rilievo non solo al lavoro svolto nei singoli Stati membri, ma anche alla dimensione comunitaria globale della lotta contro la frode.

Per quanto possibile sul piano giuridico e operativo, i membri dell'OAFCN si informano a vicenda su questioni oggetto di comunicati stampa di reciproco interesse. Analogamente, forniscono assistenza ai giornalisti nella valutazione delle informazioni ad essi trasmesse da altri membri dell'OAFCN, indipendentemente dalla loro nazionalità. Di norma, le autorità nazionali incaricate dell'applicazione della legge sono più efficaci e più a proprio agio con i media nazionali che con quelli stranieri. Uno degli obiettivi dell'OAFCN, tuttavia, è garantire che la porta di ogni servizio investigativo nazionale con cui l'OLAF coopera sia aperta a tutti i media internazionali. I membri dell'OAFCN mettono a disposizione una copertura mediatica mista (video, foto e comunicati stampa) per illustrare le attività operative dell'OLAF in cooperazione con i servizi investigativi nazionali.

Nei paesi candidati

È necessario inoltre informare l'opinione pubblica dei paesi candidati sui tipi di attività criminosa che noi tutti cerchiamo di combattere e sul potenziale rischio che rappresentano per i contribuenti. Sono in corso iniziative volte ad aprire l'adesione all'OAFCN alle AFCOS (Strutture di coordinamento antifrode) dei paesi candidati. In questi paesi verranno organizzati seminari e sessioni di formazione per comunicatori e giornalisti.

Actividades de la OAFCN

La OAFCN intenta aportar un valor añadido al trabajo de los servicios de investigación nacionales y poner de relieve no sólo el trabajo realizado por cada Estado miembro, sino también los aspectos generales de la lucha contra el fraude a escala comunitaria.

En la medida en que resulta legal y prácticamente posible, los miembros de la OAFCN intercambian información para estar al corriente de los asuntos que dan lugar a comunicados de prensa de interés recíproco. Asimismo, ayudan a los periodistas a valorar la información que reciben de otros miembros de la OAFCN con independencia de su nacionalidad. En general, los organismos que velan por que se cumpla la ley colaboran más a gusto y más eficazmente con los medios de comunicación de su país que con los extranjeros. Sin embargo, uno de los objetivos de la OAFCN consiste en que las puertas de todos los servicios de investigación nacionales con los que la OLAF colabora estén abiertas a todos los medios de comunicación internacionales.

Los miembros de la OAFCN facilitan cobertura informativa común (vídeos, fotos y comunicados de prensa) para apoyar las actividades llevadas a cabo por la OLAF con los servicios de investigación nacionales.

En los países candidatos

También es necesario familiarizar a la opinión pública de los países candidatos con los tipos de actividades delictivas que intentamos combatir, informándoles del posible peligro que encierran para los contribuyentes. Se están realizando gestiones para incluir en la OAFCN a los miembros de las estructuras de coordinación antifraude (AFCOS) existentes en los países candidatos. Se celebrarán seminarios y cursos de formación para periodistas y comunicadores en estos países.

A European platform of exchange

An awareness-raising aid for the issues of protection of the Community's financial interests The attention of the European citizen needs to be drawn to the protection of the Community's financial interests. In particular, we must provide taxpayers with an assurance that their money is being used to the best effect.

All forms of fraud against the Community's financial interests, from evasion of the taxes and duties that make up the European budget, to the misuse of financial assistance provided by the Community, entail a real and substantial loss to the European taxpayer. The OAFCN members produce joint media actions to show the national investigative services in the Member States working together with OLAF, illustrating the success of the administrative cooperation in the operational framework.

Une plate-forme d'échanges européenne

Un moyen en vue de mieux sensibiliser le public aux questions liées à la protection des intérêts financiers de la Communauté

L'attention des citoyens européens doit être attirée sur la protection des intérêts financiers de la Communauté. Il faut notamment donner au contribuable l'assurance que ses deniers sont utilisés aux meilleures fins.
Toutes les formes de fraude au détriment des intérêts financiers de la Communauté, de l'évasion des taxes et des droits qui alimentent le budget européen à l'emploi abusif de l'aide financière octroyée par la Communauté, entraînent une perte réelle et substantielle pour le contribuable européen.
Les membres de l'OAFCN mènent des actions médiatiques communes afin de faire connaître le travail de coopération entre l'OLAF et les services d'enquêtes nationaux dans les États membres, et d'illustrer le succès de la coopération administrative en matière opérationnelle.

Eine europäische Plattform für den Informationsaustausch

Sensibilisierung für Fragen des Schutzes der finanziellen Interessen der Gemeinschaft

Der Schutz der finanziellen Interessen der Gemeinschaft muss stärker in das Bewusstsein der europäischen Bürger gerückt werden. Wir müssen dem Steuerzahler die Gewissheit geben, dass mit seinen Steuergeldern effizient gewirtschaftet wird. Der gegen die finanziellen Interessen der Gemeinschaft gerichtete Betrug reicht von der Umgehung der in den Gemeinschaftshaushalt einfließenden Steuern und Zölle bis zum Missbrauch der von der Gemeinschaft gewährten Finanzhilfen, wobei er in allen seinen Formen für den europäischen Steuerzahler große und spürbare Auswirkungen mit sich bringt.
Die Mitglieder des vom OLAF eingerichteten Netzes der Betrugsbekämpfungs-kommunikatoren (OLAF Anti-fraud Communicators' Network, OAFCN) entwickeln gemeinsame Medienmaßnahmen über die Zusammenarbeit zwischen dem OLAF und den nationalen Ermittlungsdiensten, die den Erfolg der Verwaltungszusammenarbeit auf operativem Gebiet zeigen.

Una piattaforma di scambio europea

Uno strumento di sensibilizzazione sulle questioni connesse alla tutela degli interessi finanziari della Comunità

È necessario sensibilizzare i cittadini europei in merito alla tutela degli interessi finanziari della Comunità. In particolare, dobbiamo dare ai contribuenti la sicurezza che il loro denaro venga usato per il meglio.

Qualsiasi forma di frode a danno degli interessi finanziari della Comunità, dall'evasione di tasse e dazi che compongono il bilancio europeo all'abuso dell'assistenza finanziaria fornita dalla Comunità, comporta un danno reale e concreto per il contribuente europeo. I membri dell'OAFCN organizzano azioni mediatiche congiunte per far conoscere i servizi investigativi nazionali degli Stati membri che collaborano con l'OLAF e illustrare i risultati positivi della cooperazione amministrativa nel quadro operativo.

Una plataforma europea para el intercambio de información

Un medio para sensibilizar mejor a la opinión pública sobre los temas relacionados con la protección de los intereses financieros de la Comunidad

Es necesario llamar la atención de los ciudadanos europeos sobre la protección de los intereses financieros de la Comunidad. En especial, hay que garantizar a los contribuyentes que su dinero se destina a los mejores fines.

Todas las formas de fraude contra los intereses financieros de la Comunidad, desde la evasión de los impuestos y tasas que nutren el presupuesto comunitario, hasta el uso incorrecto de la ayuda económica facilitada por la Comunidad, suponen una pérdida importante y real para el contribuyente europeo.

Los miembros de la OAFCN llevan a cabo acciones de información comunes para dar a conocer los servicios de investigación nacionales que trabajan en colaboración con la OLAF, mostrando el éxito de la cooperación administrativa en el plano operativo.

OAFCN training seminars

Protecting the Communities' financial interests: Information and communication as a means of prevention of fraud

First training seminar of the OLAF Anti-Fraud Communicators' Network (OAFCN)
Finland–Sweden, 16–18 September 2002

This three-day training course was jointly organised by Finnish Customs, Swedish Customs and the Swedish Economic Crimes Bureau (Ekobrottsmyndigheten), supported by OLAF.

The seminar, which took the form of a series of lectures and workshops, dealt with the differing cultural and legal obstacles that exist in getting information across to European citizens of what is being done by OLAF and the Member States to protect the financial interests of the European Union and fight against financial and economic criminality.

The role of communication in the prevention of fraud

Second seminar of the OLAF Anti-Fraud Communicators' Network (OAFCN)

Seminar for journalists, Salamanca (Spain), 21–24 November 2002

This three-day seminar was jointly organised by the Spanish Guardia Civil and OLAF. It brought together journalists specialising in economic matters, from all EU Member States, members of different law enforcement agencies and spokespersons and directors of communication from the organisations and institutions that carry out law enforcement tasks and the fight against fraud.

The main objective of the seminar was to carry out a detailed analysis of problems that currently occur in relations between press officers and journalists tasked with reporting on these types of cases.

Protecting the Communities' financial interests: information and communication as a means of prevention of fraud in the context of EU enlargement

Third training seminar of the OLAF Anti-Fraud Communicators' Network (OAFCN)
Bucharest (Romania), 20–22 October 2003

This three-day training course was jointly organised by OLAF and the Romanian Government's Control Department. The seminar was formally opened by Mr Ion Iliescu,

President of Romania, Mrs Michaele Schreyer, European Commissioner responsible for Budget and Anti-Fraud, and Mrs Diemut Theato, Chairperson of the Budgetary Control Committee of the European Parliament, and was closed by Mr Adrian Nastase, Romanian Prime Minister and Mr Franz-Hermann Brüner, Director-General of OLAF. The presence of such a high-level group highlighted the importance attached both by the European institutions as well as the Romanian authorities to the fight against fraud and corruption.

During the course of the seminar the participants reached a consensus on a particular priority for 2003/04: the development of a communication and information concept as means of prevention of fraud, particularly in the framework of enlargement.

Deterring fraud by informing the public

Fourth training seminar of the OLAF Anti-Fraud Communicators' Network (OAFCN)
Brussels (Belgium), 24–26 November 2004

This three-day seminar was introduced by Siim Kallas, Vice-President of the European Commission, responsible for Administrative Affairs, Audit and Anti-Fraud, Mr Szabolcs Fazakas, Chairman of the Committee on Budgetary Control of the European Parliament, Mr Raymond Kendall, former Chairman of OLAF's Supervisory Committee, and Mr Franz-Hermann Brüner, OLAF's Director-General.

Participants discussed strategies and tools for the prevention of fraud and corruption by means of information and communication. The seminar was intended to serve as a platform for exchanging experiences and best practices on how to explain these issues, either via the media or directly to the general public. The event, which was organised in the framework of OLAF's activities, formed part of the implementation of OLAF's communication and information strategy, which is based on two concepts:

• information and communication as a service to the citizen, and
• information and communication as a fraud prevention tool.

Building mutual trust between anti-fraud services and journalists

Fifth training seminar of the OLAF Anti-Fraud Communicators' Network (OAFCN)
Brussels (Belgium), 28 October 2005

This one-day seminar was jointly organised by OLAF and the International Federation of Journalists (IFJ). The seminar was introduced by Mr Henrik Hololei, Head of Cabinet of Mr Siim Kallas, Vice-President of the European Commission, responsible for Administrative Affairs, Audit and Anti-Fraud, and by Mr Franz-Herman Brüner, Director-General of OLAF.

The main objective of the seminar was to discuss expectations of members from the IFJ, the International Press Association (IPA) and OLAF, and the need for transparency, openness and good communications in order to prevent fraud and corruption, by raising awareness and promoting public debate. The seminar also dealt with the role of the IFJ and IPA in improving the level of protection of working journalists and their right to report freely and work ethically and professionally, emphasising the protection of confidential resources of information.

The parties involved agreed that similar meetings should take place at least once a year in order to continue a common dialogue, therefore ensuring the flow of up-to-date information.

Transparency and media relations as a means of fighting fraud and corruption affecting EU financial interests

Sixth training seminar of the OLAF Anti-Fraud Communicators' Network (OAFCN) Sofia (Bulgaria), 8–11 October 2006

This three-day seminar was jointly organised by OLAF, the Bulgarian Ministry of the Interior and the International Federation of Journalists (IFJ). The seminar was formally opened by Mr Sergei Stanishev, the Bulgarian Prime Minister, his senior Ministers and by Mrs Rosalind Wright, Chairman of the Supervisory Committee of the OLAF.

This seminar highlighted the added value of embracing the entry of accession countries with the objective of sharing experiences and practices about communication in the fight against fraud. Journalists and their trade representatives presented their views and stated their expectations from past experience towards enhancing the flow of information.

Themes covered included:

- difficulties encountered in the post-revolution years by the accession states in the field of communication;

- mutual trust between EU states and OLAF in the exchange of relevant and accurate information and OLAF to be seen as adding value to operations as opposed to being interfering;

- constraints on investigative services' and journalists' needs.

The parties involved agreed on the need to develop and foster an atmosphere of mutual trust and cooperation to achieve what is right. Investigators must not compromise in their task, and committed journalists must do likewise.

Fight against fraud on vision: Television drama as a means of fighting fraud and corruption affecting EU financial interests

Seventh training seminar of the OLAF Anti-Fraud Communicators' Network (OAFCN), Vienna-Bratislava, 23–26 September 2007

This three-day seminar was jointly organised by OLAF, the Austrian Federal Ministry of Finance and the Government Office of the Slovak Republic. It was introduced by

Mr Wolfgang Nolz, Head of Tax Department of the Austrian Federal Ministry of Finance (BMF), by Mr Siim Kallas, European Commission Vice-President and Commissioner in charge of Administrative Affairs, Audit and Anti-Fraud and by Mr Franz-Hermann Brüner, Director-General of the European Anti-Fraud Office (OLAF).

In this seminar, experts of national television and national anti-fraud agencies shared their experiences in order to collaborate concerning the possibility of a case for dramatisation of multinational cooperation in fighting fraud affecting EU financial interests. They discussed the challenges, the difficulties, and the practical solutions. Additionally the debate explored whether the national experiences could be replicated in the wider EU context.

Anti-fraud communication and Web2.0: new technologies, new tools, new audiences

Eighth training seminar of the OLAF Anti-Fraud Communicators' Network (OAFCN) Nicosia (Cyprus), 12–14 October 2008

This two-day seminar was jointly organised by OLAF and the Cypriot Department of Customs & Excise. The seminar was formally opened by Mr Charilaos Stavrakis, Minister for Finance of the Republic of Cyprus, by Mrs Zeta Emilianides, General Director of Cypriot Customs and Excise, by Mr Luis López Sanz-Aranguez, President of the OLAF Supervisory Committee, and by Mr Keir Fitch, Member of Cabinet of Mr Siim Kallas, European Commission Vice-President, responsible for Administrative Affairs, Audit and Anti-Fraud.

The seminar focused on how to harness the new-generation Internet for the trans-border fight against fraud and corruption affecting the EU's financial interests. The seminar discussed how far blogs, video-sharing, virtual social networking, wikis and other new communication tools and channels could contribute to reaching new audiences for OLAF and its operational partners in the EU and beyond. Experts gave an update on the latest developments in the field and the experiences of national and international anti-fraud agencies were shared. Speakers included, in particular, representatives of the US Federal Bureau of Investigation (FBI), the Hong Kong Independent Commission against Corruption (ICAC) and the International Federation of Journalists (IFJ).

THE OLAF ANTI-FRAUD COMMUNICATORS' NETWORK MEMBERS

13th OAFCN meeting, Brussels 2008

Ministry of the Interior	**BALEVSKA Iveta** Chief Expert Public Relations Tel. +359 29822301 — Fax +359 29877967 Ibalevska.15@mvr.bg Gourko Street 23 — 1000 Sofia — BULGARIA
Ministry of the Interior	**BOTEVA Boryana** International Cooperation Directorate European Integration Department Tel. +359 29823366 — Fax +359 29885240 Bboteva.14@mvr.bg 6th September Street 29 — 1000 Sofia — BULGARIA
 Club — Journalists against Corruption	**TODOROVA NIKOLOVA Reneta** Chair of the Board Tel. +359 29876550 — Fax +359 29817873 renyfia@abv.bg bul. Vitosha 12 fl.6 — 1000 Sofia — BULGARIA
 National Customs Agency	**SVILAROVA Anna** Junior Specialist PR Department National Customs Agency Tel. +359 298594210/298594213 — Fax +359 298594061 www.customs.bg/ Rakowski Street 47 — 1000 Sofia — BULGARIA
State Agency for National Security	**DIMITROVA Zoya** Spokesperson Tel. +359 28147044 — Fax +359 29463234 Zoya.Dimitrova@dans.bg Cherkovna Street 90 — 1504 Sofia — BULGARIA
Public Prosecutor's Office of the Republic of Bulgaria	**POPOVA Margarita** Spokesperson of the Prosecutor General Tel. +359 29219458 mp@prb.bg Vitosha Blvd 2 — 1061 Sofia — BULGARIA

Service Public Fédéral FINANCES Central Administration of Customs and Excise	**MUYLAERT Lieven** Head of Communication Department Tel. +32 25763136 — Fax +32 25761713 Lieven.muylaert@minfin.fed.be — http://minfin.fgov.be/ 'North Galaxy' Boîte 57 — Boulevard Albert II/Koning Albert II Laan 33 1030 Bruxelles/Brussel — BELGIQUE/BELGIË
Service Public Fédéral FINANCES Central Administration of Customs and Excise	**DE SOMERE Luc** Head of Investigation Service Tel. +32 22337683 — Fax +32 22337686 luc.desomere@minfin.fed.be — http://minfin.fgov.be/ 'North Galaxy' Boîte 57 — Boulevard Albert II/Koning Albert II Laan 33 1030 Bruxelles/Brussel — BELGIQUE/BELGIË

Update of the logos: 20.4.2009

Federal Prosecutor's Office

PELLENS Lieve
Spokesperson — Prosecutor
Tel. +32 25577731 — Fax +32 25577790
lieve.pellens@just.fegov.be — http://www.just.fgov.be/
Rue des Quatre Bras/Quatre Brasstraat 19
1050 Bruxelles/Brussel — BELGIQUE/BELGIË

Police
Belgian Federal Police

DENOLF Johan
Directeur DJF
Tel. +32 27437414
Djf.direction@skynet.be — http://www.ecops.be/
Rue du Noyer/Notelaarstraat 211
1000 Bruxelles/Brussel — BELGIQUE/BELGIË

Police
Belgian Federal Police

HOLLEVOET Tine
Porte-Parole Adjoint
Tel. +32 26426505 — Fax +32 26426507/26426504
pressepolice@brutele.be — http://www.ecops.be/
Rue Fritz Toussaint/Fritz Toussaintstraat 8
1050 Bruxelles/Brussel — BELGIQUE/BELGIË

Police
Belgian Federal Police

KAISIN Astrid
Porte-Parole Adjoint
Tel. +32 26426505 — Fax +32 26426507/26426504
pressepolice@brutele.be — http://www.ecops.be/
Rue Fritz Toussaint/Fritz Toussaintstraat 8
1050 Bruxelles/Brussel — BELGIQUE/BELGIË

 ČESKÁ REPUBLIKA/CZECH REPUBLIC

General Directorate of Customs

BARTAK Jiri
Head of Public Relations, Spokesman
Tel. +420 261331921 — Fax +420 261332100
j.bartak@cs.mfcr.cz
GRC, Budejovicka 7 — 140 06 Praha 4
CZECH REPUBLIC

 DENMARK

SKAT Central Customs and Tax Administration

MADSEN Rikke
Press Officer
Tel. +45 72379657 — Fax +45 72379026
Rikke.Madsen@Skat.dk — http://www.skat.dk/
Ostbanegade 123 — 2100 Copenhagen O — DENMARK

Update of the logos: 20.4.2009

DEUTSCHLAND/GERMANY

Zollkriminalamt ZKA

SCHMITZ Wolfgang
Spokesman & Head of Press and Public Relations
Tel. +49 2216724050 — Fax +49 2216724010
wolfgang.schmitz@zollkriminalamt.de
http://www.zollkriminalamt.de/
Bergisch Gladbacher Strasse 837 — 51069 Cologne
GERMANY

EESTI/ESTONIA

Läane Police Prefecture

KUKK Kaja
Intendant, Press Officer, PR Bureau
Tel. +372 4446450 — Fax +372 5176108
kaja.kukk@laane.pol.ee — http://www.pol.ee/
Pikk 18 — 80089 Arnu — ESTONIA

Ministry of Finance

JÕESAAR Kristi
Head of Public Relations Department
Tel. +372 6113448
kristi.joesaar@fin.ee — http://www.fin.ee/
Suur-Ameerika 1 — 15006 Tallinn — ESTONIA

Estonian Tax and Customs Board

KALLAS Kaia-Liisa
Chief Expert — Development Division
Tel. +372 6762241 — Fax +372 6762127
kaia-liisa.kallas@emta.ee — http://www.emta.ee/
Lõkke 5 — 10122 Tallinn — ESTONIA

ELLADA/GREECE

DG of Customs and Excise, Ministry of Economy and Finance

YIANNIMARAS Spyridon
Customs Officer
33rd Direction of Customs Law Enforcement
Tel. +30 2107259250/210725925053
Fax +30 2107259251
d33risk@otenet.gr — http://www.e-oikonomia.gr/
Karageorgi Servias 10 — 10184 Athens — GREECE

Ministry of Economy and Finance

TSIGAKOS Apostolos
Director Special Financial Investigation Service
Tel. +30 2103375260 — Fax +30 2103428350
atsigakos@ypee.gr — http://www.ypee.gr/
Pireos 207 & Alkifronos Street 92 — 11853 Athens
GREECE

Ministry of Economy and Finance

MAVRODONTIS Ioannis
Head of Department International Cooperation and Mutual
Administrative Assistance
Tel. +30 2103401040 — Fax +30 2106982093
imavrodontis@ypee.gr — http://www.ypee.gr/
Pireos 207 & Alkifronos Street 92 — 11853 Athens
GREECE

Update of the logos: 20.4.2009

Agencia Tributaria	**GONZALEZ DE LA FUENTE Angel** Chief of the Press Office of the Tax Agency Tel. +34 915831233/34 — Fax +34 915831724 agenciatributaria.prensa@aeat.es http://www.agenciatributaria.es/ Calle Infanta Mercedes, 37 — 28020 Madrid — SPAIN
Agencia Tributaria	**LESMES ANEL Julio José** Deputy Director Tel. +34 915831229 — Fax +34 915831149 julio.lesmes@correo.aeat.es http://www.agenciatributaria.es/ San Enrique, 26 — 28020 Madrid — SPAIN
Cuerpo Nacional de Policía	**NEVADA RAJA Antonio** Jefe de la unidad de relaciones informativas y sociales Tel. +34 913223319/18 — Fax +34 913223311 antonio.nevado@policia.es — http://www.policia.es/ Calle Rafael Calvo, 33, 3a Planta — 28010 Madrid — SPAIN
Guardia Civil	**RODRIGUEZ GALAN Lourdes** Oficina de Relaciones Informativas y Sociales Tel. +34 915146012 — Fax +34 915146014 prensa@guardiacivil.org — www.guardiacivil.org/index.jsp Calle Guzman el Bueno, 110 — 28003 Madrid — SPAIN
Permanent Representation of Spain	**FERNANDEZ RANZ José Luis** Financial Counsellor Tel. +32 25098720 — Fax +32 25112630 jose-luis.fernandez@reper.maec.es Boulevard du Regent/Regentlaan 52 1000 Bruxelles/Brussel — BELGIQUE/BELGIË
Fiscalía General del Estado	**NOYA Fernando** Head of Communication Tel. +34 913352148 prensa@fiscalia.mju.es Calle Fortuny, 4 — 28071 Madrid — SPAIN

Direction Générale des Douanes et Droits Indirects	**COUDRAY Julien** Inspecteur en charge PR Tel. +33 157534984 — Fax +33 157534937 Julien.coudray@douane.finances.gouv.fr www.douane.gouv.fr/ 11 rue des Deux Communes — 93558 Montreuil Cedex FRANCE
Parquet de Paris — Palais de Justice	**MONTAGNE Isabelle** Chargée de la Communication du Procureur Tel. +33 144326810 — Fax +33 144325514 isabelle.montagne@justice.fr 14 quai des Orfèvres — 75059 Paris Louvre RP/SP FRANCE

Update of the logos: 20.4.2009

IRELAND

**Department
of Agriculture,
Fisheries and Food**

KEARNEY Martina
Press & Information Officer
Tel. +353 16072190 — Fax +353 16621165
Martina.kearney@agriculture.gov.ie
http://www.agriculture.gov.ie/
Agriculture House
Kildare Street — Dublin 2 — IRELAND

**An Garda Siochana
(Police)**

GILLIGAN John
Press & Public Relations Officer
Tel. +353 16662030 — Fax +353 16662033
John.Gilligan@garda.ie — http://www.garda.ie/
An Garda Siochana Headquarters
Phoenix Park — Dublin 8 — IRELAND

**Revenue Press —
Office of the Revenue
Commissioners**

COLEMAN David
Senior Press Officer
Tel. +353 16748069 — Fax +353 16792035
dacolema@revenue.ie — http://www.revenue.ie/
Revenue Press Office — Dublin Castle — Dublin 2
IRELAND

ITALIA/ITALY

Agenzia delle Dogane

CARUSO Corrado
Director of International Auditing
Tel. +39 0650246079/0650246043
Fax +39 0650242087
corrado.caruso@agenziadogane.it
http://www.agenziadogane.gov.it/
Via Mario Carucci 71 — 00143 Rome RM — ITALY

Agenzia delle Dogane

FENTI Cinzia
Director's Office
Tel. +39 0650246002
cinzia.fenti@agenziadogane.it
http://www.agenziadogane.gov.it/
Via Mario Carucci 71 — 00143 Rome RM — ITALY

**Comando Generale
Arma Carabinieri**

MUGGEO Pasquale
Generale
Tel. +39 0648778426 — Fax +39 064818534
pmuggeo@carabinieri.it — http://www.carabinieri.it/
Viale Romania 45 — 00197 Rome RM — ITALY

**Comando Generale
Arma Carabinieri**

CAVALLO Gian Franco
Col., capo Reparto Relazione Esterne e Comunicazione
gianfranco.cavallo@carabinieri.it — http://www.carabinieri.it/
Viale Romania 45 — 00197 Rome RM — ITALY

**Comando Generale
Arma Carabinieri**

ALONZI Vincenzo
Colonel, Head of Command Carabinieri for
Agricultural Policies
Tel. +39 06487781
http://www.carabinieri.it/
Via Torino 44 — 00184 Rome RM — ITALY

Update of the logos: 20.4.2009

Comando Generale Arma Carabinieri	**IANNOTTI Pierangelo** Ten. Col. t. ISSMI — capo Ufficio stampa Tel. +39 0680982310 — Fax +39 0680982820 pierangelo.Iannotti@carabinieri.it http://www.carabinieri.it/ Viale Romania 45 — 00197 Rome RM — ITALY
Comando Generale Guardia di Finanza	**BERRUTI Gian Luca** Cap., Ufficio stampa Tel. +39 0644222228 — Fax +39 0644222206 Berruti.gianluca@gdf.it — http://www.gdf.it/Home/ Viale XXI Aprile 51 — 00162 Rome RM — ITALY
Comando Generale Guardia di Finanza	**BOTTILLO Giuseppe** Col., capo Ufficio stampa Tel. +39 0644223520 — Fax +39 0644223590 bottillo.giuseppe@gdf.it — http://www.gdf.it/Home/
Polizia di Stato	**VIOLA Mario** Deputy Director of Press Office Tel. +39 0646536551 — Fax +39 0646549681 relazioni.est@interno.it — http://www.poliziadistato.it/ Piazza del Viminale — 00152 Rome RM — ITALY
Segreteria del Capo del Dipartimento della Polizia di Stato	**MASCIOPINTO Maurizio** Direttore Ufficio III — Relazioni esterne Tel. +39 064871489 — Fax +39 0646549798 relazioniesterne.ps@interno.it http://www.poliziadistato.it/ Piazza del Vicinale — 00152 Rome RM — ITALY
Corte dei Conti	**REBECCHI Paolo Luigi** Deputy General Financial Prosecutor Tel. +39 0638762813 — Fax +39 0638763477 paololuigi.rebecchi@corteconti.it http://www.corteconti.it/ Via Baiamonti 25 — 00195 Rome RM — ITALY
Corte dei Conti	**Avv. PINOTTI Cinthia** Vice procuratore generale, responsabile Ufficio stampa Tel. +39 0632657022 — Fax +39 0638763432 cinthia.pinotti@corteconti.it — http://www.corteconti.it/ Viale Mazzini 105 — 00195 Rome RM — ITALY
 **Nucleo della Guardia di Finanza per la repressione frodi comunitarie — Presidenza del Consiglio dei ministri — Dipartimento per le politiche comunitarie**	**FALLICA Francesco** Col. t. .st., capo della segreteria tecnica del Comitato antifrode Tel. +39 0667795002 — Fax +39 0667795337 F.fallica@palazzochigi.it http://www.politichecomunitarie.it/ Piazza Nicosia 20 — 00186 Rome RM — ITALY

Update of the logos: 20.4.2009

Nucleo della Guardia di Finanza per la repressione frodi comunitarie — Presidenza del Consiglio dei ministri — Dipartimento per le politiche comunitarie

VECCHIONE Gennaro
Gen. B. — Comandante del Nucleo
Tel. +39 0667795393 — Fax +39 0667795498
g.vecchione@palazzochigi.it
http://www.politichecomunitarie.it/
Piazza Nicosia 20 — 00186 Rome — ITALY

Nucleo della Guardia di Finanza per la repressione frodi comunitarie — Presidenza del Consiglio dei ministri — Dipartimento per le politiche comunitarie

LIBERATORE Ugo
Cap.
Tel. +39 0667795382 — Fax +39 0667795337
u.liberatore@palazzochigi.it
http://www.politichecomunitarie.it/
Piazza Nicosia 20 — 00186 Rome — ITALY

Dipartimento per le politiche europee

DE FEO Fabrizio
Capo Ufficio stampa
Tel. +39 0667795866 — Fax +39 0667795867
f.defeo@palazzochigi.it
http://www.politichecomunitarie.it/
Piazza Nicosia 20 — I00186 Rome RM — ITALY

Membro G.U.S. — Giornalisti Uffici stampa — Gruppo F.N.S.I.

CORSETTI Carlo Felice
Associated Member
Tel. +39 065806019
felix.cc@email.it
Viale Glorioso 16 — 00153 Rome — ITALY

KYPROS/CYPRUS

Cyprus Police

DEMETRIOU Chrystalla
Acting Inspector/Police Press Officer
Tel. +357 22808025 — Fax +357 22808418
pressoffice@police.gov.cy — http://www.police.gov.cy/
Evangelou Floraki Street — 1478 Nicosia — CYPRUS

Cyprus Police

STEFANIDOU Christiana
Police Press Officer/Police Constable
Tel. +357 22808367 — Fax +357 22808418
pressoffice@police.gov.cy — http://www.police.gov.cy/
Evangelou Floraki Street — 1478 Nicosia — CYPRUS

Update of the logos: 20.4.2009

 Ministry of Finance — Department of Customs & Excise	**GEORGIOU Costas** Customs Officer — Investigation and Intelligence Section — HQRS Tel. +357 24801402 — Fax +357 22302029 cogeorgiou@customs.mof.gov.cy http://www.mof.gov.cy/ce PO Box 40105 — 6301 Larnaca — CYPRUS
 Ministry of Finance — Department of Customs & Excise	**HADJIYIANNI Niki** Chief Customs Officer — Chief Investigation and Intelligence Officer Tel. +357 22601738 — Fax +357 22302029 intelligence@customs.mof.gov.cy http://www.mof.gov.cy/ce Customs Headquarters — 1440 Nicosia — CYPRUS

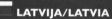 **LATVIJA/LATVIA**

 State Revenue Service (SRS)	**GRINBERGA Agnese** Head of Communication Division Tel. +371 67028733 — Fax +371 67028692 agnese.grinberga@vid.gov.lv — http://www.vid.gov.lv Smilsu Street 1 — Riga, LV-1978 — LATVIA
SRS Finance Police Board	**DIRNENS Gatis** Senior Investigator Tel. +371 67047444 — Fax +371 67047480 gatis.dirnens@vid.gov.lv K. Valdemara Street 1A — Riga, LV-1010 — LATVIA

 **LIETUVA/LITHUANIA**

 Customs Department	**VARNIENE Eugenija** Chief Inspector of the PR Division Tel. +370 52666049 — Fax +370 52666005 eugenija.varniene@cust.lt — http://www.cust.lt/ A. Jaksto g. 1/25 — LT-01105 Vilnius — LITHUANIA
 **Lithuanian Customs Criminal Service**	**KULIKAUSKAS Gediminas** Press Officer Tel. +370 52748028/52748000 — Fax +370 52748019 gediminas.kulikauskas@cust.lt — http://www.cust.lt/ Zalgirio g. 127 — LT-08217 Vilnius — LITHUANIA
 Special Investigation Service	**GOLUBOV Ruslan** Senior Specialist for Public Relations Tel. +370 52663330 — Fax +370 52622608 ruslan@STT.LT — http://stt.lt/ A. Jaksto g. 6 — LT-01105 Vilnius — LITHUANIA

Update of the logos: 20.4.2009

Financial Crime Investigation Service (FCIS), Ministry of the Interior

ANDRIUSKAITE Ruta
Spokesperson
Tel. +370 52717434 — Fax +370 52621826
ruta.andriuskaite@fntt.lt — http://www.fntt.lt/
Sermuksniu St. 3 — LT-01106 Vilnius — LITHUANIA

State Security Department

Makauskas Vytautas
Press Officer
Tel. +370 52364475 — Fax +370 2364510
spauda@vsd.it — http://vsd.lt/
Vytenio g., 1 — LT-2009 Vilnius — LITHUANIA

Prosecutor General's Office

JUODYTE Aurelija
Head of Public Relations Department
Tel. +370 52662366 — Fax +370 5662317
aurelija.juodyte@prokuraturos.lt
http://www.prokuraturos.lt
Rue A. Smetonos, 4 — LT-01515 Vilnius — LITHUANIA

LUXEMBOURG

GRAND-DUCHÉ DE LUXEMBOURG
Administration des douanes et accises

Administration des Douanes et Accises

DUSSELDORF Nico
Head of Public Relations Department
Tel. +352 290191303 — Fax +352 498790
Nico.Dusseldorf@do.etat.lu — http://www.do.etat.lu/
31, rue de Moutfort — 5355 Oetrange — LUXEMBOURG

Police Grand-Ducale

REUTER Vic
Spokesman
Tel. +352 49972010 — Fax +352 49972098
Vic.Reuter@police.etat.lu — http://www.police.public.lu/
1, Rue Marie et Pierre Curie — 2957 Luxembourg
LUXEMBOURG

MAGYARORSZÁG/HUNGARY

OLAF Coordination Bureau — Anti-Fraud Coordination Service/ Customs & Finance Guard/Ministry of Finance

SZEVERENYI David
Head of Anti-Fraud Coordination Service
Tel. +36 1456-8191 — Fax +36 1456-8143
szeverenyi.david@vam.gov.hu — http://www.vam.hu/
Hajnóczy J. u. 7–9 — 1122 Budapest — HUNGARY

Update of the logos: 20.4.2009

General Prosecutor's Office of the Republic of Hungary, Department of Special Cases, Division of Economic Crime Cases

MISKOLCZI Barna
Tel. +36 13545550 + 2550 — Fax +36 13545708
barna.miskolczi@mku.hu — http://www.mklu.hu/
Marko Utca 16 — 1055 Budapest — HUNGARY

MALTA

International Audit & Investigations Division (IAID)

SCHEMBRI Rita
Director-General — Head of AFCOS
Tel. +356 21237737 — Fax +356 21237681
rita.schembri@gov.mt — http://www.iaid.gov.mt/
IAID — Lower Ground Floor — Valetta Buildings
South Street — Valletta — VLT 1103 — MALTA

Customs Department

MALLIA Alfred
Public Relations Officer
Tel. +356 25685150 / 25685198 — Fax +356 25685242
alfred.b.mallia@gov.mt — http://www.doi.gov.mt/
Customs House — Lascaris Wharf
Valletta — CMR 1920 — MALTA

Polizia di Stato

CASSAR Michael
Assistant Commissioner of Police
Tel. +356 21241343 — Fax +356 21241343
michael.cassar@gov.mt — http://www.pulizija.gov.mt/
Police General Headquarters
Floriana — CMR 02 — MALTA

NEDERLAND/NETHERLANDS

Customs Intelligence Centre (DIC)

Van der WINDT Bram
Senior Officer (International Affairs Team)
Tel. +31 102442016 — Fax +31 102442074
a.van.der.windt@belastingdienst.nl — http://www.douane.nl
Westzeedijk 387 — 3024 EK Rotterdam
NETHERLANDS

Belastingdienst/FIOD-ECD

FIOD-ECD

VAN DEN OETELAAR Marleen
Press Officer Fiscal Tax and Investigation Service
Tel. +31 703428417
m.a.m.oetelaar@minfin.nl — http://www.belastingdienst.nl/
Postbus 20201 — 2500 EE The Hague — NETHERLANDS

Update of the logos: 20.4.2009

ÖSTERREICH/AUSTRIA

Bundesministerium für Finanzen (Federal Ministry of Finance)

Dr HELLER Herwig
Head of Enforcement, Unit IV/3 Taxes, Customs, Employment
Tel. +43 151433504080 — Fax +43 1514335907192
herwig.heller@bmf.gv.at — http://www.bmf.gv.at/
Hintere Zollamtstrasse 2b — 1030 Vienna — AUSTRIA

Bundesministerium für Finanzen (Federal Ministry of Finance)

PASQUALI Johannes
Head of Communication Department
Tel. +43 151433501028 — Fax +43 151433507087
johannes.pasquali@bmf.gv.at — http://www.bmf.gv.at
Hintere Zollamtstrasse 2b — 1030 Vienna — AUSTRIA

Bundesministerium für Finanzen (Federal Ministry of Finance)

FÜHRNSTAHL Christian
Senior Customs Officer — Anti-Fraud Division
Tel. +43 151433504083 — Fax +43 1514335907192
christian.fuehrnstahl@bmf.gv.at — http://www.bmf.gv.at/
Hintere Zollamtstrasse 2b — 1030 Vienna — AUSTRIA

Bundesministerium für Finanzen (Federal Ministry of Finance)

OBERHAUSER Hermine
Public Relations
Tel. +43 151433501029 — Fax +43 151433507087
hermine.oberhauser@bmf.gv.at — http://www.bmf.gv.at/
Hintere Zollamtstrasse 2b — 1030 Vienna — AUSTRIA

Federal Bureau for Internal Affairs (BIA)/ Ministry of the Interior

GRABENWEGER Georg Florian
Head of Unit — Prevention and External Relations
Tel. +43 1531265772 — Fax +43 1531265790
bia77@bmi.gv.at — http://www.bia-bmi.at/
Herrengasse 7 — 1030 Vienna — AUSTRIA

POLSKA/POLAND

Ministry of Finance

KWIECINSKA Dorota
Department for Protection of EU Financial Interests
Tel. +48 2226945654 — Fax +48 226945152
dorota.kwiecinska@mofnet.gov.pl — http://www.mf.gov.pl/
Swietokrzyska Street 12 — 00916 Warsaw — POLAND

Ministry of Finance

KROLIKOWSKA Agnieszka
Director of the Department for Protection of EU Financial Interests
Tel. +48 226943282 — Fax +48 226945152
agnieszka.krolikowska@mofnet.gov.pl
http://www.mf.gov.pl/
Swietokrzyska Street 12 — 00916 Warsaw — POLAND

Update of the logos: 20.4.2009

Ministry of Finance

OLEDZKA Urszula
Deputy Director of the Department for Protection of
EU Financial Interests
Tel. +48 226943282 — Fax +48 226945152
urszula.oledzka@mofnet.gov.pl — http://www.mf.gov.pl/
Swietokrzyska Street 12 — 00916 Warsaw — POLAND

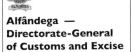

Ministry of Finance

KRZEMIEN Aleksander
Department for Protection of EU Financial Interests
Tel. +48 226943977 — Fax +48 226945152
aleksander.krzemien@mofnet.gov.pl
http://www.mf.gov.pl/
Swietokrzyska Street 12 — 00916 Warsaw — POLAND

PORTUGAL

**Alfândega —
Directorate-General
of Customs and Excise**

CURINHA Francisco
Director Customs, Cooperation and Documentation
Tel. +351 218814367/68 — Fax +351 218814396
fjcurinha@dgaiec.min-financas.pt
dscad@dgaiec.min-financas.pt
http://www.dgaiec.min-financas.pt/
Rua Terreiro do Trigo — Edifício da Alfândega
1140-060 Lisbon — PORTUGAL

**Alfândega —
Directorate-General
of Customs and Excise**

**ANGLEU TEIXEIRA GONCALVES Paula
Alexandra**
Customs Cooperation
Tel. +351 218814362 — Fax +351 218814396
paangleu@dgaiec.min-financas.pt
http://www.dgaiec.min-financas.pt/
Rua Terreiro do Trigo — Edifício da Alfândega
1140-060 Lisbon — PORTUGAL

**Republican National
Guard — Guarda
Nacional Republicana
— Brigada/Brigada
Fiscal**

COSTA PINTO
Major, Spokesman
Tel. +351 961196091
bf.gabapcmd.chefe@gnr.pt — http://www.gnr.pt/
Rua Cruz Sta. Apolónia, 16 — 1149-064 Lisboa
PORTUGAL

ROMÂNIA/ROMANIA

**Fight Against Fraud
Department (DLAF)**

PETRESCU Adina
State Secretary, Head of DLAF
Tel. +40 213181185 — Fax +40 213121005
adina.petrescu@antifrauda.gov.ro
http://www.antifrauda.gov.ro/
Bd. Regina Elisabeta nr. 3–5 — Bucharest — ROMANIA

Update of the logos: 20.4.2009

Ministry of Internal Affairs — Police

ISAC Marcel
Head of Unit — National Focal Point
Tel. +40 213160732 — Fax +40 213124239
marcel.isac1954@yahoo.com
http://www.politiaromana.ro/
Parliament Place nr. 1–5 — 13 Septembríe St.
9th floor, sector 5 — 050711 Bucharest — ROMANIA

SLOVENIJA/SLOVENIA

Ministry of Finance, Tax Administration of the Republic of Slovenia (DURS)

BOTTAZZO Violetta
Undersecretary — Information Specialist
Tel. +386 14782927 —Fax +386 14782965
Violetta.bottazzo@gov.si — http://www.durs.gov.si/
Smartinska 55 — SI-1523 Ljubljana — SLOVENIA

Ministry of Finance, Budget Supervision Office

KURE Irena
AFCO — Coordinating office for OLAF
Tel. +386 13696942 — Fax +386 13696914
irena.kure@mf-rs.si — http://www.unp.gov.si/
Fajfarjeva 33 — SI-1000 Ljubljana — SLOVENIA

Customs Administration of the Republic of Slovenia

GREGORIC Brane
Head of Director-General's Office
Tel. +386 14783805 — Fax +386 14783901
brane.gregoric@gov.si — http://www.carina.gov.si/
Šmartinska 55 — SI-1523 Ljubljana — SLOVENIA

Ministry of Finance, Customs Administration of the Republic of Slovenia, General Customs Directorate

LANGUS BOC Sabina
Public Relations Officer
Tel. +386 14783920 — Fax +386 14783901
sabina.langus-boc@gov.si — http://www.carina.gov.si/
Smartinska 55 — SI-1523 Ljubljana — SLOVENIA

Ministry of the Interior, General Police Directorate

MENEGALIJA Drago
Representative of Slovene Police for Public Relations for the Field of Criminality
Tel. +386 3114284458 — Fax +386 14285736
Drago.menegalija@policija.si — http://www.policija.si/
Stefanova Ulica 2 — SI-1501 Ljubljana — SLOVENIA

Supreme State Prosecutor's Office

VRTACNIK Mirko
Supreme State Prosecutor
Tel. +386 14341909 — Fax +386 14341936
mirko.vrtacnik@dt-rs.si — http://www.dt-rs.si/
Dunajska c.22 — SI-1000 Ljubljana — SLOVENIA

Update of the logos: 20.4.2009

 Supreme State Prosecutor's Office	 **FERLINC Andrej** Supreme State Prosecutor Tel. +386 14341905 — Fax +386 14341945 andrej.ferlinc@dt-rs.si — http://www.dt-rs.si/ Dunajska c.22 — SI-1000 Ljubljana — SLOVENIA

SLOVENSKO/SLOVAKIA

 Customs Criminal Office	**SCOBIKOVA Miroslava** Customs Criminal Officer Tel. +421 258251279 — Fax +421 253413685 miroslava.scobikova@colnasprava.sk http://www.colnasprava.sk Baijkalská 24 — 824 97 Bratislava — SLOVAKIA
 Section of Control and Fight Against Corruption — Government Office of Slovak Republic	**TETAKOVA Dorisa** Officer — Unit for Protection of EU Financial Interests and Fight Against Corruption Tel. +421 257295709 — Fax +421 257295751 dorisa.tetakova@vlada.gov.sk http://oofzeu.vlada.gov.sk/ Nám. Slobody 1 — 813 70 Bratislava — SLOVAKIA
 Government Office of Slovak Republic — SRGO	**JEZO Milan** General Director milan.jezo@vlada.gov.sk; afcossr@vlada.gov.sk http://oofzeu.vlada.gov.sk
 General Prosecution Office of Slovak Republic	**PAPCUNOVA Dagmar JUDr.** Attorney — Head of Protocol and International Relations Tel. +421 252922309 — Fax +421 252922309 dagmar.papcunova@genpro.gov.sk http://www.genpro.gov.sk Stúrov'a 2 — 812 05 Bratislava — SLOVAKIA

SUOMI/FINLAND

 **National Bureau of Investigation**	 **KYREN Tuula** Information Officer Tel. +358 718786512 — Fax +358 718786508 tuula.kyren@poliisi.fi — http://www.poliisi.fi/krp/ PO Box 285 — FI-01301 Vantaa — FINLAND
 Finnish National Board of Customs	 **AHOKAS Hannele** Director of Communication Tel. +358 204921870 — Fax +358 204921840 hannele.ahokas@tulli.fi — http://www.tulli.fi/ PO Box 512 — Erottajankatu 2 FI-00101 Helsinki — FINLAND

Update of the logos: 20.4.2009

SVERIGE/SWEDEN

Swedish Economic Crime Authority

LENNSTRAND Eva-Lisa
Head of Communication
Tel. +46 87620017 — Fax +46 86134019
eva-lisa.lennstrand@ekobrottsmyndigheten.se
http://www.ekobrottsmyndigheten.se/
Box 820 — SE-101 36 Stockholm — SWEDEN

Swedish Customs (Tullverket)

MALMBERG Annette
Head of Communication
Tel. +46 840500030 — Fax +46 8140425
malmberg@tullverket.se — http://www.tullverket.se/
Box 12854 — SE-112 98 Stockholm — SWEDEN

UNITED KINGDOM

HM Revenue & Customs (UK)

MATHEWS Paul
Senior Press Officer, Strategy and Planning
Tel. +44 2071470803
paul.mathews@hmrc.gsi.gov.uk — http://www.hmrc.gov.uk/
100 Parliament Street — London SW1A 2BQ
UNITED KINGDOM

 SFO
Serious Fraud Office

JONES David
Head of Communications
Tel. +44 2072397001 — Fax +44 2078371173
david.jones@sfo.gsi.gov.uk http://www.sfo.gov.uk/
Elm House — 10–16 Elm Street — London WC1X OBJ
UNITED KINGDOM

EUROPEAN ANTI-FRAUD OFFICE

European Anti-Fraud Office

BUTTICÉ Alessandro
OLAF Spokesman/Head of Unit Communication & Public Relations
Tel. +32 22965425 — Fax +32 22998101
Alessandro.Buttice@ec.europa.eu
http://ec.europa.eu/dgs/olaf/
Bâtiment 30, Bureau 14/72 — Rue Joseph II/Jozef II Straat
1000 Bruxelles/Brussel — BELGIQUE/BELGIË

Eurojust

THUY Joannes
Press Officer & Spokesperson
Tel. +31 704125508 — Mobile +31 645666731
Fax +31 704125005
Jthuy@eurojust.europa.eu — http://eurojust.europa.eu/
PO Box 16183 — 2500 BD The Hague — NETHERLANDS

Europol

HESZTERA Gerald
Head of Unit Corporate Communications
Tel. +31 703531563 — Fax +31 703180874
gerald.heszteraat@europol.europa.eu
www.europol.europa.eu/
PO Box 90850 — 2509 LW The Hague — NETHERLANDS

Update of the logos: 20.4.2009

EUROPEAN ANTI-FRAUD OFFICE *(continued)*

Europol

PEDERSEN Søren Kragh
Chief of Media and Public Relations
Tel. +31 703025118 — Fax +31 703180874
soren.pedersen@europol.europa.eu
www.europol.europa.eu/
PO Box 90850 — 2509 LW The Hague — NETHERLANDS